LAW AND PROTESTANTISM

The Lutheran Reformation catalyzed immense and far-reaching change in both Church and state and in both religious and secular ideas. This book investigates the transformation of law and theology born of Lutheran teachings of the sixteenth century. Profound changes in legal theory, political organization, marriage, education, and social welfare were inscribed in the legal and confessional systems of that period and have had an enduring effect on the modern Protestant world and beyond.

John Witte, Jr. uses the "binocular" of law and theology to present a panoramic picture of the Lutheran Reformation as an integrated legal and theological movement that continues to influence modern institutions of public and private law, and modern ideas of liberty, equality, and dignity. His book should be essential reading for scholars and students of Church history, legal history, Reformation history, and in adjacent areas such as theology, ethics, law, anthropology, and history of ideas.

JOHN WITTE, JR. is the Jonas Robitscher Professor of Law, Director of the Law and Religion Program, and Director of the Center for the Interdisciplinary Study of Religion at Emory University. A specialist in legal history and religious liberty, he has published 100 articles and twelve books, including *From Sacrament to Contract: Marriage, Religion, and Law in the Western Tradition* (1997) and *Religion and the American Constitutional Experiment* (2000).

D1205290

LAW AND PROTESTANTISM

The Legal Teachings of the Lutheran Reformation

JOHN WITTE, Jr.

Emory University

With a foreword by

MARTIN E. MARTY

University of Chicago

Compliments of:
Law and Religion Program
Emory University
Atlanta, Georgia 30322-2770
Telephone: (404) 727-6504
Fax: (404) 727-3374
www.law.emory.edu/LAW/REL
e-mail: lawrel@law.emory.edu

CAMBRIDGE
UNIVERSITY PRESS

PUBLISHED BY THE PRESS SYNDICATE OF THE UNIVERSITY OF CAMBRIDGE
The Pitt Building, Trumpington Street, Cambridge, United Kingdom

CAMBRIDGE UNIVERSITY PRESS
The Edinburgh Building, Cambridge CB2 2RU, UK
40 West 20th Street, New York, NY 10011-4211, USA
477 Williamstown Road, Port Melbourne, VIC 3207, Australia
Ruiz de Alarcón 13, 28014 Madrid, Spain
Dock House, The Waterfront, Cape Town 8001, South Africa

http://www.cambridge.org

First published 2002

Printed in the United Kingdom at the University Press, Cambridge

Typeface Baskerville Monotype 11 / 12.5 pt.   *System* LATEX 2ε   [TB]

A catalogue record for this book is available from the British Library

Library of Congress Cataloging-in-Publication Data
Witte, John, 1959–
Law and protestantism: the legal teachings of the Lutheran Reformation/John Witte, Jr.;
with a foreword by Martin E. Marty.
p.   cm.
Includes bibliographical references and index.
ISBN 0-521-78132-9 – ISBN 0-521-01299-6 (pb.)
1. Religion and law – Germany – History.   2. Reformation – Germany.   I. Title.
KK381.W58   2002
344.43′096 – dc21   2001043606

ISBN 0 521 78132 9 hardback
ISBN 0 521 01299 6 paperback

To Harold J. Berman

Mentor, colleague, and friend

Contents

Illustrations

Copyright on all illustrations used herein is held by the Pitts Theological Library, Emory University, and they are used with express written permission.

Foreword

Millions of people have only one eye, and still can see rather well. Some of them wear an eye-patch over the blind orb. Others with only one good eye in rare instances choose to work an effect by wearing a monocle to improve their vision and express style. For all the adjustments such improvisers make, it is hard to picture any of them – any of you, because you may be a reader of this book – preferring monocular to binocular vision.

If what I have just described is the case in the literal world of seeing, so it often is in the figurative or metaphorical world that John Witte inhabits. It is a world he would have readers share on the pages that follow. Borrowing the concept of "binocular vision" from historian of doctrine Jaroslav Pelikan, Witte asks not so much *what* are we to see but *through what lenses* should we look.

In the present case, his subject combines the two determinative subjects of "law" and "theology" in the case of sixteenth-century reformers within the Christian community in the lands that make up much of modern Germany. Too many historians, he notes, look through only the lens of law *or* the lens of theology when dealing with these conjoined topics. Fine, in some circumstances, but when a scientist looks through a microscope, only one eye gets put to work.

What happens, however, when a person wants to look at a panorama painted by figures who were in a situation where they could make few important legal moves without connecting them with theology? And *vice versa*: how should we regard the same persons, whether they were jurists or theologians, who were in circumstances where they were not in a position to make any theological moves without also seeing their legal implications?

Now Witte himself is painting a panorama. As a scholar he is equipped to include both law and theology on the vast scene he surveys in this volume. No, his scope is not vast in the global or cosmic sense. The

German territories whose legal and theological records he has plumbed and brought to view with such vigor and accuracy were themselves quite small. They remain remote from most of our experience most of the time. Yet they loom large in respect to their effect on later European and, yes, world history.

We need perspective on the choice of topics such as these. So: people in Sri Lanka or Cape Town or Boise, let us agree, are not likely to wake up in the morning thinking about the reform of law and theology. If they are, it is hard to conceive of them applying this thought to the judicial system and the ecclesiastical framework of Germany half a millennium ago. Would the latter subject *ever* come up in the ordinary course of their lives? Not likely, at least not in any direct way, unless one or another of them were a graduate student in the history of law who had been assigned an apparently irrelevant and certainly uncongenial topic having to do with theology.

In these paragraphs we have been looking at the larger world through binoculars turned around the wrong way. Such reversing effectively miniaturizes the topics of this book. In that case we will find perspective on them ever harder to gain. Witte's Germany in the sixteenth century was small, chaotic. The place to which he invites readers to pay attention was not the modern German state, patented in 1870. It was not the ominous giant that was capable of being a party to the generating of two horrible "world wars" in the century just past. His Germany had not yet become the ambitious place, imperial in outlook, and culturally ready to show off its glories: think Goethe and Beethoven and Heisenberg and Barth.

Now, it did have *some* claim to grandeur back in the 1500s because its territories made up a significant part of the Holy Roman Empire. Yet this collection of petty jurisdictions also can be seen as an archipelago of fiefdoms, principalities, and duchies, ruled by dukes and princes and bishops who might at times form coalitions and at other times make war on each other. Why pay attention to them in our century when nations like China and India use the word "billion" when speaking of their populations, not "thousands" as they did in sixteenth-century Germany? And why turn from them to Europe when the policies of the modern titans can immediately affect the whole world, directly? Why not study Chinese law and Indian religious thought to get our bearings and directions in the West?

Further risking reduction of the topic to the microscopic, notice that Witte is not even talking about all that went on in those German territories so long ago. Law and theology; theology and law; legal reform and church reform; church edict and legal adjustment: these are his topics. Aware as he is of what social historians write about, he does not have the burden or pleasure here of examining the details of home life, street lighting and waste disposal, such as they were, or changes in weaponry. He is not even being the intellectual historian writing simply about Catholicism, which was stronger and more organized then than were Witte's Lutherans, and is at home today in so many parts of our world as it summons the loyalty of a thousand million souls.

Over against the Catholicism of that day were poised two emerging forces that called themselves "evangelical" or, thanks to a minor event in 1529, often came almost accidentally to be called "Protestant" and, by their enemies, "Lutheran." It is these movements that Witte subjects to binocular vision. (Even that term "Lutheran" did not encompass the whole evangelical reality of the time. In other writings past, and still more promised, the author has turned and will turn to other Protestant themes marked "Reformed" or "Calvinist.")

While Lutherans are at home in many places of the globe and, by some reckoning, they remain the largest Evangelical or Protestant communion, their political, social, and cultural influence is dwarfed by many other religious and secular forces. Quick, now: name a Lutheran president of the United States. Answer: there have been none. It would seem easy to pass Lutherans by and therefore to strand Professor Witte somewhere amid the pages of this superbly researched and elegantly written work.

Philosopher Alfred North Whitehead did not help Witte's cause when he spoke some decades ago of not just the Lutheran but also the whole Catholic, Anglican, Reformed, and Anabaptist ventures in reform as being nothing but a domestic quarrel of northwest European peoples. New styles of scientific thought were emerging concurrently, and the reformers hardly noticed. Even the Orthodox Christians of the East tended to ignore what looked to them to be squabbles though, I think Witte demonstrates, they turned out to be of epochal significance.

Whitehead also pointed out that in many respects the once-dominating voice of Protestantism had become muffled. Its doctrines were no longer defined. Its divisions were no longer the sundering ones. Think Muslim/Jewish, rich/poor, nonwhite/white, straight/gay, women/men, if you want to find the defining and dividing issues that matter now. Not "justification by grace through faith," the Lutheran issue. You won't find it ranked high in contemporary culture.

Stop all this! John Witte is not the sort of scholar to make immodest claims, so he does not make too much of his themes by constantly stressing their relevance, their universal appeal, their urgency. But he *does* have an important story, and we do well to notice it from the beginning, though he waits until the closing pages to state the case for seeing some of the long-range and the wide-scope implications of his story.

It is not the purpose of writers of forewords to do the work of the authors whose pages they forward to readers, so I will not anticipate those modern implications that Witte draws out. But even the secular, Jewish, Roman Catholic, other-religious or other-Protestant citizens of the twenty-first century, if they bother to track back through history here, can come to see that some ideas about freedom and individuality, nursed in Lutheran Germany, are taken for granted in battles about freedom and the person today. Their origins deserve to be understood. Indeed, they demand it.

As for the potential universal character of Witte's story: Muslims, Hindus, and Buddhists alike have been on the receiving end and eventually have come into the zones of regular interaction with the Europeans who, after the times about which Witte writes, went into all the world with guns, products, missions, notions. How different these moves would have been had the Europeans made all their imperial and market moves of recent centuries as expressions of united Catholicism, reformed or not. How significant, we add, was the break-up of Christendom that started to become so evident in Martin Luther's day, long before the development of the Enlightenment in the West or before modern revolutions there and elsewhere completed the task of breaking up the world as it had been in 1500.

To speak in such sweeping terms does not do justice to the subtlety with which Witte traces themes and effects. The best case in what follows has to do with the reform of marriage laws by Luther, as well as by the theologians and jurists around him, and their immediate successors. To medieval Catholic eyes, what these leaders effected in respect to marriage looked like mere secularization. These Lutherans, however, *did* de-sacramentalize marriage and *did* make it a matter of civil law. So they *did* work to break the hold of hierarchical Catholicism on that most intimate and profound zone of life. How and why they did so are key elements in the Witte story; he is the master of this topic, and he handles it here masterfully.

Binocular vision, which in this case means using the two lenses of law and theology as Witte's main characters did, has not led him to isolate the German reformers and see them apart from the stirrings toward renewal of other Christians of the time. He makes clear that for him Luther is not a lonely heroic David who gets credit or blame for taking on the Goliath of imperial Catholicism. Yes, Witte uses a wide-angle lens on Luther, the professor of Old Testament, Wittenberg burgher, Bible translator, preacher, family man, robust raconteur uttering his "table talk," and more. But to treat the subject fairly, Witte has to bring on stage a larger cast – jurists, moralists, political figures, and others, many largely unknown today to nonspecialists, but of critical importance to the sixteenth-century Lutheran Reformation.

It becomes clear that for Witte, and in reality, the Reformation was not a single, focused event. From some angles it looks like a ruckus that erupted among the junior faculty at a new, small, backwater university in Wittenberg. It was only one locale, pitifully small when compared with Oxford and Geneva and Paris and Bologna, where law and theology became subjects of reform and new resolution. From all other angles, however, it did have world-historical significance.

While it is now high time for me to stop standing in front of the curtain of the drama that is about to unfold on these pages, I cannot resist urging readers to look for nuances that Witte, with his binocular vision, is equipped to discern and which he does then report on to us. An example that will influence me, for instance, has to do with the way he notices that the Lutheran "order," if it was hierarchical, was so not on a vertical but on a horizontal axis. The Lutherans did not do away with distinctions between ordained clergy and laity. Both belonged to "the priesthood of all believers." Yet pastors were necessary for the administration of the sacraments and the preaching of the word in that world where "everybody's job" would have been "nobody's job" had there not been some such definition. But, unlike the situation in the Catholic world, the pastors and bishops were not "above" the lay people. All the orders, replacing ranks, appear side by side.

Brilliantly, Witte spells out what the particular vocations of these sets of believers meant and mean. To do this, he has to explain the always complicated and hard to describe "two-kingdoms theory" of Luther, something Witte does as well here as I have ever seen it done. "Luther's two-kingdoms theory turned [the] traditional ontology onto its side. . . . There remained, in effect, a chain of being, an order of creation, that gave each human being and institution its proper place and purpose in this life. But, for Luther, this chain of being was horizontal, not hierarchical. . . . Luther's earthly kingdom was a flat regime, a horizontal realm of being. . . . " To the extent that this was his intention, and despite the fact that it was worked out only partially at times and frustrated or forgotten at other, often later times, this ontology and the practices based upon it have to be described as revolutionary reform.

Note also what those Evangelicals called Lutheran did *not* achieve, at least with any theological or ecclesiastical finesse. The Catholic bishops of the day would not ordain new "Lutheran" clergy, law and theology both being at stake in the situation. In any case, ordination by such bishops would have made Lutheran bishops and other pastors into "princes" or functionaries of the Holy Roman Empire. The Lutherans started ordaining clergy on their own with the prayers to the Holy Spirit and the laying on of hands by other pastors. Well and good, theologically. But remember those binoculars and keep in mind the lens of law: they had to appoint someone to run the show, to administer the Church in that late-feudal world. So, fatefully, they selected the secular princes, the "first members" of the Church. Picture in today's United States having the governor of the state or the county commissioner – depending on how one conceives the governmental analogues to those German jurisdictions – serving to administer the Church. Not only the heirs of those Lutherans have mixed heritages on which to draw.

Heritages there are, however, and here John Witte opens the trunk in which their treasures have been stored. He brings light to and then from the dusty and dark archives of law and theology, and, never deserting his role as fair-minded, disinterested, but always interesting, historian, he engages the reader in a story whose outcomes are still developing, whose plot is still unfolding.

Martin E. Marty
Fairfax M. Cone Distinguished Service Professor Emeritus
The University of Chicago

Acknowledgments

I have incurred a number of debts in the preparation of this volume. I was grateful to receive a Max Rheinstein Fellowship and Research Prize from the Alexander von Humboldt-Stiftung in Bonn in 1995 and 1996 that allowed me to serve as a visiting scholar at the Protestant Interdisciplinary Research Institute in Heidelberg, and to conduct research there and at various libraries in Dresden, Frankfurt am Main, Freiburg im Breisgau, and Hanover. I was also grateful to receive travel funds from the Jonas Robitscher Fund, furnished by Ms. Jean Bergmark and her family, to take several research trips to the Library of Congress, the Harvard Law Library, the British Library in London, and various libraries at Oxford University, Cambridge University, and the University of Edinburgh.

A number of colleagues and friends lent liberally of their advice and criticism. I would like especially to thank Harold J. Berman, Don S. Browning, R. Bruce Douglass, R. H. Helmholz, Duncan B. Forrester, Erich W. Gritsch, Carter Lindberg, Martin E. Marty, Oliver O'Donovan, and Steven Ozment, each of whom read large portions of this manuscript and made numerous edifying suggestions. Carter Lindberg was particularly generous in guiding me through the thick forests of secondary literature on the Reformation. I hope the quality of this book begins to approximate the quality of their advice. Several other colleagues and friends gave valuable advice and help on specific points, including: Frank S. Alexander, Thomas C. Arthur, Wolfgang Bock, Rebecca S. Chopp, John E. Coons, Peter Hay, Scott Hendrix, Wolfgang Huber, Timothy P. Jackson, Charles J. Reid, Jr., Robert Schapiro, Max Stackhouse, and Wolfgang Vögele.

I would like to thank my former dean and friend Howard O. Hunter for his steadfast and stalwart support of me throughout my time at Emory Law School. I would to thank Patrick Graham and Richard Wright of the Pitts Theological Library at Emory University for their help in producing the woodcut images used for the cover and illustrations herein and for the copyright release to reproduce the same. I wish also to thank Will Haines and Rosalie Sanderson for their excellent library support, and Amy Wheeler and Louise Jackson for their faithful administrative services. Several joint degree candidates in the Law and Religion Program at Emory University have provided me with able and ample research assistance on various parts of this volume and related writings – particularly Julia Belian, Penelope Brady, Brian Cook, Christy Green, Heidi Hansan, Jeffrey Hammond, Annie Jacobs, Joel Nichols, and Jimmy Rock.

I would like to thank Kevin Taylor, Senior Commissioning Editor at Cambridge University Press, and his colleagues for taking on my manuscript and working so assiduously to see to its timely publication.

I owe a special word of thanks to Professor Martin E. Marty for offering his sage criticism of several earlier manuscripts of mine and for furnishing such a generous foreword to this volume. Never before have I encountered a scholar with such boundless and bracing energy, such a lively and learned pen, and such a brilliant and catholic ken. Yet he has always found the time over the past fifteen years to send me generous notes of support, to critique my manuscripts, to contribute lectures and articles to forums and volumes I have organized, and to open to me all manner of intellectual and professional doors. This is the best example I have seen in the academy of Martin Luther's teaching of the priesthood of all believers.

This volume is dedicated to my great mentor, friend, and colleague Professor Harold J. Berman. Nearly twenty years ago, when I was a fledgling law student, Hal Berman took me under his wing and patiently began teaching me to fly. For the past fifteen years, we have worked together as colleagues at Emory Law School and in the Law and Religion Program at Emory University, sharing a deep common interest in the weightier matters of the law. Whatever I have become as a scholar and a teacher owes much to his noble instruction and example. I dedicate this volume to him with unbounded admiration, appreciation, and affection.

Abbreviations

Standard English translations are marked *. Unless otherwise noted and stated, I have used these translations.

AFR	*Archiv für Reformationsgeschichte*
Brecht	Martin Brecht, *Martin Luther*, trans. James L. Schaaf, 3 vols. (Philadelphia/Minneapolis, 1985–1993)
Bucer, *DS*	Robert Stupperich, ed., *Martin Bucers Deutsche Schriften*, 7 vols. (Gütersloh, 1960)
Bucer, *RC*	Martin Bucer, *De Regno Christi* (1550), in *Martini Buceri Opera Latina* (Paris, 1955), vol. 15, partly translated in Wilhelm Pauck, ed., *Melanchthon and Bucer* (Philadelphia, 1969), 174–394*
Coing	Helmut Coing, ed., *Handbuch der Quellen und Literatur der neueren europäischen Privatrechtsgeschichte* (Munich, 1973–77), vols. 1–2/2
Comm. Sent.	Thomas Aquinas, *Scriptum super Libras Sententiarum Petri Lombasdierisis*, in *Opera Omnia Sancti Thomae Aquinatis Doctoris Angelici* (Rome, 1882–), vol. 7.2
CR	G. Bretschneider, ed., *Corpus Reformatorum* (Brunswick, 1864) (vols. 1–28 = *Melanchthons Werke*)
Köhler	K. Köhler, *Luther und die Juristen: Zur Frage nach dem gegenseitigen Verhältnis des Rechtes und der Sittlichkeit* (Gotha, 1873)
Kunkel	Wolfgang Kunkel, Hans Thieme, and Franz Beyerle, eds., *Quellen der neueren Privatrechtsgeschichte Deutschlands* (Weimar, 1936), vols. 1–2/2
LC (1521)	Philip Melanchthon, *Loci Communes Theologici* (1521), translated in Wilhelm Pauck, ed., *Melanchthon and Bucer* (Philadelphia, 1969), 18–152*

LC (1555)   Philip Melanchthon, *Melanchthon on Christian Doctrine: Loci Communes 1555*, trans. and ed. Clyde L. Manschrek (New York/Oxford, 1965)*

LW   Jaroslav Pelikan and Helmut T. Lehmann, eds., *Luther's Works*, 55 vols. (Philadelphia, PA, 1955–68)*

MW   Robert Stupperich, ed., *Melanchthons Werke in Auswahl*, 6 vols. (Gütersloh, 1951)

Richter   Amelius L. Richter, ed., *Die evangelischen Kirchenordnungen des sechszehnten Jahrhunderts*, repr., 2 vols. (Nieuwkoop, 1967)

SCG   Aquinas, *Summa Contra Gentiles*, trans. V. J. Bourke (Notre Dame, IN, 1975)

Sehling   Emil Sehling, ed., *Die evangelischen Kirchenordnungen des 16. Jahrhunderts* (Leipzig, 1902–13), vols. 1–5, continued under the same title (Tübingen, 1955–), vols. 6–16

ST   Thomas Aquinas, *The Summa Theologiae*, English trans. by English Dominican Fathers (London, 1912–36)

Stintzing   Roderich von Stintzing, *Geschichte der deutschen Rechtswissenschaft, Erste Abteilung* (Munich/Leipzig, 1880)

Stobbe   Otto von Stobbe, *Geschichte der deutschen Rechtsquellen*, repr., 2 vols. (Aalen, 1965)

Stölzel   Adolf Stölzel, *Die Entwicklung des gelehrten Richtertums in den deutschen Territorien*, 2 vols. (Berlin, 1901, 1910),

TC   *Triglott Concordia: The Symbolic Books of the Ev. Lutheran Church German–Latin–English* (St. Louis, MO, 1921)

WA   *D. Martin Luthers Werke: Kritische Gesamtausgabe*, repr., 78 vols. (Weimar, 1883–1987)

WA Br   *D. Martin Luthers Werke: Briefwechsel*, 17 vols. (Weimar, 1930–1983)

WA TR   *D. Martin Luthers Werke: Tischreden*, 6 vols. (Weimar, 1912–)

Wieacker   Franz Wieacker, *Privatrechtsgeschichte der Neuzeit*, 2nd rev. edn. (Göttingen, 1967)

Wolf   Erik Wolf, *Grosse Rechtsdenker der deutschen Geistesgeschichte*, 4th edn. (Tübingen, 1963)

ZSS KA   *Zeitschrift der Savigny-Stiftung für Rechtsgeschichte: Kanonistische Abteilung*

Introduction

The Reformation that Martin Luther unleashed in Germany in 1517 began as a loud call for freedom – freedom of the Church from the tyranny of the pope, freedom of the laity from the hegemony of the clergy, freedom of the conscience from the strictures of canon law. "Freedom of the Christian" was the rallying cry of the early Lutheran Reformation. It drove theologians and jurists, clergy and laity, princes and peasants alike to denounce Church authorities and legal structures with unprecedented alacrity. "One by one, the structures of the church were thrust into the glaring light of the Word of God and forced to show their true colors," Jaroslav Pelikan writes.[1] Few Church structures survived this scrutiny in the heady days of the 1520s. The Church's canon law books were burned. Church courts were closed. Monastic institutions were confiscated. Endowed benefices were dissolved. Church lands were seized. Clerical privileges were stripped. Mendicancy was banned. Mandatory celibacy was suspended. Indulgence trafficking was condemned. Annates to Rome were outlawed. Ties to the pope were severed. The German people were now to live by the pure light of the Bible and the simple law of the local community.

Though such attacks upon the Church's law and authority built on two centuries of reformist agitation in the West, it was especially Luther's radical theological teachings that ignited this movement in Germany. Salvation comes through faith in the Gospel, Luther taught, not through works of the Law. All persons stand directly before God; they are not dependent upon clerics for divine mediation. All believers are priests to their peers; they are not divided into a higher clergy and lower laity. All persons are called by God to serve in vocations; clerics have no monopoly on the Christian vocation. The Church is a communion of saints, not a corporation of law. The consciences of its members are to be guided

---

[1] Jaroslav Pelikan, *Spirit versus Structure: Luther and the Institutions of the Church* (New York, 1968), 5.

by the Bible, not governed by human traditions. The Church is called
to serve society in love, not to rule it by law. Law is the province of the
magistrate, not the prerogative of the cleric. When put in such raw and
radical terms, these theological doctrines of justification by faith, the
priesthood of believers, the distinction of Law and Gospel, and others
were highly volatile compounds. When sparked by Luther's pugnacious
rhetoric and relentless publications, they set off a whole series of explosive
reforms in the cities and territories of Germany in the 1520s and 1530s,
led by scores of churchmen and statesmen attracted to the Reformation
cause.

In these early years, Luther's attack on the Church's canon law and
clerical authority sometimes ripened into an attack on human law and
earthly authority as a whole. "Neither pope nor bishop nor any other
man has the right to impose a single syllable of law upon a Christian
man without his consent," Luther wrote famously in 1520.[2] The Bible
contains all the law that is needed for proper Christian living, both individual and corporate. To subtract from the law of the Bible is blasphemy.
To add to the law of the Bible is tyranny. "Wise rulers, side by side with
Holy Scripture, [are] law enough."[3] When jurists of the day objected
that such radical biblicism was itself a recipe for blasphemy and tyranny,
Luther turned on them harshly. "Jurists are bad Christians," he declared
repeatedly.[4] "Every jurist is an enemy of Christ."[5] When the jurists persisted in their criticisms, Luther reacted with vulgar anger: "I shit on
the law of the pope and of the emperor, and on the law of the jurists as
well."[6]

The rapid deconstruction of law, politics, and society that followed
upon such shrill rhetoric soon plunged Germany into an acute crisis –
punctuated and exacerbated by the peasants' war, the knights' uprising,
and an ominous scourge of droughts and plagues in the 1520s and early
1530s. On the one hand, the Lutheran reformers had drawn too sharp a
contrast between spiritual freedom and disciplined orthodoxy within the
Church. Young Lutheran churches, clerics, and congregants were treating their new liberty from the canon law as license for all manner of doctrinal and liturgical experimentation and laxness. Widespread confusion
reigned over preaching, prayers, sacraments, funerals, holidays, and pastoral duties. Church attendance, tithe payments, and charitable offerings
declined abruptly among many who took literally Luther's new teachings

---

[2] *LW* 36:70.   [3] *LW* 44:203–4.
[4] *WA TR* 3, No. 2809b; see also *WA TR* 6, Nos. 7029–30.   [5] *WA TR* 3, Nos. 2837, 3027.
[6] *WA* 49:302. See many further such sentiments below pp. 119–20.

of free grace. Many radical egalitarian and antinomian experiments were engineered out of Luther's doctrines of the priesthood of believers and justification by faith – ultimately splintering the German Reformation movement into rival Evangelical, Anabaptist, and Free Church sects, as well as various religious revolutionaries (*Schwärmer*).

On the other hand, the Lutheran reformers had driven too deep a wedge between the canon law and the civil law. Many subjects traditionally governed by the canon law of the Catholic Church remained without effective civil regulation and policy in many of the cities and territories newly converted to Lutheranism. The vast Church properties that local magistrates had confiscated lingered long in private hands. Prostitution, concubinage, gambling, drunkenness, and usury reached new heights. Crime, delinquency, truancy, vagabondage, and mendicancy soared. Schools, charities, hospices, and other welfare institutions fell into massive disarray. Requirements for marriage, annulment, divorce, and inheritance became hopelessly confused. A generation of orphans, bastards, students, spinsters, and others found themselves without the support and sanctuary traditionally afforded by monasteries, cloisters, and ecclesiastical guilds. All these subjects, and many more, the Catholic canon law had governed in detail for many centuries in Germany. The new Protestant civil law, where it existed at all, was too primitive to address these subjects properly.

In response, the Lutheran reformation of theology and the Church quickly broadened into a reformation of law and the state as well. Deconstruction of the canon law for the sake of the Gospel gave way to reconstruction of the civil law on the strength of the Gospel. Castigation of Catholic clerics as self-serving overlords gave way to cultivation of Protestant magistrates as fathers of the community called to govern on God's behalf. Old rivalries between theologians and jurists gave way to new alliances, especially in the new Lutheran universities. In the 1530s and thereafter, Lutheran theologians began to develop and deepen their theological doctrines in sundry catechisms, confessions, and systematic writings, now with much closer attention to their legal, political, and social implications. Lutheran jurists joined Lutheran theologians to craft ambitious legal reforms of Church, state, and society on the strength of this new theology. These legal reforms were defined and defended in hundreds of monographs, pamphlets, and sermons published by Lutheran writers from the 1530s to the 1560s. They were refined and routinized in hundreds of new reformation ordinances promulgated by German cities, duchies, and territories that converted to the Lutheran cause. By the time of the Peace of Augsburg (1555) – the imperial law that temporarily settled the constitutional order of Germany – the Lutheran Reformation had brought fundamental changes to theology and law, to spiritual life and temporal life, to church and state.

Critics of the day, and a steady stream of theologians and historians ever since, have seen this legal phase of the Reformation as a corruption of the original Lutheran message. For some, it was a bitter betrayal of the new freedom and equality that Luther had promised. For others, it was a distortion of Luther's fundamental reforms of theology and Church life. For others, it was a simple reversion to traditional canonical norms dressed in new theological forms. For still others, it was a naked seizure of power by the original reformers eager to canonize their formulations and to guarantee their control of the Reformation movement.

My argument in this volume is that it was the combination of theological and legal reforms that rendered the Lutheran Reformation so resolute and resilient. The reality was that Luther and the other theologians needed the law and the jurists, however much they scorned them. It was one thing to deconstruct the framework of medieval Catholic law, politics, and society with a sharp theological sword. It was quite another thing to reconstruct a new Lutheran framework of law, politics, and society with only this theological sword in hand. Luther learned this lesson the hard way in the crisis years of the 1520s, and it almost destroyed his movement. He quickly came to realize that law was not just a necessary evil but an essential blessing in this earthly life. Equally essential was a corps of professional jurists to give institutional form and reform to the new theological teachings. It was thus both natural and necessary for the Lutheran Reformation to move from theology to law. Radical theological reforms had made possible fundamental legal reforms. Fundamental legal reforms, in turn, would make possible further radical theological reforms. From the 1530s onwards, the Lutheran Reformation became in its essence both a theological and a legal reform movement. It struck new balances between law and Gospel, rule and equity, order and faith, structure and spirit.

Contrary to assertions by Luther's critics, this move from theology to law was not a corruption of the original Lutheran message but a bolstering of it. It was not a betrayal of the founding ideals of liberty and equality, but a balancing of them with the need for responsibility and authority. It was not a distortion of Luther's reforms of theology and Church life but a grounding of them in a deeper constitutional order. It was not a seizure of power by the theologians, but a sharing of power with the jurists and the law-makers. It was not a reversion to traditional canon law norms, but a conversion and convergence of old canon law and new civil law norms in the service of the Reformation cause.

Such is the main argument of this book. What follows in the next section is a summary of the high points of the argument, with some attention to the medieval context in which the Lutheran Reformation was situated. The section thereafter compares this argument briefly with the modern historiography of the Lutheran Reformation.

LAW AND THEOLOGY IN THE LUTHERAN REFORMATION

The two-kingdoms framework

The starting point of the revamped Lutheran Reformation was Luther's complex theory of the two kingdoms, which came together in the later 1520s and 1530s. In this two-kingdoms theory, Luther repeated much of his original theological message. But he wove his early more radical doctrines into a considerably more nuanced and integrated theory of being and order, of the person and society, of the Church and the priesthood, of reason and knowledge, of righteousness and law.

God has ordained two kingdoms or realms in which humanity is destined to live, Luther argued: the earthly kingdom and the heavenly kingdom. The earthly kingdom is the realm of creation, of natural and civil life, where a person operates primarily by reason and law. The heavenly kingdom is the realm of redemption, of spiritual and eternal life, where a person operates primarily by faith and love. These two kingdoms embrace parallel heavenly and earthly, spiritual and temporal forms of righteousness and justice, government and order, truth and knowledge. These two kingdoms interact and depend upon each other in a variety of ways, not least through biblical revelation and through the faithful discharge of Christian vocations in the earthly kingdom. But these two kingdoms ultimately remain distinct. The earthly kingdom is distorted by sin and governed by the Law. The heavenly kingdom is renewed by grace and guided by the Gospel. A Christian is a citizen of both kingdoms at once and invariably comes under the distinctive government of each. As a heavenly citizen, the Christian remains free in his or her conscience, called to live fully by the light of the Word of God. But as an earthly citizen, the Christian is bound by law, and called to obey the natural orders and offices that God has ordained and maintained for the governance of this earthly kingdom.

Luther's two-kingdoms theory was a rejection of traditional hierarchical theories of being, society, and authority. For centuries, the Christian West had taught that God's creation was hierarchical in structure – a vast chain of being emanating from God and descending through various levels and layers of reality. In this great chain of being, each creature found its place and its purpose, and each human society found its natural order and hierarchy. It was thus simply the nature of things that some persons and institutions were higher on this chain of being, some lower. It was the nature of things that some were closer and had more ready access to God, and some were further away and in need of greater mediation in their relationship with God. This was one basis for traditional Catholic arguments of the superiority of the pope to the emperor, of the clergy to the laity, of the spiritual sword to the temporal sword, of the canon law to the civil law, of the Church to the state.

Luther's two-kingdoms theory turned this traditional ontology onto its side. By distinguishing the two kingdoms, Luther highlighted the radical separation between the Creator and the creation, and between God and humanity. For Luther, the fall into sin destroyed the original continuity and communion between the Creator and the creation, the organic tie between the heavenly kingdom and the earthly kingdom. God is present in the heavenly kingdom, and is revealed in the earthly kingdom mainly through "masks." People are born into the earthly kingdom, and have access to the heavenly kingdom only through faith. Luther did not deny the traditional view that the earthly kingdom retained its natural order, despite the fall into sin. There remained, in effect, a chain of being, an order in creation, that gave each human being and institution its proper place and purpose in this life. But, for Luther, this chain of being was horizontal, not hierarchical. Before God, all persons and all institutions in the earthly kingdom were by nature equal. Luther's earthly kingdom was a flat regime, a horizontal realm of being, with no person and no institution obstructed or mediated by any other in relationship to and accountability before God.

Luther's two-kingdoms theory also turned the traditional hierarchical theory of human society onto its side. For centuries, the medieval Church had taught that the clergy were called to a higher spiritual service in the realm of grace, the laity to lower temporal service in the realm of nature. The clergy were accordingly exempt from many earthly obligations and foreclosed from many natural activities, such as marriage.

For Luther, clergy and laity were both part of the earthly kingdom, and were both equal before God and before all others. Luther's doctrine of the priesthood of all believers at once "laicized" the clergy and "clericized" the laity. Luther treated the traditional clerical office of preaching and teaching as just one other vocation alongside many others that a conscientious Christian could properly and freely pursue in this life. He treated all traditional lay offices as forms of divine calling and priestly vocation, each providing unique opportunities for service to God, neighbor, and self. Preachers and teachers of the church must carry their share of civic duties, pay their share of civil taxes, and participate in their share of earthly activities just like everyone else.

Luther's two-kingdoms theory also turned the traditional hierarchical theory of authority onto its side. Luther rejected the medieval two-swords theory that regarded the spiritual authority of the cleric and the canon law to be naturally superior to the temporal authority of the magistrate and the civil law. In Luther's view, God has ordained three basic forms and forums of authority for governance of the earthly life: the domestic, ecclesiastical, and political authorities, or, in modern terms, the family, the church, and the state.[7] *Hausvater*, *Gottesvater*, and *Landesvater*; *paterfamilias*, *patertheologicus*, and *paterpoliticus*: these were the three natural offices ordained at creation. All three of these authorities represented different dimensions of God's presence and authority in the earthly kingdom. All three stood equal before God and before each other in discharging their natural callings. All three were needed to resist the power of sin and the Devil in the earthly kingdom. The family was called to rear and nurture children, to teach and discipline them, to cultivate and exemplify love and charity within the home and the broader community. The Church was called to preach the Word, to administer the sacraments, to discipline its wayward members. The state was called to protect peace, to punish crime, to promote the common good, and to support the church, the family, and various other institutions, such as schools and charities, that were derived from them.

Not only were these three natural estates of family, Church, and state created equally, rather than hierarchically: only the state, in Luther's view, held legal authority – the authority of the sword to pass and to enforce positive laws for the governance of the earthly kingdom. Contrary

---

[7] The terms "family" (*Familie*; *Stamm*), "church" (*Kirche*; *Geistlichkeit*), and "state" (*Staat*; *Obrigkeit*), while used as shorthand expressions herein, were highly loaded and plastic terms that shifted considerably in the sixteenth century, in part under the influence of the Reformation. See below, pp. 70–2, 76–7, 89–94, 97–9, 107–13, 136–8, 151–2, 161–4, 217–32.

to medieval Catholic views, Luther emphasized that the Church was not a law-making authority. The Church had no sword, no jurisdiction. To be sure, Church officers and theologians must be vigilant in preaching and teaching the law of God to magistrates and subjects alike, and in pronouncing prophetically against injustice, abuse, and tyranny. But formal legal authority lay with the state, not with the Church, with the magistrate, not with the cleric.

Luther regarded the magistrate as God's vice-regent called to elaborate divine law and to reflect divine justice in the earthly kingdom. The best source and summary of divine law, in his view, was the Ten Commandments and their elaboration in the moral principles of the Bible. It was the Christian magistrate's responsibility to cast these general principles of divine law into specific precepts of human law, designed to fit local conditions. This was to be an exercise of faith, reason, and tradition at the same time. The magistrate was to pray to God earnestly for wisdom and instruction, yielding when apt to the homiletic and prophetic directions of Lutheran theologians and ministers. He was to maintain an untrammeled reason in judging the needs of his people and the advice of his counselors. He was to consider the wisdom of the legal tradition – particularly that of Roman law, which Luther called a form of "heathen wisdom" – as well as that of early Christian canon law once freed from its medieval papalist accretions and distortions.

Luther also regarded the magistrate as the "father of the community" (*Landesvater, paterpoliticus*). He was to care for his political subjects as if they were his children, and his political subjects were to "honor" him as if he were their parent. Like a loving father, the magistrate was to keep the peace and to protect his subjects in their persons, properties, and reputations. He was to deter his subjects from abusing themselves through drunkenness, sumptuousness, prostitution, gambling, and other vices. He was to nurture his subjects through the community chest, the public almshouse, the state-run hospice. He was to educate them through the public school, the public library, the public lectern. He was to see to their spiritual needs by supporting the ministry of the local church, and encouraging attendance and participation through civil laws of Sabbath observance, tithing, and holy days. He was to see to his subjects' material needs by reforming inheritance and property laws to ensure more even distribution of the parents' property among all children. He was to set an example of virtue, piety, love, and charity in his own home and private life for his faithful subjects to emulate and to respect.

These twin metaphors of the Christian magistrate – as the lofty vice-regent of God and as the loving father of the community – described the basics of Lutheran political theory. Political authority was divine in origin, but earthly in operation. It expressed God's harsh judgment against sin but also his tender mercy for sinners. It communicated the Law of God but also the lore of the local community. It depended upon the Church for prophetic direction but it took over from the Church all jurisdiction – governance of marriage, education, poor relief, and other earthly subjects traditionally governed by the Church's canon law. Either metaphor of the Christian magistrate, standing alone, could be a recipe for abusive tyranny or officious paternalism. But both metaphors together provided Luther and his followers with the core ingredients of a robust Christian republicanism and budding Christian welfare state.

Law, politics, and society

A whole coterie of sixteenth-century jurists and moralists built on Luther's core insights to construct intricate new Lutheran theories of law, politics, and society. Foremost among these were: (1) Philip Melanchthon, the great linguist, moral philosopher, systematic theologian, and Roman law scholar at the University of Wittenberg, known in his day as the "Teacher of Germany"; (2) Johannes Eisermann, a student of Melanchthon, the founding law professor of the new Lutheran University of Marburg, and counselor to one of the strongest Lutheran princes of the day, Landgrave Philip of Hesse; and (3) Johann Oldendorp, Melanchthon's correspondent and Eisermann's colleague at the University of Marburg, and the most original and prolific jurist of the Lutheran Reformation. These three legal scholars, and scores of other German jurists and moralists who worked under their influence, brought many of Luther's cardinal theological teachings to direct and dramatic legal application.

Most sixteenth-century Lutheran jurists started their theories with Luther's two-kingdoms framework, and the legal, political, and social implications that Luther had drawn from the same. But while Luther tended to emphasize the distinctions between these two kingdoms, most Lutheran jurists tended to emphasize their cooperation. While Luther tended to view the domestic, ecclesiastical, and political orders as natural and equal in their governance of the earthly kingdom, most Lutheran jurists gave new emphasis and power to the political order of the magistrate, and paradoxically placed new limitations on that power as well.

First, the Lutheran jurists emphasized, more than did Luther, that the Bible was an essential source of earthly law. Luther was all for using the Bible to guide life in the earthly kingdom. But for all his early radical biblicism, he was ambivalent about the Bible's precise legal role. He tended to use the Bible as a convenient trope and trump in arguing for certain legal reforms, without spelling out a systematic theological jurisprudence. By contrast, Lutheran jurists of the day viewed the Bible as the highest source of law for life in the earthly kingdom. For them, it was the fullest statement of the divine law. It contained the best summary of the natural law. It provided the surest guide for positive law.

The jurists laid special emphasis on the Ten Commandments. The First Table of the Ten Commandments, they believed, laid out the cardinal principles of spiritual law and morality that governed the relationship between man and God. The Second Table laid out the cardinal principles of civil law and morality that governed the basic relationships among individuals. The Commandments against idolatry, blasphemy, and Sabbath-breaking undergirded the new religious establishment laws of Lutheran communities: laws governing orthodox doctrine and liturgy, ecclesiastical polity and property, local clergy and Church administrators. The Commandment "Thou shalt not steal" was the source of the law of property, as well as a source of criminal law alongside the Commandment "Thou shalt not kill." The Commandments requiring one to honor parents and to forgo adultery and coveting another's wife were the source of a new civil law of sex, marriage, and family. The Commandment "Thou shalt not bear false witness" was the organizing principle of the law of civil procedure, evidence, and defamation. The Commandment "Thou shalt not covet" undergirded a whole battery of inchoate crimes and civil offenses. Not all positive law, of course, fit under the Ten Commandments. But the Ten Commandments provided the Lutheran jurists with a useful framework for organizing a good number of the new legal institutions of the Lutheran state.

Secondly, the Lutheran jurists adduced, more readily than did Luther, Catholic canon law as a valid source of Protestant civil law. Luther eventually made his grudging peace with some of the early canon law, acknowledging its utility for defining the disciplinary standards of the church and the equitable norms for the state. But Luther remained firmly opposed to the use of later medieval papal legislation, either in law-making or in legal education. The Lutheran jurists were less reticent. They made ready use of the whole *Corpus iuris canonici* in their texts, courses, consilia, judicial opinions, and legislative drafting.

The Lutheran jurists grounded their more ample use of the canon law in innovative theories of both the church and the state. The invisible church of the heavenly kingdom, they argued, might well be able to survive on the Bible alone, freed from the accretions of the canon law. But the visible Church of the earthly kingdom, filled with both sinners and saints, required both biblical and canonical rules and procedures to be governed properly. Medieval canon law, insofar as it extended biblical norms, was a proven law for the governance of the visible Church, and should be used. The magistrate, as God's vice-regent and father of the community, they further argued, was required to attend to both the civil and spiritual needs of his subjects. He was to rule using Christian and equitable laws. The canon law was viewed as a valid and valuable source of Christian equity and justice, grounded as it often was in the Bible and in the early apostolic constitutions. Canon law was thus a valuable prototype on which the Protestant Christian magistrate could call. This new ecclesiology and jurisprudence, together, provided a sturdy rationale for the ample conversion and convergence of the medieval Catholic canon law and the new Lutheran civil law.

Thirdly, the Lutheran jurists emphasized, more than did Luther, the three uses of the law in the governance of the earthly kingdom. Luther had developed the "uses of the law" doctrine as part of his theology of salvation, and as part of his answer to the radical antinomians. Legal works played no role in the drama of salvation, he continued to insist. Yet, the law itself was still useful in the earthly kingdom. It had a "civil use" of restraining sin and a "theological" use of driving sinners to the repentance that was necessary for faith in Christ and thus entrance into the heavenly kingdom. Lutheran jurists repeated these two uses of the law, but stressed a third, "educational" use of the law. When properly understood and applied, they argued, law not only coerced sinners, it also educated saints. It yielded not only a basic civil morality, but also a higher spiritual morality. This was a further argument that the jurists used to insist on positive laws that established religious doctrine, liturgy, and morality in each polity. The positive law was to teach not only the civil morality of the Second Table of the Decalogue, but also the spiritual morality of the First Table. It was to teach citizens not only the letter of the moral law, but also its spirit. The law thereby was useful in defining and enforcing not only a "morality of duty" but also a "morality of aspiration."[8]

---

[8] The phrases are from Lon L. Fuller, *The Morality of Law*, rev. edn. (New Haven, CT, 1964), passim.

Fourthly, the Lutheran jurists emphasized, more than did Luther, the need to establish an overtly Evangelical[9] order of law, society, and politics in the earthly kingdom. Luther certainly had something of the same aspiration. But the Lutheran jurists were less reserved than Luther about building bridges between the two kingdoms, even rendering the earthly kingdom an approximation of the heavenly kingdom. The Marburg jurist Johannes Eisermann provided the most expansive argument. Eisermann acknowledged that the precise form and function of every Christian commonwealth will differ, for each community will strike its own balance among the norms of "nature, custom, and reason" and have its own unique interpretation of the Commandments of Scripture and tradition. But certain features of a Christian commonwealth will be inevitable. Eisermann repeated the notion that the positive law of each such polity must reflect and project the natural law, particularly as summarized in the Decalogue and the Gospel. He also repeated the notion that the positive law was to support a higher spiritual morality, through establishment by law of the right doctrine, liturgy, confession, canon, and Church structure that should prevail in that polity. A true Christian commonwealth, he further argued, should seek to be the very body of Christ on earth – a miniature *corpus Christianum*. It should seek to follow St. Paul's image that all are "individual members one of another." This meant that each person and each vocation must count and must be supported in a Christian commonwealth. Each person must respect the dignity, property, and privacy of others, and discharge the charity, care, and priestly service that become the Christian faith. A true Christian commonwealth should also follow St. Paul's image that some members of the body are greater and some are lesser. This, for Eisermann, supported an intricate hierarchy of estates, orders, and professions within the local polity, each with its own distinctive callings in serving the common good and reforming the commonwealth. Eisermann's early formulation of an overtly Protestant republicanism gave rise to a whole series of later Lutheran commonwealth theories, most notably those of the Strasbourg reformer Martin Bucer and the Württemberg reformer Johannes Brenz.

Fifthly, the Lutheran jurists developed an intricate theory of both political power and the limitations on political power. Luther had endorsed

---

[9] Throughout this volume, I shall be using the term "Evangelical(ism)" as a synonym for "Lutheran(ism)." The term "Lutheran," though now common, was historically a term of opprobrium that Catholics used to describe those who followed Luther rather than Christ. Luther preferred to call himself and his followers "Evangelicals," those who followed the Gospel (*evangelium* in Latin). *WA* 8:685.

a robust theory of political authority, calling the magistrate the vicar of Christ, the father of the community, and the only law-making authority of the earthly kingdom. But Luther had put strong limits on political power with his emphasis on the inherent limitation of the magistrate's jurisdiction to earthly matters, the internal checks provided by the magistrate's civil retinue (called the *Obrigkeit*), and the external checks provided by the concurrent orders of the family and the Church.

The jurists often repeated Luther's teachings, but they also undercut them. By granting the magistrate the power over religious doctrine and liturgy, they effectively extended his power at least partly into the heavenly kingdom. By glorifying the magistrate as the highest legal authority within the earthly kingdom, they severely compromised the checks and balances of the lower *Obrigkeit*. By giving the magistrate exclusive power to define the legal form and function of the Church and the family, they jeopardized the institutional checks and balances these orders might have provided on the political order. This theory seemed to provide magistrates with all that was needed for absolute power.

But the Lutheran jurists also placed a number of safeguards against tyranny: the need for written, published laws that the magistrate himself obeyed; the responsibility of the clergy to preach and prophesy against injustice; the need for civil disobedience against positive laws that openly violated the Bible and the Christian conscience. Moreover, the Lutheran jurists' arguments for enhancing the power and prestige of the political office also paradoxically put safeguards on it. One safeguard lay in their theory of the Ten Commandments as the source of positive law. This enhanced the magistrate's power to reach both civil and spiritual matters. But it also restrained the magistrate in the use of his power. For the Ten Commandments were best interpreted by the Church and its theologians, not by the state and the *Obrigkeit*. The magistrate was thus obligated to draw on theologians and clergy to understand the moral and religious dimensions of the law. He was to appoint them to the legislature. He was to request their opinions on discrete questions. He was to consult the whole theology faculty on difficult cases. A second safeguard lay in the jurists' flattering descriptions of the magistrate as the paragon of Christian virtue. This enhanced the splendor and glory of the political office. But it also held its occupant to a very high moral standard. Those officials who defied this description should not and could not serve, and risked resistance or all-out revolt if they persisted. When this view came to be coupled with a theory of election to office, it provided a critical restriction on tyranny. A third safeguard lay in the intense pluralism of

Germany, with its 350-plus separate and often very small polities. The small size of these polities did allow for the ready realization of a unitary local Lutheran commonwealth under the plenary legal authority of the Lutheran magistrate. But the small size of these polities also made it easier for people to leave – taking with them their labor, their expertise, their taxes, their services, and other essential contributions to the local commonwealth. The sterner the local tyranny, the smaller the local population, was the theory. When the right of a dissenter to emigrate was guaranteed by the Peace of Augsburg (1555), this became a further strong impediment to tyranny.

Sixthly, Johann Oldendorp led the Lutheran jurists in the development of an innovative theory of Christian equity that built on Luther's understanding of the Christian conscience. Every law was, by its nature, a strict law, Oldendorp argued, and every law, by definition, thus required equitable application. To do equity was an exercise of both the mind and the soul of the judge. It required the judge to apply civil reason, to separate salient from superficial fact, to reason from precedent and analogy. It also, however, required the judge to use natural reason, to consult the natural law inscribed on his conscience, to meditate prayerfully on Scripture, and so decide on the right application or reformation of the rule. Such conscientious application of rules was required not only in exceptional cases but in all cases. It was concerned not only with being just and merciful to the party in the particular case, but also with serving the letter and the spirit of the law itself. Oldendorp's theory of equity was a unique form of Christian practical reasoning, on the one hand, and pious judicial activism on the other.

Traditionally, equity was considered to be a unique quality of the canon law and a unique ability of the ecclesiastical judge. Thus in medieval Germany, most cases that required formal equity were filed in or removed to Catholic Church courts for resolution. Oldendorp's theory effectively merged law and equity. Every law required equity in order to be just, and all equity required a law in order to be applied. Law and equity belonged together and completed each other. The legislator had to build equity into each new law that was passed. The judge had to do equity in every case. Oldendorp's theory had direct implications for legal reform in evangelical Germany. It helped to support the merger of Church courts and state courts in Lutheran Germany; separate Church courts of equity were no longer required. It helped to support the convergence of canon law and civil law in Lutheran Germany; the canon law as a source of equity was an invaluable resource for the civil law.

And it helped to support the growing professionalization of the German judiciary in the sixteenth century, and the requirement that judges be educated both in law and in theology, in civil law and in canon law.

Lutheran reformation laws

These new Lutheran theories of law, politics, and society did not remain confined to the lectern or the letter desk. They came to direct and dramatic application in sixteenth-century Lutheran Germany. Building on a century-long German tradition of issuing "legal reformations" often in defiance of local Church leaders, the Lutheran reformers translated this new theological jurisprudence directly into new legal terms. Many leading Lutheran jurists sat on local courts as judges and notaries, or on local urban or territorial councils as secretaries and legal advisors, and thereby took a direct hand in shaping the new laws. Lutheran jurists and theologians issued formal opinions (*consilia*) on legal questions on request from courts, councils, or individual litigants. Civil courts regularly consulted the law faculties and sometimes also the theology faculties of local Lutheran universities to help them resolve cases raising difficult legal and moral issues. These were important channels for translating the new Lutheran gospel into law.

More directly influential were the hundreds of new "legal reformations" issued by cities and territories that had converted to the Lutheran cause. Initially, these legal reformations were simple statements of the new Lutheran faith of the local polity and simple declarations of the new subjects that Lutheran magistrates had taken over from the Church. After two or three decades of amendment and reformulation, however, many of these local Lutheran laws had become sophisticated legal documents that set out the new faith and the new legal order in copious detail, and instituted learned executive and judicial mechanisms for the implementation and enforcement of these laws.

Many of the leading Lutheran theologians and jurists helped to draft and enforce these new reformation laws. The reformers whose names we have encountered already were among the most active in this effort: Luther, Melanchthon, Oldendorp, Eisermann, Bucer, and Brenz, as well as the Wittenberg reformers Johannes Bugenhagen and Justus Jonas, among several others. The reformers made ample use of scissors and paste in crafting these new reformation laws. They regularly duplicated their own formulations and those of their closest coreligionists in drafting new laws. They corresponded with each other about the laws, and frequently circulated draft laws among their inner circle for comment and critique. They referred to and paraphrased liberally the writings of the leading reformers in crafting the legal provisions. This close collaboration led to considerable uniformity among the new reformation laws and considerable legal appropriation of the reformers' cardinal theological ideas.

While these Lutheran reformation laws were very wide-ranging in subject matter, they typically had lengthy provisions on: (1) religious dogma, liturgy, and worship; (2) public religious morality; (3) sex, marriage, and family life; (4) education and public schools; and (5) poor relief and other forms of social welfare.

The first two sets of legal provisions, on dogma and morality, were less innovative in form. Sometimes they approximated the caricature of simply being traditional canon laws wrapped in new Lutheran forms and now administered by Lutheran civil authorities. The actual changes, especially to the theology, were substantial, but the forms of law used to enforce them were largely familiar. In theology, the new civil laws reflected the Lutheran resystematization of dogma, the truncation of the sacraments, the reforms of liturgy and the religious calendar, the vernacularization of the Bible, the expansion of catechesis and religious instruction, the revamping of corporate worship and congregational music, the reforms of ecclesiastical discipline and local church administration, and more. In morality, new Sabbath-day laws prohibited all forms of unnecessary labor and uncouth leisure on Sundays and holy days, and required faithful attendance at services. Other new laws prohibited blasphemy, sacrilege, witchcraft, sorcery, magic, alchemy, false oaths, and similar offenses. New sumptuary laws proscribed immodest apparel, wasteful living, and extravagant feasts and funerals. New entertainment laws placed strict limits on public drunkenness, boisterous celebration, gambling, and other games that involved fate, luck, and magic. Neither the Lutheran magistrates' emphasis on these moral offenses, nor their definition of them, strayed far from the formulations of the medieval canon law. What was new was that these new subjects now fell primarily under civil law rather than under canon law.

The new Lutheran laws on marriage, education, and social welfare involved far greater theological and jurisprudential innovation. Each of these subjects had been at the heart of medieval theology and canon law. Each was at the heart of the new Lutheran theology and jurisprudence, and among the first pressing subjects that early Lutherans sought to reform. Lutheran theologians took the lead in critiquing the traditional lore and law and developing innovative theories that skillfully interwove some strands of older Catholic theology and canon law into a new Lutheran tapestry of theology and law. Lutheran jurists took the lead in working out the legal implications of these theological reforms, sometimes with ample revisions and reservations. On these three subjects, provisional legal reforms were on the books very early in Reformation, and then greatly expanded in the new wave of legal reforms in the 1530s and thereafter.

The institution of marriage, as one of the three great estates of the earthly kingdom, attracted a great deal of theological and legal attention. Prior to the sixteenth century, marriage was regarded as a sacrament of the Church. It was formed by the mutual consent of a fit man and a fit woman in good religious standing. When properly contracted, this union of husband and wife symbolized the enduring union of Christ and His Church, and conferred sanctifying grace upon the couple and their children. The parties could form this union in private, but once properly formed it was an indissoluble bond broken only by the death of one of the parties.

As a sacrament, marriage was subject to the jurisdiction of the Church. A whole network of canon law and confessional rules governed sex, marriage, and family life. The Church did not regard the family as its most exalted estate, however. Though a sacrament and a sound way of Christian living, marriage and family life were not considered to be spiritually edifying. Marriage was a remedy for sin, not a recipe for righteousness. Marriage was considered subordinate to celibacy. Clerics and monastics were required to forgo marriage as a condition for ecclesiastical service. Those who could not, were not worthy of the Church's holy orders and offices.

Lutheran theologians treated marriage not as a sacramental institution of the heavenly kingdom, but as a social estate of the earthly kingdom. Marriage, they taught, was a divinely created institution that served the goods and goals of mutual love and support of husband and wife, the procreation and nurture of children, and mutual protection of both spouses from sexual sin. All adult persons, preachers and others alike, should pursue the calling of marriage, for all were in need of the comforts of marital love and the protection from sexual sin. Moreover, the marital household served as a model of authority, charity, and pedagogy in the earthly kingdom and as a vital instrument for the reform of Church, state, and civil society. Parents served as "bishops" to their children. Siblings served as priests to each other. The household altogether, particularly the Christian household of the married minister, was a source of Evangelical impulses in society.

Though divinely created and spiritually edifying, however, marriage and the family remained a social estate of the earthly kingdom. All parties could partake of this institution, regardless of their faith. Though subject to divine law and clerical counseling, marriage and family life came within the jurisdiction of the magistrate, not the cleric. The magistrate was to set the laws for marriage formation, maintenance, and dissolution; child custody, care, and control; family property, inheritance, and commerce.

Lutheran magistrates rapidly translated this new Protestant gospel into civil law, in some polities building on late medieval civil laws that had already controlled some aspects of the marital institution. These new civil marriage laws shifted primary marital jurisdiction from the Church to the state. They strongly encouraged the marriage of clergy, discouraged celibacy, and prohibited monasticism. These new civil laws further denied the sacramentality of marriage and the religious tests and impediments traditionally imposed on prospective marital couples. They modified the doctrine of consent to betrothal and marriage, and required the participation of parents, peers, priests, and political officials in the process of marriage formation and dissolution. They sharply curtailed the number of impediments to betrothal and to putative marriages. And they introduced absolute divorce, in the modern sense, on proof of adultery, desertion, and other faults, with a subsequent right to remarriage at least for the innocent party.

The school, as a platform for the transmission of Lutheran lore and as a preparation for each person's Christian vocation, was also the subject of intense theological and legal reform. Prior to the sixteenth century, the Church had established a refined system of religious education for Germany and beyond. Cathedrals, monasteries, chantries, ecclesiastical guilds, and large parishes offered the principal forms of lower education, governed by general and local canon law rules of the Church. Young students were trained in the trivium and quadrivium, and taught the creeds, catechisms, and confessional books. Gifted graduates were sent on to Church-licensed universities for advanced training in the core faculties of law, theology, and medicine. The foundation of this Church-based educational system lay in Christ's Great Commission to his apostles and their successors "to teach all nations" the meaning and measure of the Christian faith. The vast majority of students were trained for clerical and other forms of service in the Church.

The Lutheran Reformation transformed this pan-Western system of Church-based education into sundry local systems of state-based education in Germany. Luther, Melanchthon, Bugenhagen, Brenz, and other leading Protestant reformers castigated the Church leadership both for its professional monopolization of education and for its distortions of religious and humanistic learning. They introduced a system of public education that leveled traditional social distinctions between clergy and laity in defining the goods and goals of education, and gave new emphasis to civil officials and civic concerns in the organization and operation of the schools. In the reformers' view, the magistrate, as "father of the community," was primarily responsible for education. Education was to be mandatory for boys and girls alike, fiscally and physically accessible to all, and marked by both formal classroom instruction and civic education through community libraries, lectures, and other media. The curriculum was to combine biblical and evangelical values with humanistic and vocational training. Students were to be stratified into different classes, according to age and ability, and slowly selected for any number of vocations.

The theological reformers of the sixteenth century built on the work of the legal reformers of the fourteenth and fifteenth centuries. The system of state-run public education that they established built squarely on the Latin and vernacular schools already established in larger medieval cities in Germany. The system of state-run charities and guilds to support poor students built on the prior practice of princes, estates, and monasteries to maintain educational endowments. The curricula of the lower schools kept religion at their core, and retained the seven liberal arts as well as a number of texts prescribed by the Catholic canon law.

The reformers, however, cast these traditional pedagogical principles and practices into their own distinctive ensemble, grounded in the two-kingdoms theory. Over time, the Protestant magistrate replaced the Catholic cleric as the chief protector and cultivator of the public school and university. The state's civil law replaced the Church's canon law as the chief law governing education. The Bible replaced the scholastic text as the chief handbook of the curriculum. German replaced Latin as the universal tongue of the educated classes in Germany. The general callings of all Christians replaced the special calling of the clergy as the *raison d'être* of education. Education remained fundamentally religious in character. But it was now subject to broader political control and directed to broader civic ends.

Social welfare institutions, many of which had been confiscated or destroyed during the radical Reformation period, also demanded the reformers' immediate attention, particularly given the explosion of poverty and vagabondage in Germany in the 1520s and 1530s. Prior to the six-teenth century, the Church taught that both poverty and charity were spiritually edifying. Voluntary poverty was a form of Christian sacrifice and self- denial that conferred spiritual benefits upon its practitioners and provided spiritual opportunities for others to accord them their charity. Itinerant monks and mendicants in search of alms were the most worthy exemplars of this ideal, but many other deserving poor were at hand as well. Voluntary charity, in turn, conferred spiritual benefits upon its practitioner, particularly when pursued as a work of penance and purga-tion in the context of the sacraments of penance or extreme unction. To be charitable to others was to serve Christ, who had said, "In as much as ye have done it unto one of the least of these my brethren, ye have done it unto me" (Matthew 25:40).

These teachings helped to render the medieval Church the primary object and subject of charity and social welfare. To give to the Church was the best way to give to Christ, since the Church was the body of Christ on earth. The Church thus received alms through the collec-tions of its mendicant monks, the charitable offerings from its many pilgrims, the penitential offerings assigned to cancel sins, the final be-quests designed to expedite purgation in the life hereafter, and much more. The Church also distributed alms through the diaconal work of the parishes, the hospitality of the monasteries, and the welfare services of the many Church-run almshouses, hospices, schools, chantries, and ecclesiastical guilds. A rich latticework of canonical and confessional rules calibrated these obligations and opportunities of individual and ecclesiastical charity, and governed the many corporations, trusts, and foundations of charity under the Church's general auspices.

The Lutheran reformers rejected traditional teachings of both the spiritual idealization of poverty and the spiritual efficaciousness of charity. All persons were called to do the work of God in the world, they argued; they were not to be idle or impoverished. Voluntary poverty was a form of social parasitism to be punished, not a symbol of spiritual sacrifice to be rewarded. Only the worthy local poor deserved charity, and only if they could not be helped by their immediate family members, the family being the "first school of charity." Charity, in turn, was not a form of spiritual self-enhancement; it was a vocation of the priesthood of believers. Charity brought no immediate spiritual reward to the giver; it was designed to bring spiritual opportunity to the receiver. Luther's doctrine of justification by faith alone undercut the spiritual efficacy of charity for the giver. But Luther's doctrine of the priesthood of all believers enhanced the spiritual reward for the receiver. It induced him to see the good works brought by faith, and so be moved to have faith himself.

The Lutheran reformers also rejected the traditional belief that the Church was the primary object and subject of charity. The Church was called to preach the Word, to administer the sacraments, and to discipline the saints. For the local church to receive and administer charity beyond its immediate congregation detracted from its primary ministry. For the church to run monasteries, almshouses, charities, hospices, orphanages, and more detracted from its essential mission. The local parish church should continue to receive the tithes of its members, as biblical laws taught. It should continue to attend to the immediate needs of its local members, as the apostolic Church had done. But most other gifts to the Church and the clergy were, in the reformers' view, misdirected. Most other forms of ecclesiastical charity, particularly those surrounding pilgrimages, penance, and purgation, were, for the reformers, types of "spiritual bribery," predicated on the fabricated sacraments of penance and extreme unction and on the false teachings of purgatory and works righteousness.

In place of traditional ecclesiastical charities, the reformers instituted a series of local civil institutions of welfare, centered on the community chest, administered by the local magistrate, and directed to the local, worthy poor and needy. The community chest usually comprised the Church's endowments and other properties that had been confiscated. These community chests were eventually supplemented by local taxation and private donation. In larger cities and territories, several such community chests were established, and the poor closely monitored in the use of their services. At minimum, this system provided food, clothing, and shelter for the poor, and emergency relief in times of war, disaster, or pestilence. In larger and wealthier communities, the community chest eventually supported the development of a more comprehensive local welfare system featuring public orphanages, workhouses, boarding schools, vocational centers, hospices, and more, administered or supervised by the local magistrate. These more generous forms of social welfare the Lutheran reformers considered to be an essential service of the Christian magistrate, the father of the community called to care for his political children. As with education, so with social welfare: the Lutheran reformers built on some two centuries of experimental civil regulation of the poor and private administration of charity in some of the stronger cities and territories of the German Empire. But again it was Lutheran theology that brought these legal reforms into common focus and common practice in later sixteenth-century Germany.

State, Church, family, school, and charity: these were the five areas where the Lutheran Reformation effected the most dramatic institutional changes in the first half of the sixteenth century. These five areas attracted the most searching theological critique. These five areas promoted the most sustained legal reforms. In these five laboratories, Lutheran theologians and jurists, together, forged the most original political theology and theological jurisprudence.

It must be emphasized that these were not the only legal changes born of the Lutheran Reformation. There were many other changes in sixteenth-century German private laws of defamation and slander, primogeniture and inheritance, foundations and trusts, and more. There were several sweeping changes in German legal science – in the resytematization of private law, in new styles of legal pedagogy and legal rhetoric, in new theories of precedent and judicial reasoning, in new hermeneutical approaches to ancient law, in new collations and syntheses of Roman law, canon law, and customary law. There were also major reforms of public law – in the reorganization and growing sophistication of the civil courts and their rules of procedure, evidence, and appeal; in the many new codes of criminal law, territorial law, and public policy law. These and other legal changes in Germany are usually associated with the "reception of Roman law" and the "rise of legal humanism," movements which clearly had a landmark influence on sixteenth-century German law. Some of these legal changes were also related to changes born of the Lutheran Reformation, and to the work of Lutheran jurists and theologians.

It must also be emphasized, however, that the Lutheran Reformation did not entirely eclipse the medieval canon law tradition in sixteenth-century Germany. Several German cities and territories remained Catholic, preserved the traditional Roman faith and liturgy, and continued to administer the canon law in traditional Church courts. These German Catholic polities were ultimately protected in their faith and in their law by the Peace of Augsburg (1555), whose principle of *cuius regio, eius religio* established in each German principality the preferred religion of the prince, whether Catholic or Lutheran.

Even in many avowedly Lutheran polities of Germany, the break with the medieval legal tradition was not so radical as some of the reformers had envisioned. Despite the fiery anti-papal and anti-canonical rhetoric of their early leaders – symbolized most poignantly in Martin Luther's burning of the canon law and confessional books in 1520 – Lutheran theologians and jurists eventually accepted and appropriated a good deal of the traditional canon law. This could only be expected. After all, the canon law had ruled German spiritual and temporal life for many centuries before the Reformation, and late medieval Germany was considerably more faithful to Rome than most other nations at the time. Indeed, the canon law, along with Roman law and customary law, was considered to be part of an integral common law (*jus commune*) of Germany. Most of the jurists and theologians who had joined the Reformation cause were trained in the canon law; several, in fact, held the *doctor iuris canonici* or *doctor iuris utriusque*. In the heady days of revolutionary defiance in the 1520s, it was easy for Protestant neophytes to be swept up in the radical cause of eradicating the canon law and establishing a new Evangelical order. When this revolutionary plan proved unworkable, however, theologians and jurists invariably returned to the canon law that they knew. Theologically offensive ecclesiastical structures and legal provisions, such as those directly rooted in notions of papal supremacy or spurned sacraments, were still critiqued and avoided. But a good deal of what remained was put to ready use in service of the new Protestant theology and law.

The Lutheran Reformation is thus best seen as a watershed in the flow of the Western legal tradition – a moment and movement that gathered several streams of German, Roman, and Roman Catholic legal ideas and institutions, remixed them and revised them in accordance with the new Lutheran norms and forms of the day, and then redirected them in the governance and service of the German people. The legal influence of Lutheran theology varied significantly over time, across jurisdictions, and among subject matters. Numerous other factors, besides Lutheran theology – economics, politics, psychology, sociology, and technology prominent among them – worked a formidable influence on the development of law. But the Lutheran theological reformation had a formidable legal influence. Such is the main story of this volume.

ERNST TROELTSCH AND THE HISTORIOGRAPHY OF THE LUTHERAN REFORMATION

Some readers will recognize that the subtitle to this volume – "The *Legal Teachings* of the Lutheran Reformation" – is a variation on the classic title of Ernst Troeltsch, *The Social Teachings of the Christian Churches* (1911). Troeltsch was one of the great polymaths of Germany at the turn of the twentieth century, professionally trained as a theologian but also deeply learned in history, philosophy, ethics, law, and cultural science.[10] He wrote in the grand panoramic style of nineteenth-century German intellectuals, a style made famous by G. W. F. Hegel nearly a century before and by Max Weber in his own day.[11] Troeltsch's writings are a banquet for the mind, filled with all manner of delicious interpretations that have nurtured theologians, philosophers, ethicists, historians, and jurists to this day. Troeltsch had a special gift for seeing the big picture, for crafting the clever dialectic, for tracing ideas across vast expanses of cultural space and time. These gifts were on full display in his massive two-volume work on *The Social Teachings of the Christian Churches* and several other works that amplified parts of this story. Even the casual student of Troeltsch will know of this remarkable tour of nearly two millennia of Christian theology and social ethics, organized in part around the dialectic of "church-type" versus "sect-type" movements, of "world-avertive" versus "world-embracing" Christian theologies.[12]

When it came to describing the sixteenth-century Lutheran Reformation, however, Troeltsch's trademark gift of generalization tended to obscure if not ignore the sources, particularly the legal sources. Troeltsch recognized full well the power of the original Protestant critique of the Catholic tradition, and noted several changes to Catholic dogma, liturgy, and sacramental life that Luther and his followers introduced in Germany. He also took note of the Lutheran reformers' new emphasis on the Decalogue as a source and summary of natural law and political morality. And he allowed that, with regard to such "legal relations" as marriage and education, the Lutheran Reformation "has not been without influence" – albeit a rather mixed influence, since in Troeltsch's judgment the reforms largely served to consolidate the power of the *paterfamilias* over the family and the dominance of the Protestant magisters over German learning.[13]

The heart of Troeltsch's argument, however, was that in law the Lutheran Reformation "simply continued the medieval conditions."[14]

---

[10] See discussion and sources in Sarah Coakley, *Christ without Absolutes: A Study of the Christology of Ernst Troeltsch* (Oxford, 1988); Robert Morgan, "Introduction" to Robert Morgan and Michael Pye, eds., *Ernst Troeltsch: Writings on Theology and Religion* (Louisville, KY, 1977), 1–53.

[11] See Ernst Cassirer, *The Problem of Knowledge: Philosophy, Science, and History Since Hegel*, trans. William H. Woglom and Charles W. Hendel (New Haven, CT, 1950), 217–325; George J. Yamin, Jr., *In the Absence of Fantasia: Troeltsch's Relation to Hegel* (Gainesville, FL, 1993).

[12] Ernst Troeltsch, *The Social Teachings of the Christian Churches*, trans. Olive Wyon, 2nd impr. (London, 1949).

[13] Ernst Troeltsch, *Protestantism and Progress: A Historical Study of the Relation of Protestantism to the Modern World*, trans. W. Montgomery (New York, 1912), 93–9, 145–8.

[14] Ibid., 100–1.

Lutheranism, Troeltsch argued, was fundamentally a "church-type" movement with little interest in, or theological capacity to engage with, matters of law, politics, and society. Given its founding dualism of Law and Gospel, Troeltsch argued, Lutheranism tended to make law and theology mutually irrelevant. Luther and his followers developed only a "crude, raw, and aphoristic" understanding of law that departed little from the commonplaces of scholastic and patristic jurisprudence.[15] In criminal law, the Lutheran Reformation simply "carried on the traditions of the old barbaric justice, and further, on its own part, based it on the thought of original sin and of civil authority as the representative of the retributive justice of God."[16] "In Civil Law, also, it is impossible to speak of any kind of innovations of principle," save perhaps the reformers' support for the "adoption of Roman law," which even so subtle a thinker as Philip Melanchthon simply equated with the Decalogue.[17] Rather than change the medieval law, Troeltsch concluded, the Lutheran reformers simply took it over unreflectingly, and used it to consolidate their power in Germany. "[D]espite its anti-Catholic doctrine of salvation," sixteenth-century Lutheranism was "a thoroughly ecclesiastical culture in the medieval sense of the term. It sought to regulate the state and society, education and science, economics and law, according to the supernatural standards of revelation." Like medieval Catholics, sixteenth-century Lutherans "incorporated the concept of natural law into their general understanding by equating it with the law of God," whose interpretation they monopolized.[18]

This deprecation of sixteenth-century Lutheran reforms of law and theology was part and product of Troeltsch's broader ambition to show that the Lutheran Reformation was no watershed moment in the Western tradition, and certainly was not the font of modernity. It was the eighteenth-century Enlightenment, Troeltsch wrote repeatedly, that was "the beginning and foundation of the intrinsically modern period of European culture and history, in contrast to the previously dominant ecclesiastically and theologically determined culture."[19] The "dominant

[15] Ernst Troeltsch, "Das christliche Naturrecht–Ueberblick," in id., *Gesammelte Schriften*, 4 vols. (Tübingen, 1922–1925), 4:156–65, at 161–4; id., "Das stoisch-christliche Naturrecht und das moderne profane Naturrecht," in id., *Gesammelte Schriften*, 4:166–90, at 180–3. See also Troeltsch's first book, *Vernunft und Offenbarung bei Johann Gerhard und Melanchthon* (Berlin, 1891).

[16] Troeltsch, *Protestantism and Progress*, 97.

[17] Ibid., 98–100.

[18] Quoted by Toshimasa Yasukata, *Ernst Troeltsch: Systematic Theologian of Radical Historicality* (Atlanta, 1986), 50–1. See elaboration in Troeltsch, *Social Teachings*, 2:523–39.

[19] Ernst Troeltsch, "Die Aufklärung," in *Gesammelte Schriften*, 4:338–9. See further id., "Luther, der Protestantismus und die Moderne Welt," in ibid., *Schriften*, 4:202–53, esp. 207ff.; id., *Religion*

ideas" of the sixteenth-century Reformation grew "directly out of the continuation and impulse of the medieval idea" and were only "new solutions [to] medieval problems."[20]

On the one hand, Troeltsch's arguments were a tacit plea for Christian ecumenism – an attempt to show the fundamental continuity between Catholic and Protestant thought, even at the greatest flashpoints of confessional difference in the sixteenth century. One happy consequence of such thinking is that an impressive school of historiography has emerged in the past century to reveal the many medieval Catholic antecedents to the Protestant Reformation – in nominalism, conciliarism, humanism, monastic pietism, and other movements. Accordingly, a good deal of the sixteenth-century Protestant Reformation is now understood to be a veritable "harvest of medieval theology," in Heiko Oberman's famous phrase.[21] And these same medieval movements inspired their own sundry reforms in sixteenth-century Catholic circles – in the great canons and catechism of the Council of Trent (1545–63), and in the reformist writings of Luther's Catholic contemporaries Thomas More, Erasmus of Rotterdam, and Francisco de Vitoria, among others.[22]

On the other hand, Troeltsch's arguments were a direct rejoinder to the new Lutheran triumphalism of his day – particularly that of his teacher Albrecht Ritschl as well as the German philosopher and historian Wilhelm Dilthey, whom Troeltsch had read closely while a student. These and several other German intellectuals had set out to reform the pietistic, socially avertive Lutheranism of later nineteenth-century Germany. Armed with a new critical edition of Luther's *Werke*, and a growing body of historical evidence of the "cultural significance" of the Lutheran Reformation, these German intellectuals pressed their Evangelical coreligionists to count Luther and his followers among the greatest prophets and founders of modernity, and to restore his influence in

---

   in History, trans. and ed. James Luther Adams and Walter F. Bense (Minneapolis, 1991), 3–4, 216–218, 226–227.

[20] Quoted by Yasukata, *Ernst Troeltsch*, 54.

[21] Heiko Oberman, *The Harvest of Medieval Theology: Gabriel Biel and Late Medieval Nominalism* (Cambridge, MA, 1963). See also id., *Forerunners of the Reformation: The Shape of Medieval Thought* (New York, 1966); id., *The Dawn of the Reformation: Essays in Late Medieval and Early Reformation Thought* (Edinburgh, 1986); Alister McGrath, *The Intellectual Origins of the European Reformation* (Oxford, 1987).

[22] See sources and discussion in John W. O'Malley, *Trent and all That: Renaming Catholicism in the Early Modern Era* (Cambridge, MA, 2000); Guido Kisch, *Erasmus und die Jurisprudenz seiner Zeit: Studien zum humanistischen Rechtsdenken* (Basel, 1960); Francisco de Vitoria, *Political Writings*, ed. Anthony Pagden and Jeremy Lawrance, (Cambridge and New York, 1991); Brian Tierney, *The Idea of Natural Rights: Studies on Natural Rights, Natural Law, and Church Law, 1150–1625* (Atlanta, 1997), 207ff.

modern German culture.[23] Parallel movements were afoot in European Calvinist communities, yielding Abraham Kuyper's sterling *Lectures on Calvinism* (1898) that argued for the Calvinist origins of modern politics, science, and aesthetics. More famous still was Max Weber's *Protestant Ethic and the Spirit of Capitalism* (1904–5), a robust apologia for the Calvinist origins of modern capitalism and democratic economy.

Troeltsch worked assiduously to undercut this Protestant triumphalism, especially with respect to German Lutheranism.[24] The social anemia, political acquiescence, and legal quietism of modern-day Lutheranism, he argued, was not a betrayal of the sixteenth-century Lutheran Reformation but a fulfillment of it. Luther and his followers might have reformed theology and the church, but in legal and political matters they did little but accept the status quo. The later tragedies of the Second World War, and the relative quietness of the Lutheran churches in the face of the same, seemed a grim vindication of Troeltsch's thesis. A whole industry of writing began to emerge in the mid-twentieth century drawing direct and easy lines from Luther to Hitler, from Reformation sermons against the Jews to the horrors of the Holocaust.[25]

Troeltsch's interpretation of the law and theology of the Lutheran Reformation anticipated if not shaped a good deal of more recent historiography. Church historians, legal historians, and social historians alike have echoed and elaborated various parts of his thesis.

Like Troeltsch, many church historians have tended to deprecate the legal contributions of the Lutheran Reformation. They have tended to focus their analysis on the writings of Luther, Melanchthon, and other magisterial reformers and found therein only a rudimentary legal understanding, haphazardly arranged and sometimes bombastically proclaimed. They have tended to neglect the legal elaboration and political reification of Lutheran teachings by dozens of influential German jurists

---

[23] Karl Holl, "Die Kulturbedeutung der Reformation" (1911), in id., *Gesammelte Aufsätze zur Kirchengeschichte*, 7th edn., 3 vols. (Tübingen, 1948), 1:468. See analysis in Heinrich Bornkamm, *Luther im Spiegel der deutschen Geistesgeschichte* (Heidelberg, 1955); Steven Ozment, *The Age of Reform, 1250–1550: An Intellectual and Social History of Late Medieval and Reformation Europe* (New Haven, CT, 1980), 26off.; id., *Protestants: The Birth of a Revolution* (New York, 1992), 1–7, 119ff.; Helmut Walser Smith, *German Nationalism and Religious Conflict: Culture, Ideology, Politics, 1870–1914* (Princeton, 1995); James Stayer, *Martin Luther, German Saviour: German Evangelical Theological Factions and the Interpretation of Luther, 1917–1933* (Montreal, 2000).

[24] See detailed sources and discussion in Brent W. Sockness, *Against False Apologetics: Wilhelm Herrmann and Ernst Troeltsch in Conflict* (Tübingen, 1998).

[25] See, e.g., William M. McGovern, *From Luther to Hitler: The History of Fascist-Nazi Political Philosophy* (Boston, 1941), and a summary and evaluation of more recent literature in James D. Tracy, ed., *Luther and the Modern State in Germany* (Kirksville, MO, 1986); Heiko Oberman, *The Roots of Anti-Semitism in the Age of Renaissance and Reformation*, trans. J. I. Porter (Philadelphia, 1984).

in the course of the sixteenth century. Furthermore, many church historians have tended to confine their attention to the Lutheran reforms of dogma, liturgy, and church polity, and have thus treated Lutheranism primarily as a spiritual, sometimes even a mystical, movement. "Luther's Church," writes Hajo Holborn, "was confined exclusively to the Word and to the spiritual comfort of the individual. . . . Luther [was] wary of attaching any significance to the details of a secular order."[26] Reinhold Niebuhr wrote similarly, and castigated Luther and his followers for their "quietist tendencies" and "defeatism." For Luther, "no obligation rests upon the Christian to change social structures so that they might conform more perfectly to the requirements of brotherhood."[27]

Like Troeltsch, many legal historians have tended to deprecate the sixteenth century in general, and Lutheran theology in particular. Most standard legal history texts today treat the sixteenth-century Reformation era as a mere transition period in the Western legal tradition, if they treat it at all.[28] "Sixteenth-century jurists," a leading jurist writes, "were merely the doorkeepers to the modern age" of Western law and legal thought. Sixteenth-century legislators and judges "performed a few of the experiments necessary to prepare for the great codification movements of the modern age" but they "were largely incapable of entering new legal ideas of their own." At best, sixteenth-century law was an open conduit by which the West moved from medieval canon law to modern civil law. At best, sixteenth-century legal theory provided a transition between the legal communitarianism of Gratian, Aquinas, and Ockham and the legal individualism of Grotius, Hobbes, and Locke. When legal historians do treat the sixteenth century, they tend to emphasize other themes – the rise of legal humanism, the reception of Roman law, the emergence of Machiavellian politics, and the like – leaving Lutheran theological contributions largely untouched.[29]

Even more than Troeltsch, some social historians today have dismissed the "Reformation" altogether as a historian's fiction and a historical

---

[26] Hajo Holborn, *A History of Modern Germany: The Reformation* (New Haven, CT, 1959), 188, 190.

[27] Reinhold Niebuhr, *The Nature and Destiny of Man*, 2 vols. (New York, 1964), 2:192–3, with further quotations and analysis in Carter Lindberg, *Beyond Charity: Reformation Initiatives for the Poor* (Minneapolis, 1993), 161 ff.

[28] See critique of the legal literature in Harold J. Berman and John Witte, Jr., "The Transformation of Western Legal Philosophy in Lutheran Germany," *Southern California Law Review* 62 (1989): 1573–660, at 1575–9, 1650–60; Harold J. Berman, *Faith and Order: The Reconciliation of Law and Religion* (Atlanta, 1993), 86–103.

[29] Herman Dooyeweerd, *Encyclopaedie der Rechtswetenschap*, 2 vols. (Amsterdam, 1946), 1:93. See similarly Wieacker, 189ff.; Ernst Cassirer, *The Myth of the Modern State*, trans. Charles W. Hendel (New Haven, CT, 1946), 116ff.

failure. Martin Luther and other sixteenth-century figures certainly called for reforms of all sorts, recent interpretations allow. But they inspired no real reformation. Their ideas had little impact on the beliefs and behaviors of common people. Their policies perpetuated elitism and chauvinism more than they cultivated equality and liberty. Their reforms tended to obstruct nascent movements for democracy and market economy and to inspire new excesses in the patriarchies of family, Church, and state. As the editors of the *Handbook of European History 1400–1600* put it, "the Reformation" must now be viewed as an ideological category of "nineteenth century Protestant historical belief," which served more to defend the self-identity of modern mainline Protestants than to define a cardinal turning point in Western history. Recent historiography, the editors continue, has brought "changes of sensibility" that have now "robbed" the term "Reformation" of any utility and veracity. Particularly, "the rise of economic and social history tended to carve the boundary between modern and older Europe ever more deeply into the era between 1750 and 1815." Moreover, "the ebbing prestige of individualism and Christianity in European high culture undermined the [Reformation] concept's explanatory power."[30]

This volume invites historians, among many others, to look afresh at the Lutheran Reformation, now through the "binocular" of law and theology.[31] It invites church historians to look more closely at the legal dimensions of the Reformation, where a good deal of the new theology was cast in its most enduring forms. It invites legal historians to look more closely at the religious dimensions of the Reformation, where a good deal of the new law found its most enduring norms. And it invites social historians to take more seriously both the theology and the law of the Reformation, sources of ideas and institutions that were much more than simply the totems of the elite or the bludgeons of the powerful. The binocular of law and theology, I submit, brings into focus a considerably wider and fuller picture of the Lutheran Reformation than can be seen through the monocular of law or the monocular of theology alone – let alone through naked modern eyes focused primarily on sixteenth-century social particulars. When viewed through this binocular the Lutheran Reformation is hardly the ideological concept or idle category that some recent historiography suggests.

---

[30] Thomas A. Brady *et al.*, eds., *Handbook of European History, 1400–1600* (Leiden/New York, 1994), xiii–xvii.

[31] The phrase is from Jaroslav Pelikan, "Foreword" to John Witte, Jr. and Frank S. Alexander, eds., *The Weightier Matters of the Law: Essays on Law and Religion* (Atlanta, 1988), xii.

By running counter to traditional lines of historical analysis, this volume will invariably draw criticisms from those whose favorite arguments have been traversed or avoided. By rummaging anew through the desks of many sixteenth-century theologians and jurists, it will invariably draw fire from specialists who have organized these desks in a particular way. By adducing and combining afresh historical arguments and concepts, and showing their enduring influence on the Western legal tradition, this volume will invariably draw charges of both historicism and iconoclasm. This is the bane of any serious work of interdisciplinary scholarship.

Such methodological grumbling, however, is generally as transient as it is inevitable. After these inevitable grumbles of discontent have been raised, the question that will remain is whether specialists will look up from their favorite formulas and see in this volume a glimpse of a new way to understand law and the Reformation, law and theology, law and history, law and ideology. Will students and new readers gain from this volume fresh historical inspiration and instruction that is not afforded either by the traditional accountings of first one thing happening and then another, or by the new vogue of flattening all past texts and traditions into particularistic narratives? Will theologians and churchfolk, politicians and public policy analysts, sociologists and anthropologists see in this story theological and legal methods and lessons that have pertinence for our day? Will Protestants and Catholics see in these early confluences and convergences of canon law and civil law useful sources and resources for a deeper Christian ecumenism and political activism?

This is the broader challenge of this book. I have tried to press the case as forcefully as the data allow. I have adduced ample evidence for my thesis from many sixteenth-century theological and legal sources that are not much known or used today. I have tried, in the conclusion, to draw out a few of the modern implications of this story while trying to avoid the sins of both chronological snobbery and "winner's history."[32]

---

[32] The phrase is from R. H. Helmholz, *Canon Law and English Common Law* (London, 1983), 15.

1. Title Page from *Der Stat Nuremberg verneute Reformation* (Nuremberg, 1564)

Moses is shown on the right with one of the tablets of the law from Sinai, and the Holy Roman Emperor, likely Ferdinand, is on the left.

Canon law and civil law on the eve of the Reformation

In his 1520 manifesto, *To the Christian Nobility of the German Nation Concerning the Reform of the Christian Estate*, Martin Luther described the law of Germany as a "wilderness" of confusion. Confronted by the masses of "rambling and farfetched" laws that prevailed in his day, Luther threw up his hands in frustration as he sought to map out appropriate legal reforms. He scratched a couple of quick lines about the superiority of civil law to canon law, and of territorial law to imperial law. He spoke of the need to tailor laws to the "gifts and peculiar characteristics" of local polities. But then, uncharacteristically, Luther gave up. He recommended simply that "wise rulers, side by side with Holy Scripture, would be law enough," and expressed hope that others would give "more thought and attention to the matter."[1] Luther himself would soon return to the matter of law reform with a vengeance, but for the moment his mind was on more pressing questions – not least the growing perils to his own body and soul occasioned by the papal bull calling for his excommunication.

Luther had ample reason to be frustrated in his attempts to take the measure of the German law of his day. In 1520, the German-speaking lands of the Holy Roman Empire had no fewer than 364 registered polities, most with their own local legal systems. Nearly half of these were ecclesiastical polities, run by powerful prince-bishops and prelates, who exercised both spiritual and temporal jurisdiction within their domains. The remainder were civil polities of various sorts and sizes – several large and powerful principalities, scores of lesser principalities, duchies, graveships, lordships, and free cities, most with their own forms of local civil law.[2]

---

[1] *LW* 44:203–4.

[2] The numbers are drawn from the imperial tax schedule (*Reichsmatrikel*) of the Diet of Worms, reprinted in Gerhard Benecke, *Society and Politics in Germany, 1500–1700* (London, 1974), appendix II, 382–93. For alternate numbers, based on other imperial and territorial registers, see Holborn, *A History of Germany: The Reformation*, 39 (120 ecclesiastical princes and prelates, 30 secular princes,

Germany was part of both the Western Christian Church and the Holy Roman Empire. Accordingly, it was subject to the jurisdiction of both the pope and the canon law, and the emperor and the imperial law. At the turn of the sixteenth century, the canon law was considerably more effective and authoritative. Germany was a rather conservative Catholic bastion at the time, and German bishops and prelates were more faithful to Rome than many of their foreign co-clerics. Particularly in ecclesiastical principalities, the general canon law norms of the pope and the Church councils, and the local canon law norms of German bishops and local synods, dominated spiritual and temporal life. A hierarchy of Church courts and other administrative offices saw to the effective implementation of canon law, with a refined system of litigation, judgment, and appeal.

By contrast, the law of the Holy Roman Emperor was increasingly subject to the local control of the German princes, cities, and estates. The emperor did pass several "imperial reformations" and "peace statutes" for Germany in the later fifteenth century, and in 1495 put in place an Imperial Supreme Court to enforce imperial law among the feuding German estates. But rather little came of these efforts prior to the middle of the sixteenth century. Considerably more effective were some of the so-called "legal reformations" of the cities and territories of late medieval Germany. These legal reformations both consolidated the legal power and prestige of local princes and city councils and empowered some of them to impose increasing restrictions on the power and property of local bishops and prelates. But in circa 1500 neither the Holy Roman Emperor nor any of these local princes or city councils could match the power or the prestige of the Church and its canon law.

The task of this brief chapter is to describe (1) the nature of canon law and the sources of ecclesiastical jurisdiction; (2) the forms of civil law and the impetus for the new legal reformations; and (3) the increasing friction between civil law and canon law that helped prepare the way for the Lutheran Reformation.

---

100 plus counts and dukes, and 66 cities); *New Cambridge Modern History* vol. 1 (Cambridge, 1970), 194 (6 electors, 120 prelates, 30 lay princes, 140 counts and lords, 85 towns); F. R. H. DuBoulay, *Germany in the Later Middle Ages* (London, 1983), 93–4 (7 electoral and 25 secular principalities, 90 archbishoprics, bishoprics, and abbeys, 100-plus countships, and many lesser lordships); Ozment, *The Age of Reform*, 190ff. (75 free cities and roughly 3,000 towns). The German-speaking regions of the Empire included not only modern-day unified Germany, but also sections of the modern-day Netherlands, Switzerland, Austria, Slovakia, and the Czech Republic. For maps, see *The New Cambridge Modern History*, 16:66–7, 122–3; Geoffrey Barraclough, *The Origins of Modern Germany* (New York, 1957), 359–60.

CANON LAW

On the eve of the Lutheran Reformation, the Catholic Church was a formidable legal and political body that ruled throughout much of Germany. In 1517, the German-speaking sections of the Holy Roman Empire were divided among three electoral territories, four archbishoprics, forty-six bishoprics, and eighty-three monasteries and other prelatries. The three electoral territories of Cologne, Mainz, and Trier, and thirty of the bishoprics – collectively comprising about a quarter of the land of Germany – were ecclesiastical principalities, where prince-bishops ruled without strong local civil rivals. The remaining ecclesiastical polities overlapped with civil polities, and clerics and magistrates ruled concurrently.[3] The Church operated most of the schools, hospices, almshouses, and charities in Germany through its cathedrals, monasteries, chantries, and ecclesiastical guilds. Thousands of clerics served in the Church, many of them trained in both theology and canon law in one of the dozen German universities that had been chartered by the Church, or abroad in Italy, France, Spain, or the Netherlands.[4] In 1500, canon law dominated the law faculties of the German universities: the majority of chairs were occupied by canonists, and the majority of law students pursued canon law studies.[5]

With this elaborate structure, the Church claimed a vast *spiritual* jurisdiction in Germany. The Church claimed exclusive personal jurisdiction over clerics and monastics, over Jews, Muslims, and heretics, over transient persons like pilgrims, students, crusaders, sailors, and foreign merchants, and over such *personae miserabiles* as widows, orphans, and the poor. It also claimed subject matter jurisdiction over religious doctrine

---

3 Benecke, *Society and Politics*, 382–93; Willy Andreas, *Deutschland vor der Reformation*, 5th edn. (Berlin, 1932), 61 ff.; Lawrence G. Duggan, *Bishop and Chapter: The Governance of the Bishopric of Speyer to 1552* (New Brunswick, NJ, 1978), 3ff.

4 The thirteenth German university, at Wittenberg, was not chartered by the church on its establishment in 1502. See Heiko A. Oberman, "University and Society on the Threshold of Modern Times: The German Connection," in James M. Kittelson and Pamela J. Transue, eds., *Rebirth, Reform, and Resilience: Universities in Transition, 1300–1700* (Columbus, OH, 1984), 19, 28. On the training of canon lawyers in Germany and abroad, see Stölzel, 1:45–111; Rainer C. Schwinges, *Deutsche Universitätsbesucher im 14. bis 15. Jahrhundert. Studien zur Sozialgeschichte des alten Reiches* (Stuttgart, 1986); Erich Genzmer, "Kleriker als Berufsjuristen im späten Mittelalter," in *Etudes d'histoire du droit canonique dédiées à Gabriel le Bras*, 2 vols. (Paris, 1965), 2:1207–36.

5 See generally Stintzing, 21ff.; Stobbe, 2:16ff.; Coing, 1:835–46. Karl H. Burmeister, *Das Studium der Rechte im Zeitalter des Humanismus im deutschen Rechtsbereich* (Wiesbaden, 1974), 31–57, 73–7, 181–93, shows that in pre-Reformation Germany, on average, 60% of law faculty chairs were devoted to canon law study, and the vast majority of students pursued either the *doctor juris canonici* or *doctor juris utriusque*.

and liturgy; ecclesiastical property, patronage, benefices, and tithes; clerical ordination, appointment, and discipline; sex, marriage, and family relations; wills, testaments, and intestacy; oaths and pledges of faith; and a host of moral offenses against God, neighbor, and self. The Church repeated its claims of spiritual jurisdiction in numerous concordats and letters from the later thirteenth century onward.[6]

The Church also claimed *temporal* jurisdiction over subjects and persons that fell within the concurrent jurisdiction of one or more civil authorities. Through prorogation or choice-of-law provisions in contracts or treaties, or through prorogation agreements executed on the eve of trial, parties could mutually agree to litigate their civil disputes in accordance with canon law. Through removal procedures, cases could be transferred from a civil court to a Church court if the civil relief or procedures available were adjudged unfair or unfit.[7]

These jurisdictional claims rendered Church officials both legislators and judges in Germany. From the twelfth century onward, Church authorities issued a steady stream of papal decretals and bulls, conciliar decrees and edicts that were to prevail throughout Western Christendom. These general legislative documents circulated singly and in heavily glossed German collections. A formidable body of supplementary legislation promulgated by German bishops and synods also circulated, both in original form and in glossed local collections and pastoral handbooks.[8] Bulky confessional manuals by Johannes von Freiburg, Johannes von Bruder Berthold, Angelus de Clavasio, and others provided elaborate summaries and illustrations of canon law rules.[9] Handsomely decorated handbooks such as *The Decretal Pearl, The Golden Compendium*, and *The Abridged Decretum and Decretals* provided useful introductions to canonical legislation.[10] More seasoned readers could turn to the learned

---

[6] See Udo Wolter, "Amt und Officium in mittelalterlichen Quellen vom 13. bis 15. Jahrhundert: Eine begriffsgeschichtliche Untersuchung," *ZSS KA* 78 (1988): 246; Harold J. Berman, *Law and Revolution: The Formation of the Western Legal Tradition* (Cambridge, MA, 1983), 260ff.; Coing, 1:467–504, 835–46.

[7] Winfried Trusen, *Anfänge des gelehrten Rechts in Deutschland. Ein Beitrag zur Geschichte der Frührezeption* (Wiesbaden, 1962), 63ff.

[8] On the development of the *Corpus iuris canonici* (so named for the first time in 1671), see Coing, 1:835–46, 2/1:615, 664–7; Roderich von Stintzing, *Geschichte der populären Literatur des römisch-kanonischen Rechts in Deutschland am Ende des fünfzehnten und im Anfang des sechszehnten Jahrhunderts* (Leipzig, 1867) 7–50, 151–96; Stobbe, 2:17ff.

[9] See lists in Ludwig Hain, *Repertorium bibliographicum in quo libri omnes ab arte typographica inventa usque ad annum MD typis expressi ordine alphabetico vel simpliciter enumerantur vel adcuratius recensentur*, 4 vols. (Milan, 1948) and discussion in Trusen, *Anfänge*, 135ff.; Thomas N. Tentler, *Sin and Confession on the Eve of the Reformation* (Princeton, NJ, 1977), 28ff.

[10] *Margarita decreti seu tabula martiniana. . . .* (Erlangen, 1481); *Repertorium aureum mirabili artificio contextum continens titulos quinque librorum decretalium* (Cologne, 1495); Paulus Florentinus, *Breviarium decretorum et decretalium* (Louvain, 1484).

commentaries and opinions of Johannes Andreae, Sebastian Brant, and scores of other German canonists whose writings circulated widely in early sixteenth-century Germany given the advent of printing.[11]

Church courts adjudicated cases in accordance with the substantive and procedural rules of the canon law. Most cases were heard first in the consistory court, presided over by the archdeacon or a provisory judge. Major disputes, however, involving annulment, heresy, or clerical felonies, were generally heard by the consistory court of the bishop, presided over by the bishop himself or by his principal official. Periodically, the pope or a strong bishop would deploy itinerant ecclesiastical judges, called *inquisitores*, with original jurisdiction over discrete questions that would normally lie within the competence of the consistory courts. The pope also sent out his legates who could exercise a variety of judicial and administrative powers in his name. Cases could be appealed up the hierarchy of Church courts, ultimately to the papal rota. Cases raising particularly serious or novel questions could be referred to distinguished canonists or law faculties called assessors, whose learned opinions (*consilia*) on the questions were often taken by the Church court as edifying if not binding.[12]

The Church's jurisdictional claims to make and enforce canon law rested on three main arguments.

First, the Church predicated its jurisdictional claims on its authority over the sacraments. Since the twelfth century, theologians had recognized seven liturgical sacraments: baptism, confirmation, penance, eucharist, marriage, ordination, and extreme unction, a sacramental theology finally and formally confirmed by the Council of Trent (1545–63). These seven liturgical sacraments, unlike other sacred symbols and rituals, were considered to be, in Peter Lombard's words, both "signs" and "causes" of God's grace, which Christ had instituted for the sanctification of His Church.[13] If properly administered and received, sacraments transformed the souls of their participants and conferred sanctifying grace upon the Christian community. The administration of such solemn ceremonies could not turn simply on the predilections of parish priests or the preferences of individual believers. Christ had vested authority over the sacraments in St. Peter and, through apostolic succession, in the papal and other ruling offices of the Church. The pope and his clergy thus

---

[11] See discussion in Stintzing, *Literatur*, 451–62.

[12] See sources and discussion in James R. Sweeney and Stanley A. Chodorow, eds., *Popes, Teachers, and Canon Law in the Middle Ages* (Ithaca, NY, 1989).

[13] Petrus Lombardus, *Libri IV sententiarum*, 2nd rev. edn. (Florence, 1916), bk. 4, Dist. 2.1. See further Joseph Martos, *Doors to the Sacred: A Historical Introduction to Sacraments in the Catholic Church* (Garden City, NY, 1981), 65–96.

had authority to promulgate and enforce canon law rules (literally to "speak the law" – *jus dicere*) that would govern sacramental participation and procedure.

The Church had exercised this jurisdiction over the sacraments since apostolic times, and with increasing alacrity since the twelfth century. By 1517, the Church had woven around certain sacraments whole systems of canon law rules and procedures. The sacrament of marriage supported the canon law of sex, marriage, and family life. The sacrament of penance supported the canon law of crimes and torts (delicts) and, indirectly, the canon law of contracts, oaths, charity, and inheritance. The sacrament of ordination became the foundation for a refined canon law of corporate rights and duties of the clergy. The sacrament of baptism and confirmation undergirded a constitutional law of natural rights and duties of Christian believers.[14]

Secondly, the Church predicated its jurisdictional claims on Christ's famous delegation to the Apostle Peter: "I will give you the keys of the kingdom of heaven, and whatever you bind on earth shall be bound in heaven, and whatever you loose on earth shall be loosed in heaven."[15] According to conventional canonical lore, Christ had conferred on St. Peter two keys: a key of knowledge to discern God's word and will, and a key of power to implement and enforce that word and will throughout the Church. St. Peter had used these keys to help define the doctrine and discipline of the apostolic Church. Through apostolic succession, the pope and his clergy had inherited these keys to define the doctrine and discipline of the contemporary Church. This inheritance, the canonists believed, conferred on the pope and his clergy a legal power, a power to make and enforce canon laws.[16] "In deciding cases the authority of the Roman pontiffs prevails," wrote a thirteenth-century canonist, "for ... not only knowledge is needed, but also power is needed ... power, that is jurisdiction."[17]

This argument of the keys readily supported the Church's claims to subject matter jurisdiction over core spiritual matters of doctrine and liturgy – the purpose and timing of the mass, baptism, eucharist,

---

[14] See generally Paul Wilpert, ed., *Lex et Sacramentum im Mittelalter* (Berlin, 1969); Peter Landau, "Sakramentalität und Jurisdiktion," in Gerhard Rau *et al.*, eds., *Das Recht der Kirche*, 3 vols. (Gütersloh, 1995), 2:58–95; Berman, *Law and Revolution*, 165–254; R. H. Helmholz, *The Spirit of the Classical Canon Law* (Athens, GA/London, 1996), 200–28.

[15] Matthew 16:19 (RSV).

[16] Brian Tierney, *The Origins of Papal Infallibility, 1150–1350* (Leiden, 1972), 39ff.

[17] Quoted by Brian Tierney, *Religion, Law, and the Growth of Constitutional Thought, 1150–1650* (Cambridge, 1982), 32.

confession, and the like. The key of knowledge, after all, gave the pope and his clergy access to the mysteries of divine revelation, which, by use of the key of power, they communicated to all believers through the canon law. The argument of the keys, however, could be easily extended. Even the most mundane of human affairs ultimately have spiritual and moral dimensions. Resolution of a boundary line dispute between neighbors implicates the commandment to love one's neighbor. Unaccountable failure to pay one's civil taxes or feudal dues is a breach of the spiritual duty to honor those in authority. Printing or reading a censored book is a sin. Strong clergy, therefore, readily used the argument of the keys to extend the subject matter jurisdiction of the Church to matters with more attenuated spiritual and moral dimensions, particularly in jurisdictions where they had no strong civil rivals.[18] A 1435 declaration by the Archbishop of Mainz, for example, claimed

jurisdiction over all and individual cases, criminal and civil, spiritual and temporal, beneficial and profane . . . and [over] all matters [involving] prelates, chapters, assemblies, corporations, universities, as well as individual persons, clerics and laymen, of whatever status and grade, dignity and preeminence, by reason of orders or condition.[19]

Thirdly, the Church predicated its jurisdictional claims on the belief that the canon law was the true source of Christian equity. Canon law, in the words of the early sixteenth-century jurist Nicolaus Everardus, was rooted in "the teachings of the Bible, the Church Fathers, and the seven ecumenical councils, and inspired by the Holy Spirit." Civil law, by contrast, was of "pagan origin" and inspired by "secular reason." In the minds of many canonists, therefore, canon law was perforce superior in authority and in sanctity. Civil law was perforce "secondary, subordinate, and subsidiary."[20]

The canon law was considered not only a Christian law but also an equitable law. Late medieval canonists referred to it variously as "the mother of exceptions," "the epitome of the law of love," and "the mother of justice." As the mother of exceptions, canon law was flexible, reasonable, and fair, capable either of bending the rigor of a rule in an individual case through dispensations and injunctions, or punctiliously insisting on

---

[18] See examples in Trusen, *Anfänge*, 45ff.

[19] Quoted by Georg May, *Die geistliche Gerichtsbarkeit des Erzbischofs von Mainz im Thüringen des späten Mittelalters* (Tübingen, 1950), 111.

[20] Nicolaus Everardus, *Loci argumentorum legales* (Amsterdam, 1603), locus 130. See further L. J. van Apeldoorn, *Nicolaas Everaerts (1462–1532) en het recht van zijn tijd* (Amsterdam, 1935), 9–14.

the letter of an agreement through orders of specific performance or reformation of documents. Canon law thereby "smoothed the hard and coarse edges of strict Roman [i.e., civil] law," in Everardus' words.[21] As the epitome of love, canon law afforded special care to the disadvantaged – widows, orphans, the poor, the handicapped, abused wives, neglected children, maltreated servants, and the like. It provided them with standing to press claims in Church courts, competence to testify against their superiors without their permission, methods to gain succor and shelter from abuse and want, opportunities to pursue pious and protected careers in the cloister.[22] As the mother of justice, canon law provided a method whereby the individual believer could reconcile himself or herself at once to God and to neighbor. "Herein lies the essence of canonical equity," Eugen Wohlhaupter maintains, and perhaps the principal reason why litigants would tend to be drawn to Church courts over civil courts. Church courts treated both the legality and the morality of the conflicts before them. Their remedies enabled litigants to become "righteous" and "just" not only in their relationships with opposing parties and the rest of the community, but also in their relationship to God.[23]

This system of canon law and ecclesiastical jurisdiction was not without ample detractors, both within the Church hierarchy and without. As early as 1324, for example, Marsilius of Padua issued a withering attack on the Church's claims to temporal jurisdiction and the papacy's claims to superiority within the clerical hierarchy. These views were echoed by a number of later critics in the German Empire, notably John Hus of Prague and Nicholas of Cusa, who spent a good deal of his career in Germany.[24] Nicholas of Cusa also laid the foundation for Lorenzo Valla's famous exposure of the forged fourth-century "Donation" of power by Emperor Constantine to Pope Sylvester. This Donation of Constantine had been a key early canonical text that supported a whole welter of later medieval arguments for the superiority of the pope to the emperor, and of the spiritual power to the temporal power. This philological deconstruction was of a piece with several other humanist

---

[21] Ibid., 12. See further sources quoted in Pier Giovanni Caron, "Aequitas et interpretatio dans la doctrine canonique aux XIIIe et XIVe siècles," *Monumenta Iuris Canonici Series C* 4 (1971): 131.

[22] Berman, *Faith and Order*, 55–82.

[23] Eugen Wohlhaupter, *Aequitas canonica. Eine Studie aus dem kanonischen Recht* (Paderborn, 1931), 16–17. See also Stobbe, 2:110ff.; Trusen, *Anfänge*, 22ff.

[24] See Marsilius of Padua, *The Defensor Pacis Translated with an Introduction*, trans. and ed. Alan Gewirth (New York, 1956), Discourse II. For its circulation in fifteenth-century Germany, see Hermann Heimpel, "Characteristics of the Late Middle Ages in Germany," in Gerald Strauss, ed., *Pre-Reformation Germany* (New York, 1972), 43–72, at 59ff.; Paul E. Sigmund, "The Influence of Marsilius of Padua on XVth-Century Conciliarism," *Journal of the History of Ideas* 23 (1962): 392.

challenges to the authenticity of other important canon law texts, and with the agitation for the development of critical editions of the original canonical sources, freed from the (sometimes self-serving) medieval glosses and commentaries.[25]

These humanist attacks on some of the canon law texts also provided fuel for the growing movement of conciliarism within the Church. Since 1378 the papacy had been bitterly divided, with rival popes in Avignon and Rome, and for a brief time a third rival pope in Pavia. Given the widespread confusion within the Church hierarchy, and in the operation of the canon law, Emperor Sigismund in 1415 convoked at Constance the first of a series of great Church councils that declared the Church council to be the final authority over Church polity and canon law, despite papal disapproval. This was partly a fresh canonical and theological invention to restrict papal tyranny and to restore the canon law to its preeminent authority in Christendom. But it was also a return to long-obscured earlier canonical texts that the humanists had helped to bring to new light and life.[26]

The weakness of the papacy during and around this period of the Great Schism also empowered strong kings in Europe to take a measure of control over the Church's law and property. In England, for example, the Statutes of Provisors (1351) and Praemunire (1353) truncated the original and appellate jurisdiction of the Church courts.[27] In the Pragmatic Sanction of Bourges (1438) and again in the Concordat of Bologna (1516), French kings banned various papal taxes, limited appeals to Rome, required French bishops to be elected by French Church councils called by the king, subjected the clergy in France to royal discipline, and increased royal control over Church property.[28] Comparable movements to restrict the power of the clergy and the canon law were afoot in Germany, but in the absence of a strong central monarch, they came to more sporadic local application.

---

[25] For a modern edition of the Donation see Walter Schwahn, ed., *De falsa credita et ementita Constantini Donatione declamatio* (Stuttgart, 1994), with discussion in Donald R. Kelley, *Foundations of Modern Historical Scholarship: Language, Law, and History in the French Renaissance* (New York, 1970), 19ff.; Myron P. Gilmore, *Humanists and Jurists: Six Studies in the Renaissance* (Cambridge, MA, 1963), 3ff.; Ernst Cassirer, *The Individual and the Cosmos in Renaissance Philosophy*, trans. Mario Domandi (Philadelphia, 1963), 78ff.

[26] See Brian Tierney, *Foundations of the Conciliar Theory: The Contribution of the Medieval Canonists from Gratian to the Great Schism*, new enlarged edn. (Leiden/New York, 1998).

[27] Reprinted in Carl Stephenson and Frederick G. Marcham, eds., *Sources of English Constitutional History*, rev. edn. (New York/San Francisco, 1972), 226–8.

[28] Reprinted and analyzed in Sidney Z. Ehler and John B. Morrall, *Church and State Through the Centuries* (Westminster, MD, 1954), 96–144.

CIVIL LAW

The hierarchy of canon law structures that prevailed in pre-Reformation Germany stood in marked contrast with the honeycomb of civil law structures. In 1500, German civil authority was divided among the four electoral principalities of Bohemia, Brandenburg, Saxony, and the Palatinate, thirty-one additional secular principalities, some 138 smaller duchies and lordships, some eighty-five "free" imperial and territorial cities, and nearly 3,000 tiny towns and villages.[29] Many of these local civil polities had their own internal laws and courts, some of them predicated on centuries-old charters of rights and privileges, which local leaders fiercely defended against civil and ecclesiastical detractors.

In theory, these sundry civil authorities of Germany were all confederated within the Holy Roman Empire of the German Nation. Formal constitutional law of the day declared the Holy Roman Emperor to be the preeminent civil authority of Germany. The emperor discharged executive authority through his Chancery and Treasury, as well as through the Imperial Council of Regency (*Reichsregiment*) that sat in his absence. He exercised legislative authority through the imperial diets – literally imperial meeting "days" (from *dies* in Latin). These were itinerant parliamentary meetings with representative princes, nobles, and city officials called by the emperor and empowered to vote on general ordinances and imperial peace statutes prepared by the Chancery and Regency. The emperor discharged judicial authority through the high imperial courts: the *Reichshofgericht* of the thirteenth century that eventually fell into desuetude, and the Supreme Imperial Court (*Reichskammergericht*) established in Germany in 1495.[30] The emperor was an important source and symbol of national identity in late medieval Germany, and a great deal of political pageantry and nationalist liturgy was attached to his court and office. Individual emperors sometimes exercised a considerable influence over the military, material, and moral tone and temperature of the German people.[31]

In reality, however, the Holy Roman Emperor and Empire were largely under the control of the German princes and estates by the end of the fifteenth century. Already in the imperial Golden Bull of 1356, a severely weakened and overextended Emperor Charles IV had given the right to elect his successors to the seven "electoral" princes of Germany – the

[29] Benecke, *Society and Politics*, 382–93.
[30] Denys Hay, *Europe in the Fourteenth and Fifteenth Centuries* (New York, 1966), 193ff.
[31] Guy E. Swanson, *Religion and Regime: A Sociological Account of the Reformation* (New York, 1967), 85ff.

three prince-bishops of Mainz, Trier, and Cologne, and the four secular princes of Bohemia, Saxony, Brandenburg, and the Palatinate – who were jealous of their own local interests. This Bull also tacitly rendered the seven electoral princes the preeminent civil authorities of Germany, touching off more than a century of intermittent rivalries among them and the lesser principalities, duchies, cities, and estates of nobles and imperial knights.

In 1495, Emperor Maximilian I sought to quell these perennial German feuds and to regularize his procurement of imperial taxes and soldiers. He declared a territorial peace (*Landfriede*) in the Empire and established the Supreme Imperial Court (*Reichskammergericht*) with jurisdiction over sundry disputes between and within local German civil polities. What might have been a strong assertion of imperial authority in Germany, however, ultimately proved to be a further abdication of the same. The 1495 Ordinance that created the Court put power to appoint the Court's judges and notaries in the hands of the German princes and estates. Invariably, they appointed judges who tended to be more favorable to local German rather than imperial interests. The same Ordinance also stipulated, however, that at least half the judges of the court must be legal professionals trained in Roman law, and that the court must follow written procedures and issue formal written judgments.[32] In the sixteenth century, this insistence on legal formality and professionalism would render the *Reichskammergericht* an influential and distinguished tribunal in German legal life, especially when the Peace of Augsburg (1555) granted it further power and autonomy. But in the fifteenth century, the imperial court and the emperor became and remained rather weak.

While German emperors waned in authority in the course of the fifteenth century, many German principalities and cities waxed. Indeed, the century before the theological reformation of Luther was an era of intense "legal reformation" in Germany. In the early fifteenth century, German jurists began to call for a thoroughgoing "reformation" (*reformatio*) of the doctrines, structures, and methods of private and criminal law. Beginning with Cologne in 1437, several German cities passed what they called "legal reformations" (*Rechtsreformationen*). These were major new pieces of legislation, some in excess of 100 dense folio pages.

---

[32] Barraclough, *The Origins of Modern Germany*, 249ff.; Fritz Hartung, "Imperial Reform, 1485–1495: Its Course and its Character," in Gerald Strauss, ed., *Pre-Reformation Germany* (New York, 1972), 73–135; Hans Gross, "The Holy Roman Empire in Modern Times: Constitutional Reality and Legal Theory," in James Vann and Steven Rowan, eds., *The Old Reich: Essays on German Political Institutions, 1495–1806* (Brussels, 1974), 1–30, at 5ff.

They included the legal reformations of Nürnberg (1479), Hamburg (1497), Tübingen (1497), Worms (1499), Frankfurt am Main (1509), and Freiburg im Breisgau (1520) as well as reform measures in several smaller towns. They also included the new reformation laws of the principalities and duchies of Baden (1511), Franken (1512), Bavaria (1518), Erbach (1520), and several others.[33] Also important was a whole series of statutes that sought to reform criminal law, criminal procedure, and criminal courts in Würzburg (1447), Nuremberg (1481), Tyrol (1499), Bamberg (1507), and Laibach (1514), among others.[34]

These local legal reformations aimed, in part, to routinize and reform the civil laws and procedures of these local polities. At minimum, they reduced a good deal of local customary law to writing, often thereby supplanting the ancient urban and territorial laws of the twelfth and thirteenth centuries.[35] More fully, these legal reformations aimed to update and integrate these local laws to some extent – sometimes plucking various substantive and procedural provisions from the many learned medieval texts and commentaries on Roman law and canon law as well as from the new reformation laws already on the books in neighboring German polities.[36] Later and more sophisticated legal reformations, such as the Reformation of Worms (1498) and the Statute of Freiburg im Breisgau (1520), were veritable codes of the local private laws of contracts, property, inheritance, and more.[37] The same is true of some of the territorial laws of the 1500s and 1510s on criminal law and procedure (*Halsgerichtsordnungen*) that put in place comprehensive new rules of evidence, proof, and punishment in criminal cases, incorporating a number of rules drawn from the medieval canon and medieval Roman law.[38]

Many of these local reformations also began to reform local courts and local methods of adjudication. Prior to the legal reformation movements, most late medieval cities and territories of Germany had courts of lay judges called "assessors" (*Schöffen*) to implement and enforce local civil

---

[33] The most important of these are collected in Kunkel, vol. 1. See analysis in Stobbe, 2:279–480; Wieacker, 189ff.

[34] Stobbe, 2:237ff.

[35] On these medieval city laws, see Berman, *Law and Revolution*, 371ff.

[36] For a detailed analysis of these Roman and canon law texts available, see Stintzing, *Literatur*.

[37] Reprinted in Kunkel, 1:95–220; 241–320, with detailed analysis in Carl Koehne, *Die Wormser Reformation vom Jahre 1499* (Berlin, 1897); id., *Der Ursprung der Stadtverfassung in Worms, Speier und Mainz* (Berlin, 1890); Hansjürgen Knoche, *Ulrich Zasius und das Freiburger Stadtrecht von 1520* (Karlsruhe, 1957); Hans Thieme, "Die 'Nuewen Stattrechten und Statuten der löblichen Staat Fryburg' von 1520," in W. Müller, ed., *Freiburg im Mittelalter* (Baden, 1970), 96–108.

[38] See sources and discussion in John H. Langbein, *Prosecuting Crime in the Renaissance: England, Germany, France* (Cambridge, MA, 1974); id., *Torture and the Law of Proof: Europe and England in the Ancien Régime* (Chicago, 1977).

and criminal law. Most of these *Schöffen* were drawn from distinguished families, guilds, or estates and known more for their institutional wisdom than for their professional legal acumen. They tended to adjudicate by giving specific written answers to specific written questions about (the often unwritten) local law. The *Schöffen* would sit together as a court (the *Schöffengericht*) to discuss the local law in light of the questions put to them, and to render a written decision. There was rarely occasion for formal pleadings, written briefs, or adversarial procedure, let alone for formal appeal to a higher court. Hearings in a case, if allowed at all, were usually oral, informal, and without the presence of legal counsel. The written judgment of the *Schöffen* was often a highly distilled statement of fact and of judgment, with little by way of citation to authority, *ratio decidendi*, or concern for precedent.[39] This did not mean that these judgments were intrinsically unjust. Particularly the judgments of more distinguished *Schöffen* courts in the big cities (often called *Oberhöfe*) were highly coveted and prized. But this was a highly localized and plastic form of adjudication, with little obvious predictability as one moved from one polity to the next. This was a notable factor for merchants, bankers, shippers, and others with legal interests in more than one venue. This was one further reason why German litigants often found Church courts to be more convenient tribunals: they all, at least in theory, applied the same substantive law, and allowed for litigation and adjudication following formal written procedures.

Following the example of the Church courts, the legal reformations of the fifteenth and early sixteenth centuries introduced formal rules of procedure into local civil courts. This, in turn, triggered the development of new rules of pleading, evidence, argument, appeal, and more. Even more important, it placed a growing premium on and demand for professional judges, lawyers, and notaries in local courts, most of them trained in the new law faculties of the local German universities. Increasingly at the turn of the sixteenth century, professional lawyers came to represent clients in adversarial proceedings in local courts in accordance with written rules and procedures. Increasingly, professional judges now issued formal opinions, at least in major cases, with an eye to interpreting local legal reformation laws, to adducing Roman law and canon law authorities in support of their positions, and to being consistent with precedents of the local courts. Increasingly, the learned opinions of professorial jurists, and sometimes of whole law faculties of

---

[39] See detailed discussion in Stölzel, passim; John P. Dawson, *The Oracles of the Law* (Ann Arbor, MI, 1968), 158ff.

German universities, were solicited in important cases, both by litigants
and by courts, and these juridical opinions became important sources
of law in their own right. This gradual rationalization, systematization,
professionalization, and "scientization" (*Verwissenschaftlichung*) of German
law, born of the legal reformation movement, are now regarded as the
most salient features of what traditionally had been called "the reception
of Roman law" in Germany.[40]

CANON LAW AND CIVIL LAW

The German civil authorities generally respected and protected the
spiritual jurisdiction of the Church, and the spiritual privileges and prerogatives of the pope and the clergy. Dozens of late medieval imperial
statutes, as well as concordats between German princes and bishops,
dukes and archdeacons, confirmed the persons and subjects over which
the Church claimed spiritual jurisdiction. These same instruments guaranteed the clergy their immunities from civil taxes, services, and prosecution – though strong secular princes and dukes sometimes exacted a
high price for their acquiescence. These instruments also obligated ecclesiastical and civil officials to aid and accommodate each other. When
Church courts or inquisitors condemned heretics, civil authorities were
to torture and execute them. When Church courts encountered contu-
macious defendants or witnesses, civil authorities were to punish them.
When the clergy or property of the Church needed protection, civil authorities were to supply the troops. When the Church's goods were stolen
or misplaced, the civil authorities were to retrieve them. Church officials,
in turn, were to support and protect the civil authorities. When civil authorities sought to execute a felon, a ranking ecclesiastic was required to
give his acquiescence. When a prince sought to discipline or depose a
lower official, the bishop was expected to lend his suasion and sanction.
When a city or territory faced a natural calamity or military emergency,
local churches were to open their doors and coffers freely.[41]

    These statutes and concordats did not, however, prevent civil authori-
ties from seeking to govern matters at the edges of the Church's spiritual

[40] The terms are from Wieacker, 131ff. See also comparable judgments by Dawson, *Oracles of the
Law*, 238ff.; Stobbe, 2:83ff.; Berman, *Faith and Order*, 92ff.; Wolfgang Kunkel, "The Reception of
Roman Law in Germany," in Strauss, ed., *Pre-Reformation Germany*, 263–80; Georg Dahm, "On
the Reception of Roman and Italian Law in Germany," in ibid., 281–315.

[41] See, e.g., May, *Die geistliche Gerichtsbarkeit des Erzbischofs von Mainz*, 143ff.; Paul Kirn, "Der mittelalterliche Staat und das geistliche Gericht," *ZSS KA* 46 (1926): 162, 185ff.; Lawrence Duggan,
"The Church as an Institution of the Reich," in Vann and Rowan, eds., *The Old Reich*, 149–64.

jurisdiction – particularly where local clerics were delinquent or inclined to overreach. The 1438 Reformation of Emperor Sigismund, for example, after decrying the swollen ranks and dockets of the Church courts, ordered cryptically that "[m]atters of jurisdiction and punishment are to be observed according to the old imperial law."[42] A 1440 statute of the City of Ulm, in an effort to curb exploitative betrothals and secret marriages allowed under the canon law, authorized the local civil court to order a man who had seduced a virgin either to marry her or to pay her dower; to fine a secretly betrothed couple and order them to seek parental and clerical approval of their marriage; and to enforce in civil court the canon law of marital impediments.[43] A 1495 territorial ordinance of Baden concerned with both the dwindling number of priests and monks and the manipulation of children into the cloisters, set out detailed instructions and formulas for enrollment in these Church offices.[44] The 1498 City Reformation of Worms, after citing the corruption of the Church courts and the complexity of canon law procedures, set forth a series of simple procedures for gaining relief from defamation, for preparing and proving last wills and testaments, and for disposing of an intestate estate.[45] A comprehensive 1520 statute of Freiburg prohibited a number of "immoral acts" that the Church had not adequately punished – sacrilege, slander, breach of faith, oath-breaking, blasphemy, and unconscionable contracts. The same statute, though it deferred to the canon law of marital formation and dissolution, carefully delineated the secular matters of marriage and family life that were subject to civil law – dowries, prenuptial contracts, wife and child abuse, child support after separation, and the like. The same statute simply supplanted altogether the traditional canon law of guardianship, adoption, and inheritance with new civil rules.[46] By the later fifteenth century, as we shall see in

---

[42] Heinrich Koller, ed., *Reformation Kaiser Siegmunds* (Stuttgart, 1964), 296–97. See further Heinrich Werner, ed., *Die Reformation des Kaiser Sigismund: Die erste Reformschrift eines Laien vor Luther* (Berlin, 1908).

[43] Quoted in Walter Köhler, "Die Anfänge des protestantischen Eherechtes," *ZSS KA* 74 (1941): 277.

[44] Landesordnung (1495), art. 3, in Rudolf Carlebach, ed., *Badische Rechtsgeschichte* (Heidelberg, 1906), 1:95ff.

[45] Worms Reformation (1498), bk. 3, part 1, and bk. 4, parts 2–3, in Kunkel, 1:109ff., 150ff. See further Koehne, *Der Ursprung*, 139ff.

[46] Der Staat Freyburg im Brisgow Statuten und Stattrechten (1520), tract 5, xciii ("On Slander, Outrage, and Evil Deeds"), in Kunkel, 1:276ff. On unconscionable contracts, see tract 2, part 9, reprinted in ibid., 1:261ff. See also tract 3, part 2 ("On Marriage and Preparations for Marriage"), tract 3, parts 3–7 ("On Inheritances and Other Solicitudes Between Married People and Their Children," "On the Settlement of Inheritances Between Children," "On Testaments and Wills," "On Adopted Children and Their Inheritance"), in Kunkel, 1:278–308.

later chapters, a number of city councils came to exercise considerable control over the operation of schools, charities, guilds, poor relief, and family life.

While they generally respected the Church's spiritual jurisdiction except at the edges, the German civil authorities did not often take kindly to the Church's expansive *temporal* jurisdiction. Already a century before the Reformation, the emperor and several strong princes and city councils took steps to restrict the Church's temporal powers, privileges, and properties. The 1438 Reformation of Sigismund, for example, ordered that "temporal and spiritual justice must be kept distinct. If a cleric has a claim against a layman, let the case be tried before a [civil] magistrate. Similarly, if a layman litigates against a cleric, they should go before a spiritual judge." At the same time, bishops should restrict the use of the ban and the interdict to instances of true injustice in spiritual matters, and civil judges must resist attempts at removal of simple civil cases to the Church courts. The same 1438 Reformation also sought to curb abuses among clerics and monks that the canon law in action had come to tolerate. Priests who persisted in the sin of concubinage and "despoiling women" were ordered simply to marry their concubines, to desist from sexual activity on Sabbath and holy days, and to provide shelter and support for their illegitimate children. Mendicant monks were ordered to stay in their cloisters and cease their begging; almsgivers were forbidden to support them. Rich monasteries were ordered to curb their sumptuousness, to cease their commerce, to limit the income of their abbots and the size of their endowments, and to return to their original tasks of prayer, contemplation, education, and poor relief.[47]

Similar provisions were introduced in some of the legal reformations of the German cities and territories.[48] The City Reformations of Nuremberg (1479) and Frankfurt am Main (1509), for example, both included stern restrictions on the use of prorogation clauses in private contracts and treaties and strict prohibitions against judicial removal of cases from civil to Church courts. Civil courts were required to remove to Church courts "purely spiritual cases," but only so long as Church courts, in turn, would remove to civil courts "purely temporal cases."[49] These same City Reformations, together with the City Reformation of Frankfurt am Main (1578), also took increasing control of the traditional

[47] Koller, ed., *Reformation Kaiser Siegmunds*, 152–57, 187–211, 230–34, 298–303. See further Erich Molitor, *Die Reichreformbestrebungen des 15. Jahrhunderts bis zum Tode Kaiser Friedrichs III* (Breslau, 1921).
[48] See further analysis of these early legal reformations, below pp. 177ff.
[49] Reprinted in Kunkel, 1:1, 1:221.

canon laws of inheritance and marital property, introducing a number of changes drawn from various medieval Roman law tracts and commentaries.[50] A number of territories and cities passed new laws that limited gifts and legacies of property to the Church, regulated the amortization of Church property, subjected the Church's secular properties to taxation, and controlled the disposition of income from Church endowments.[51] The preambles to many of these statutes, and the growing numbers of pamphlets and formal grievances (*gravamina*) defending the same, castigated the Church for its greed and opulence – its excessive court fees, high tithes and taxes, indulgence trafficking, self-interested laws of testate and intestate succession, vast holdings of tax-exempt realty and personalty, and luxurious clerical and monastic livings.[52] In a few territories, such as Bavaria, Württemberg, and the Palatinate, territorial rulers simply took over much of the Church's traditional jurisdiction over tithes, benefices, and Church properties.[53]

CONCLUSIONS

These growing instances of popular complaint and civil control of the Church's property and temporal jurisdiction at the turn of the sixteenth century were important storm signals of the Lutheran Reformation to come. They were of a piece with several other reform movements of the day: conciliar restrictions on the excesses of papal monarchy, humanist

---

[50] See Helmut Coing, *Die Frankfurter Reformation von 1578 und das Gemeine Recht ihrer Zeit* (Weimar, 1935), 63ff.; id., *Die Rezeption des römischen Rechts in Frankfurt am Main* (Frankfurt am Main, 1962), 75ff., 134ff.; id., "Zur romanistischen Auslegung von Rezeptionsgesetzen," *ZSS KA* 69 (1936): 264; E. Ziehen, *Frankfurt, Reichsreform und Reichsgedanke 1486–1504*, repr. (Vaduz, 1965); Andreas Gedeon, *Zur Rezeption des römischen Privatrechts in Nürnberg* (Nürnberg, 1957), 44ff.

[51] See Eugen Mack, *Die kirchliche Steuerfreiheit in Deutschland seit der Dekretalengesetzgebung*, repr. (Aalen, 1965), 211ff.; John A. F. Thomson, *Popes and Princes, 1417–1517* (London, 1980), 145ff.; Albert Werminghoff, "Die deutschen Reichskriegssteuergesetze von 1422 bis 1427 und die deutsche Kirche," *ZSS KA* 5 (1915): 1–111.

[52] For contemporary examples, see Ulrich von Hutten's lengthy diatribe *Vadiscus* (1520), in Eduard Boecking, ed., *Ulrich von Huttens Schriften*, repr. (Aalen, 1963–6), 4:145–268; Gerald Strauss, ed., *Manifestations of Discontent in Germany on the Eve of the Reformation* (Bloomington, IN, 1971), 52–62; Anton Störmann, *Die städtischen Gravamina gegen den Klerus am Ausgange des Mittelalters und in der Reformationszeit* (Münster, 1916); Detlof Ploese and Günter Vogler, eds., *Buch der Reformation. Ein Auswahl zeitgenössischer Zeugnisse (1476–1555)* (Berlin, 1989). See summary in Ozment, *Protestants: The Birth of a Revolution*, 11–18.

[53] See sources and discussion in Henry J. Cohn, "Church Property in the German Protestant Principalities," in E. I. Kouri and Tom Scott, eds., *Politics and Society in Reformation Europe: Essays in Honor of Sir Geoffrey Elton on his Sixty-Fifth Birthday* (New York, 1987), 158–187, at 161; id., *The Government of the Rhine Palatinate in the Fifteenth Century* (Oxford, 1965), 140ff.; Paul Mikat, "Bemerkungen zum Verhältnis von Kirchengut und Staatsgewalt am Vorabend der Reformation," *ZSS KA* 93 (1981): 300.

attacks on the authenticity of some of the Church's canons, nationalist agitation against the universalist ambitions of Rome, pietist exposures of the moral and material excesses of the clergy, and more. Taken together, these attacks rendered late medieval Germans highly suspicious of abuses of power and privilege by the pope and other high clergy, and of the high costs and intense casuistry of some of the Church courts and their canon law. When Luther later attacked the "Babylonian" qualities of the Roman papacy, and the "tyrannical abuses" of the canon law, he was sounding very familiar themes.

It was a long way, however, from these *gravamina* of discontent to the outright rejection of canon law and ecclesiastical jurisdiction. No fifteenth-century critic or magistrate in Germany seriously questioned the reality of maintaining one Christian faith and one Catholic Church. No one seriously questioned that the Church was a divinely appointed legal and political corporation in Christendom, with authority to rule spiritual affairs by inner norms and outer laws. No one seriously questioned the natural superiority of the clergy to the laity, of the spiritual sword to the temporal sword, of the canon law to the civil law. When Luther began his theological reformation in 1517, he was very much of the same mind. He, too, at first, sought to reform the Church from within, to call it back to some of its neglected biblical and canonical sources that had become obscured and obfuscated through centuries of power papal politics and plain clerical greed. Luther soon went much further.

2. Woodcut from Johannes Freiherr von Schwarzenberg, *Beschwerung der alten Teüfelischen Schlangen mit dem Götlichen wort* (Augsburg, 1525)

The resurrected Christ, standing beside, and giving his blessing to, a tree bearing the banners "work," "love," "faith" – perhaps representing the tree of life.

2

Loving thine enemy's law: The Evangelical conversion of Catholic canon law

On December 10, 1520, before a group of his students and colleagues at the University of Wittenberg, Martin Luther burned the books of the canon law and of the sacramental theology that supported it. Consigned to the flames were Gratian's *Decretum* (ca. 1140) and four books of later papal laws that formed the *Corpus iuris canonici*. Also included were the popular confessional book *Summa angelica* (1486) and the papal bull that threatened Luther's excommunication. Luther's colleagues Johann Agricola and Philip Melanchthon, who had organized the event, had also hoped to burn the works of Thomas Aquinas and John Duns Scotus, two of the greatest theologians of the medieval Church. But they could not find anyone in Wittenberg who would donate their copies for the fire. They selected instead some works by Luther's antagonists, Johann Eck and Jerome Emser. Luther later wrote of his canonical bonfire: "I am more pleased with this than any other action in my life."[1]

If there were a single event that signaled Luther's permanent break with Rome, this was the event.[2] Three years before, on October 31, 1517, Luther had posted and published his *Ninety-Five Theses*, attacking the Church's crass commercialization of salvation through the selling of indulgences. In several publications over the next few months, Luther had questioned with increasing stridency the biblical integrity of the Church's theology of salvation and the sacraments.[3] On October 8–9,

---

[1] *LW* 48:192; see also *LW* 48:186–7; Brecht 2:424–27; Heinrich Böhmer, "Luther und der 10. Dezember 1520," *Luther-Jahrbuch* 2/3 (1920/1): 7–53. It is not certain what books, besides the papal bull, Luther himself consigned to the flames. See Erich W. Eritsch, *Martin – God's Court Jester: Luther in Retrospect* (Philadelphia, 1983), 38.

[2] See generally Scott H. Hendrix, *Luther and the Papacy: Stages in a Reformation Conflict* (Philadelphia, 1981).

[3] *LW* 31:35–70, 77–252; *LW* 35:3–113; *LW* 39:3–22; *LW* 42:95–115; *LW* 44:3–14, 15–114.

1518, Luther had answered a summons to appear in Augsburg before the pope's representative, Cardinal Cajetan, but had refused to recant his views. On November 28, 1518, Luther had appealed directly to the pope, insisting upon his rights, as a professor of theology, to an open hearing of his views at a general church council.[4] On July 4–14, 1519, with no such church council forthcoming, Luther had engaged in a sensational public debate at the University of Leipzig with Johann Eck over whether the papacy was of divine or human origin – a debate that revealed the increasing radicality of Luther's theological doctrines of justification by faith, the primacy of the Bible, the nature of the Church, and the priesthood of all believers.[5] On June 15, 1520, Pope Leo X had issued *Exsurge, Domine*, the bull that condemned the teachings of that "wild boar" Martin Luther as "heretical," "scandalous," "offensive," "seductive," and "repugnant to Catholic truth."[6] The bull had given Luther sixty days after receipt to recant and return to the Catholic fold. December 10, 1520 was the sixtieth day. On that day, Luther had his bonfire, burning his last bridge with Rome.

Luther had premeditated this act for some time. In the preceding six months, he had published his manifestoes – *To the Christian Nobility*, *The Babylonian Captivity of the Church*, and *Freedom of a Christian*.[7] These tracts and several accompanying letters were filled with angry denunciations of what Luther judged to be fatal fallacies of the canon law and of the sacramental system.[8] Several times in these writings, Luther recommended

---

[4] *LW* 31:253–92.   [5] Ibid., 307–26.

[6] Carl Mirbt, ed., *Quellen zur Geschichte des Papsttums und des römischen Katholizimus*, 2nd edn. (Tübingen/Leipzig, 1901), 183–5.

[7] Respectively *LW* 44:115–217; *LW* 36:3–126; *LW* 31:327–77. See also ibid., 379–95; *LW* 39:239–300.

[8] Though most of these and contemporaneous tracts contained broadsides against the canon law, Luther cited chapter and verse to more than three dozen canon law provisions that he considered to be particularly unjust and unbiblical. Johannes Heckel, "Das *Decretum Gratiani* und das deutsche evangelische Kirchenrecht," *Studia Gratiana* 3 (1955), 512–14; Wilhelm Maurer, "Reste des kanonischen Rechtes im Frühprotestantismus," *ZSS KA* 95 (1965), 192–5. A more favorable assessment of the canon law (of asylum) appears in a short pamphlet, published anonymously in 1517 and republished under Luther's name in 1520: *De his qui ad Ecclesias confugiunt tam iudicibus secularibus quam Ecclesie Rectoribus et Monasteriorum Prelatis perutilis* (1517), in *WA* 1:3–7, reprinted with a 1520 version and modern German translation in Barbara Emme and Dietrich Emme, eds., *Martin Luther: Traktat über das kirchliche Asylrecht* (Regensburg, 1985). The tract is an irenic presentation of the commonplaces of Mosaic, Roman, and canon laws of asylum. See R. H. Helmholz, *The Ius Commune in England: Four Studies* (Oxford, 2001), chap. 1. The right of asylum had been at issue in Wittenberg on the eve of the Reformation: On November 21, 1512, the Bishop of Brandenburg accused the city council of Wittenberg of falsely imprisoning a cleric who had escaped from civil custody and had sought asylum in a monastery. The bishop threatened to put Wittenberg under interdict if the cleric was not released. The case was appealed all the way to Rome before the city relented and apologized in April, 1515.

simply razing the canon law altogether and returning afresh to the Bible: "In the entire canon law of the pope there are not even two lines which could instruct a devout Christian," he wrote. "[T]here are so many mistakes and dangerous laws that nothing would be better than to make a bonfire of it." And again: "it would be a good thing if canon law were completely blotted out, from the first letter to the last, especially the [papal] decretals. More than enough is written in the Bible about how we should behave in all circumstances." "Unless they abolish their laws and ordinances and restore to Christ's churches their liberty and have it taught among them, they are to blame for all the souls that perish under this miserable captivity, and the papacy is truly the kingdom of Babylon and of the very Antichrist."[9] After such pronouncements, Luther's canonical bonfire was no surprise.

Luther's attack

Luther defended his iconoclasm in a whole torrent of arguments in the early 1520s. First, Luther argued, the canon law fostered papal tyranny. The canonists treated the pope not only as "lord of the world," but also as "the vicar of Christ," a veritable "demigod."[10] The pope thus enjoyed unbridled powers of legislation, adjudication, and administration that no one in Christendom – not even an ecumenical council – could effectively review, rejoin, or resist. Neither the pope nor his delegates were obliged to abide by Scripture, tradition, or conciliar decree. Instead, they had power "to break up, change, or eliminate" rules of law as they saw fit. They passed laws and cast judgments for all of Christendom, yet they

---

The party who wrote the legal opinion (*consilium*) on appeal was known to be an Augustinian monk, from Luther's monastery. See Brecht, 1:155; cf. *WA Br* 1:97–8. Whether Luther wrote the tract is disputed. Its irenic presentation of the canon law is out of character for Luther, and the suspicion is that the publisher attributed the 1520 edition to Luther to augment sales. See notes in *WA* 60:311ff. It must be said, however, that Luther was thoroughly familiar with the ample provisions of the Mosaic law that are adduced, and the analysis of them is typical of Luther's early biblical commentaries. Luther also knew the canon law texts that are adduced and analyzed in this tract – those of Panormitanus, Hostiensis, and various titles and cases in the *Corpus iuris canonici*; he refers to these same basic canon law texts in his other writings in the 1510s and 1520s. While the density and precision of the citations of Roman law were not typical of Luther's writings, the Roman law texts adduced are obvious sources to cite for anyone familiar with the issue of asylum, and Luther could well have found them himself or with the help of a local lawyer, such as the Wittenberg jurist Jerome Schürpf whom Luther had befriended by 1517 and who had also written on the law of asylum. See below pp. 67–8 on Luther and Schürpf. I am grateful to R. H. Helmholz for bringing this tract to my attention, and to Scott Hendrix for apprising me of current scholarly opinion about its authenticity.

9 *LW* 44:179, 202–3; *LW* 36:72. See also *LW* 44:182; *LW* 36:71–73, 79; *LW* 48:274–276.
10 *LW* 31:341–342. See also *LW* 44:136.

neither subjected themselves to law nor submitted to the judgments of others.[11] Luther found particularly arbitrary the power of the pope and his delegates to grant equitable dispensations from vows, oaths, contracts, and other canonical strictures that worked injustice in particular cases. "These days," Luther grumbled, "canon law is not what is written in the books of law, but whatever the pope and his flatterers want. Your cause may be thoroughly established in canon law, but the pope always has his chamber of the heart in the matter, and all law, and with it the world, has to be guided by that." The very powers of dispensation that had made the medieval canon law the "mother of equity," Luther charged, had made the pope the father of tyranny.[12]

Secondly, Luther charged, the canon law was abusive and self-serving. The canonists over the centuries had spun a thick tangle of special benefits, privileges, exemptions, and immunities that elevated the clergy above the laity, and inoculated them from legal accountability to local magistrates. Local clergy, Luther charged, used these prerogatives to amass huge holdings of tax-exempt property, supported by ample foundations and endowments, and controlled by parishes, cathedrals, monasteries, guilds, chantries, and other Church institutions. These ecclesiastical units, in turn, used their properties to foster luxurious clerical livings and to engage in lucrative lending practices. To Luther's mind, these were flagrant violations of the canon laws of poverty and usury that had served to "suck Germany dry."[13] When parties challenged these practices, local clergy used their privileges of forum to remove their cases to local church courts. Local church courts, in turn, used the false threats of the interdict and the ban to usurp the jurisdiction of the secular courts and to apply the canon law to subjects and persons far beyond their spiritual ken.[14]

Thirdly, Luther charged, the Church's canon law was an instrument of greed and exploitation. To support its luxury and bureaucracy, the Church imposed heavy annates, tithes, and other religious taxes on the German people. The Church invented all manner of relics, obits, ceremonies, altars, and pilgrimages to fleece the people of their charity. It reserved and sold German benefices and other lucrative Church offices only to the highest bidder – often a foreigner with enough money to pay

[11] *LW* 31:383–95; *LW* 36:336–43; *LW* 44:86–9, 136–38, 141–4, 152–7, 164–8, 203.
[12] *LW* 44:202–3. See also ibid., 151–7; *LW* 36:79–80.
[13] *LW* 44:141. See also ibid., 95–6, 155–6, 163–4, 191–2, 213, 237–9, and his later full treatise on the subject in *LW* 45:231–310, esp. 295–308.
[14] *LW* 44:130–3, 160–1, 181–2; *LW* 45:58–61.

the "reservation fees" to receive his office, but without the pastoral or administrative skills needed to discharge it effectively. The Church even sold salvation and purgation through its penitential works and indulgences.[15] Luther wrote:

[T]oday nothing comes from Rome but a fair of spiritual wares which are bought and sold openly and shamelessly: indulgences, parishes, monasteries, bishoprics, deaconries, benefices, and everything else that was originally founded for the service of God throughout the world. As a result, not only is all the money and wealth of the world drawn and driven to Rome, but the parishes, bishoprics, and prelacies are pulled to pieces and laid waste. Consequently, the people are neglected, and the word of God and God's name and honor perish and faith is destroyed.[16]

This is "bare-faced robbery, deceit, and tyranny of hell's portals."[17]

Fourthly and most fundamentally, Luther argued, the canon law was devoid of authority. In Luther's view, God vested His legal authority in the prince, not the pope. The prince and other civil magistrates were for Luther God's vice-regents called to appropriate and apply God's law in governing human society. The pope and all clerics, by contrast, were called to preach the Word, to administer the sacraments, to admonish the sinful, and to guide human consciences. This was the true meaning of "the power of the keys" described by Matthew 16:18–19.[18] By promulgating and enforcing canon law, the pope and his bishops had usurped the prince's authority and "obscured the Gospel, faith, grace, and true divine service." "Neither pope nor bishop nor any other [clerical] man has the right to impose a single syllable of law upon a Christian. . . ."[19]

Moreover, in Luther's view, the canon law opposed both the teaching and the authority of the Bible. The Bible, as Luther understood it, teaches that each person (1) stands in direct relation to God when confessing his or her sin and receiving God's grace; (2) is justified not by works but solely by faith in God's grace; and (3) is commanded to lead life in all its aspects in accordance with the Word of God in the Bible. By conferring on clerics the authority to dispense God's grace and to intercede for the souls of the laity, the canon law intruded upon the Christian's personal relation with God. It made clerics indispensable mediators between God and humanity, falsely according to them a greater sanctity

---

[15] *LW* 44:141–4, 155–7, 169–72, 181; *LW* 31:175–7, 233; *LW* 45:109.
[16] *LW* 44:88–89.   [17] Ibid., 156.
[18] *LW* 44:83–96, 127–30; *LW* 45:106–9, 118–26. See also his earlier exposition, *Luther: Lectures on Romans* [1516], trans. and ed. W. H. Pauck (Philadelphia, 1961), 358–66, and his later exposition in *The Keys* (1530), *LW* 40:321–77.
[19] *LW* 36:23–4, 55, 70–2, 96.

and greater accessibility to God. By defining an hierarchy of meritorious works, the canon law sanctioned a salvation by works, not by faith; it elevated spiritual acts and vocations and deprecated those of the earthly life. By governing every step of the Christian walk with human rules and regulations, the canon law "tyrannized the Christian's conscience," "Judaized Christianity," and "destroyed the spiritual love and freedom of the Gospel."[20]

The most flagrant distortion of the Gospel, in Luther's view, was the complex system of sacraments that supported a good deal of the canon law. In Luther's view, the Church had fabricated the sacraments of ordination, confirmation, extreme unction, and marriage to augment its power.[21] It had misconstrued the remaining three sacraments of baptism, the eucharist, and penance.[22] "Nowhere in all of the Holy Scriptures is this word *sacramentum* employed in the sense in which we use the term today; it has an entirely different meaning. For whenever it occurs it denotes not the sign of a sacred thing, but the sacred secret thing itself." The Gospel, the word of Christ, Luther believed, is the "only true sacrament." The promises of the Gospel are manifested through the "three sacramental signs" of baptism, eucharist, and penance.[23] Moreover, the Church unnecessarily complicated the sacraments with its thick layers of legalistic and liturgical accretions. In Luther's view, the simple sacramental procedures mandated by Christ in Scripture were all that was required.[24] The vast systems of canon law rules that governed sacramental participation and procedure were, in his view, "distorting inventions."[25]

On the strength of these criticisms, Luther in the early 1520s urged that all legal authority be removed from the clergy and consigned to the magistracy. The Church is a community of faith and love, not a corporation of law and politics. The consciences of its members are to be guided by Scripture and the Spirit, not governed by human traditions and priestly injunctions. All its members are priests and stand equal before God; they are not divided into a higher clergy and a lower laity. The Church is called to serve society, not to rule it. All legal authority and government belong to the Christian magistrate. He is called to govern the

---

[20] *LW* 31:345–54.   [21] *LW* 36:91–126.

[22] In his early years, Luther betrayed considerable ambivalence about the sacramental quality of penance. This ambivalence is reflected in his lengthy tract on *The Babylonian Captivity of the Church* (1520). At the beginning of the tract, he elected "for the present [to] maintain that there are but three [sacraments]: baptism, penance, and the bread [i.e., the eucharist]": *LW* 36:18. By the end of the tract, he was quite unsure that penance could be regarded as a sacrament, for "it lacks the divinely instituted visible sign, and is . . . simply a way to return to [the promise of] baptism" (ibid., 124).

[23] *LW* 36:18, 93.   [24] Ibid., 52; see also 162–98.   [25] Ibid., 32.

secular affairs of all persons, to maintain public order, peace, and justice, and to facilitate the growth of the Church and the moral improvement of civil society.

Luther's allies

Luther's radical remarks were the opening shots in what Roderich von Stintzing aptly called "the battle over the canon law."[26] To be sure, many of Luther's remarks simply echoed the sentiments of more than a century of dissent in Germany.[27] They might, similarly, have come to naught had the papal bull *Exsurge, Domine* had the intended effect of silencing Luther for good.[28] Luther's critique of the canon law, however, proved more resilient, in part because of its deeper theological moorings, in part because of its widespread dissemination and appeal among theologians and legislators in the early years of the Lutheran Reformation.[29]

Many new Evangelical converts echoed and elaborated Luther's critique of the canon law. "We would dearly love to live by God's Word," the Bavarian noblewoman Argula von Grumbach grumbled in a pamphlet of 1523. "But the jurists and advocates are against it, for their law contradicts the Lord's command to 'do unto others as you would have them do unto you'."[30] The pope and his lawyers have "invent[ed] laws out of their own heads and not from the Word of God." They have "greedily" put themselves in a position of luxury and "coerced" us laity into a "state of coin-pinching poverty." "So-called spiritual princes and prelates have their money, while the purse of the secular princes lies empty." Their vast cathedrals, benefices, monasteries, cemeteries, and estates lie free from taxation, yet they impose crushing taxes on us and threaten our magistrates with spiritual sanctions if we do not pay them. So "the sweat of the poor is used to serve the devil." And so the magistrates are "led along like monkeys on a chain by these so-called spiritual rulers." "My heart goes out to our princes whom they have seduced and betrayed so deplorably."[31]

---

[26] Stintzing, 273.   [27] See above pp. 46–9.

[28] See details in James Atkinson, *The Trial of Luther* (New York, 1971).

[29] See sources and discussion in Mark U. Edwards, Jr., "The Reception of Luther's Understanding of Freedom in the Early Modern Period," *Luther-Jahrbuch* 62 (1995): 104–120; id., *Printing, Propaganda, and Martin Luther* (Berkeley/Los Angeles, 1994).

[30] Argula von Grumbach, *Ein Christennliche Schrift einer erbaren Frawe vom Adel* (Bamberg, 1523), Bv, quoted in the translation by Gerald Strauss, *Law, Resistance, and the State: The Opposition to Roman Law in Reformation Germany* (Princeton, NJ, 1986), 6.

[31] Von Grumbach, *Ein Christenliche Schrift*, Bii–iv; eadem, *Wye ein Christliche Fraw des Adels . . . in Gotlicher schrifft, wolegrundtenn Sendbrieffe, die hohenschul zu Ingolstadt, umd das sie eynen Evangelischen*

Philip Melanchthon complained similarly in 1521 that the clergy "have passed laws for themselves concerning immunities of churches, their own revenues, etc. which are both godless and tyrannical to an outstanding degree." They carry on as if "they were rulers of the world" above the jurisdiction of anyone. They "outlaw and curse with dire threats anyone who demands from a priest tribute or tax or any other things which are collected from all for the public good." All this is blatantly contrary to "the divine law that subjects priests to civil magistrates, kings, and rulers."[32]

Similar sentiments came from the pen of Melanchthon's colleague Justus Jonas, a jurist and a theologian who had been appointed in 1521 to a chair in canon law at the University of Wittenberg. Shortly after his appointment, Jonas became so convinced that the canon law "reeked of self-serving" and "betrayed biblical truth" that he abandoned his canon law chair. Upon intervention by Luther and Melanchthon, Jonas was appointed to a chair of theology at the University of Wittenberg, from which he issued a steady bombardment of lectures and sermons against the canon law.[33]

Several Evangelical writers urged the expulsion of discrete canon law rules that, to their minds, worked the greatest injustices in Germany. The Nürnberg reformer Wenceslaus Linck and the Strasbourg reformer Wolfgang Capito both strongly advocated the abolition of clerical immunities from civil prosecution and clerical exemptions from taxes, services, and other civic duties. They viewed such privileges as "against God, against the love of one's neighbor, against all sense of fair play, against human nature and reason, and detrimental to the community at large."[34] Clergy, they argued, should discharge the duties of citizenship like everyone else in the community.

Jungeling, zu widersprechung des wort Gottes, betrangt haben straffet (Erfurt, 1523), Aiii–Aiiib. See Peter Matheson, ed., *Argula von Grumbach: A Woman's Voice in the Reformation* (Edinburgh, 1998), 77–81, 106–08; Silke Halbach, *Argula von Grumbach als Verfasserin reformatorischer Flugschriften* (Frankfurt am Main, 1992).

[32] *LC* (1521), 62. See also *MW* 3:170ff; Maurer, "Reste des kanonischen Rechtes," 214–22.

[33] Justus Jonas, *Der Briefwechsel des Justus Jonas*, ed. Gustav Kawerau, 2 vols. (Hildesheim, 1964), vol. 1, nos. 54, 65. See Hans Liermann, "Das kanonische Recht als Gegenstand des gelehrten Unterrichts in den protestantischen Universitäten Deutschlands in den ersten Jahrhunderten nach der Reformation," *Studia Gratiana* 3 (1955): 539, 543–54; Köhler, 33–4. See also *WA Br* 2:368–9; *LW* 48:275 n. 3.

[34] Wolfgang Capito, *Das die Pfaffhait schuldig sey Burgelichen Ayd zuthün. On verletzung jrer Eeren* (1525), A7, quoting translation in Steven Ozment, *The Reformation in the Cities: The Appeal of Protestantism to Sixteenth Century Germany and Switzerland* (New Haven, CT, 1975), 87. Wenceslaus Linck, *Ob die geystlichen Auch schuldig sein Zinsze, geschoss, etc. zügeben vnd andere gemeyne bärde mit zutragen. Eyn Sermon Auffs Euangelion Mat. 22. Ob sich getzymme dem Keyser Zinns geben* (Altenburg, 1524).

The ex-Franciscan Johann Eberlin von Günzburg complained that Germany was beset "by false and bad faith, from which there is no escape because it is upheld by Roman law and canon law. No one can now be certain of his case given the loopholes that can always be found in it, through which the common people are chased from pillar to post." Günzburg traced these abuses to several canon law rules and policies which he urged the emperor especially to expunge: the constant appeal of local cases to Rome, the easy dispensations from canon law rules, the excessive use of the interdict and the ban, and the hefty augmentation of the staff and the finances of Church offices and courts. Moreover, to remove other abuses created by the canon law, he urged the emperor to outlaw payment of papal annates, taxes, and indulgences, to authorize clerical marriage, to remove most canon law impediments to lay marriage, to limit the property accumulations of the cloisters and charities, to outlaw mendicancy and begging, and to allow the good faith breach of monastic and clerical vows.[35]

Johann Freiherr von Schwarzenberg – a distinguished jurist, who drafted two major criminal codes for Germany, the *Bambergensis* (1507) and the *Carolina* (1532) – issued several editions of a pamphlet denouncing the "ungodly scandal" of drunkenness, gluttony, sumptuousness, profligacy, and loose living that had reduced Germany to "a kingdom of the devil." Schwarzenberg laid the blame squarely on the failure of local spiritual authorities to enforce their moral laws, or even to live by them. He urged adoption of a comprehensive new civil law of moral discipline, enforceable by imperial and local civil authorities alike.[36]

In 1524, Schwarzenberg issued another pamphlet denouncing a Bamberg monastery that had held his daughter in what he called a "hellish prison" and that had embezzled the funds he had donated, presumably to effectuate her release.[37] Encouraged by Luther and others, Schwarzenberg took the occasion to expose what he called "the diabolical teachings of those monkish snakes" and the "perverted and profligate living" of some of the monks and nuns.[38] Schwarzenberg's

---

[35] Johann Eberlin von Günzburg, *Ein klägliche Klag an den christlichen römischen kayser* (1521), in *Johann Eberlin von Günzburg, Ausgewählte Schriften*, ed. Ludwig Enders (Halle, 1896), 1:107–31. See Bernard Riggenbach, *Johann Eberlin von Günzburg und sein Reformprogram* (Tübingen, 1874); Susan G. Bell, "Johan Eberlin von Günzburg's *Wolfaria*: The First Protestant Utopia," *Church History* 36 (1967): 122.

[36] Johann Freiherr von Schwarzenberg, *Der Zudrincker und Prasser Gesatze, Ordenung und Instruction* (Oppenheim, 1512; repr. 1513, 1523, 1524).

[37] Id., *Ein schöner Sendbrieff des wolgepornen und Edeln herrn Johannsen herrn zu Schwartzenberg an Bischoff zu Bamberg aussgangen* (Nuremberg, 1524).

[38] Id., *Diss Büchlyn Kuttenschlang genant die Teuffels lerer macht bekant* (Nuremberg, 1526).

son, a devout Catholic nobleman in Bavaria, objected to his father's strident anti-monasticism. He urged his father to remain subject to papal authority and canon law, and enlisted his friend Kaspar Schatzgeyer to send his father an exposition on the proper meaning of Christian freedom and canonical authority. This prompted the elder Schwarzenberg to write a 383-page apologia for the Reformation – with meaty chapters, amply sprinkled with biblical citations, on the nature of the Church and the clergy, celibacy and oathswearing, the power of the keys, the relationship of faith and works, the seven Christian sacraments, the nature of Christian freedom, and more. Schwarzenberg laid particular stress on the Evangelical doctrines of justification by faith alone and the priesthood of all believers as reason enough to reject much of the canon law and ecclesiastical structure as an "abomination of God's Word."[39] The document, which tracked Luther's and Melanchthon's writings rather closely, won high praise from Luther as a faithful presentation of Evangelical doctrine. But it permanently alienated Schwarzenberg from his son.

The canon law of monastic and clerical celibacy was a sore subject that occupied several other pamphleteers in the 1520s – and would become a major institution for reform.[40] Argula von Grumbach, for example, regarded celibacy laws as sources of great sin: "The pope has followed the advice of the devil; he has forbidden [his clergy] to have wives, but for the sake of money permitted them to have concubines."[41] The Strasbourg reformer Martin Bucer, an ex-monk, argued that canon law prohibitions of clerical marriage were "contrary to both spiritual and imperial law" and must be removed.[42] The ex-canonist Johann Apel, in pleading his cause for clerical marriage, declared to his bishop: "Who

---

[39] Id., *Beschwerung der alten teüfelischen Schlangen mit dem götlichen Wort* (Zwickau, 1527); cf. Kaspar Schatzgeyer, *De vera libertate evangelica* (Tübingen, 1527). See Luther's comments on Schwarzenberg in *WA Br* 2:601 and further Willy Scheel, *Johann Freiherr zu Schwarzenberg* (Berlin, 1905), 328–46; Wolf, 128–30. In 1539, when describing who should be invited to an ecumenical church council, Luther said it should also "include a few intelligent and reliable laymen." If "Schwarzenberg were living, he and men like him could be trusted": *LW* 41:140–41.

[40] See below pp. 215–16, 223–4.

[41] Grumbach, *Ein Christennliche Schrift*, Biii. See also the lengthy tract against monasticism attributed to her: *Grund und Ursach auss gotlichen Rechten, warumb Prior und Convent in Sant Annen Closter zu Augspurg jren standt verendert haben* (Augsburg, 1526). A more gentle and gradual approach to dissolving the monasteries is recommended in *LW* 45:169–72, 341.

[42] Bucer, *DS*, 2:154. For comparable arguments by Melanchthon who had a strong influence on Bucer in his early years, see *MW* 4:8ff., 20ff. and further quotations in Maurer, "Reste des kanonischen Rechtes im Frühprotestantismus," 199–214. See also Martin Luther, *On Monastic Vows* (1521), *LW* 44:243–400; Stefan Klingebeil, *Von Priesterehe . . . mit Vorrede Mart. Luther* (Wittenberg, 1528) and below pp. 223–4.

does not see the fornication and concubinage? Who does not see the defilement and the adultery?" A cleric's breaking of "this little man-made rule of celibacy is very slight when compared to these sins of fornication and breaking the law of the Lord."[43] The Evangelical pamphleteer Hans Schwalb pressed even further: "If a married man sleeps with another woman, one of them must leave the city [i.e., be banished]. But our squires, the worthy clergy, forcefully seize the wives and daughters of pious townsmen and peasants, holding them against God, honor, and law . . . Why are such pastors – and it is not an isolated case but many – not excommunicated?"[44] No one was harsher in his rebuke of clerical celibacy than Erasmus of Rotterdam, himself the illegitimate son of an enterprising priest. Celibate priests who casuistically defended their celibacy while living sexually active lives were for Erasmus no less than "barbarians, monkeys, asses, hypocrites, philistines, pharisees, scribes, publicans, Essenes, sycophants, pseudo-apostles, prophets, [and] demons."[45]

Such antipathy toward the canon law and Church structures did not remain confined to the pulpit and the pamphlet. In the early years of the Lutheran Reformation, civil magistrates rapidly translated these anticanonical sentiments into new civil laws and policies. By 1530, six territories, sixteen major cities, and scores of smaller towns in Germany had promulgated new Lutheran reformation ordinances.[46] By 1540, these numbers had more than doubled. Each of these polities followed its own path of reform, bearing the accents and interests of its local leadership. Some polities were fervently Protestant and seized on an ambitious reformation program with alacrity. Others were more tepid, transient, and selective in their Evangelical sympathies. Others experimented with the reformation but then rejected it altogether or insisted on toleration of both Catholic and Protestant forms. But, whatever their local differences, virtually all of these newly converted polities began their reformations

---

43 A 1523 case in *Politische Reichshandel. Das ist allerhand gemeine Acten Regimentssachen und weltlichen Discursen* (Frankfurt am Main, 1614), 785–95, further described in Apel's *Defensio Johannis Apelli ad Episcopum Herbipolensem pro svo conivgio* (Wittenberg, 1523).

44 Hans Schwalb, *Beklagung eines Laien, gennant Hans Schwalb über viel Missbräuche christlichen Lebens* (1521), translation in Joel F. Harrington, *Reordering Marriage and Society in Reformation Society* (Cambridge, 1995), 37.

45 See ibid., 36–7, 61–3 and detailed discussion in Emile V.-Telle, *Erasme de Rotterdam et le septième sacrement* (Geneva, 1954), 81ff., 233ff.

46 The territories of Prussia, Halle, Brandenburg-Ansbach, Hesse, Lüneburg, and Saxony and the cities of Leisnig, Elbogen, Magdeburg, Nordlingen, Stralsund, Wittenberg, Halle, Bern, Basel, Hamburg, Zurich, Meissen, Brunswick, Frankfurt am Main, Göttingen, and Rostock, together with several smaller villages and rural districts. These ordinances are collected in Richter and Sehling. See further below pp. 182–90.

by seizing the power and property of the Church and its clergy, and challenging the authority of the pope and his canon law.

Virtually all the new reformation ordinances promulgated in the later 1520s and early 1530s accorded civil magistrates new control over religious doctrine and liturgy, over the selection and supervision of local parish clergy, and over the use and maintenance of chapels, cloisters, charities, and Church schools. Many such Church properties became subject to civil taxation and, in several instances, were simply confiscated by local magistrates for use as public schools or charities. Payments of annates, indulgences, and other forms of ecclesiastical taxes and fees were curtailed, and in some polities forbidden altogether.[47] Appeals to Rome were curbed. Removal of cases from local Church courts to local civil courts became increasingly common. Prorogation clauses, stipulating the use of canon law and Church courts in the event of dispute, were voluntarily expunged from contracts and treaties, and in some polities firmly forbidden by civil law. Clerics began to lose their exemptions and immunities at civil law, and became subject to the personal jurisdiction of secular courts, in both criminal and civil cases. Urban and territorial councils and courts began to claim exclusive subject-matter jurisdiction over marriage, education, inheritance, charity, and other matters that had previously lain within the Church's jurisdiction. The law faculties began to replace chairs and courses in canon law with those in civil law.

In a few instances, the new reformation ordinances explicitly outlawed use of the canon law. The 1526 Church Reformation of Hesse, for example, commanded bluntly that "we prohibit all provisions of the canon law."[48] The 1535 Church Ordinance of Pomerania ordered citizens not to conduct marital and related domestic matters in accordance with "the inequitable and unjust (*unrecht*) papal law."[49] The 1536 Hanover Church Ordinance likewise declared: "The canon law forbids too much and then dispenses from its restrictions for money. Our magistrate will not have this."[50] Most of these early reformation ordinances, however, simply sidestepped and supplanted the canon law without comment.

---

[47] See sources and discussion in Cohn, "Church Property in the German Protestant Principalities," 162ff.; Walter Zimmermann, *Die Reformation als rechtliches-politisches Problem in den Jahren, 1524–1530/31* (Göttingen, 1978); Dietrich Kratsch, *Justiz-Religion-Politik: Das Reichskammergericht und die Klosterprozesse im ausgehenden sechzehnten Jahrhundert* (Tübingen, 1990), 19ff. For a good local case study of later uses of church property, see Helga-Maria Kühn, *Die Einziehung des geistlichen Gütes im albertinischen Sachsen, 1539–1553* (Cologne/Graz, 1966).

[48] Richter, 1:68.   [49] Sehling, 4:328, 331.   [50] Richter, 1:276–77.

CRISIS AND CRITICISM

By the late 1520s and early 1530s, Luther's radical goal of a complete eradication of the canon law began to prove unworkable both for the Evangelical churches and for the German states.

On the one hand, the Lutheran reformers had drawn too sharp a contrast between spiritual freedom and disciplined orthodoxy within the Church. Young Evangelical churches, clerics, and congregants were treating their new liberty from the canon law as a license for doctrinal and liturgical laxness. There have been "many wild illusions" about Christian freedom, Luther and Melanchthon lamented in an instruction manual of 1528: "[S]ome people think they are free in the sense that they need no government and even that they need to pay no taxes. Others interpret Christian freedom to mean that they can eat meat, refrain from confession and fasting and the like."[51] This was fundamentally misguided, Luther and Melanchthon believed, and they took the occasion to offer a crisp primer on the true meaning of Christian freedom.

This new instruction, evidently, did not have the desired effect. A year later, Luther again complained loudly about the ill state of the new Evangelical churches: "Pastorates are declining and going to ruin."

The common people...have no knowledge whatever of Christian doctrine, and, alas, many pastors are altogether incapable and incompetent to teach.... [T]hey do not understand and cannot even recite the Lord's Prayer, or the Creed, or the Commandments. They live like dumb brutes and irrational hogs; and yet, now that the Gospel has come, they have nicely learned to abuse all liberty like experts.[52]

Other reformers decried the widespread confusion over prayers, the sacraments, funeral rituals, festivals, the religious calendar, and the division of responsibility among pastors and other officers of the Church. Others lamented the abrupt decline in almsgiving and Church offerings among those congregants who took too literally the Evangelical teachings of free grace. Still others were shocked to find how quickly pastors and theologians had misinterpreted the Scriptures, twisted cardinal Evangelical doctrines, or reverted to an abridged Roman Catholicism.[53] Traditionally, a system of canonical and penitential rules had governed such doctrinal and liturgical matters in copious detail. The rudimentary

[51] *LW* 40:263–320, at 302–3.   [52] *TC*, 532–3; see also *LW* 49:133–6.
[53] See discussion and sources in Ozment, *Protestants*, 89–117; Brecht, 2:439–51.

civil laws on religion newly in place proved incapable of defining and preserving religious order and orthodoxy.

On the other hand, the reformers had driven too deep a wedge between the civil law and the canon law, the magistrate and the cleric. They had vested in the civil magistrate plenary authority over law. But they had removed the canon law as a legitimate source of civil law, and the clergy as a legitimate resource for its formation and enforcement. By the mid-1530s, many subjects over which Evangelical civil magistrates had claimed jurisdiction from the Catholic Church – poor relief, charity, marriage, education, public morality, inheritance, and the like – remained without effective civil regulation and policy. Many Evangelical magistrates lacked the will or the means to implement effective civil law reforms of these subjects. Many Evangelical pastors lacked the license or the ability to intervene in such legal affairs. By the early 1530s, chroniclers and pamphleteers were complaining that the Church properties and endowments which the magistrates had confiscated still lingered in private hands while the needs of the widows, orphans, the poor, the sick, and the young were mounting without relief. Others complained of the erosion of public morality in Germany – the fresh outbreak of prostitution, concubinage, gambling, drunkenness, and usury. Others pointed out the widespread confusion over marriage, divorce, and inheritance requirements, and the precipitous drop in school and Church attendance.

Luther himself pointed to the "great disagreement among the princes and the estates," especially the independent guilds, which had effectively ground civil administration to a halt in several polities. "[U]sury and avarice have burst in like a flood, and have become lawful," he wrote. Germany is racked with "wantonness, lewdness, extravagance in dress, gluttony, gambling, idle display, various bad habits and wickedness, insubordination of subjects, of domestics, and of laborers, of every trade."[54] Melanchthon wrote with equal alarm about the "evil madness" and "insanity" of those capricious magistrates who, "under the false pretext of the Christian name, shake and overthrow the basis of civil affairs" without putting new laws and structures in place. He was particularly concerned about the foot-dragging of the magistrates told to implement the new reformation ordinances. "If you give the magistrate the power to establish whatever he pleases, see into what slavery you will throw us."

[54] *TC*, 453, 459; see further quotes from Luther in Köhler, 46–7.

The magistrates will seize our properties and offices at whim. "Neither our homes, nor our children, nor our wives, nor even our own life will be safe." If this new "plague of antinomianism" is not remedied soon, Melanchthon wrote, "all good things, piety, humanity, all study and arts which love leisure and pleasure will be banished."[55] The reformers' radical ideal of a pure Church governed only by the Gospel, and of a pure state governed only by the Christian magistrate's civil law, had soon plunged Germany into a more acute legal and social crisis.

The leading jurists of the day, despite their sympathies with the Evangelical cause, blamed much of this crisis on Luther and other theologians who had attacked the canon law.[56] The reaction of Luther's Wittenberg colleague and friend Jerome Schürpf was quite typical. Schürpf had been among Luther's closest friends and supporters in the early years of the Reformation. As new colleagues at the University of Wittenberg, Schürpf and Luther had engaged in regular conversation about matters theological, legal, and ecclesiastical. Schürpf had advised Luther on how to respond to the early attacks of Johann Eck and Jerome Emser on Luther's *Ninety-Five Theses*, how to answer the summons of Cardinal Cajetan in 1518, and what to do with the threatened bull of excommunication in 1520. Schürpf stood by when Luther burned the canon law books in 1520. He accompanied Luther to the Diet of Worms in 1521, and served as his legal counsel during the first hearing. He helped to mediate relations between Electoral Prince Frederick and Luther during and after Luther's hiding at the Wartburg Castle in 1521–3. He participated in the celebration of the ex-monk Martin Luther's wedding to the ex-nun Katherine von Bora in 1525. He was among the first "superintendents" Luther sent out in the later 1520s to inspect the condition of the new Evangelical churches.[57]

---

[55] *CR* 11:68, 74–5, 79.

[56] For Catholic reactions to Luther, see Edwards, *Printing*, 57ff., 149ff.

[57] For favorable references to Schürpf in Luther's letters, see *LW* 48:218–19, 227; *LW* 49:13, 36, 168, 184. See also his comments in *LW* 40:272; *LW* 54:150, 180, 236, 246, 262, 338 and Melanchthon's comments in *CR* 11:215, 357, 917; *CR* 12:86. See analysis in Theodor Muther, *Aus dem Universitäts- und Gelehrtenleben im Zeitalter der Reformation* (Erlangen, 1866; repr. Graz, 1966), 190–202; Brecht, 2:43–5; Wiebke Schaich-Klose, *D. Hieronymus Schürpf: Leben und Werk des Wittenberger Reformationsjuristen, 1481–1554* (Tübingen, 1967). In Berman and Witte, "The Transformation of Western Legal Philosophy," 603 n. 64, I included this misleading statement: "'It was Schürpf's example most of all,' Luther wrote later in his life, that "'inspired me [in 1517] to write of the great error of the Catholic Church.'" While Schürpf was generally supportive, Luther in fact reports in his *Table Talk* of 1538 that "Dr. Jerome Schurff advised against writing the [*Ninety-Five Theses*]. 'You wish to write against the pope? What are you trying to do? It won't be tolerated'": *WA TR* 3, No. 3722, *LW* 54:264.

Nevertheless, Schürpf rejected Luther's call for the eradication of canon law and the confiscation of Church property.[58] Schürpf viewed the state's usurpation of the Church's spiritual jurisdiction over doctrine, liturgy, and moral offenses as "blasphemous and scandalous." He regarded the state's abolition of canon law as "unchristian" and "sinful." He described the state confiscation and taxation of church properties as blatant acts of "thievery, robbery and iconoclasm" and the prince's new control over clerical appointments and benefices as "barbarous."[59] "Clerics must be free from all jurisdictional claims of the laity, and all civil taxes, as a matter of divine right," Schürpf wrote in a later legal opinion. "In spiritual matters, [local religious] leaders are the bishops of their benefices. The canon law prohibits any lay person from possessing and controlling these benefices.... The civil law must submit to this canon law."[60]

The distinguished Freiburg jurist Ulrich Zasius, who was initially supportive of the Reformation, likewise came to regard Luther's anti-canonicalism as both unprincipled and unfair.[61] "Luther calls the canon law insipid and frigid," Zasius wrote. But this charge rests on "too gross and general a view" of the canon law. Luther "seems to think that all of canon law has equal authority," though obviously some provisions are more authoritative than others. Luther seems to think that canon law provisions always rival civil law provisions, though in reality "the two laws often run in the same course" and are thoroughly intermixed. "How, then, can [he] say that the whole canon law must be outlawed?"[62] "[I]t is wrong to overturn an arrangement that has for so long been

---

[58] See summary of their differences over the canon law in Muther, *Aus dem Universitäts- und Gelehrten-leben*, 203–13.

[59] Hieronymus Schurpf, *Consilia seu responsa* (Basel, 1559), 1:87, 176. Luther rejected this position: see, e.g., *WA TR* 6, No. 5663.

[60] Schurpf, *Consilia*, 1:79, 86, 108, 150, 151.

[61] In the late 1510s and early 1520s, Zasius endorsed the Evangelical cause, purchased the works of Luther, Melanchthon, and other reformers as late as 1530, and refused the call of the Freiburg faculty to burn Luther's tracts in symbolic retaliation for Luther's burning of the canon law books. See generally Steven W. Rowan, *Ulrich Zasius: A Jurist in the German Renaissance, 1461–1535* (Frankfurt am Main, 1987), 144–9. By the early 1520s, however, Zasius broke with Luther, in part over his views on canon law and sacramental marriage, in particular over his defiance of papal authority. "Here I must leave Luther," Zasius wrote at the end of 1522, "for I regard it as safer to remain here with the [Roman Catholic] Church, with its sacred institutions and the doctrines of the doctors." Ulrich Zasius, Letter to Thomas Blaurer, quoted ibid., 155. Zasius remained a loyal supporter of his fellow Freiburger Desiderius Erasmus, whose own initial reservations about Luther had hardened into open rejection by the mid-1520s: ibid., 135–44, 149–62; Wolf, 79–82, 93; Kisch, *Erasmus und die Jurisprudenz seiner Zeit*.

[62] Ulrich Zasius, Letter of 1520, quoted by Roderich von Stintzing, *Ulrich Zasius: Ein Beitrag zur Geschichte der Rechtswissenschaft im Zeitalter der Reformation* (Basel, 1857), 224. See further Ulrich Zasius, *Von wahrer und falscher Jurisprudenz*, ed. Erik Wolf (Frankfurt am Main, 1948), 20; Köhler, 35.

accepted as right." "[I]t is not only imprudent but also unfair to spurn a source of law that for centuries has been valid." It leaves legislators without "an ancient, equitable, and tested" source of law. It leaves citizens without a fair and honorable standard by which to conduct their affairs. It leaves civil judges with too wide a discretion to work injustice and abuse, since they can now "simply ignore one part of the law."[63] It leaves the Church and the faith without a central authority – save Luther and his followers in Wittenberg. "You assert Evangelical liberty," Zasius wrote to Luther's supporter Thomas Blaurer, "but you do not tell us of what this liberty must consist. . . . Is Luther's opinion alone to be preferred to all the doctors in the last thousand years? Tell me why!"[64]

Luther's opinion on sundry spiritual and temporal matters had, in fact, become highly coveted in many Evangelical quarters of Germany during the crisis of the 1520s and early 1530s. In 1529, Luther complained that "each day, I am inundated with so many letters that my table, chair, footstool, desk, chests, bookshelves, and everything else are covered with letters, inquiries, disputes, complaints, pleas, and so on."[65] Luther was not at all comfortable with his role as de facto Protestant pope, nor with Wittenberg's role as de facto Protestant Rome. He prefaced the 1528 *Instruction to Saxon Visitors* with the caveat that these were not "a new form of papal decretals."[66] He prefaced the 1526 Wittenberg ordinance on the *German Mass and Order of Service* with the caveat that "it is not my intention that the whole German nation must adopt this Wittenberg ordinance."[67] He prefaced his 1530 treatise on marriage with the strong caveat: "I want to do this not as a judge, official, or regent, but by way of advice, such as I would in good conscience give as a special service to my good friends."[68] He objected strongly when a colleague painted him and his Pomeranian co-religionist Johannes Bugenhagen as "the pope of Germany and the cardinal of Pomerania."[69] But, with the abolition of the canon law and the pope, the Evangelical Church and state were left with no other final authority.

---

[63] Ulrich Zasius to Martin Luther (September 1, 1520), in *WA Br*, 2:182; and further quotes from Zasius in Stintzing, *Ulrich Zasius*, 234; Köhler, 35.

[64] Ulrich Zasius, Letter to Thomas Blaurer (December 21, 1521), in Ambrosius and Thomas Blaurer, *Briefwechsel der Brüder Ambrosius und Thomas Blaurer*, 3 vols. (Freiburg im Breisgau, 1908–12), vol. 1, no. 8.

[65] *WA Br* 5, No. 100. Cf. *WA Br* 12, no. 60.

[66] *LW* 40:272 (rendering the original term "Decretalen" in Richter, 1:83 as "decretals" not "decrees").

[67] Sehling, 1/1:10, 11.   [68] *LW* 46:267–8.

[69] A statement made by a Wittenberg colleague, Nuntius Vergerio (1535), quoted by Hans Liermann, *Der Jurist und die Kirche: Ausgewählte kirchenrechtliche Aufsätze und Rechtsgutachten* (Munich, 1973), 183–4.

COMPROMISE: THE EVANGELICAL CONVERSION
OF THE CANON LAW

From the 1530s onward, Evangelical theologians and jurists forged an innovative compromise on the relationship of canon law and civil law, of ecclesiastical and political authority. Evangelical theologians developed a theory of the Church that struck a new balance between order and liberty, orthodoxy and innovation, and that accorded both civil law and canon law a place in the definition of ecclesiastical polity and religious liberty. Evangelical jurists developed a theory of the state that struck a new balance among divine law, canon law, and civil law, and that accorded both magistrates and clerics new responsibilities for law and order. Both theories supported the slow Evangelical conversion and convergence of canon law and civil law.

Theological compromise

The newly emerging theory of the Church was rooted in the reformers' two-kingdoms theory.[70] The Lutheran reformers distinguished between the pure invisible Church of the heavenly kingdom, and the sin-tainted visible Church of the earthly kingdom.[71] The invisible Church is a perfect community of saints, where all stand equal in dignity and sanctity before God, all enjoy perfect Christian liberty, and all govern their affairs in accordance with the commandments of love and the Gospel. The invisible Church remains an ideal form for the current fallen world, hidden from full view and obstructed from full realization until the return of Christ.[72] The invisible Church is, in Luther's words, "so deeply hidden that no one can see or know it but can only grasp and believe it in baptism, the Lord's Supper, and the Word."[73]

---

[70] See detailed discussion of this doctrine below pp. 87–105.

[71] *WA* 31/2:586–789; *LC* (1555), chaps. 27, 28, and 34. Within the vast literature on Lutheran ecclesiology, see esp. Maurer, "Reste des kanonischen Rechtes," 223ff.; Gertrud Schwanhäusser, *Das Gesetzgebungsrecht der evangelischen Kirche unter dem Einfluss des landesherrlichen Kirchenregiments im 16. Jahrhundert* (Munich, 1967), 15–31; Johannes Heckel, "Das blinde, undeutliche Wort 'Kirche'," in *Gesammelte Aufsätze*, ed. Siegfried Grundmann (Cologne, 1964), 132–242; Hans Liermann, *Deutsches evangelisches Kirchenrecht* (Stuttgart, 1933); id., *Grundlagen des kirchlichen Verfassungsrecht nach lutherischer Auffassung* (Berlin, 1954); Wilhelm Maurer, "Von Ursprung und Wesen kirchlichen Rechts," *Zeitschrift des evangelischen Kirchenrechts* 5 (1956): 1.

[72] *WA* 1:639; *WA* 9:196; *WA* 10:140. See discussion in Martin Heckel, *Gesammelte Schriften: Staat, Kirche, Recht, Geschichte*, 4 vols. (Tübingen, 1989–97), 1:327ff.

[73] See *WA* 10/1:140.

The visible Church, by contrast, is the actual Church of this sinful world. It embraces saints and sinners alike: true believers and spiritual imposters; Christians whose piety at times renders them capable of living by the Gospel alone, but whose sinfulness at other times renders them in need of structures of government and strictures of law.[74] As in the invisible Church, so in the visible Church, members still stand directly before God and are individually accountable for their lives. They still are justified by faith alone, not by works. They still enjoy liberty of conscience, which includes the liberty to leave the visible Church itself – the right of exit and pilgrimage that was so vital to the constitutional protection of religious liberty in Germany after promulgation of the Peace of Augsburg (1555).[75] But, unlike the invisible Church, the visible Church uses law together with the Gospel to govern its members' relationships with God and with fellow believers. Compliance with this law does not earn salvation for its members. It merely protects the individual parishioner and the Church as a whole against the distortion and confusion introduced by sin. And it preserves a measure of order, organization, and orthodoxy within the visible Church.[76] As the Württemberg reformer Johannes Brenz put it, Church law

is created not in the belief that by the observance of its good works men repent of their sin and earn God's grace, for only Christ can redeem man's sin, and he has already earned God's grace for us. Rather this Church order is prescribed in the belief that a true and orderly discipline of the congregation of the Church provides both the occasion and the motivation to attend the preaching of God's word more diligently and to receive the sacrament more earnestly.[77]

The visible Church of the earthly kingdom has from its apostolic beginnings, therefore, governed itself and its members by canon laws – both as adumbrated in the Scriptural canon and as elaborated in human canons.

---

[74] Augsburg Apology, Arts. 7/8. The Apology cites the canon law in support of this proposition: "And the *Decretum* of Gratian says that the Church in its wide sense embraces good and evil; likewise, that the wicked are in the Church only in name, not in fact; but that the good are in the Church both in fact and in name" (*TC*, 229).

[75] See esp. Augsburg Apology, Arts. 7/8, 18; *LC* (1555), chaps. 5, 29.

[76] Augsburg Apology, Art. 18, *TC*, 335–7. See also *LC* (1555), 306: "There are various grades and kinds of customs [i.e., laws]. Some are commanded by God [through] divine law. Some are for worldly authority, to establish general peace or morality.... Some are external manners and rules concerning special days and exercises [of worship] such as a bishop might order.... These human ceremonies... are serviceable in an external sense for discipline, for teaching, for guiding, for introducing virtue. But we should be careful about how highly we esteem them." Melanchthon went on to list "errors which the papists enact into their laws," especially their view that "compliance with these traditions merits forgiveness of sins": ibid., 258, 308–9.

[77] Richter, 1:176, 177. See also Schwanhäusser, *Das Gesetzgebungsrecht*, 61ff.

The Scriptural canon teaches basic norms and forms of Christian living. It prescribes respect for the Bible, observance of the Sabbath Day and holy days, faithful payment of tithes, obedience to authorities, and the like. It proscribes blasphemy, false swearing, idolatry, and other sins that offend God and erode community discipline. These basic biblical norms must be obeyed no matter what form the visible Church takes. The Bible does not, however, furnish a complete handbook for proper Christian living.[78] From the beginning, therefore, the Church has made canons that translate general biblical principles into specific human precepts to guide the faithful. "We know that the Fathers had good and useful reasons for instituting ecclesiastical discipline in the manner described in the ancient canons," the 1531 Augsburg Apology reads. Such canons must and do have currency in the contemporary Evangelical Church as well.[79] "We gladly keep the old traditions set up in the Church, for they are useful and promote tranquility. . . . Our enemies falsely accuse us of abolishing good ordinances and Church discipline. We can truthfully claim that in our churches . . . we are more faithful to the ancient canons than our opponents are."[80]

This was not idle theological rhetoric. In the 1530s and thereafter, Evangelical theologians and churches in Germany came to view the early canon law as a valuable source for contemporary Church law and discipline. They looked with particular favor on Gratian's *Decretum* of 1140, the first book of the *Corpus iuris canonici* which collected and integrated numerous passages from the apostolic canons, the Church Fathers, and the decrees of the early Church councils. Thus in 1530, Melanchthon collected and published "some odds and ends from Gratian," principally the "acts and decrees of the old Church . . . so that the [contemporary Evangelical] Church might have an authoritative statement of [religious] dogma and ecclesiastical order."[81] The booklet enjoyed wide circulation

---

[78] See, e.g., *LC* (1555), 257, 307–8; Paul Althaus, *The Theology of Martin Luther*, trans. Robert C. Schultz (Philadelphia, 1966), 335ff.

[79] Augsburg Apology, Art. 14, *TC*, 315; see also Art. 15, ibid., 319: "No tradition was instituted by the holy Fathers with the design that it should merit the forgiveness of sins, or righteousness, but they have been instituted for the sake of good order in the Church and for the sake of tranquility."

[80] Art. 15, ibid., 325. True to its teachings, the Apology cited the canon law thirteen times in support of its arguments. See esp. Arts. 7/8, 12, 23, with discussion in Jaroslav Pelikan, " '*Verius servamus canones*': Church Law and Divine Law in the Apology of the Augsburg Confession," *Studia Gratiana* 11 (1967): 367–88. For comparable sentiments by other reformers, see Rudolf Shäfer, "Die Versetzbarkeit de Geistlichen im Urteil der evangelisch-theologischen Autoritäten des 16. Jahrhunderts," *ZSS KA* 9 (1919): 99–176.

[81] *CR* 23:733–752.

in Evangelical parishes and schools throughout Germany and Scandinavia. Luther was sympathetic to this effort: "There are many things in the *Decretum* of Gratian, gathered from the Church Fathers, which are of outstanding value," he commented. "For in them can be perceived the state of the old and primitive Church."[82]

Also in 1530, Lazarus Spengler of Nürnberg published his own selection of canon law texts – from the *Decretum* as well as the *Decretales* (1234) – for use in the local Evangelical churches. Eight years before, Spengler had offered a crisp fourteen-page primer on the essentials of Evangelical theology, entitled *A Short Concept and Instruction on the Whole Truth of Christianity*.[83] Despite wide circulation, this theological text had not had its desired effect. In an effort to offset the widespread doctrinal and liturgical confusion he continued to encounter in Nürnberg, Spengler published a sixty-nine-page legal tract with a similar design, entitled *A Short Extract From the Papal Laws of the Decretum and the Decretals, Which Set Forth the Articles of the Word of God and the Gospel Which are Unalterable, or At Least Do Not Contradict It*.[84] "It has become clear that our clergy have established a number of Christian articles that are actually false heresy and error, when judged in good faith and conscience against the Holy Scripture," Spengler wrote in his foreword. It seems expedient to demonstrate this error on the basis "not only of God's revelation but also the authoritative order of the [apostolic] Church, the learning and example of the Holy Fathers, and the statutes of the old councils." Spengler thus proceeded to select from the canon law texts ancient provisions as well as more recent promulgations that, in his view, "were consistent with the Word of God and Holy Scripture, and compatible with human justice and equity."[85]

Spengler's selection was quite spare – comprising some 49 folio pages in total. From Gratian's *Decretum*, he excerpted 39 of the 101 distinctions in Part I, 21 of the 36 cases in Part II, and the five distinctions on consecration

---

[82] *WA* 30/2:219. See also *WA TR* 5, No. 6483: "Gratian, a man learned in the law, held this as his sole pursuit and as the final cause of the *Decretum*, that he might be able to reconcile canons and find the mean between good and bad canons. He meant well, but it happened to him that he rejected the better and approved the worse, because he . . . was terrified by the glossator who said this is not to be held because it is contrary to the pope."

[83] Lazarus Spengler, *Ain kurtzer Begriff vnd Underrichtung aines gantzen wahrhaften Christlichen wesens* (Wittenberg, 1522).

[84] Lazarus Spengler, *Ein kurtzer auszug auss den Babstlichen recht der Dekret und Decretalen / Inn denn artickeln die ungeverlich Gottes wort un dem Evangelio gemetz seind / oder zum wenigsten nit wider streben* (Nuremberg, 1530).

[85] Ibid., Aiii–Aiv.

in Part III.[86] In most instances, Spengler cryptically summarized only that part of Gratian's text that quoted or confirmed apostolic, patristic, or early conciliar authorities, citing the original texts in the margins. Much of the nuance of the earlier texts, and much of the integration achieved by Gratian, were lost in these cryptic selections. For example, in Part II of his *Decretum*, Gratian had devoted nine long cases (filling 154 large folio columns) to difficult questions of marriage, divorce, celibacy, annulment, impediments, rape, and the like, integrating an array of widely discordant Christian sources collected from the first millennium.[87] Spengler distilled all this into a one-and-half page paraphrase of patristic and early conciliar authorities that upheld favorite Evangelical teachings on the equal spiritual status of marriage and celibacy and the prohibition of divorce or desertion without cause.[88] From Gregory's *Decretales*, Spengler extracted a few sentences from twenty-one titles, most of them dealing with proper clerical life and Church governance. On the strength of these titles, he issued a sharp attack on clerical corruption, papal primacy, and mandatory celibacy within the Catholic Church, and a firm warning against the recurrence of such "abuses" in the budding Evangelical churches.[89]

Luther was so pleased with Spengler's treatise that he had it republished in Wittenberg, and commended its use at the University of Wittenberg.[90] He added his own preface to the tract, beginning with the comment: "I myself should have long ago drawn such a book from the *Decretum* and the canon laws."[91] In a long tract on the theology and law of marriage published that same year of 1530, Luther again recommended use of "the Bible, the civil law, and the ancient canons and the best points of canon law."[92] Luther even offered a rather charitable interpretation of the papacy, whose rule in Christendom he had so long condemned:

[T]here is much that is Christian and good under the papacy; indeed, everything that is Christian and good is to be found there and has to come to us from this source. For instance, we confess that in the papal Church there are the true holy Scriptures, true baptism, the true sacrament of the altar, the true keys to the

---

[86] From *Decretum*, Part I, Dist. VIII–XIII, XVIII, XX, XXI, XXIII, XXIIII, XXVI, XXVIII, XXXI, XXXII, XXXV–XXXVIII, XL, XLI, XLIII–XLVII, XLIX, LXIII, LXXIX, LXXXI–LXXXV, LXXXVII, LXXXVIII, LXXXX, LXXXXV, LXXXXVI. From *Decretum*, Part II, Causae I–III, V, VII, VIII, X–XIII, XVI, XXI–XXVII, XXX, XXXII, XXXIIII., Dist. I–III (*Tractatus de poenitentia*), Causa XXXV. From *Decretum*, Part III, Dist. I–V.

[87] C.XXVII–C.XXXVI; see Friedberg, *Corpus iuris canonici*, vol. I, cols. 1050–158, 1246–92.

[88] C. XXVII, q. 1; C. XXX, q. 5; C. XXXII, q. 4; C. XXXIII, q. 2.   [89] Ibid., Jiiii–Kiiii.

[90] Lazarus Spengler, *Ein kurczer auszug auss den Bebstlichen rechten der Decret und Decretalen . . . mit einer schönen Vorrhede Mart. Luth.* (Wittenberg, 1530). See Harold J. Grimm, *Lazarus Spengler: A Lay Leader of the Reformation* (Columbus, OH, 1978), 143.

[91] 1530 Wittenberg edition, Aiii.   [92] *LW* 46:267–68.

forgiveness of sins, the true office of the ministry, the true catechism in the form of the Lord's Prayer, the Ten Commandments, and the articles of the creed. . . . I contend that in the papacy there is true Christianity, even the right kind of Christianity, and many great and devoted saints.[93]

It was theological sentiments such as these that provided the basis for the ready importation of medieval canon laws into the doctrinal, liturgical, and administrative life of the Evangelical churches of Germany. Occasionally, the churches were quite overt about this. A 1543 Consistory Ordinance of Kurbrandenburg, for example, ordered that "the members of the consistory must practice and adjudicate in accordance with both the canon and the civil law."[94] A 1543 Church Ordinance of Wolfenbüttel required that at "least two canonists be among the principal jurists on the consistory" to ensure the church's compliance with the "ancient canon law."[95] Joachim von Beust's frequently reprinted handbook on domestic matters, commissioned for use in the Evangelical churches in Saxony, simply rolled together into one body of authority some 140 Lutheran and Catholic, civil law and canon law sources. Where there was conflict, Beust would generally place side by side quotes from each of the authorities, generally preferring Protestant voices over Catholic, and theologians over jurists.[96]

In the more usual case, the later sixteenth-century Evangelical churches simply followed the rules, structures, and procedures of the canon law with rather little fanfare or advertisement. A good deal of the remainder of this book will seek to demonstrate this Evangelical conversion and convergence of canon law and civil law in the governance of marriage, education, and social welfare. Several other writers have already shown this same conversion and convergence in the new regulations of doctrine, liturgy, ritual, and holy days, the organization of Evangelical ecclesiastical polities, the division and distribution of bishoprics, parishes and benefices, their selection and supervision of bishops, pastors and other clergy, the organization of courts and administrators, the collection of tithes and Church rates, the maintenance and support

---

[93] *LW* 40:231–2.

[94] Quoted by Rudolf Schäfer, "Die Geltung des kanonischen Rechts in der evangelischen Kirche Deutschlands von Luther bis zur Gegenwart," *ZSS KA* 5 (1915): 165, 187.

[95] Richter, 2:56.

[96] Joachim von Beust, *Tractatus de iure connubiorum et dotium ad praxin forensem accommodatus* (Frankfurt am Main, 1591). Among canonists, Beust most frequently cited Gratian, Hostiensis, Johannes Andreae, Paulus de Castro, Angelus Aretinus, Antonius Rosellus, Innocent III, Innocent IV, Johannes de Imola, and Lucas de Penna.

of sanctuaries, cemeteries, parsonages, and the like.[97] In all these aspects of ecclesiastical life, the new Evangelical churches and magistrates drew readily on canon law antecedents and analogues.

Jurisprudential compromise

This new theological theory of the Church and the sources of Church law went hand in hand with a new legal theory of the state and the sources of civil law. This new legal theory, too, made ample room for the transplantation and use of the canon law.

Many sixteenth-century German jurists began with Luther's and Melanchthon's basic theory of the Christian magistrate, which we shall discuss at greater length in succeeding chapters.[98] As God's vice-regent in the earthly kingdom, the magistrate governed with divine authority and in accordance with the natural law revealed in the Bible and in the reason and conscience of each person. As the "father of the community" (*Landesvater*), the magistrate was to protect peace, punish crime, and govern the multiple relationships among persons and their collective relationship with God through civil laws and processes. Absent his traditional legal rival, the cleric, the magistrate had plenary jurisdiction – that is, law-making power – over matters spiritual and temporal within the earthly kingdom.[99]

Philip Melanchthon's elaboration of Luther's basic political theory was particularly influential among the German jurists and magistrates of the day. Like Luther, Melanchthon believed that political rulers were called to be God's "mediators" and "ministers" in the earthly kingdom. Persons within the jurisdiction of these magistrates were called to obey them.[100] Going beyond Luther, however, Melanchthon argued that the divinely imposed task of political authorities was to promulgate "rational positive laws" for the governance of both the Church and the state in the earthly kingdom.[101] To be rational, Melanchthon argued, positive laws have to be based on both the general principles of natural law and practical considerations of social utility and the common good.

---

[97] See sources cited above notes 71, 79, 94. See also Anneliese Sprengler-Ruppenthal, "Das kanonische Recht in Kirchenordnungen des 16. Jahrhunderts," in R. H. Helmholz, ed., *Canon Law in Protestant Lands* (Berlin, 1992), 49–122; Karla Sichelschmidt, *Recht aus christlicher Liebe oder obrigkeitlicher Gesetzesbefehl? Juristische Untersuchungen zu den evangelischen Kirchenordnungen in 16. Jahrhundert* (Tübingen, 1995), esp. 83–182; Hans Grünberger, "Institutionalisierung des protestantischen Sittendiskurses," *Zeitschrift für historische Forschung* 24 (1997): 215–56.

[98] See below pp. 119ff.   [99] See below pp. 108ff.

[100] *CR* 11:69–70; *CR* 21:1011.   [101] *CR* 16:230; *CR* 22:611–12.

In discharging this new authority for the spiritual and social lives of their subjects, Melanchthon argued, Christian magistrates were to look to both Roman law and canon law precedents as useful prototypes for their own state laws. Melanchthon placed special emphasis on the Roman law, praising the *Corpus iuris civilis* (565) of the Christian emperor Justinian for its sophistication, detail, and written character. Though some of the provisions in Justinian's vast collection may have been of "heathen origin," Melanchthon wrote, many of its provisions "are the very voice of God, offered to the human race through wise rulers whose minds God ruled by a special inspiration so that they saw the sources of justice and showed them to others." Roman laws were not simply "written by human ingenuity," Melanchthon argued against the anti-Romanist detractors of his day. They were "derived either by firm demonstrations of, or at least by solid arguments from the solid principles" of natural law, of "the rays of divine wisdom poured into us." Indeed, some of the Christianized Roman law can be viewed as "a visible appearance of the Holy Spirit" in the world.[102]

While he preferred Roman law, Melanchthon also viewed the canon law as a legitimate source of the new civil law. The medieval canon law not only provided many examples of insightful interpretation of certain provisions of the classical Roman law.[103] It also provided the best example of a Christian and equitable interpretation of the natural law. "The secret wisdom which God has revealed to his Church through his Word is vastly different from the wisdom which comes through reason," Melanchthon wrote.[104] The Church, over the centuries, has captured some of this wisdom in the canon law. Melanchthon thus repeated several times the medieval commonplaces that the canon law was "a Christian law," "a law of equity," "the epitome of justice," a "rule of Christian love."[105] Though he continued throughout his career to point out "the many errors which the papists enact into their laws," he also pointed to this source as a "a great font of learning" for the Christian magistrate.[106]

Melanchthon's theory of the Christian magistrate and the sources of civil law had a great influence among Germany's leading Evangelical jurists.[107] Following Melanchthon's lead, many of these jurists viewed

---

[102] *CR* 11:921–2; see also ibid., 352–6, 361–2, and discussion in Guido Kisch, *Melanchthons Rechts- und Soziallehre* (Berlin, 1967), 116–56; Wilhelm Maurer, *Die Kirche und ihr Recht: Gesammelte Aufsätze zum evangelischer Kirchenrecht* (Tübingen, 1976), 254–9; Strauss, *Law, Resistance, and the State*, 224–30.
[103] See generally Kisch, *Melanchthons Rechts- und Soziallehre*, 127, 150–1 n.
[104] *LC* (1555), 306.
[105] Schäfer, "Die Geltung des kanonischen Rechts," 215ff.
[106] *LC* (1555), 309; *CR* 16:118.   [107] Kisch, *Melanchthons Rechts- und Soziallehre*, 51–76.

canon law, alongside Roman law, as a valid and valuable source of the
new civil law. Their basic assumption was that "the canon law contains
both good and bad provisions, but in general is useful."[108] We must
be "like the spider," Lazarus Spengler exhorted his colleagues, "and
suck, draw, and discard" from the books of canon law that which is
"opposed and repugnant to divine and human truth, Scripture, virtue,
and fairness." Theologically offensive provisions in the canon law, such
as those rooted in papal supremacy or spurned sacraments, must be
discarded. Politically offensive provisions, such as those guarding clerical
privileges or episcopal dispensations and appeals, also can have little
place. But a good number of the remaining provisions of the canon law
are "godly, Christian, founded in Scripture, and conducive to an upright,
honest, and pious life" and should be put to ready use.[109]

A number of jurists echoed Spengler's sentiments, emphasizing the
great utility of the canon law for civil legislatures and civil courts.[110]
"Some have declared the canon law to be a sentence of iniquity and
impiety," Johann Oldendorp wrote. "But they ascribe these features to
those things [in the canon law] which are of no use."[111] Much in "the
canon law ought properly and licitly to prevail [and] be taught and
observed . . . by reason of its social utility and human necessity."[112] Jacob
Omphalius wrote similarly of the *Decretales*: "There are many that contain
sound [legal] doctrine and are of great value and should be established
and retained in the state."[113] Jerome Schürpf emphasized the traditional
interdependence of canon law and civil law, and urged that the alliance
continue among Evangelical magistrates: "When some matter is found
decided by the Church, then it should be preserved in the secular forum,
because one law aids the other, just as one power aids the other. For if
recourse is had to custom in some case where doubt remains, even more
so should recourse be had to canon law, which is of greater authority and
which prevails in force over custom." Again, "where the civil law fails to
dispose of the matter, or where there are various opinions [among the
civilians], then the canon law is to be kept in each forum."[114] Chancellor
Rehus of Basel declared similarly at the Reichstag at Worms: "In human

[108] Udo Wolter, *Ius canonicum in iure civili* (Cologne/Vienna, 1975), 62.
[109] Spengler, *Ein kurczer auszug*, quoting translation in Strauss, *Law, Resistance and the State*, 219–20.
[110] See quotes in Schäfer, "Die Geltung des kanonischen Rechts," 203–8; Wolter, *Ius canonicum*, 59–64.
[111] Quoted ibid., 62.
[112] Eberhard von der Weihe, quoted in Schäfer, "Die Geltung des kanonischen Rechts," 208.
[113] Jakob Omphalius, *De civili politica libri tres* (Cologne, 1563), c.17, n. 39.
[114] Schürpf, *Consilia*, 71.

affairs, there is nothing better than to hold to the statutes and laws of old, for the commonwealth cannot long endure without statutes. Where our predecessors did not maintain salutary [civil] laws, however, there is nothing wrong with applying canon laws so as to maintain the highest peace and continuity."[115]

The 1543 *Tract on Matrimonial Cases* by Melchior Kling, a colleague of Luther and Melanchthon at the University of Wittenberg, illustrates and explains this appetite for traditional canon law forms. Kling opened his tract by sifting through available sources for the new civil marriage law of Germany: Mosaic law, the New Testament, Roman law, customary law, and canon law among them. He stated several times that he accepted the "new [Evangelical] theology of marriage." But, he said: "I have generally followed the canon law in this writing, which at the time of the Empire was used to frame opinions in matrimonial cases. For even though other laws may have been extant, which might seem more worthy and out-standing – customs and examples both predating and following the time of Moses, the law of Moses itself, the New Testament, and Roman law – these are not completely sufficient or comprehensive for our time."[116] The canon law, Kling believed, had appropriated the most valuable parts of the Old and New Testaments, Roman law, and local custom, and had refined its doctrine over centuries. "Surely, we could not go back to the simple Mosaic rules of marital impediments" or "return to the pre-Mosaic customs of concubinage and polygamy," he reasoned. "Nor could we easily follow both the Mosaic [and] . . . New Testament laws of divorce," let alone try to "observe the multiple causes for divorce [rec-ognized in Christian] imperial law." The canonists had worked through all these conflicting authorities, and had systematized a "Christian and equitable" source of law. Modern Evangelicals should not, and could not, simply cast this work aside. To begin on a biblical *tabula rasa* was foolish, Kling concluded. "We should begin with tradition," and amend and emend it as the Bible and new theological doctrines compel.[117]

Kling practiced what he preached. Though he cited most frequently to the Bible, the *Digest*, the "doctors," and the "theologians" (presumably meaning Lutheran theologians), his tract is peppered throughout with references to the *Decretum*, the *Decretales*, and the tracts of Panormitanus,

---

[115] Quoted in Köhler, 36–7.
[116] Melchior Kling, *Matrimonialium causarum tractatus, methodico ordine scriptus* (Frankfurt am Main, 1543).
[117] Ibid., proemium, A2–A3. See also Melchior Kling, *Das gantze Sachsich Landrecht, mit Text und Gloss* (Leipzig, 1572), I, I, tit. X, fol. 14b, arguing for the role of custom and tradition.

Hostiensis, Johannes Andreae, and several other canonists.[118] Ten years later, Kling prepared a lengthy commentary on various parts of the canon law, including its provisions on marriage. This commentary was thereafter usually bound with his *Tract on Matrimonial Causes*, and the sources used together in Protestant law faculties.[119]

The devout Lutheran jurist Johann Oldendorp made similar use of the canon law. In his oft-reprinted *Dictionary of the Law*,[120] *Collection of Canon and Civil Laws*,[121] and *Topics of Law*,[122] Oldendorp set out in detail prevailing canon law and civil law rules and maxims arranged alphabetically under topics – from "absence" and "accusations" to "usucapio" and "usury." All three sources mixed ancient and contemporary, canonist and civilian, Catholic and Protestant authorities – making heavy use of Gratian, Hostiensis, Panormitanus, and Johannes Andreae, among other canonists.[123]

Particularly in his *Collation of Laws* and his *Topics of Law*, Oldendorp sought to demonstrate the substantial compatibility of canon law and civil law sources on many points. In a series of entries on "marriage," "divorce," and "parent and child," for example, he brought together a wide range of civil law and canon law authorities to show that marriage was the natural union of one man and one woman, formed by mutual consent and for the purpose of love, procreation, and avoidance of evil. All other sexual unions were per se unnatural, and thus illegal. Sexual activity within this institution was licit; sexual activity outside it was improper. Children born of this union were legitimate; those born outside of this union were illegitimate. The *paterfamilias* was the leader of the household, the wife and children subordinate to his authority. Improper conduct by either party could lead to dissolution of the union, with heavy obligations of care falling on the guilty party. On all these positions, the canonists and civilians largely agreed. Oldendorp recognized the conflicts between these sources as well; in such instances, he preferred modern civil law over medieval canon law, and biblical law

---

[118] In this 44-folio-page tract, Kling cited Panormitanus 31 times, Hostiensis 14 times, and Johannes Andreae 6 times.

[119] Melchior Kling, *In praecipuos, & eos qui ad usum forensem prae caeteris faciunt. Secundi libri, Antiquarum Decretalium Titulos Commentaria* (Frankfurt am Main, 1550). See Stintzing, 305–9.

[120] Johann Oldendorp, *Lexicon iuris* (Frankfurt am Main, 1553).

[121] Id., *Collatio iuris civilis et canonici, maximam afferens boni et aequi cognitationem* (Cologne, 1541).

[122] Id., *Topicorum legalium . . . exactissima traditio* (Marburg, 1545), in id., *Opera omnia* (Basel, 1559), 1:83–256.

[123] In his *Lexicon iuris*, for example, which is quite spare on citations throughout, Oldendorp does mention the *Decretum* (58b, 248b), Hostiensis (203a), Gratian (194), Joannes Andreae (194), and Panormitanus (203b, 245).

over both. Canon law allowed for clandestine marriages; Roman law and Protestant theology demanded parental consent and witnesses to unions. Oldendorp preferred the latter. Canon law prohibited divorce and remarriage, granting only separation from bed and board; modern civil law allowed it on proof of the adultery, desertion, or quasi-desertion of one of the parties.[124] Again, Oldendorp preferred the civil law rule, though this was still inferior to the rule of the Gospel: "What God hath brought together, let no man put asunder." "[W]e must constantly be on guard that the canons we use ... do not contradict divine law and natural law," he later wrote.[125]

Jurists at the University of Wittenberg translated these favorable impressions of the canon law into pedagogical practice.[126] Johann Apel – despite his earlier conviction under canon law and ultimate excommunication from the Catholic Church for breaching oaths of celibacy and holy orders – offered lectures on the *Decretales* after 1528, together with fellow Lutheran jurist Kaspar von Teutleben.[127] Lazarus Spengler's collation of canon law texts, discussed above, came to be used as a text in the faculties of both law and theology at the University of Wittenberg. Melchior Kling began to offer lectures on the *Decretales* in 1532, and later added lectures on the *Liber sextus*, a later collection of papal laws.[128] Konrad Lagus, emulating the topical method of systematic theology developed by his teacher Philip Melanchthon, developed an innovative course on legal science that systematized canon law, Roman law, and customary law under various topics, and developed new rules for resolving conflicts among these sources of law.[129] A 1536 revision of the charter of the University of Wittenberg required the establishment of three chairs in civil law, but also a chair in canon law, whose occupant was to offer regular courses

---

[124] See Oldendorp, *Collatio*, 38–40, 46–8, 77–9; id., *Lexicon iuris*, 138–9. See also Friederich Merzbacher, "Johann Oldendorp und das kanonische Recht," in Siegfried Grundmann, ed., *Für Kirche und Recht: Festschrift für Joh. Heckel* (Cologne, 1959), 235–40.

[125] Johann Oldendorp, *Consiliorum et responsorum doctorum et professorum facultatis juridicae in academia Marpurgensi* (Marburg, 1606–7), 1:11, consilium 5, item 23.

[126] See Liermann, "Das kanonische Recht."

[127] Udo Wolter, "Die Fortgeltung des kanonischen Rechts und die Haltung der protestantischen Juristen zum kanonischen Recht in Deutschland bis in die Mitte des 18. Jahrhunderts," in R. H. Helmholz, ed., *Canon Law in Protestant Lands* (Berlin, 1992), 13–48, at 19n.

[128] Stintzing, 281.

[129] See Theodor Muther, "Doctor Conrad Lagus: Ein Beitrag zur Geschichte der Systematik des Zivilrechts und der Lehre von Autorrecht," in id., *Zur Geschichte der Rechtswissenschaft und der Universitäten in Deutschland* (Jena, 1876; repr. Amsterdam, 1976), 299–359; and the summary of recent literature in Hans Erich Troje, "Konrad Lagus (ca. 1500–1546): Zur Rezeption der Loci-Methode in der Jurisprudenz," in Heinz Scheible, ed., *Melanchthon in seinen Schülern* (Wiesbaden, 1997), 255–84.

in the canon law and also to advise and occasionally sit on the *Hofgericht*.
Kling first held the chair, followed by Johannes Schneidewin, a friend
of Luther and Melanchthon (and a frequent guest in Luther's home),
and Matthaeus Wesenbeck, a supporter of the Reformation throughout
his life.[130] Civil law instruction clearly predominated at the University of
Wittenberg after the Reformation, but canon law retained a formidable
influence.

Other Evangelical universities gradually made comparable accommodations to the canon law. The founding charters of the Evangelical
universities of Marburg (1527), Königsberg (1544), and Jena (1548) made
no provision for canon law chairs or instruction. Within a generation of
their founding, however, canon law texts and lectures found their way
into each of these law faculties; by the later sixteenth century, Königsberg
and Jena each had a chair in canon law as well.[131] The norm at other
German Evangelical universities was similar: to retain one of their three
to five chairs in law for a canonist, and to retain lectures, courses, and
degree program based on the *Decretum* (1140) and *Decretales* (1234), and
selections from later papal and conciliar legislation.[132]

Luther was sympathetic to much of this new legal theory and pedagogy, save the retention of later medieval papal legislation. "Oh, you
jurists!" he wrote with exasperation. "I could put up with you if you
stayed with imperial law but not the canon law. But all you doctors of
both [civil and canon] laws defend the pope and his canons more than
civil law and the emperor."[133] Luther was particularly galled that his
colleagues at the University of Wittenberg insisted on teaching the later
papal decretals. "These jurists have the audacity to give public lectures
to our youngsters on this papal crap, the canon law," he lamented near
the end of his life. "So much for our efforts to banish it! . . . We see them
bloated with pride as they now reintroduce this stinking crap."[134] "The
whole canon law and all the decretals . . . are born out of the ass of the
Devil."[135]

Three decades before, Luther's diatribes against the canon law
had revolutionized Germany. Now they rung feeble and false. The

---

[130] Liermann, "Das kanonische Recht," 548.

[131] Liermann, *Der Jurist und die Kirche*, 116; Burmeister, *Das Studium der Rechte*, 56.

[132] See, e.g., the following ratios of canon law to civil law chairs at selected German universities (as
prescribed by statute): Frankfurt an der Oder (1541): 1/3; Heidelberg (1558): 1/3; Jena (1558):
1/2; Leipzig (1555): 1/2; Rostock (1549): 1/3; Tübingen (1535): 1/5. Burmeister, *Das Studium
der Rechte*, 116ff.; Stintzing, 28off.

[133] *WA TR* 2, No. 2496b.   [134] *WA TR* 4, No. 4382b. See also ibid., 5663.

[135] *LW* 41:328.

Evangelical jurists of Germany had created a new ensemble of legal ideas and institutions that could accommodate both the old canonical order and Luther's new revolutionary ideals. Not only the ancient canons, but also the more recent papal legislation could have a place in the new civil law of Lutheran Germany. Their place in the new civil law turned not on their ancient pedigree and authorship, but on their modern utility and conformity with Scripture and the natural law. This was no easy test for the canon law. For the Reformation had given Scripture and natural law its own distinctive interpretations. Evangelical jurists thus spurned much more of the canon law than they accepted. But a good deal of the canon law came to survive and flourish, now under Evangelical inspiration.

SUMMARY AND CONCLUSIONS

In 1520, Luther set out to free Germany from the tyranny of the papacy and the hegemony of the canon law. He burned the canon law books. He castigated the Catholic clergy. He derided the Roman papacy. He called for the destruction of centuries-old systems of Church government and law, and a return to the simple norms of the Bible.

This spare legal diet soon proved insufficient to sustain the Reformation. Doctrinal and liturgical confusion abounded within the Evangelical churches. Laws governing marriage and family life, contracts and oaths, wills and testaments, charity and welfare, crime and punishment, and many other subjects that had previously been governed by the canon law fell into massive disarray. Germany plunged into an increasingly acute social, political, and ecclesiastical crisis in the 1520s and 1530s – punctuated and exacerbated by the peasants' war, the knights' uprising, and an ominous scourge of droughts, plagues, and other forms of *force majeure*.

In response, Luther, Melanchthon, and other leading reformers came to embrace a wider array of sources of law than had initially been their wont. Particularly the older canon law came to be viewed as a valid and valuable source of Christian equity and justice, grounded as it was in the Bible, apostolic canons, patristic learning, and various decrees of the first ecumenical councils. Lutheran theologians developed an ecclesiology that facilitated the importation of canon law structures into the doctrinal, liturgical, and administrative life of the Evangelical churches. Lutheran jurists developed a political theory that facilitated the importation of canon law structures into the public, private, and criminal laws and procedures of the German state. By the mid-1550s, the medieval canon law had returned afresh to Evangelical German society, but now largely under the control of civil authorities and under the color of civil law.

"We have *converted* ["ummkert"] the canon law to our cause," Johannes Bugenhagen, Luther's confessor and coworker, declared triumphantly in 1545.[136] Perhaps so – but perhaps in a more ambiguous sense than Bugenhagen had in mind. The term *conversion* bears a double meaning today. For most theologians, *conversion* means a change in core convictions, in fundamental beliefs. From the perspective of Bugenhagen, Luther, and other sixteenth-century Lutheran theologians, this is doubtless what the conversion of canon law meant to them. They had returned the inherited canon law to its core biblical teachings, much as Christ had returned the inherited Jewish law to His Father's cardinal teachings 1500 years before. They had stripped the canon law of its casuistry and self-serving papalist accretions, and returned to its core interpretations and applications of biblical and natural norms.

For most jurists, however, *conversion* also means the unlicensed and unwelcome taking of the goods of another – a legal offense that can give rise to a private suit in tort, sometimes also a public prosecution for crime. From the perspective of Catholic canonists and Church leaders of the sixteenth century, this is doubtless what the conversion of canon law would have meant to them. The Lutheran reformers simply took over the ideas and institutions of the canon law and converted them to their own use in theology and law – often without attribution. They simply took over hundreds of Church properties, endowments, foundations, charities, almshouses, schools, cathedrals, cemeteries, Church courts, and other properties and institutions that were part of the canon law administration – often ostracizing and occasionally killing former occupants in the process.[137]

Through "false legends, blasphemous idolatry of our own works, as well as corruption of worldly estates, murder, and every kind of trouble . . . he has stolen our bishoprics and possessions . . . and made a horror and confusion" of "everything in Christendom."[138] So reads a bitter pamphlet of 1545. It might well have been written by the pope against Luther. But, in fact, it was written by Luther against the pope. It is an ironic self-indictment. It warns Luther's champions against undue

---

[136] Johannes Bugenhagen, *Was man vom Closter leben halten sol* (Wittenberg, 1545), Civ (emphasis added).

[137] It must be said that Luther repeatedly counseled against violent ejection of monks and nuns, preferring instead to let current monastics remain in place but prohibit the enrollment of any new monks. See, e.g., *LW* 44:172, *LW* 45:67–8, 167–72.

[138] *LW* 41:328–9.

triumphalism about the birth of the Reformation. It also warns Luther's antagonists against undue denunciation of Luther's efforts at reform. Luther might well have been justified in pointing to the material excesses, legal abuses, and theological fallacies of a system of canon law and papal authority gone awry. And Luther would doubtless have approved some of the sweeping canon law reforms introduced by the Catholic Church in the Council of Trent (1545–1563), shortly after his death: several of those reforms were of a piece with those he had begun urging already in 1517. But it is also important to remember that a good number of Lutheran churches and institutions were born out of what Luther's Wittenberg colleague Jerome Schürpf called "barbarous" acts of "thievery, robbery and iconoclasm" against the Catholic Church. And it is important to remember that not a few Lutheran legal teachings were simply lifted straight from the canon law books before being cast in Evangelical forms. Four centuries and more later, this ample intermixing of Catholic and Lutheran theology and law has provided extraordinary opportunities for ecumenical cooperation. At the time, however, it was a recipe for religious rivalry and warfare that racked Germany for decades until the Religious Peace of Augsburg (1555) called a temporary truce.

3. Woodcut from Martin Luther, *Das Allte Testament deutsch* (Wittenberg, 1523)
God in the clouds, flanked by decorative cherubs on columns, and Moses kneeling
before him, with eagle below representing civil authority on earth.

3

A mighty fortress: Luther and the two-kingdoms framework

One of the great ironies of the Lutheran Reformation was that it adopted some of the very same canon law norms that it had at first set out to destroy. In 1520, Luther burned the canon law books. By 1530, he was commending their use in his own University of Wittenberg. In the 1520s, the first reformation ordinances banned canon law norms. By the 1530s, new reformation ordinances were commanding their use in the governance of both Church and state. This adoption of the canon law was, in part, a product of inertia. As the biblical radicalism of the early Reformation plunged Germany into deep crisis, the reformers simply returned to the canon law norms that they had learned in their youth. The adoption of the canon law was also, however, a product of innovation. As Luther's theological distinctions between Law and Gospel began to betray their institutional limitations, the reformers developed innovative new theories of the relationship of Church and state, ecclesiastical and political authority, canon law and civil law.

These innovative new theories were, in fact, only a small part and product of a complex rethinking of Luther's original theological message. Luther's radical theological doctrines of Law and Gospel, of justification by faith alone, of the priesthood of all believers, of *sola Scriptura*, and more had proved pungent and powerful enough to deconstruct traditional norms and forms. But left in raw and radical terms, these theological doctrines raised more questions than they answered. If the Gospel is all that really counts, what use is the law? If justification comes only through faith, why bother with works? If all persons are equal as priests, who is Dr. Martin to tell us what to do? If the Bible alone is be our guide, what is the place of reason and conscience in this earthly life? These and many other sobering questions led Luther and his followers rather quickly from radical attacks on the old order to patient reconstruction of a new order.

87

Luther's complex reconstruction came to be known as the two-kingdoms theory (*Zweireichelehre*), a theory that a number of Lutheran theologians and jurists eventually adopted at least in broad outline. Luther's two-kingdoms theory did not only provide his answer to many of the thorny institutional and intellectual questions thrown up during the radical phase of the Reformation. It also provided the foundation for the reformation of German law, politics, and society on explicit Evangelical terms.

This chapter spells out various dimensions of Luther's two-kingdoms theory, and then draws out their respective implications for his theology of law, politics, and society.[1] The next chapter analyzes the new legal theories that sixteenth-century Lutheran jurists and moralists built with Luther's two-kingdoms framework at their core.

A WILDERNESS OF CASUISTRY

In 1957, the great Reformation historian Johannes Heckel called Luther's two-kingdoms theory a veritable *Irrgarten*, literally "garden of errors," where the wheats and tares of interpretation had grown indiscriminately together.[2] Some half a century of scholarship later, Heckel's little garden of errors has become a whole wilderness of confusion, with many thorny thickets of casuistry to ensnare the unsuspecting.[3] It is tempting to find another way into Lutheran contributions to legal theory. But Luther's two-kingdoms theory was the framework on which both he and many of his followers built their enduring views of law and authority, justice and equity, society and politics. We must wander in this wilderness at least long enough to get our legal bearings.

Luther was a master of the dialectic – of holding two doctrinal opposites in tension and of exploring ingeniously the intellectual power of this tension. Many of his favorite dialectics were set out in the Bible and well rehearsed in the Christian tradition: spirit and flesh, soul and body, faith and works, heaven and hell, grace and nature, the kingdom of God versus the kingdom of Satan, the things that are God's and the

---

[1] Some of the material in this chapter and the next is adapted from Berman and Witte, "The Transformation of Western Legal Philosophy" (hereafter "Transformation").

[2] Johannes Heckel, *Im Irrgarten der Zwei-Reiche-Lehre* (Munich, 1957).

[3] For detailed bibliography see "Transformation," nn. 21–3. See further sources and discussion in Ulrich Duchrow, *Christenheit und Weltverantwortung: Traditionsgeschichte und systematische Struktur der Zweireichelehre* (Stuttgart, 1983); Helmar Junghaus, ed., *Leben und Werk Martin Luthers* (Berlin, 1983); Per Frostin, *Luther's Two Kingdoms Doctrine: A Critical Study* (Lund, 1994); Bernhard Lohse, *Luthers Theologie* (Göttingen, 1995); Andreas Pawlas, *Die lutherische Berufs- und Wirtschaftsethik: Eine Einführung* (Neukirchen-Vluyn, 2000), and the classic work of Franz Lau, *"Äeusserliche Ordnung" und "Weltlich Ding" in Luthers Theologie* (Göttingen, 1933).

things that are Caesar's, and more.[4] Some of the dialectics were more uniquely Lutheran in accent: Law and Gospel, sinner and saint, servant and lord, inner man and outer man, passive justice and active justice, alien righteousness and proper righteousness, civil uses and theological uses of the law, among others.

Luther developed a good number of these dialectical doctrines separately in his writings from 1515 to 1545 – at different paces, in varying levels of detail, and with uneven attention to how one doctrine fit with others. He and his followers eventually jostled together several doctrines under the broad umbrella of the two-kingdoms theory. This theory came to describe at once: (1) the distinctions between the fallen realm and the redeemed realm, the City of Man and the City of God, the Reign of the Devil and the Reign of Christ; (2) the distinctions between the sinner and the saint, the flesh and the spirit, the inner man and the outer man; (3) the distinctions between the visible Church and the invisible Church, the Church as governed by civil law and the Church as governed by the Holy Spirit; (4) the distinctions between reason and faith, natural knowledge and spiritual knowledge; and (5) the distinctions between two kinds of righteousness, two kinds of justice, two uses of law.

When Luther, and especially his followers, used the two-kingdoms terminology, they often had one or two of these distinctions primarily in mind, sometimes without clearly specifying which. Rarely did all of these distinctions come in for a fully differentiated and systematic discussion and application, especially when the jurists later invoked the two-kingdoms theory as part of their jurisprudential reflections. The matter was complicated even further because both Anabaptists and Calvinists of the day eventually adopted and adapted the language of the two kingdoms as well – each with their own confessional accents and legal applications that were sometimes in sharp tension with Luther's and other Evangelical views.[5] It is thus worth spelling out Luther's understanding of the two kingdoms in some detail, and then drawing out its implications for law, society, and politics.

THEORY OF BEING

First and foremost for Luther, the two-kingdoms theory was an ontology, a theory of the two-fold nature of being or reality. In his early writings,

---

[4] See Oliver O'Donovan, *The Desire of the Nations: Rediscovering the Roots of Political Theology* (Cambridge, 1996), 82ff., 193ff.

[5] See Robert Friedmann, *The Theology of Anabaptism* (Scottdale, PA, 1973), 38ff. and my "Moderate Religious Liberty in the Theology of John Calvin," *Calvin Theological Journal* 31 (1996): 359–403.

Luther often described this in the familiar Augustinian terms that he had learned in the monastery.[6] Augustine's City of God was the perfect heavenly kingdom in the life hereafter. It was already experienced but not yet fully realized by Christians who sojourned in the City of Man, in this earthly kingdom of space and time.[7] Sometimes, Luther described this distinction in the grand terms of the Bible, as the kingdom of God (*Reich Gottes, regnum Dei*) and the kingdom of Satan (*Teufels Reich, regnum diaboli*) locked in perennial battle for the souls of humankind until the second coming of Christ and the ultimate overthrow of the Devil.[8] Sometimes, Luther focused on the contrast between two classes of citizens in the world – Christians who have accepted the lordship of Christ in the heavenly kingdom and non-Christians who submit only to the authorities of the earthly kingdom.[9] These were quite different renderings of a basic ontological dualism, but they often came tumbling out together in Luther's torrential prose. For example, in a famous 1523 passage, Luther wrote:

Here we must divide the children of Adam and all mankind into two parts, the first belonging to the kingdom of God (*reych Gottis*), the second to the kingdom of the world (*reych der welt*).

Those who belong to the kingdom of God are all true believers who are in Christ and under Christ, for Christ is king and lord in the kingdom of God.... [T]hese people need no worldly law or sword. If all the world were composed of real Christians, that is, right believers, there would be no need for or benefits from prince, king, lord, sword, or law. They would serve no purpose, since Christians have in their heart the Holy Spirit, who both teaches and makes them to do injustice to no one, to love everyone, and to suffer injustice and even death willingly and cheerfully at the hands of anyone....

All who are not Christians belong to the kingdom of the world and are under the law. There are few true believers, and still fewer who live a Christian life, who do not resist evil and indeed themselves do no evil. For this reason, God has provided for them a different government (*Regiment*) beyond the Christian estate (*Stand*) and kingdom of God. He subjected them to the sword so that, even though they would like to, they are unable to practice their wickedness,

---

[6] See Hans-Ulrich Delius, *Augustin als Quelle Luthers: Eine Materialsammlung* (Berlin, 1984).

[7] *LW* 45:88–92, 104–8; *LW* 46:242–3; *WA* 36:385; *WA* 45:252ff.; *WA TR* 6, No. 7026.

[8] Ibid. Luther writes: "Man's will is like an animal standing between two riders. If God is the rider, man goes and wills where God goes.... If Satan is the rider, man wills and goes where Satan goes" (*WA* 18:635). See Luther's intense autobiographical reflection on this dialectic in Heiko Oberman, *Luther: Man Between God and Devil*, trans. Eileen Walliser-Schwarzbart (New Haven, CT, 1983).

[9] *LW* 21:109; *LW* 23:316–19; *WA* 36:385. In this early period, Luther believed that while God operates in both kingdoms, Christ operates only in the heavenly kingdom. See *LW* 14:19–27; *LW* 45:88.

and if they do practice it they cannot do so without fear or with success and impunity....

God has ordained two governments: the spiritual (*geystliche*), by which the Holy Spirit produces Christians and righteous people under Christ; and the temporal (*welltliche*), which restrains the non-Christian and the wicked.[10]

As the quotation reveals, Luther believed that the two kingdoms (*Reiche*) were ruled by two authorities or governments (*Regimente, Stände*). In his early years, Luther viewed these two authorities primarily through his favorite binocular of the Law and the Gospel.[11] The earthly kingdom was governed by Law. The heavenly kingdom was governed by Gospel. Both the Law and the Gospel were ultimately forms of God's authority and revelation. But they had to be carefully distinguished.[12] The Law was an authority of the Sword; it brought coercion, bondage, and restraint. The Gospel was an authority of the Word; it promised love, freedom, and charity. In this world of space and time, both these authorities ruled concurrently, and a Christian believer needed to submit to each, and to resist their conflation:

Paul says in 1 Timothy 1 [:9], "the Law is not laid down for the righteous but for the lawless." Why is this? It is because the righteous man of his own accord does all and more than the Law demands. But the unrighteous do nothing that the Law demands; therefore, they need the Law to instruct, constrain, and compel them to do good . . . In the same way a savage wild beast is bound with chains and ropes so that it cannot bite and tear as it would normally do, even though it would like to; whereas a tame and gentle animal needs no restraint, but is harmless despite the lack of chains and ropes. . . .

If anyone attempted to rule the world by the Gospel and to abolish all earthly law and sword on the plea that all are baptized and Christian, and that, according to the Gospel, there shall be among them no law or sword – or need for either – . . . he would be loosing the ropes and chains of the savage wild beasts and letting them bite and mangle everyone. . . .

For this reason one must carefully distinguish between these two authorities. Both must be permitted to remain; the one to produce righteousness, the other to bring about external peace and prevent evil deeds. Neither one is sufficient in the world without the other. No one can become righteous in the sight of God by means of the earthly government, without Christ's spiritual government. Christ's government does not extend over all men; rather, Christians are

---

[10] *WA* 11:249–52.
[11] See *WA* 40:486: "Of this distinction between Law and Gospel, you will find nothing in the books of the monks, canonists, or theologians, whether recent or ancient. Augustine understood this difference somewhat and showed it. Jerome and others were wholly ignorant of it."
[12] See, e.g., *WA TR* 1, No. 590, *LW* 54:105–7.

always a minority in the midst of non-Christians. Now where earthly government or law alone prevails, there sheer hypocrisy is inevitable, even though the
commandments be God's very own. For without the Holy Spirit in the heart
no one becomes truly righteous, no matter how fine the work he does. On the
other hand, where the spiritual government alone prevails over land and peoples, there wickedness is given free rein and the door is open for all manner of
rascality, for the world as a whole cannot receive or comprehend it.[13]

As this quotation reveals, Luther in this early period tended to conflate
(1) the theological category of Law – the Old Testament dispensation of
God that antedated the Gospel – with (2) the political category of law –
the positive laws promulgated by the magistrate. The Law of God and
the law of the magistrate were both part of the government of the earthly
kingdom, and Luther at first did little to distinguish them. The dangers of
this early position soon became apparent. For Luther, in this early period,
also tended to conflate the image of the earthly kingdom as the evil realm
of the Devil with that of the earthly kingdom as the political realm of
the magistrate. This double conflation led the early Luther dangerously
close to intimating that not only the law of the magistrate but also the
Law of God was part of the earthly kingdom of the Devil. Add Luther's
repeated and bitter attacks on Mosaic law, canon law, and Roman law
alike, and it was easy to see how Luther's early theory could lead an
earnest Evangelical follower straight into antinomianism – wholesale
rejection of all law in favor of the freedom of the Christian Gospel.

By the late 1520s, Luther thus moved to a more nuanced view of the
temporal government that governed the earthly kingdom. Luther's earlier Augustinian picture of the earthly kingdom as the fallen and formless
City of Man under the reign of the Devil faded into the background. To
the foreground came Luther's new picture of the earthly kingdom as
the natural realm, once a brilliant and perfect creation of God, but now
darkened and distorted by the fall into sin. Despite the fall, however, God
in his grace had allowed the earthly kingdom to continue to exist. God
had also allowed the various natural laws and natural orders to continue
to operate. Luther referred many times to the natural laws of marriage
and family, property and business born of God's primal command to
Adam and Eve in Paradise: "Be fruitful and multiply, replenish the earth
and subdue it, and have dominion over [it]" (Genesis 1:28).[14] Luther also
pointed to the natural laws on the proper worship and honor of God, on
coveting and homicide, on evidence and judicial procedure, adumbrated

---

[13] Ibid. See also *LW* 9:136.   [14] *LW* 1:69ff.

in God's primal confrontation with Cain immediately after Paradise (Genesis 4:1–17).[15] For Luther, each of these natural laws, created by God, continued to govern the earthly kingdom after the fall into sin.

Not only the natural laws, but also the natural orders of creation continued to govern after the fall into sin. "God has ordained three orders or governments (*hierarchias/Regimente*)" to embody, elaborate, and enforce natural laws in the earthly kingdom, Luther wrote in 1539: "the household, the state, and the Church," or the *ordo economicus, ordo politicus,* and *ordo ecclesiasticus* as he elsewhere put it.[16]

> The first government (*Regiment*) is that of the home, from which the people come. The second is that of the "state" (*civitas*), that is, the country, the people, princes, and lords, which we call the temporal government. These [two governments] embrace everything – children, property, money, animals, and so on. The home must produce, whereas the city must guard, protect, and defend. Then follows the third, God's own home and city, that is, the Church, which must obtain people from the home and protection and defense from the state. These are the three hierarchies ordained by God, the three high divine governments, the three divine, natural, and temporal laws of God.[17]

All three of these orders, governments, or estates, Luther insisted, represented different dimensions of God's authority and law in the earthly kingdom. All three stood equal before God and before each other in discharging their essential natural tasks. All three were needed to resist the power of sin and the Devil in the earthly kingdom. All three deserved equally the obedience of those under their authority. All three were essential to the preservation of life and law, order and obligation in the earthly kingdom. All three not only exercised the justice and wrath of God against sin, but also anticipated the more perfect life and law of the heavenly kingdom.[18] As Luther put it: "God wants the government of the earthly kingdom to be a symbol of . . . the heavenly kingdom, like a mime or a mask."[19]

This "three-estate theory" (*drei Ständelehre*) became one of the signature doctrines of Lutheran jurisprudence, which later theologians and jurists expounded at length, as we shall see.[20] It provided Luther with

---

[15] Ibid., 259ff.
[16] *WA* 39:/2:42. See also *LW* 3:217; *LW* 37:364ff.; *LW* 41:177ff. For anticipations of this doctrine in Luther's earlier writings, see F. Edward Cranz, *An Essay on the Development of Luther's Thought on Justice, Law, and Society* (Cambridge, MA/London, 1959), 153–78.
[17] *WA* 50:509.   [18] See *LW* 13:169.   [19] *WA* 51:241.
[20] See Wilhelm Maurer, *Luthers Lehre von den drei Hierarchien und ihr mittelalterlicher Hintergrund* (Munich, 1970).

a considerably more nuanced and positive theory of earthly law and government than some of his earlier statements had allowed. His ontological picture of the world remained a basic dualism between a lower earthly kingdom and a higher heavenly kingdom. But the earthly kingdom was now much more clearly a realm of divinely ordained authority and law, albeit perennially distorted by sin. And the earthly kingdom was naturally subdivided into three orders of domestic, political, and ecclesiastical authority, each called to embrace and enforce God's law, and each empowered to prohibit and punish human sin.

THEORY OF THE PERSON

The two-kingdoms theory was not only an ontology, a theory of the twofold nature of reality. It was also an anthropology, a theory of the twofold nature of the Christian person. All persons in Christendom, Luther argued, share equally in a doubly paradoxical nature. Each Christian is at once a saint and a sinner, righteous and reprobate, saved and lost – *simul iustus et peccator*.[21] At the same time, each Christian is at once a free lord who is subject to no one, and a dutiful servant who is subject to everyone.

Every Christian "has a two-fold nature," Luther argued in expounding his famous doctrine of *simul iustus et peccator*. We are at once body and soul, flesh and spirit, sinner and saint, "outer man and inner man." These "two men in the same man contradict each other" and remain perennially at war.[22] On the one hand, as bodily creatures, we are born in sin and bound by sin. By our carnal natures, we are prone to lust and lasciviousness, evil and egoism, perversion and pathos of untold dimensions.[23] Even the best of persons, even the titans of virtue in the Bible – Abraham, David, Peter, and Paul – sin all the time.[24] In and of ourselves, we are totally depraved and deserving of eternal death. On the other hand, as spiritual creatures, we are reborn in faith, and freed from sin. By our spiritual natures, we are prone to love and charity, goodness and sacrifice, virtue and peacefulness. Even the worst of persons, even the reprobate thief nailed on the cross next to Christ's, can be saved from sin. In spite of ourselves, we are totally redeemed and assured of eternal life.[25]

---

[21] *LW* 31:344–7, 358–61. See also *LW* 12:328; *LW* 27:230ff.; *LW* 32:173; *WA* 39/1:21, 492, 552.
[22] *LW* 31:344.   [23] Ibid., 344, 358–61; see also *LW* 25:120–30, 204–13.
[24] *LW* 19:47–8; *LW* 23:146.   [25] *LW* 31:344–54, 368–77.

It is through faith in the Word of God, Luther argued, that a person moves from sinner to saint, from bondage to freedom. This was the essence of Luther's doctrine of justification by faith alone. No human work of any sort – even worship, contemplation, meditation, charity, and other supposedly meritorious conduct – can make a person just and righteous before God. For sin holds the person fast, and perverts his or her every work. "One thing, and only one thing, is necessary for Christian life, righteousness, and freedom," Luther declared. "That one thing is the most holy Word of God, the Gospel of Christ."[26] To put one's faith in this Word, to accept its gracious promise of eternal salvation, is to claim one's freedom from sin and from its attendant threat of eternal damnation. And it is to join the communion of saints that begins imperfectly in this life and continues perfectly in the life to come. But a saint by faith remains a sinner by nature, Luther insisted, and the conflict of good and evil within the same person remains until death.[27]

This brought Luther to a related paradox of human nature – that each Christian is at once a lord who is subject to no one, and a priest who is servant to everyone. On the one hand, Luther argued, "every Christian is by faith so exalted above all things that, by virtue of a spiritual power, he is [a] lord."[28] As a redeemed saint, an "inner man," a Christian is utterly free in his conscience, utterly free in his innermost being. He is like the greatest king on earth, who is above and beyond the power of everyone. No earthly authority – whether pope, prince, or parent – can impose "a single syllable of the law" upon him.[29] No earthly authority can intrude upon the sanctuary of his conscience, or endanger his assurance and comfort of eternal life. This is "the splendid privilege," the "inestimable power and liberty" that every Christian enjoys.[30]

On the other hand, Luther wrote, every Christian is a priest, who freely performs good works in service of his or her neighbor and in glorification of God.[31] "Christ has made it possible for us, provided we believe in him, to be not only his brethren, co-heirs, and fellow-kings, but also his fellow-priests," Luther wrote. And thus, in imitation of Christ, we freely serve our neighbors, offering instruction, charity, prayer, admonition, and sacrifice.[32] We abide by the law of God so far as we are able so that others may see our good work and be similarly impelled to seek God's

---

[26] Ibid., 345.
[27] *Lectures on Romans* (1515–16), trans. and ed. Wilhelm Pauck (Philadelphia, 1961), 120. See also *LW* 23:146; *LW* 12:328–30; *LW* 8:9–12.
[28] *LW* 31:354.   [29] *LW* 36:70; see also *LW* 31:344–6.   [30] *LW* 31:355–8.
[31] Ibid., 355–6; see also *LW* 36:112–16, 138–40; *LW* 40:21–3; *LW* 13:152; *LW* 39:137–224.
[32] *LW* 31:355; see also *LW* 36:241.

grace. We freely discipline and drive ourselves to do as much good as we are able, not so that we may be saved but so that others may be served. We live so far as we are able the life of the Beatitudes, the virtues of poverty, meekness, humility, mercy, and peacefulness.[33] "A man does not live for himself alone," Luther wrote, "he lives only for others."[34] The precise nature of our priestly service to others depends upon our gifts and upon the vocation in which God calls us to use them.[35] But we are all to serve others freely and fully as God's priests.

Not everyone who is charitable has faith, Luther insisted, but everyone who has faith is charitable. Charity is a form of divine worship, of priestly service, that serves God and neighbor at once. "[T]here is no greater worship or service of God (*Gottesdienst*) than Christian love which helps and serves the needy," Luther wrote.[36] "Out of faith flows the love of and desire for God, and out of love, a free, willing, and gladsome desire to serve one's neighbor."[37]

Such are the paradoxes of human nature, Luther believed. We are at once sinners and saints; we are at once lords and servants. We can do nothing good; we can do nothing but good. We are utterly free; we are everywhere bound. The more a person thinks himself a saint, the more sinful in fact he becomes. The more a person thinks herself a sinner, the more saintly she in fact becomes. The more a person acts like a lord, the more he is called to be a servant. The more a person acts as a servant, the more in fact he has become a lord. This is the paradoxical nature of human life.

Luther's first distinction between the saint and the sinner tracked closely his ontological distinction between the City of God and the City of Man, the reign and realm of Christ versus those of the Devil.[38] Sinners are earthly citizens. Saints are heavenly citizens. Every Christian is both a sinner and a saint. Every Christian is a citizen of both the earthly and the heavenly kingdoms. Earthly citizenship comes with birth. Heavenly citizenship comes through faith.

Luther's second distinction between free lord and priestly servant did not track his ontological distinctions so neatly. In one sense, this

---

[33] *LW* 45:87.   [34] *LW* 31:364–5; see also *LW* 51:86–7.   [35] *LW* 38:188; *LW* 28:171–2.
[36] *LW* 45:172–3.
[37] *WA* 7:35–6. See detailed sources and discussion in Lindberg, *Beyond Charity*, 95ff.; Abby Phyllis Knobler, "Luther and the Legal Concept of the Poor in the Sixteenth Century German Church Orders" (PhD Diss., UCLA, 1991), 133ff.
[38] Indeed, Luther developed his anthropological dualism in detail already in his *Freedom of a Christian* (1520), while he developed his ontological dualism in detail only in his *Temporal Authority* (1523).

lord–priest distinction was a description only of the Christian saint, only of a member of the heavenly kingdom. Both lordship and priesthood after all were qualities of the Christian believer, the party who had been justified by faith, and had thus become a citizen of the heavenly kingdom. As lord, such a heavenly citizen was utterly free from the strictures and structures of the law of the earthly kingdom. As priest, he or she was utterly free to do good works for neighbors, even if such works could never fully comply with God's Law.

In another sense, however, the lord–priest distinction did track the two-kingdoms distinction. To be a lord was to be above everyone in the earthly kingdom, to be "an inner man," to "live for oneself alone," to have the assurance and luxury of being in utter community and compatibility with God, above the sinful din of the earthly crowd. To be a priest, however, was to be servant to everyone – in the heavenly and the earthly kingdoms alike. It was to be an "outer man," a "person for the sake of others" – not least those sinful nonbelievers of the earthly kingdom who would see in this service a reflection of and an invitation to a saintly Christian life in the heavenly kingdom. Luther's doctrine of the priesthood of all believers did not connote a priesthood *to* believers only. It connoted a priesthood *by* believers both to fellow believers in the heavenly kingdom and to nonbelievers in the earthly kingdom – in imitation of Christ's priestly service on earth. As Luther put it: "The fact that we are all priests and kings means that each of us Christians may go before God and intercede for the other, asking God to give him his own faith."[39] Thus a Christian believer, in discharging the services of the priesthood of believers, inevitably moved between the heavenly and the earthly kingdoms.

THEORY OF THE CHURCH

Luther's two-kingdoms theory also drew to itself an ecclesiology, a theory of the two-fold nature of the Church. Parts of this ecclesiology we just saw foreshadowed in Luther's discussion of a Christian as a saint of the heavenly kingdom and a priest of the earthly kingdom. Other parts of this theory we saw earlier in Luther's description of the Church as one of the three natural orders of the earthly kingdom, and in his gradual acceptance of the early Catholic canon law as a legitimate norm for organizing the visible Church.[40]

Luther distinguished the invisible Church of the heavenly kingdom from the actual Church of the earthly kingdom. For Luther, the "invisible

---

[39] *WA* 10/3:108.   [40] See above pp. 74–5.

Church" was the communion of saints (*communio sanctorum*). By *communio*, Luther meant a congregation or assembly (*Gemeinde, Sammlung*) of parties who were committed to the mutual sharing (*communicare*) of all things and experiences in this life, not least Christ himself.[41] By *sanctorum*, Luther meant primarily all those sinners who had accepted Christ in faith and had so become saints. To be a saint was to be in community with other living persons who had accepted Christ in faith. It was also to be in communion with Christ and with all Christian believers who had died and had come into more perfect communion with Christ – those "saints in heaven" described so graphically in the final book of the Bible, The Revelation of St. John.[42] The communion of saints thus began imperfectly in this life and continued perfectly in the life to come. The true Church of the heavenly kingdom began temporally in this world of space and time, and continued eternally in the new world beyond space and time.

The invisible Church was a community of faith, hope, and love, Luther argued.[43] It featured a pure spiritual fellowship, a perennial ethic of mutual sharing and caring, each party ministering to the other in accordance with his or her special gifts.[44] It was

the most divine, the most heavenly, the noblest fraternity . . . the community of holiness in which we are all brothers and sisters, so closely united that a closer relationship could not be conceived. Herein we have one baptism, one Christ, one sacrament, one food, one Gospel, one faith, one spirit, one spiritual body, with each person being a member of the other."[45]

While this spiritual Church remained an aspirational ideal for the world, it could only be seen "through a glass darkly," and only then by the keenest eyes of faith. In the earthly kingdom, Luther wrote, "the Church is hidden, the saints are hidden."[46] "Just as that rock [Jesus Christ], sinless, invisible and spiritual, is perceptible by faith alone, so perforce the Church is sinless, invisible and spiritual, perceptible by faith alone."[47]

The actual Church of the earthly kingdom is only a shadow of this shining ideal, Luther argued, but dependent upon this ideal Church as a shadow is dependent upon light for its being and form. The earthly Church is comprised of both saints and sinners. Some are true believers, some are just imposters. Sometimes the true believers behave as saints, other times they behave as sinners. Thus God has established a visible

---

[41] *WA* 7:219; *WA* 10/2:89; *WA* 28:149. See also Althaus, *The Theology of Martin Luther*, 294ff.
[42] See esp. *LW* 35:389–411.   [43] *WA* 6:131.   [44] *WA* 10/3:407ff.; *WA* 17/2:255.
[45] *WA* 2:756.   [46] *WA* 18:652.   [47] *WA* 7:710.

Church, as one of the orders of the earthly kingdom. God has called this Church to dispense his unique "gifts" to the earthly kingdom: the preaching of the Word, the administration of the sacraments, the discipline of the keys. All Christians, as members of the priesthood of all believers, have a general responsibility to help dispense these gifts. But from within the universal priesthood of believers, God also calls some to be the "priests" of the Church: pastors, teachers, sextons and other Church officers. These "priests" of the earthly Church enjoy no special status in the earthly kingdom: like the parent and the prince, they simply have a distinctive office, neither more nor less important to God than other offices in the earthly kingdom. It is the responsibility of these priests, in tandem with the other earthly officers and orders, to see that the earthly Church remains true to its office and faithful to its calling.[48] This included, as we saw in the last chapter, adopting and adapting early canon law norms to structure and organize the visible Church.[49] It also included adopting and enforcing moral codes for both the officers and members of the Church.

THEORY OF KNOWLEDGE

Luther's two-kingdoms theory also drew to itself an epistemology, a theory of two sources and forms of knowledge. In his early years, Luther often described this in his favorite language of Law and Gospel. The knowledge of the Law brought death, the knowledge of the Gospel brought life. The truth revealed by the Law is that we all are sinners. The truth revealed by the Gospel is that we all can be saints. To move from sinner to saint, from death to life, from the earthly kingdom to the heavenly kingdom, required earnest cultivation and application of the knowledge of Christ taught in the Gospel.[50] The implications of this epistemology for Luther's theory of education will occupy us at some length in a later chapter.[51]

In his later years, Luther also came to describe this epistemological distinction in terms of faith versus reason, of revealed knowledge versus

---

[48] See esp. *LW* 40:325–47; *LW* 41:3–178; *LW* 38:188ff. See elaboration in Rudolf Schäfer, "Die Versetzbarkeit der Geistlichen im Urteil der evangelischen-theologischen Autoritäten des 16. Jahrhunderts," *ZSS KA* 9 (1919): 99–176; Hans Liermann, "Laizismus und Klerikalismus in der Geschichte des evangelischen Kirchenrechts," *ZSS KA* 39 (1952): 1.

[49] See above pp. 70–6.

[50] This is the central thesis of Luther's *Commentary on Galatians* (1535), which argument he summarized in *LW* 26:4–12.

[51] See chapter 7 below.

hidden knowledge. In the heavenly kingdom, Luther argued, God reveals Himself directly through the Bible and through the Christian conscience. His Word and will are utterly clear to all those who have true faith. In the earthly kingdom, however, God is hidden, shrouded by the sin that has fallen over this kingdom. He is the "hidden God" (*deus absconditus*), whose truth and knowledge are revealed and known only through "masks" *larvae*).

One such set of "masks," Luther argued, is a person's natural reason, which God has created with an inborn inclination to do good and to seek God.[52] Cultivation of one's natural reason is essential to surviving in the earthly kingdom and to preparing oneself for the heavenly kingdom. "The light of reason is everywhere kindled by the divine light," Luther declared. "The light of reason is a part and beginning of the true light provided it recognizes and honors him by whom it is kindled." "For wherever reason goes, there the will follows. And wherever the will goes, there love and desire follow."[53] But the Devil, too, is hidden in human reason and will, and distorts the natural knowledge and truth that God has implanted. Therefore, a person must not think that by willing to do good or by reasoning to find God, he or she will be able to move from the earthly kingdom to the heavenly kingdom, to attain salvation.[54] Faith alone (*sola fides*) brings salvation. Human reason and human will are always bound by sin – a point Luther pressed with great alacrity in his debate with Erasmus over the "bondage of the will."[55] "Reason when illuminated [by the Holy Spirit] helps faith by reflecting on something, but reason without faith isn't and can't be helpful."[56]

A second set of "masks" through which the hidden God can be partly seen in the earthly kingdom are the various offices of authority in the earthly orders of household, Church, and state. These offices not only rule the earthly kingdom on God's behalf, as we saw. They also communicate God's truth and knowledge, God's word and will, so far as they are able.[57] "[T]he magistrate, the emperor, the king, the prince, the counsul, the teacher, the preacher, the [parent] – all these are masks [of God]," Luther argued. God wants us to "respect and to acknowledge" them as His creatures and His teachers. These authorities are competent to teach much that is needed for life in the earthly kingdom, and a rational person would do well to heed their instruction. "But when the

---

[52] *LW* 1:66ff.　　[53] *LW* 52:57, 79.　　[54] *WA* 7:73; see also *WA* 39:374; *WA* 40:42, 66.
[55] *LW* 33:295ff.　　[56] *WA TR* 1, No. 71 *LW* 54:71.　　[57] *LW* 26:94–6; *LW* 14:114; *LW* 24:67.

issue is one involving religion, conscience, the fear of God, faith, and the worship of God, then we must not fear or trust any [such earthly] order or look to it for consolation or rescue, either physical or spiritual." This would "offend God," and be a "denial of His truth."[58]

A third set of "masks" by which the hidden God is partly revealed is the conscientious work of Christian believers in the earthly kingdom. It is the duty of Christians of all sorts "to work the work of God in the world," Luther argued.[59] As citizens of the earthly kingdom, Christians were not to withdraw ascetically from the "things of the world," abstaining from its activities and institutions as certain Anabaptists of the day taught.[60] Rather, Christians were to participate actively in these earthly institutions and activities, to confirm their natural origin and function, and to use human will and reason, however defective, to do as much good and to attain as much understanding as possible. "God himself ordained and established this earthly realm and its distinctions," Luther wrote. "[W]e must remain and work in them so long as we are on earth."[61]

THEORY OF RIGHTEOUSNESS

Finally, the two-kingdoms theory drew to itself a soteriology, a theory of two forms of justice or righteousness (*justitia, Gerechtigkeit*) and two corresponding uses of the law (*duplex usus legis*). We have already seen the heart of Luther's doctrine of justification by faith alone: Sinners become saints, earthly citizens become heavenly citizens, only through faith in Christ, Luther insisted. No human works, however seemingly meritorious, will earn a person salvation. Luther's discussion of two forms of righteousness and two uses of the law presented another dimension of this cardinal teaching, but now with an eye to explaining how and why good works might still be useful.

Earthly righteousness, Luther taught, "the righteousness of law or of works," is a natural righteousness whose norms, though ordained by God at creation, are perceived and carried out by the reason and will of sinners. This Luther variously called "active," "proper," "political," or "civil" righteousness. While this form of righteousness has no effect on one's citizenship in the heavenly kingdom, it does help to improve one's citizenship in the earthly kingdom. Earthly life for oneself and for all

---

[58] *LW* 26:95–6.   [59] *WA* 31/1:437; *WA* 40/3:271ff.
[60] *WA* 21:342ff. Cf. Walter Klaasen, *Anabaptism in Outline: Selected Primary Sources* (Scottsdale, PA, 1981.
[61] *WA* 32:390. See also *LW* 14:114–15; Linberg, *Beyond Charity*, 108ff.

others is more livable and tolerable if one does good, rather than evil. Heavenly righteousness, by contrast, "the righteousness of the Gospel or of faith," is a spiritual righteousness in which God alone acts. By grace, God inspires faith in a person's heart, and then by grace God responds to their faith, delivering them from sin and forgiving them. Luther thus variously called this a form of "passive," "alien," or "foreign" righteousness.[62] Luther summarized:

> We set forth two worlds, one of them heavenly and the other earthly. Into these we place two kinds of righteousness, which are distinct and separate from each other. The righteousness of the Law is earthly and deals with earthly things; by it we perform good works. But as the earth does not bring forth fruit unless it first has been watered and made fruitful from above . . . so also by the righteousness of the Law we do nothing even when we do much; we do not fulfill the Law, even when we fulfill it. Without any merit or work of our own we must first be justified by Christian righteousness, which has nothing to do with the righteousness of the Law or with earthly and active righteousness. But this righteousness is heavenly and passive. We do not have it of ourselves; we receive it from heaven. We do not perform it; we accept it by faith, through which we ascend beyond all laws and works.[63]

The corollary to this doctrine of the two forms of righteousness was the doctrine of the two uses of the law.[64] Once it is granted that salvation does not depend upon the works of the law, the question arises: Why does God continue to maintain the Law of God and the law of the magistrate? What are, from God's point of view, its "uses" in the life of the earthly kingdom? Luther set forth two uses of the law, and touched on a third.

One use of the law, Luther argued, is to restrain people from sinful conduct by threat of punishment.[65] Luther called this the "civil" or "political" use of the law. God wants even the worst of sinners to observe the law, Luther argued – to honor their parents, to avoid killing and stealing, to respect marriage vows, to testify truthfully, and the like – so that "some measure of earthly order, concourse and concord may be

---

[62] *WA* 1:293ff.; *LW* 5:213ff.; *LW* 12:328ff.; *LW* 31:297–306. See also Heinrich Bornkamm, "Iustitia dei in der Scholastik und bei Luther," *AFR* 4 (1942): 1; Althaus, *Theology of Martin Luther*, 224–50; Cranz, *Development*, 73–112.

[63] *LW* 26:8.

[64] See John Witte, Jr. and Thomas C. Arthur, "Three Uses of the Law: A Protestant Source of Criminal Punishment?" *Journal of Law and Religion* 10 (1994): 433.

[65] Luther generally spoke of the "civil use" as the "first use of the law," and the "theological use" as the "second use of the law," though the latter was the more important to him. See *WA* 10:454ff.; *WA* 40:486ff.; Frank S. Alexander, "Validity and Function of Law: The Reformation Doctrine of *usus legis*," *Mercer Law Review* 31 (1980): 509.

preserved."[66] Sinners, not naturally inclined to observe the law, may be induced to do so by fear of punishment – divine punishment as well as human punishment. "Stern hard civil rule is necessary in the world," Luther wrote, "lest the world be destroyed, peace vanish, and commerce and common interest be destroyed."[67] He emphasized that to maintain order it is important that there be precise legal rules, not only to deter lawbreakers but also to restrain magistrates from their natural inclination to wield their powers arbitrarily.[68] This first use of the law applied both to the Law of God and to the law of the magistrate. It induced in earthly citizens a "civil" or "political righteousness," a justice of law.

A second use of the law is to make people conscious of their duty to give themselves completely to God while at the same time making them aware of their utter inability to fulfill that duty without divine help. Luther called this the "theological use" of the law. The law in this sense serves as a mirror in which a sinner can reflect upon his depravity and to see behind him the beckoning hand of a gracious God ready to forgive him and welcome him into the heavenly kingdom. Through the law the sinful person is induced to acknowledge his sin and to seek God's gracious forgiveness.[69] Here Luther relied on St. Paul's explanation of the significance of the Law – to make people conscious of their inherent sinfulness and to bring them to repentance.[70] Luther sometimes put this in harsh terms:

The true office and the chief and proper use of the law is to reveal to man his sin, blindness, misery, wickedness, ignorance, hate, contempt of God, death, hell, judgment, and the well-deserved wrath of God. . . . When the law is being used correctly, it does nothing but reveal sin, work wrath, accuse, terrify, and reduce minds to the point of despair.[71]

From out of the depths of this despair, the sinner will cry to God for forgiveness and salvation. This second use of the law applied primarily to the Law of God, though the laws of a true Christian magistrate could have the same effect. It induced in persons a "passive righteousness," a justice of faith, a recognition that one is entirely helpless in his own pursuit of heaven, but need only have faith in God's grace to be saved.

Luther also touched lightly on a third use of the law. This use, grounded in St. Paul's discussion of the law as "our schoolmaster to bring us unto Christ" (Galatians 3:24), became known in the Protestant world as the

---

[66] *WA* 10:454; see also *WA* 11:251.   [67] *WA* 15:302.
[68] *WA TR* 3, No. 3911.   [69] See, e.g., *WA* 40:481–6.
[70] See esp. Romans 7:7–25; Galatians 3:19–22 and discussion in *WA* 16:363–93.
[71] *WA* 40:481.

"educational," "didactic," or "pedagogical" use of the law.[72] Law, in this sense, serves to teach the faithful, those who have already been justified by faith, the good works that please God. Luther recognized this concept without explicitly expounding a doctrine of the third use of the law. He recognized that those who are justified by faith remain sinful and in need of God's constant instruction through the law. He recognized that sermons, commentaries, and catechism lessons on the many Old Testament passages on law are directed, in no small part, to teaching the faithful the meaning of God's law.[73] He wrote cryptically early in his career of the "three-fold use of the law."[74] Later, in his *Table Talk*, he distinguished among "written law," "oral law," and "spiritual law" and then wrote that the spiritual law "touches the heart and moves it, so that a man not only ceases to persecute, but ... desires to be better."[75] It is clear that, for Luther, law could serve not only as a harness against sin and an inducement to faith but also as a teacher of Christian virtue.

But Luther never systematically expounded a third use of the law, in ways that Melanchthon and many Protestant theologians and jurists did after 1535. Part of his resistance was exegetical: St. Paul's Galatians passage, after all, speaks of the law as "our schoolmaster *unto* Christ" (*paedagogus noster fuit in Christum*). Those who are already justified, by definition have Christ, thus rendering the teacher's role fulfilled. Luther thus treated the teaching function of the law as part of its civil use. The law was like a stern schoolteacher who kept unruly pupils in line until they had matured to self-restraint.[76]

Part of Luther's resistance was jurisdictional: Law was the province of the earthly kingdom, Gospel was the province of the heavenly kingdom. To acknowledge that Christians, members of the heavenly kingdom, still

---

[72] Philip Melanchthon, in *Loci communes* (1535), was the first to expound systematically all three uses of the law. See *CR* 21:405–6 and Gerhard Ebeling, *Word and Faith*, trans. J. Leitsch (Philadelphia, 1963), 62–78. See discussion of his later expositions below pp. 127–9.

[73] In his *Large Catechism* (1529), which he described as "a set of instructions for the daily lives of Christian believers," Luther devoted more than fifty pages to exegesis of the Decalogue, concluding that "outside of the Ten Commandments, no work can be good or pleasing to God, however great or precious it may appear in the eyes of the world" (*TC*, 670–1). He included a similar exegesis in his *Treatise on Good Works* (1520), *WA* 6:196ff., and his *Disputations Against the Antinomians* (1539), *LW* 47:99ff.

[74] In his 1522 *Commentary on Galatians* 3, Luther spoke of "three-fold use of the law" (*drey wysse am brauch des gesetz*), though in this tract as well as his 1531 *Commentary on Galatians*, he focused only on the civil and theological uses of the law (*WA* 10/1:449, 457). Martin Bucer, in his 1525 Latin translation of Luther's sermon, rendered Luther's German phrase as *triplex usus legis*, a Latin phrase that other reformers adopted (*WA* 10/1:457 n. 2).

[75] *The Table Talk or Familiar Discourses of Martin Luther*, trans. W. Hazlitt (London, 1848), 135–36. See also *WA* 38:310.

[76] *LW* 26:345–7; *LW* 27:278–9.

needed law to teach them was tacitly to admit that law might have a role in the heavenly kingdom, and the Gospel alone might not teach enough. This Luther could never allow. It was one thing to bring the Gospel down into the earthly kingdom, which Luther condoned happily. It was quite another thing to elevate the law to the heavenly kingdom. This could not be.

Part of Luther's resistance was also circumstantial: Unlike many later Protestant theologians, Luther did not develop a detailed doctrine of sanctification – a notion that a believer, upon justification by faith, might become holier, more sanctified, through subsequent good works defined by the law.[77] A strong theological doctrine of the "third use of the law" went hand in hand with a strong doctrine of sanctification. Without the latter, Luther saw no need to develop the former, although he endorsed without qualification those Evangelical confessions and treatises in which both these doctrines were set forth.[78]

IMPLICATIONS FOR THEORIES OF LAW, POLITICS, AND SOCIETY

This was the essence of Luther's two-kingdoms theory: God has ordained two kingdoms or realms in which humanity is destined to live, the earthly kingdom and the heavenly kingdom. The earthly kingdom is the realm of creation, of natural and civic life, where a person operates primarily by reason and law. The heavenly kingdom is the realm of redemption, of spiritual and eternal life, where a person operates primarily by faith and love. These two kingdoms embrace parallel forms of righteousness and justice, government and order, truth and knowledge. They interact and depend upon each other in a variety of ways. But they ultimately remain distinct. The earthly kingdom is distorted by sin, and governed by the Law. The heavenly kingdom is renewed by grace and guided by the Gospel. A Christian is a citizen of both kingdoms at once and inevitably comes under the distinctive government of each. As a heavenly citizen, the Christian remains free in his or her conscience, called to live fully by the light of the Word of God. But as an earthly

---

[77] See esp. Romans 8:28–30 and Galatians 3:21–9 and Luther's interpretations in *LW* 25:371–8; *LW* 26:327–58. See further Carter Lindberg, "Do Lutherans Shout Justification But Whisper Sanctification?" *Lutheran Quarterly* 13 (1999): 1; Elmer L. Towns, "Martin Luther on Sanctification," *Bibliotheca Sacra* 125 (1969): 114.

[78] See Wilfred Joest, *Gesetz und Freiheit: Das Problem des tertius usus legis bei Luther und die neutestamentliche Parainese* (Göttingen, 1968); Werner Elert, *Law and Gospel*, trans. Edward H. Schroeder (Philadelphia, 1967), 38ff.

citizen, the Christian is bound by law, and called to obey the natural orders and offices of household, state, and Church that God has ordained and maintained for the governance of this earthly kingdom.

This elegant dialectical theology provided the framework for several fundamental reforms of traditional theories of society, politics, and law. These Luther adumbrated and his followers elaborated.

Social implications

First, Luther's two-kingdoms theory was a rejection of traditional hiearchical theories of being, authority, and society. For centuries, the Christian West had taught that God's creation was fundamentally hierarchical in structure: a vast chain of being emanating from God and extending down through the various kingdoms of humans, animals, plants, and physical things. In this great chain of being, each creature found its place and its purpose, and the whole creation found its natural order.[79] And in this chain of being, human society found its natural order and hierarchy. It was thus simply the nature of things that some persons and institutions were higher on this chain of being, some lower. It was the nature of things that some were closer and had more access to God, and some were further away and in need of greater mediation in their relationship with God. This was one basis for traditional arguments of the superiority of the pope to the emperor, the clergy to the laity, the canon law to the civil law, the Church to the state. It was also one basis for the hierarchical doctrine of purgatory and paradise depicted so graphically in Dante's *Divine Comedy* – that vast hierarchy of purgation and sanctification that a confessed sinner slowly ascended in the afterlife in pursuit of re-communion with God.

Luther's two-kingdoms theory turned this traditional ontology onto its side. By separating the two kingdoms, Luther highlighted the radical separation between the creator and the creation, and between God and humanity. For Luther, the fall into sin destroyed the original continuity and communion between the creator and the creation, the tie between the heavenly kingdom and the earthly kingdom. There was no series of emanations of being from God to humanity. There was no stairway

---

[79] See Arthur Lovejoy, *The Chain of Being: A Study of the History of an Idea* (Cambridge, MA, 1933); Paul G. Kuntz and Marion L. Kuntz, eds., *Jacob's Ladder and the Tree of Life: Concepts of Hierarchy and the Great Chain of Being* (New York, 1987). On the legal and ecclesiological implications of this ontology, see Tierney, *Religion, Law, and the Growth of Constitutional Thought* 8ff.; id., *Foundations of Conciliar Theory*, 98ff.

of merit from humanity to God. There was no purgatory. There was no heavenly hierarchy. God is present in the heavenly kingdom, and is revealed in the earthly kingdom primarily through "masks." People are born into the earthly kingdom, and have access to the heavenly kingdom only through faith.

Luther did not deny the traditional view that the earthly kingdom retains its natural order, despite the fall into sin. There remained, in effect, a chain of being, an order of creation that gave each creature, especially each human creature and each natural institution, its proper place and purpose in this life. But, for Luther, this chain of being was horizontal, not hierarchical. Before God, all persons and all institutions in the earthly kingdom were by nature equal. Luther's earthly kingdom was a flat regime, a horizontal realm of being, with no person and no institution obstructed or mediated by any other in access to and accountability before God.

Secondly, and relatedly, Luther's two-kingdoms theory turned the traditional hierarchical theory of human society onto its side. For many centuries, the Church had taught that the clergy were superior to the laity. The clergy were, to adapt Luther's language, special officers of the higher heavenly realm of grace, while the laity were simply members of the lower earthly realm of nature. As members of the higher heavenly realm, the clergy had readier access to God and God's mysteries. They thus mediated the channel of grace between the laity and God – dispensing God's grace through the sacraments and preaching, and interceding for God's grace by hearing confessions, receiving charity, and offering prayers on behalf of the laity. In this sense, the lowliest cleric was superior to the noblest emperor. All the clergy, from the lowliest parson to the greatest pope, were exempt from earthly laws, taxes, and other duties, and foreclosed from earthly pursuits such as marriage and family life.

Luther rejected this traditional social theory. Clergy and laity were fundamentally equal before God and before all others, he argued. Luther's doctrine of the priesthood of all believers at once "laicized" the clergy and "clericized" the laity. It treated the traditional "clerical" office of preaching and teaching as just one other vocation alongside many others that a conscientious Christian could properly and freely pursue. He treated all traditional "lay" offices as forms of divine calling and priestly vocation, each providing unique opportunities for service to one's peers. Preachers and teachers of the visible Church must carry their share of civic duties and pay their share of civil taxes just like everyone else. And they could and should participate in earthly activities such as marriage and family life just like everyone else.[80]

Luther expanded on this natural egalitarianism with his robust understanding of the Christian "calling" (*Beruf*) or "vocation" (*vocatio*). Every "good, decent, and useful" occupation in which a Christian conscientiously engages should be treated as a Christian vocation, Luther believed. Each vocation was an equally virtuous and effective calling of God, though none was a pathway to salvation.[81] Both the carpenter and the prince, the mineworker and the judge, the housewife and the banker should accept their Christian responsibility to perform their tasks conscientiously and, so far as possible, in the service of God and others.[82] Public officials, in particular, Luther argued, have a special calling to serve the community. This calling may require them to adopt a Christian social ethic that differs from a Christian personal ethic. A Christian's duty in his direct relationship with God "as a private person, a person for himself alone," is to love his enemy and to suffer injustice and abuse from his neighbor without resistance and without revenge. As a public person, serving in such offices as the military or the judiciary, however, a Christian might well be required to resist his neighbor and to avenge injustice and abuse, even to the point of violence and bloodshed.[83]

Luther did not press his natural egalitarianism to communitarian extremes. He saw no incompatability between insisting on the equal status of all persons and vocations before God, and accepting the ample disparities in wealth, power, privilege, and respectability among persons and positions in daily life. Some are more blessed, some less so. Some work harder, some play more. Some enjoy goods, some spurn them. Some start with noble inheritances, some start with nothing. Some vocations require more pageantry and property than others. None of these empirical disparities, however, changes the normative reality of human equality before God.

Political implications

Luther's two-kingdoms theory also turned the traditional hierarchical theory of spiritual and temporal authority onto its side. For centuries, the Church had taught that the pope is the vicar of Christ, in whom

---

[80] See esp. Ozment, *The Reformation in the Cities*, 84ff. [81] *LW* 46:93ff.
[82] See Gustaf Wingren, *The Christian Calling: Luther on Vocation*, trans. Carl C. Rasmussen (Edinburgh, 1957); Pawlas, *Die lutherische Berufs- und Wirtschaftsethik*.
[83] *LW* 21:108–15; *LW* 46:93–9.

Christ has vested the "plentitude of his power." This power was symbolized in the "two swords" discussed in the Bible (Luke 22:38): the spiritual and the temporal swords. Christ had handed these two swords to the highest being in the human world: the pope, the vicar of Christ. The pope and his clerical delegates wielded the spiritual sword, in part by establishing canon law rules for the governance of all Christendom. The pope, however, was too holy to wield the temporal sword. He therefore delegated this sword to those authorities below the spiritual realm: emperors, kings, dukes, and their civil retinues. These civil magistrates were to promulgate and enforce civil laws in a manner consistent with canon law and other Church teachings. Under this two-swords theory, civil law was by its nature inferior to canon law. Civil jurisdiction was subordinate to ecclesiastical jurisdiction. Political authority was subordinate to clerical authority.[84]

Medieval popes could rarely make good on these grand claims to universal, preemptory legal authority in Christendom. Indeed, the strongest expressions of the two-swords theory came with Pope Boniface VIII's bull *Unam Sanctam* (1302) and its progeny when the papacy was losing its power and clutching ever more firmly at a waning ideal. But the two-swords theory remained a staple of traditional political theory in Germany. And a good number of strong German bishops and ecclesiastical princes in Luther's day were still making good on its claims in their local polities.

Luther rejected this hierarchical view of government. For Luther, the earthly kingdom featured three natural forms and forums of government: the domestic, ecclesiastical, and political, or in modern terms, the family, the Church, and the state. These three institutions stood equal before God, and were each called directly by God to discharge complementary tasks in the earthly kingdom. The family, as we shall see in a later chapter, was called to rear and nurture children, to teach and to discipline them, to cultivate and exemplify love and charity within the home and the broader community.[85] The Church was called to preach the Word, to administer the sacraments, to discipline their wayward members. The state was called to protect peace, punish crime, promote the common

---

[84] On medieval formulations, see Otto von Gierke, *Political Theories of the Middle Age*, trans. F. W. Maitland, repr. (Cambridge, 1958), 7–21; Ewart Lewis, *Medieval Political Ideas* (New York, 1954), 2:506–38; and key documents in Brian Tierney, *The Crisis of Church and State, 1050–1300* (Englewood Cliffs, NJ, 1964). For patristic antecedents, and their interpretation, see, e.g., Gerard E.Caspary, *Politics and Exegesis: Origen and the Two Swords* (Berkeley, CA, 1979); Lester L. Field, *Liberty, Dominion, and the Two Swords: On the Origins of Western Political Theology* (Notre Dame, IN, 1998).

[85] See below chapter 6.

good, and to support the Church, family, and other institutions derived from them.

Not only were these three estates equal, rather than hierarchical, in authority, status, and responsibility, Luther argued. Only the state had *legal* authority – the authority of the sword to pass and enforce positive laws for the governance of the earthly kingdom. Contrary to the two-swords theory, Luther emphasized that the Church was not a law-making authority. The church had no sword. It had no jurisdiction. It had no business involving itself in the day-to-day administration of law or in the vesting of magistrates in their offices. The Church's ministry and mission lay elsewhere. To be sure, each local church needed internal rules of order and discipline to govern its members and officers, and external legal structures to protect its polity and property. But it was up to the local magistrate to pass and enforce these ecclesiastical laws, in consultation and cooperation with the local clergy and theologians. And, to be sure, Church officers and theologians had to be vigilant in preaching and teaching the law of God to magistrates and subjects alike, and in pronouncing prophetically against injustice, abuse, and tyranny. But formal legal authority lay with the state, not with the Church.[86]

Luther was more concerned with the function than with the form of the state. Luther had, at first, hoped that the emperor would endorse the Reformation, and accordingly included in his early writings some lofty panegyrics on the imperial authorities of the Holy Roman Empire of his day and of the Christian Roman Empire of a millennium before. When the emperor failed him, Luther turned at various times to the nobility, the peasantry, the city councils, and the princes, and in turn wrote favorably about each of them, and then sometimes unfavorably when they failed him.[87] Such writings must be read in their immediate political context,

---

[86] See above pp. 97–9 and good summaries in *LW* 45:105ff.; *LW* 36:106ff.

[87] See variously, K. Trüdinger, *Luthers Briefe und Gutachten an weltliche Obrigkeit zur Durchführung der Reformation* (Münster, 1975); Bernd Moeller, *Imperial Cities and the Reformation: Three Essays*, trans. and ed. H.C. Erik Midelfort and Mark U. Edwards, Jr. (Philadelphia, 1972); Ozment, *Reformation of the Cities*; Hans Baron, "Religion and Politics in the German Imperial Cities during the Reformation," *English Historical Review* 52 (1937): 405, 614; Martin Brecht, "Die gemeinsame Politik der Reichsstädte und die Reformation," *ZSS KA* 63 (1977): 180; Harold J. Grimm, "The Reformation and the Urban Social Classes in Germany," in John C. Olin *et al.*, eds. *Luther, Erasmus, and the Reformation* (New York, 1969), 75; Hajo Holborn, "Luther and the Princes," in ibid., 67; Gerhard Müller, "Martin Luther and the Political World of his Time," in E. I. Kouri and Tom Scott, eds., *Politics and Society in Reformation Europe: Essays in Honor of Sir Geoffrey Elton on his Sixty-Fifth Birthday* (New York, 1987), 35–50.

however, and not used to paint Luther as a theorist of political abso-
lutism, or elitist oligarchy, or constitutional democracy. Luther had no
firm theory of the forms of political office. He did not systematically sort
out the relative virtues and vices of monarchy, aristocracy, or democracy.
He spent very little time on the thorny constitutional questions of the nature and purpose of executive, legislative, and judicial powers, let alone
finer questions of checks and balances, judicial review, and other such
questions that occupied other sixteenth-century Protestant and humanist
writers.[88] These were not Luther's primary concern.

Luther was more concerned with the general status and function of
the political office, both before God and within the community. On the
one hand, Luther believed, the magistrate was God's vice-regent in the
earthly kingdom, called to elaborate and enforce God's Word and will,
to reflect God's justice and judgment on earthly citizens. The magistracy
was, in this sense, a "divine office," a "holy estate," a "Godly calling,"
within the earthly kingdom. Indeed, the magistrate was a "god" on earth,
as Psalm 82:6 put it, to be obeyed as if God himself.[89] "Law and earthly
government are a great gift of God to mankind," Luther wrote with
ample flourish. "Earthly authority is an image, shadow, and figure of
the dominion of Christ." Indeed, "a pious jurist" who serves faithfully
in the Christian magistrate's retinue is "a prophet, priest, angel, and
savior . . . in the earthly kingdom."[90]

The magistrate and his retinue not only represented God's authority
and majesty, however: they also exercised God's judgment and wrath
against human sin. "Princes and magistrates are the bows and arrows of
God," Luther wrote, equipped to hunt down God's enemies in the earthly
kingdom.[91] The hand of the Christian magistrate, judge, or soldier "that
wields the sword and slays is not man's hand, but God's; and it is not
man, but God, who hangs, tortures, beheads, slays, and fights. All these
are God's works and judgments."[92]

On the other hand, Luther believed, the magistrate was the "father
of the community" (*Landesvater, paterpoliticus*). He was to care for his political subjects as if they were his children, and his political subjects were

---

[88] See Quentin Skinner, *The Foundation of Modern Political Thought*, 2 vols. (Cambridge, 1978); A.
London Fell, *Origins of Legislative Sovereignty and the Legislative State*, 4 vols. published to date
(Königstein/Cambridge, MA, 1983–).

[89] See *LW* 2:139ff.; *LW* 13:44ff.; *LW* 44:92ff.; *LW* 45:85ff.; *LW* 46:237ff. and detailed citations to
the secondary literature in "Transformation," nn. 39ff.

[90] *WA* 30/2:554.   [91] *LW* 17:171.

[92] *WA* 19:626. See also *WA* 6:267; *LW* 45:113; *LW* 46:95ff.

to "honor" him as if he were their parent.[93] This was the essence of the *ordo politicus*, of the political authorities and their subjects that comprise "the state." Like a loving father, the magistrate was to keep the peace and to protect his subjects from threats or violations to their persons, properties, and reputations.[94] He was to deter his subjects from abusing themselves through drunkenness, sumptuousness, prostitution, gambling, and other vices.[95] He was to nurture and sustain his subjects through the community chest, the public almshouse, the state-run hospice.[96] He was to educate them through the public school, the public library, the public lectern.[97] He was to see to their spiritual needs by supporting the ministry of the locally established church, and encouraging their attendance and participation through the laws of Sabbath observance, tithing, and holy days. He was to see to their material needs by reforming inheritance and property laws to ensure more even distribution of the parents' property among all children.[98] He was to set an example of virtue, piety, love, and charity in his own home and private life for his faithful subjects to emulate and to respect. The Christian magistrate was to complement and support the God-given responsibilities of parents and family members for their children and dependants, without intruding on the paternal office. And he was to support the preaching and sacramental life of the local church without trespassing on the ecclesiastical office, let alone that of the invisible Church of the heavenly kingdom.[99]

These twin metaphors of the Christian magistrate – as the lofty vice-regent of God and as the loving father of the community – described the basics of Luther's and Lutheran political theory. For Luther political authority was divine in origin, but earthly in operation. It expressed God's harsh judgment against sin but also his tender mercy for sinners. It communicated the Law of God but also the lore of the local community. It depended upon the Church for prophetic direction but it took over from the Church all jurisdiction – governance of marriage, education, poor relief, and other earthly subjects traditionally governed by the Church's canon law. Either metaphor standing alone could be a recipe for abusive tyranny or officious paternalism. But both metaphors together provided

---

[93] *WA* 30/1:152ff.; *LW* 13:58ff. See also *TC* 626–627; *LW* 44:81–99.
[94] *LW* 13:44ff; *LW* 45:88ff., 103; *LW* 46:225ff.
[95] *LW* 44:95ff., 212ff.; *LW* 46:94ff.   [96] See chapter 5 below.   [97] See chapter 7 below.
[98] See Ozment, *Protestants: The Birth of a Revolution*, 71ff., and more generally Paula Sutter Fichtner, *Protestantism and Primogeniture in Early Modern Europe* (New Haven, CT, 1989).
[99] *LW* 45:83–84, 104–13; cf. *LW* 36:106–17.

Luther and his followers with the core ingredients of a robust Christian republicanism and budding Christian welfare state.[100]

Legal implications

Luther's two-kingdoms theory effectively "flattened" the traditional hierarchical theories of being and order, clergy and laity, ecclesiastical and political authority. His earthly kingdom was a horizontal realm with each person, each order, and each official called directly by God to discharge discrete offices and vocations. What kept this earthly kingdom and its activities intact, Luther believed, was the Law of God, and its elaboration by earthly authorities and subjects.

Luther defined the Law of God as the set of norms ordained by God in the creation, written by God on the hearts of all people, and rewritten by God on the pages of the Bible. Luther called this variously the "law of nature," "natural law," "divine law," "Godly law," "the law of the heart," "the teachings of conscience," "the inner law," among others – terms and concepts that he did not clearly differentiate either from each other or from traditional formulations.[101] His main point was that God's natural law, set at the creation, continued to operate after the fall into sin, and that it provided the foundation for all positive law and public morality in the earthly kingdom.

The natural law defined the basic obligations that a person owed to God, neighbor, and self. The clearest expression of these obligations, for Luther, was the Ten Commandments which God inscribed on two tables and gave to Moses on Mt. Sinai. The First Table of the Decalogue set out basic obligations to honor the Creator God, to respect God's name, to observe the Sabbath, to avoid idolatry and blasphemy. The Second Table set out basic obligations to respect one's neighbor – to honor authorities, and not to kill, commit adultery, steal, bear false

---

[100] See pp. 139–54 on Johannes Eisermann and Nicolaus Hemming, and Bucer, *RC* also Tracy, ed., *Luther and the Modern State in Germany*.

[101] See the collection of quotations in Hermann W. Beyer, *Luther und das Recht: Gottes Gebot, Naturrecht, Volksgesetz in Luthers Deutung* (Munich, 1935). Among numerous studies, see esp. Johannes Heckel, *Lex charitatis: Eine juristische Untersuchung über das Recht in der Theologie Martin Luthers* (Munich, 1953); W. D. J. Cargill Thompson, *The Political Thought of Martin Luther* (Brighton, Sussex, 1984); John Tonkin, *The Church and the Secular Order in Reformation Thought* (New York, 1971), 37–72; Paul Althaus, *The Ethics of Martin Luther* trans. Robert C. Schultz (Philadelphia, 1972), 25–36; Cranz, *Development*, 73–112; Joseph Binder, "Zur Hermeneutik der Rechtslehre Martin Luthers," *Archiv für Rechts- und Sozialphilosophie* 51 (1965): 337; John T. McNeill, "Natural Law in the Thought of Luther, *Church History* 10 (1941): 211.

witness, or covet.[102] Luther believed this to be a universal statement of the natural law binding not only the Jews of the Old Testament but on everyone. "The Decalogue is not the law of Moses . . . but the Decalogue of the whole world, inscribed and engraved in the minds of all men from the foundation of the world."[103] "[W]hoever knows the Ten Commandments perfectly must know all the Scriptures, so that, in all affairs and cases, he can advise, help, comfort, judge, and decide both spiritual and temporal matters, and is qualified to sit in judgment upon all doctrines, estates, spirits, laws, and whatever else is in the world."[104] And again: "[A]lthough the Decalogue was given in a particular way and place and ceremony . . . all nations acknowledge that there are sins and iniquities."[105]

Knowledge of this natural law comes not only through revealed Scripture, Luther argued, but also through natural reason – one of those "masks" by which the hidden God is partly revealed in the earthly kingdom. Luther built on St. Paul's notion that even the heathen have a "law written in their hearts, their conscience also bearing witness" to a natural knowledge of good and evil (Romans 2:15). Every rational person thus "feels" and "knows" the Law of God, even if only obliquely. The basic teaching of the natural law "lives and shines in all human reason, and if people would only pay attention to it, what need would they have of books, teachers, or of law? For they carry with them in the recesses of the heart a living book which would tell them more than enough about what they ought to do, judge, accept, and reject."[106]

But sinful persons do not, of their own accord, "pay attention" to the natural law written on their hearts, and rewritten in the Bible. Thus God has called upon other persons and authorities in the earthly kingdom to elaborate its basic requirements. All Christians, as priests to their peers, must communicate the natural law of God by word and by deed. Parents must teach it to their children and dependents. Preachers must preach it their congregants and catechumens. And magistrates must elaborate and enforce it through their positive laws and public policies.

The magistrate's elaboration and enforcement of the natural law was particularly important, Luther believed, since only the magistrate held formal legal authority in the earthly kingdom. "Natural law is a practical first principle in the realm of public morality," Luther wrote; "it forbids

---

[102] See esp. LW 44:15–114; TC 581–677. See further Heinrich Bornkamm, *Luther and the Old Testament*, trans. Eric W. Gritsch and Ruth C. Gritsch (Philadelphia, 1969).
[103] *WA* 39/1:478.   [104] *TC* 573.
[105] *WA* 39/1:540; see also *WA* 18:72; *WA* 30:192.   [106] *WA* 17/2:102.

evil and commands good. Positive law is a decision that takes local conditions into account," and "credibly" elaborates the general principles of
the natural law into specific precepts to fit these local conditions. "The
basis of natural law is God, who has created this light, but the basis of
positive law is the earthly authority," the magistrate, who represents God
in this earthly kingdom.[107] The magistrate must promulgate and enforce
these positive laws by combining faith, reason, and tradition. He must
pray to God earnestly for wisdom and instruction. He must maintain
"an untrammelled reason" in judging the needs of his people and the
advice of his counsellors.[108] He must consider the wisdom of the legal
tradition – particularly that of Roman law, which Luther called a form
of "heathen wisdom."[109] "The polity and the economy" of the earthly
kingdom, Luther wrote, "are subject to reason. Reason has first place.
There [one finds] civil laws and civil justice."[110]

SUMMARY AND CONCLUSIONS

A mighty fortress is our God,
A bulwark never failing;
Our helper He, amidst the flood
Of mortal ills prevailing.
For still our ancient foe
Doth seek to work us woe;
His craft and power are great
And armed with cruel hate
On earth is not his equal.

Did we in our own strength confide,
Our striving would be losing;
Were not the right Man on our side,
The Man of God's own choosing.
Dost ask who that may be?
Christ Jesus, it is he;
Lord Sabaoth His name,
From age to age the same.
And He must win the battle.

And though this world, with devils filled,
Should threaten to undo us,

---

[107] *WA TR* 3: 3911; see also *WA* 51:211.   [108] *LW* 45:120–6. See also below pp. 164, 167.
[109] *WA* 51:242. See also *WA* 12:243; *WA* 14:591, 714; *WA* 16:537; *WA* 30/2:557; *WA* 51:241 and
discussion in Heckel, *Lex charitatis*, 82ff.
[110] *WA* 40:305.

We will not fear, for God has willed
His truth to triumph through us.
The prince of darkness grim,
We tremble not for him;
His rage we can endure,
For lo! his doom is sure,
One little Word shall fell him.

That Word above all earthly powers –
No thanks to them – abideth;
The spirit and the gift are ours.
Through him who with us sideth.
Let goods and kindred go.
This mortal life also.
The body they may kill,
God's truth abideth still.
His kingdom is forever.

These are the powerful words of Luther's famous hymn, *A Mighty Fortress is our God*, published in 1529. They capture many of the cardinal convictions at the core of Luther's two-kingdoms theory: the contrasts between Satan and Christ, body and soul, works and faith, folly and truth, despair and hope, death and life, the mortality of the earthly kingdom and the eternity of the heavenly kingdom. They also capture Luther's abiding faith that God and His Word ultimately remain in charge of both kingdoms, even if the Devil and his minions temporally vie for power in the earthly kingdom.

While driven by the simple biblical piety reflected in this song, the two-kingdoms theory provided Luther and the Lutheran Reformation with the start to an intricate new framework of thought. This two-kingdoms theory held together Luther's emerging theories of being, the person, the Church, knowledge, and righteousness all at once. Or, in loftier academic language, the two-kingdoms theory allowed Luther to move toward an integrated ontology, anthropology, ecclesiology, epistemology, and soteriology.

Sixteenth-century Evangelical jurists and moralists began their theories of law, politics, and society where Luther left off. Most Lutheran jurists and moralists accepted some variation on Luther's two-kingdoms framework, incorporating almost by reference and reflex its complex tangle of theories and referring readers to Luther's writings if they needed to read more. Most Lutheran jurists and moralists also repeated the radical social, political, and legal implications that Luther had drawn from this theory. The theoretical challenge that remained was to work out in detail the implications of Luther's views for new Evangelical theories of the origin, nature, and purpose of law, society, politics, authority, power, equity, and more. In the course of the sixteenth century, a host of Evangelical jurists and moralists rose to this challenge, sometimes pressing Luther's theological insights to startling new conclusions that Luther himself would have been hesitant to embrace.

4. Woodcut from Johannes Cogelerus, *Imagines elegantissimae: quae multum lucis ad intelligendos doctrinae Christianae locos adferre possunt, Collectae, partim ex praelectionibus Domini Philippi Melanthonis, partim ex scriptis Patrum a Iohanne Cogelero, Verbi diuini ministro Stetini cum praefatione D. Georgij Maioris* (Wittenberg, 1558)

Moses raises the two stone tablets overhead, and in the distance Israel worships the golden calf. In the background Moses receives the tablets from God on Mt. Sinai.

4

Perhaps jurists are good Christians after all: Lutheran theories of law, politics, and society

LUTHER AND THE JURISTS

"Jurists are bad Christians."[1] This is one of Luther's most famous aphorisms about law that every German schoolboy still learns and that every pious Protestant still ponders when considering the legal profession. The phrase was of a piece with many other derogatory comments that Luther made about jurists. "Of the Gospel, jurists know nothing, and therefore they are justly excluded from the circuit of divinity."[2] "Every jurist is an enemy of Christ."[3] "We theologians have no worse enemies than jurists."[4] "There is eternal strife and war between jurists and theologians."[5] "Every jurist is either a good-for-nothing or a know-nothing."[6] "A jurist should not speak until he hears a pig fart" for only then will his words have a proper climate to be appreciated.[7] And more scatological still: "I shit on the law of the pope and of the emperor, and on the law of the jurists as well."[8]

Luther's shrill comments were, in part, the fallout of his bitter struggles with the University of Wittenberg's law faculty about teaching papal laws to Evangelical students.[9] They were, in part, general echoes of centuries-long antipathies between the faculties of law and theology in German and other Western universities. They were, in part, more specific echoes of contests among sixteenth-century Germans about the propriety of replacing German customary law with Roman law and Romanist and civilian jurisprudence.[10] They were, in part, expressions of Luther's theological contempt for any jurist who pretended to extend his ken and

---

[1] *WA TR* 3, No. 2809b; see also *WA TR* 6, No. 7029–30.
[2] *Table Talk of Martin Luther*, trans. Hazlitt, 135.   [3] *WA TR* 3, No. 2837, 3027.
[4] *WA TR* 5, No. 5663.   [5] *WA TR* 6, No. 7029.   [6] *WA TR* 5, No. 5663.   [7] Ibid.
[8] *WA* 49:302. See further Hans Liermann, "Der unjuristische Luther," *Luther-Jahrbuch* 24 (1957): 69; Roderich von Stintzing, *Das Sprichwort 'Juristen böse Christen' in seiner geschichtlichen Bedeutung* (Bonn, 1875).
[9] See above pp. 82–3.   [10] See Strauss, *Law, Resistance and the State*.

jurisdiction into the heavenly kingdom. They were, in part, just another contribution to the vats of vitriol that every generation has poured over its jurists and lawyers for their hair-splitting casuistry, pretentious self-indulgence, and cleverly cloaked theft from their clients.[11]

But Luther eventually made his grudging peace with some of the jurists of his day, much as he had made his grudging peace with some of the canon law of earlier days. The reality was that Luther needed the jurists to support his reformation, as much as he had needed the canon law to support his Evangelical Church. It was one thing to deconstruct the institutional framework of medieval law, politics, and society with a sharp and skillfully wielded theological sword. It was quite another thing to try to reconstruct a new institutional framework of Evangelical law, politics, and society with only this theological sword in hand. Luther learned this lesson the hard way in witnessing the bloody peasants' revolt in Germany in 1525, and the growing numbers of radical egalitarian and antinomian experiments engineered out of his doctrines of the priesthood of all believers and justification by faith alone. He came to realize that law was not just a necessary evil, it was an essential blessing for life in the earthly kingdom. Equally essential was a corps of well-trained jurists, eager and able to given institutional form to the best theological teachings of the Reformation.[12]

Jaroslav Pelikan has written famously that one of the stories of the Lutheran Reformation is a swing of the pendulum, first from structure to spirit, and then from spirit to structure.[13] This image, which Professor Pelikan used to describe the two-fold reformation of the German Church, also describes nicely the two-fold reformation of German law. Luther and the theologians directed the first swing of the pendulum, moving Germany from canon law structure to biblical spirit. The jurists joined the theologians to direct the second swing of the pendulum, moving Germany from a spiritual freedom run awry to a newly structured Evangelical order.

This chapter analyzes the theoretical moves made by jurists and moralists to help accomplish this second reform movement. It focuses on the new legal theories of Lutheran Germany through the mid-sixteenth century, using close case studies of Philip Melanchthon, Johannes Eisermann, and Johann Oldendorp to illustrate the range of new Lutheran theories of law, politics, and society. Subsequent chapters will document the institutional moves made by theologians and jurists

---

[11] See, e.g., Luther's comments on lawyers' tricks in *TC* 665ff. and further Stintzing, *Das Sprichwort* and Wilfried Prest, ed., *Lawyers in Early Modern Europe and America* (London, 1981).
[12] *LW* 46: 240–2.   [13] Pelikan, *Spirit versus Structure*.

together to translate the new Lutheran lore into new legal forms and norms.

THE LEGAL PHILOSOPHY OF PHILIP MELANCHTHON

It has been said that while Martin Luther taught "the justice of God," Philip Melanchthon taught "the justice of society," and that his legal teachings "deserve to be viewed alongside the teachings of an Aristotle, a Thomas Aquinas, a Leibniz, and . . . the German school of jurisprudence of the nineteenth century."[14] Wilhelm Dilthey called Melanchthon "the ethicist of the Reformation" and the "greatest didactic genius of the sixteenth century, [who] liberated the philosophical sciences from the casuistry of scholastic thought. . . . A new breath of life went out from him."[15] Indeed, in his own time Melanchthon was called "the teacher of Germany" (*praeceptor Germaniae*).[16]

Born in 1497, Melanchthon was a child prodigy. He received his bachelor's degree at the University of Heidelberg in 1511 and his master's degree at the University of Tübingen in 1514. In 1518, he was appointed to the University of Wittenberg to serve as its first professor of Greek. In his inaugural address on *The Improvement of Education*, he urged his colleagues to abandon the "arid, barbaric fulminations of the scholastics" and to return to the study of pure classical and Christian sources.[17]

In part under Luther's personal inspiration, Melanchthon joined the Evangelical cause. In his first year at the University of Wittenberg, he studied theology while teaching Greek and rhetoric, and in 1519 he received the bachelor's degree in theology. He soon became a gifted professor of theology; as many as 600 students attended his lectures. He also became an eloquent exponent of Lutheran theology. In 1519 and 1520, he wrote several learned defenses of Luther against his opponents and a number of short popular theological pamphlets. In 1521, he published his famous *Common Topics of Theology* (*Loci communes*) the first systematic treatise on Protestant theology and a standard classroom text in Evangelical and broader circles for centuries to come.[18] During the

---

[14] H. Fild, *Justitia bei Melanchthon* (Theol. Diss., Erlangen, 1953), 150.

[15] Wilhelm Dilthey, *Gesammelte Schriften*, 23 vols. (Leipzig, 1921), 21:193.

[16] Karl Hartfelder, *Philipp Melanchthon als Präceptor Germaniae* (Berlin, 1899). See further pp. 265–77 below on his educational reforms. For biography, see Heinz Scheible, *Melanchthon: Eine Biographie* (Munich, 1997); Robert Stupperich, *Philip Melanchthon: Gelehrter und Politiker* (Zurich, 1996); Wilhelm Maurer, *Der junge Melanchthon zwischen Humanismus und Reformation*, 2 vols. (Munich, 1969).

[17] *MW* 3:29–42.

[18] *LC* (1521); see Paul Joachimsen, "*Loci communes*: Eine Untersuchung zur Geistesgeschichte des Humanismus und der Reformation," *Luther-Jahrbuch* 8 (1926): 27; Quirinius Breen, "'Loci communes' and 'Loci' in Melanchthon," *Church History* 16 (1947): 197.

1520s and 1530s, Melanchthon played a leading role in the debates between the Lutheran reformers and their multiple Catholic and Protestant opponents. He drafted the chief declaration of Lutheran theology, the Augsburg Confession (1530), and its Apology (1531). He prepared a number of Lutheran catechisms and instruction books and published more than a dozen commentaries on biblical books and ancient Christian creeds as well as several revised and expanded editions of his *Loci communes*.[19]

In the course of all this, Melanchthon wrote a good deal about law, chiefly in the context of theology and natural and moral philosophy.[20] He lectured and taught widely on Roman law, and on the theological and philosophical foundations of legal and political institutions. He also participated in the drafting of several reformation ordinances, and was frequently consulted on cases that raised intricate legal, political, and moral questions. Through these writings and activities, Melanchthon had a formidable influence on the legal and theological reforms of marriage, education, and social welfare, as we shall see in subsequent chapters. He also had a formidable influence on Lutheran legal theory, developing several important new strands of argument and influencing scores of Evangelical jurists who attended his lectures or read his writings.[21]

Natural law and biblical law

Melanchthon started with Luther's two-kingdoms framework[22] and its founding theological doctrines of Law and Gospel, total depravity, and justification by faith alone.[23] He endorsed Luther's notion of the natural

[19] The 1535, 1543, 1555, and 1558 editions of his *Loci communes* appear respectively in *CR* 21:81, 229, 561; *CR* 22:47.

[20] See discussion in Sachiko Kusukawa, *The Transformation of Natural Philosophy: The Case of Philip Melanchthon* (Cambridge, 1995) and sample texts in Kisch, *Melanchthons Rechts- und Soziallehre*, 189–287.

[21] On Melanchthon's legal philosophy, see among many others, ibid.; Clemens Bauer, "Melanchthons Rechtslehre," *AFR* 42 (1951): 64; id., "Der Naturrechtsvorstellungen des jungeren Melanchthon," in *Festschrift für Gerhard Ritter zu seinem 60. Geburtstag* (Tübingen, 1950), 244; Albert Hänel, "Melanchthon der Jurist," *Zeitschrift für Rechtsgeschichte* 8 (1869): 249; Walter Sohm, "Die Soziallehren Melanchthons," *Historische Zeitschrift* 115 (1916): 68; Stintzing, 287ff.; Alfred Voigt, "Die juristische Hermeneutik und ihr Abbild in Melanchthons Universitätsreden," in Carl Joseph Hering, ed., *Staat, Recht, Kultur: Festgabe für Ernst von Hippel zu seinem 70. Geburtstag* (Munich, 1965), 265. On Melanchthon's influence on sixteenth-century jurists, see Stintzing, 241–338; Kisch, *Melanchthons Rechtslehre*, 51–73.

[22] See esp. *TC* 328–33; *LC* (1555), 39–44, 274–9, 323–44; *CR* 11:68ff., 357ff., 917ff. and detailed discussion in Adolf Sperl, *Melanchthon zwischen Humanismus und Reformation* (Munich, 1959).

[23] See *LC* (1521), 49–111; *LC* (1555), 83–174, with further sources and discussion in Kusukawa, *Natural Philosophy*, 27–74; Timothy J. Wengert, *Philip Melanchthon's Exegetical Dispute with Erasmus of Rotterdam* (New York/Oxford, 1998).

primacy and equality of the three estates of family, Church, and state in the governance of the earthly kingdom.[24] And he accepted Luther's notion that a God-given natural law was written on the hearts of all people, rewritten on the pages of the Bible, and accessible by human reason to guide and govern life in the earthly kingdom.[25]

Already in his early writings, however, Melanchthon was more explicit than Luther in expounding the content of this natural law. While the Decalogue, the Beatitudes, and the Golden Rule were all useful biblical summaries of the natural law, he argued, classical and post-biblical sources provided additional insights into its content. Melanchthon ultimately identified at least ten principles of natural law that he considered to be common to classical and Christian sources: (1) to worship God and to honor God's law; (2) to protect life; (3) to testify truthfully; (4) to marry and raise children; (5) to care for one's relatives; (6) to harm no one in their person, property, or reputation; (7) to obey all those in authority; (8) to distribute and exchange property on fair terms; (9) to honor one's contracts and promises; and (10) to oppose injustice.[26]

Melanchthon also went well beyond Luther in grounding this natural law philosophically. Building on the two-kingdoms theory, Melanchthon taught that God has implanted in all individuals certain "inborn elements of knowledge" ("notitiae nobiscum nascentes"). These he called variously a "light from above," a "natural light," "rays of divine wisdom poured into us," "a light of the human faculty" without which we could not find our way in the earthly kingdom.[27] These *notitiae* included various "theoretical principles" of logic, dialectics, geometry, arithmetic, physics, and other sciences: that two plus two equals four, that an object thrown into the air will eventually come down, that the whole is bigger than any one of its parts, and the like. These *notitiae* also include certain "practical principles" ("principia practica") of ethics, politics, and law: that "men were born for civil society," that offenses which harm society should be punished, that "promises should be kept," and many others.[28] "All these natural elements of knowledge," Melanchthon believed, "are congruent with the eternal and unchanging norm of the divine mind that God has

---

[24] See *LC* (1555), 323; pp. 135ff., 217–18, 230–2 below; Rolf B. Huschke, *Melanchthons Lehre vom ordo politicus* (Gütersloh, 1968).

[25] *MW* 4:164; *CR* 21:116–17; *CR* 16:167ff.

[26] See notes in *CR* 21:25–7. See another early summary in *CR* 21:119–20; and in Maurer, *Der junge Melanchthon*, 2:288ff.

[27] *CR* 13:150, 647; *CR* 11:920–1; *CR* 21:7121. See also *CR* 13:642ff.; *CR* 20:695ff., 748ff.; Melanchthon, *Dialectices Philippi Melanchthonis* (Louvain, 1534), esp. bks. II–III; Dilthey, *Gesammelte Schriften*, 2:162ff.; Heinrich Bornkamm, *Das Jahrhundert der Reformation: Gestalten und Kräfte* (Göttingen, 1966), 69ff.

[28] *CR* 21:117, 398–400, 711–13; *CR* 11:918–19.

planted in us." They provide the starting point for life and learning in this earthly kingdom.[29]

Melanchthon often equated the natural law with these "practical principles," these "natural elements of knowledge concerning morals" that undergird life and law in the earthly kingdom.[30] The ten natural law principles that he had identified early in his career remained in place, but he now tended to distill them into more general virtues as well:

The greatest and best things in the divine mind, that of the creator of the human race, are wisdom, distinguishing honorable from shameful things, and justice, truth, kindness, clemency, and chastity. God planted seeds of these best things in human minds, when He made us after His own image. And He wished the life and behavior of men to correspond to the standard of His own mind. He also revealed this same wisdom and doctrine of the virtues with His own voice [in the Bible].

This knowledge, divinely taught both by the light that is born in us and by the true divine voice, is the beginning of the laws and of the political order [of the earthly kingdom]. God wishes us to obey them not only for the sake of our needs, but more, so that we may acknowledge our creator and learn from this same order that this world did not arise by chance, but that there is a creator who is wise, just, kind, truthful, and chaste and who demands similar virtues in us. We may also learn that He is an avenger who punishes violations of this order.[31]

Human reason, Melanchthon argued, cannot prove the existence of these natural law principles.[32] They are facts and facets of human nature, forms of innate knowledge that are in the mind of God, and "placed in our mind by God" at creation.[33] They are beyond the power of even the purest reason to prove or disprove. This was a deliberate departure from conventional medieval teachings that human reason can prove moral propositions that are consistent with divine revelation. Like Luther, Melanchthon distrusted the capacity of human reason to understand, far less to prove, what was in the mind of God.[34]

Nor can human reason apprehend or apply these natural law principles without distortion. "Our nature is corrupted by original sin," Melanchthon wrote, echoing Luther's doctrine of total depravity. "Thus the law of nature is greatly obscured."[35] This, too, was a decided departure from conventional teaching. Medieval writers recognized that all individuals have an innate or natural knowledge of good and evil,

---

[29] *CR* 16:228.   [30] *MW* 3:208.   [31] *CR* 11:918–19.
[32] *CR* 21:399–400; see also *CR* 13:547–55; 21:116–17.
[33] Quoted in Kusukawa, *Natural Philosophy*, 94.
[34] See Dilthey, *Gesammelte Schriften*, 2:175–6; *Philip Melanchthon: Orations on Philosophy and Education*, ed. Sachiko Kusukawa (Cambridge, 1999), xvii–xviii.
[35] *MW* 4:146ff.; *TC* 157–9; *CR* 21:399–402.

which they sometimes called "synderesis." Through proper discipline, a person could come to understand and apply this knowledge and so do good and avoid evil. A person must use reason to apprehend the natural law. He must use conscience to apply it in concrete circumstances. Thus, for example, through the exercise of reason a person apprehends and understands the principle of love of neighbor; through the exercise of conscience he connects this principle with the practice of aiding the poor and helpless or of keeping his promises. For many medieval writers, reason was a cognitive or intellectual faculty, conscience a practical or applicative skill.[36] Melanchthon, like Luther, would have none of this fine casuistry.[37] God planted a perfect natural knowledge of the nature of good and evil in our minds. But our sin keeps us from apprehending or applying it without distortion.

Melanchthon's emphasis on the limitations of human reason, however, rendered his doctrine of natural law paradoxical. On the one hand, he argued that "the law of nature itself, divinely written in the minds of men, is the law of God concerning those virtues which the reason understands and which are necessary for civil life."[38] On the other hand, he argued that "in this enfeebled state of nature," human reason is "darkened" and thus "the law of nature is distorted . . . and invariably misunderstood."[39]

Melanchthon resolved this paradox by subordinating the natural law that is discerned but distorted by reason to the biblical law that is revealed and understood by faith.[40] The biblical law that he had in mind was the rich set of moral teachings set out in parts of the Torah, the Beatitudes, various parables and maxims of Christ, and various epistles of St. Paul. These biblical moral teachings he variously called the "divine law," "the law of God," "the law of morality," "the law of virtue," "the judgment of God," "the eternal immutable wisdom and rule of justice in God Himself."[41] The best summary of biblical moral law, in his view, was the Ten Commandments set out in Exodus 20 and Deuteronomy 5. Accordingly, the best source of knowledge of the content of the natural law was the Decalogue.[42] "[W]hy then did God proclaim the Ten

---

[36] Eric D'Arcy, *Conscience and its Right to Freedom* (New York, 1961); Johannes Stelzenberger, *Syneidesis, Conscientia, Gewissen* (Paderborn, 1963).

[37] For Luther's rejection of this doctrine, see Michael G. Baylor, *Action and Person: Conscience in Late Scholasticism and the Young Luther* (Leiden, 1977), 157ff. For Melanchthon's, see Kusukawa, *Natural Philosophy*, 94ff.

[38] *CR* 16:23.   [39] Ibid., 24; *CR* 21:400–1.   [40] *CR* 21:392.

[41] *CR* 21:1077; 22:201–2. Following tradition, Melanchthon distinguished the ceremonial, judicial, and moral laws of the Bible. Only the moral law remained in effect after Christ (*CR* 21:294–6, 387–92; *LC* (1521), 53–7). Johann Oldendorp made more of these ceremonial and juridical laws in his interpretation of natural law than did Luther or Melanchthon: see pp. 158–61.

[42] *CR* 21:392; see also *CR* 12:23.

Commandments?" Melanchthon wrote:

[First], in the wake of sin, the light in human reason was not as clear and bright as it had been before. . . . Against such blindness, God not only proclaimed his law on Mt. Sinai, but has sustained and maintained it since the time of Adam in his Church. . . . The other reason is that it is not enough for a person to know that he is not to kill other innocent persons, nor rob others of their wives and goods. Rather, one must know who God is and know that God earnestly wants us to be like Him, and that he assuredly rages against all sins. Therefore, He proclaims his commandments Himself, so that we know that they are not only our thoughts but that they are God's law, and that God is the judge and punisher of all sinners, and that our hearts may recognize God's wrath and tremble before it. . . . Still another reason why God proclaims His law is this: human reason, without God's word, soon errs and falls into doubt. If God Himself had not graciously proclaimed His wisdom, men would fall still further into doubt about what God is, who He is, about what is right and wrong, what is order and what is disorder.[43]

The Ten Commandments presented Melanchthon with a somewhat different iteration of the core principles of natural law from the ten principles he had listed earlier in his career based on his reading of the classical sources. The Ten Commandments, he stressed, are not the only valid iteration of natural law. Classical formulations, particularly those of Greek philosophy and Roman law, continue to be effective. Indeed, the overlap between classical and biblical teachings attests to the universality of these natural law norms.[44] But, given their authorship by God Himself on Mt. Sinai, the Ten Commandments are the most authoritative rendering of the meaning of the natural law. A pious Christian magistrate and citizen would do well to start with these.

Following Luther and the medieval tradition, Melanchthon divided the Ten Commandments into two tables. The First Table is comprised of the first three commandments: to acknowledge one God and make no graven image, to utter no blasphemy, and to keep the sabbath day holy. These are the basic natural law principles that define a person's relationship with God. The Second Table comprises the remaining seven commandments: to honor one's parents and authorities, to preserve life, to protect marriage and the family, to respect property, to maintain truth, and to avoid envy and greed. These are the basic natural law principles that correspond with a person's need for community.[45] Melanchthon

---

43 *CR* 22:256–7; see also *CR* 16:70.   44 Ibid.; *CR* 11:66–86, 919–24.
45 See Bo Reicke, *Die Zehn Worte in Geschichte und Gegenwart* (Tübingen, 1973) describing three distinct Jewish and Christian traditions for numbering and arranging the Ten Commandments. The Lutheran reformers' scheme followed Augustine and the medieval scholastics. In the Bible, the

insisted that compliance with the First Table of the Decalogue – especially the First Commandment prohibiting the worship of false gods or graven images – is a prerequisite for understanding and complying with all the other commandments, and indeed should be part of all subsequent commandments.[46] For without having the faith and love of God mandated by the First Commandment, it is impossible to have faith and love for oneself and one's neighbors.

Melanchthon, building on Luther, transformed traditional legal theory by making not reason but the Bible, and more particularly the Ten Commandments, the basic source and summary of natural law in the earthly kingdom. To be sure, medieval writers had also discussed and interpreted the Ten Commandments at some length. They had also argued, in Thomas Aquinas's words, that the Ten Commandments "clearly set forth the obligations of the natural law."[47] Most medieval writers, however, had relied on the Ten Commandments to develop a moral law for the inner spiritual life rather than a natural law for the outer civil life. Accordingly, most discussion of the Ten Commandments in the medieval tradition occurred in the confessional books, not in the law books.[48] For Melanchthon, by contrast, the Ten Commandments were the ultimate source and summary of the natural law and hence a model for the positive law enacted by the earthly rulers.

The uses of natural law

Like Luther, Melanchthon insisted on justification by faith alone, not by works of the law.[49] Also like Luther, he believed the natural law still "remains useful" for life in the earthly kingdom. Once it is properly understood and administered, Melanchthon argued, the natural law serves civil, theological, and pedagogical uses.[50]

The first use of the law is "civil" or "political." Melanchthon described this much as Luther did. Law serves to coerce people to avoid evil and to do good. In this sense,

law teaches, and with fear and punishments forces one to keep his external members under moral discipline, concerning all the commandments about external works. . . . This civil use is binding on all persons whatsoever, even if

Commandments are not numbered or divided into tables. See Exodus 20:1–17; Deuteronomy 5:6–21.

[46] *CR* 22:220. See also *TC*, 166–215.   [47] *ST* I–II, q. 98, art. 5.
[48] See Ozment, *The Reformation in the Cities*, 17ff.; Reicke, *Zehn Worte*, 9ff.
[49] *LC* (1521), 88–108; *LC* (1555), 150–86.
[50] *CR* 1:706–9; *CR* 11:66; *CR* 21:405–6, 716–19; *LC* (1555), 54–7, 122–8.

they are not holy. This external obedience is possible for all persons to some extent.... It is God's earnest will that all men live in external discipline; He punishes external vice in this life with public plagues, with the sword of the *Obrigkeit*, and with illness, poverty, war, dispersion, distress in children, and many kinds of misfortunes. And he who is not converted to God falls into eternal punishment.[51]

Law thereby creates what Melanchthon variously called a "civil," "external," "public," or "political" morality.[52] Although this form of morality "does not merit forgiveness of sin," Melanchthon wrote, "it is pleasing to God."[53] For it allows people of all faiths to live peaceably together within the earthly kingdom that God has created.[54] It enables Christians to fulfill the vocations to which God has called them. And it allows "God continually to gather to himself a Church among men."[55]

The second use of the law is "theological": to make people conscious of their inability, by their own will and reason, to avoid evil and do good, and so impel them to seek grace.[56] Melanchthon followed Luther's description of this use of the law almost to the letter.[57]

The third use of the law is "educational": to teach the faithful, those who have already been justified, the higher spiritual morality that becomes Christians.[58] Melanchthon's exposition of this third use of the law built on Luther's teaching that the Christian believer is at once a saint and sinner, a citizen of both the heavenly and the earthly kingdoms.[59] But Melanchthon went beyond Luther in insisting that all Christian believers still need the instruction of the law, "for they carry with them . . . weakness and sin," and they "are still partly ignorant of God's will and desire for their lives."[60] The law teaches them not only the "public" morality that is common to all persons, but also the "private" morality that is required only of Christians. As a teacher, the law not only coerces them against violence and violation of others, but also cultivates in them charity and love. It not only punishes harmful acts of murder, theft, and adultery, but also prohibits evil thoughts of hatred, covetousness, and lust. Through the exercise of this private morality, the saints glorify God, exemplify God's law, and impel other sinners in the earthly kingdom to seek God's grace. Indeed, Melanchthon believed, the more a believer allows himself to be taught by the law, the better teacher of the law he himself can become for others. This was a new variation on Luther's doctrine of the priesthood of all believers.[61]

---

[51] *CR* 22:250.   [52] Ibid.; *CR* 11:70ff., 219ff., 920ff.   [53] *CR* 22:250.   [54] Ibid., 151, 249.
[55] *CR* 22:249.   [56] *CR* 21:69–70; *CR* 22:250–1.   [57] Ibid., 152.   [58] *CR* 21:255.
[59] *LC* (1521), 138–40.   [60] Ibid., 127, 132.   [61] Ibid., 175–86.

For Luther, with his emphasis on the justice of God, the theological use of the law was primary: to drive sinners to see their sin and to seek forgiveness. For Melanchthon, with his emphasis on the justice of society, the educational use of the law was primary: to teach the meaning and measure of both public and private morality, outer and inner righteousness in the earthly kingdom. Indeed, in some of his expositions Melanchthon folded the civil use of the law into the pedagogical use:

Paul says in Galatians 3[:24] that the law is a teacher in Christ, and that a child should be subject to the law, as though he were subject to teachers, until he matures in Christ. . . . Nevertheless, God has also subjected to this teaching all who are not in Christ or who are weak . . . [for] the multitude must be instructed, ruled, and coerced in this manner even now by laws and by certain offices. . . . This political pedagogy, which is justice, forms morals and includes both religious rites and human and civil offices. Through teaching and exercise it accustoms children [of God] to the proper worship of God, and it restrains foolish people from vices.[62]

Rational positive law

Melanchthon's twin emphases on the role of the Bible in teaching the contents of natural law, and on the role of the natural law in teaching the elements of Christian morality, brought the heavenly and earthly kingdoms into rather close cooperation. Melanchthon pressed this cooperation even closer by arguing that the purpose of the positive law of the state is to foster the Christian morality taught by the natural law, particularly the Ten Commandments.

Like Luther, Melanchthon regarded political rulers, whatever their form, to be God's "ministers" and "vice-regents" in the earthly kingdom, to be rendered the same obedience rendered to God.[63] Also like Luther, he recognized that many political officials abuse their political office, but that these abuses reflect the depravity only of the political official, not of the political office itself, which is a great "creation, blessing, and order of God."[64]

Melanchthon went beyond Luther, however, in articulating the divinely imposed task of Christian magistrates to promulgate what he called "rational positive laws" ("rationes iuris positivi") for the governance of the earthly kingdom.[65] To be "rational," Melanchthon argued,

[62] *CR* 1:706–8; see further Köhler, 104ff.; Strauss, *Law, Resistance, and the State*, 228ff.
[63] *CR* 11:69–70; *CR* 21:1011.   [64] *CR* 22:602–6; see also *WA* 32:529ff.; *LW* 45:113ff.
[65] *CR* 16:230; *CR* 22:611–12.

positive laws must be based on both (1) the general principles of natural law and (2) practical considerations of social utility and the common good. Unless both criteria are met, a positive law is neither legitimate nor binding on his subjects.

Conformity with natural law

In elaborating the first criterion, Melanchthon started from the position that the Christian magistrate is the "custodian" of both tables of the Decalogue, "a voice of the Ten Commandments" within the earthly kingdom.[66] "When you think about *Obrigkeit*, about princes or lords," Melanchthon wrote, "picture in your mind a man holding in one hand the tables of the Ten Commandments and holding in the other a sword. Those Ten Commandments are above all the works which he must protect and maintain," using the sword if necessary. Those Ten Commandments are "also the source from which all teaching and well-written laws flow and by which all statutes should be guided."[67]

Melanchthon took this image directly into his understanding of the nature and purpose of the positive law. The Christian magistrate is to enforce and elaborate the natural law principles set out in the Decalogue. His positive laws are to be organized and informed by the two main tables of the Decalogue. The First Table is to support positive laws that govern spiritual morality, the relationship between persons and God. The Second Table is to support positive laws that govern civil morality, the relationships between persons.[68]

As custodians of the First Table of the Decalogue, Melanchthon wrote, magistrates must pass laws against idolatry, blasphemy, and violations of the Sabbath – offenses that the First Table prohibits on its face.[69] Magistrates are also, however, to pass laws to "establish pure doctrine" and right liturgy, "to prohibit all wrong doctrine," "to punish the obstinate," and to root out the heathen and the heterodox.[70] "[W]orldly princes and rulers who have abolished idolatry and false doctrine in

---

[66] *CR* 22:87, 286, 615.

[67] *CR* 22:615. Luther used a similar image, albeit more generic: "a prince must have the law in hand as the sword. . . . " (*LW* 45:118).

[68] This was a different understanding of civil and spiritual morality from the one Melanchthon pressed under the "uses of the law" doctrine. Under the uses doctrine, Melanchthon distinguished external versus internal morality – living the letter versus living the spirit of all Ten of the Commandments. In his exegesis of the Decalogue, however, Melanchthon tied "civil morality" to compliance with the Second Table, and "spiritual morality" to compliance with the First Table. Both dialectics, he believed, were present in the earthly kingdom, and both needed to be fostered by the positive law of the Christian magistrate.

[69] *CR* 16:87–8; *CR* 22:615–17.   [70] *CR* 22:617–18.

their territories and have established the pure doctrine of the Gospel and the right worship of God have acted rightly," Melanchthon argued. "All rulers are obliged to do this."[71]

Melanchthon's move toward the establishment of religion by positive law was a marked departure from Luther's original teaching. In 1523, for example, Luther had written: "Earthly government has laws that extend no further than to life, property, and other external things on earth. For God cannot and will not allow anyone but Himself alone to rule over the soul. Thus when the earthly power presumes to prescribe laws to souls, it encroaches upon God and His government and only seduces and corrupts souls."[72] Luther eventually softened this stance, particularly in his late-life railings against Jews, antinomians, and Anabaptists.[73] But he remained firmly opposed to the magistrate defining by positive law which doctrines and liturgies were orthodox and which heterodox.

Melanchthon had held similar views in the 1520s and 1530s. But he eventually retreated from this position, despite Luther's objections that he was thereby betraying the essence of the two-kingdoms theory.[74] Melanchthon, even more than Luther in his later life, had been party to two decades of intense religious rivalries between and among Catholics and Protestants in Germany. He had become increasingly dismayed at the fracturing of German society and the perennial outbreaks of violent antinomianism and spiritual radicalism. He had become especially incensed at the "great many frantic and bewildered souls" who were blaspheming God and His law with their "monstrous absurdities" and "diabolical rages."[75] To allow such blasphemy and chaos to continue without rejoinder, Melanchthon believed, was ultimately to betray God and to belie the essence of the political office. After all, he reasoned,

earthly authority is obliged to maintain external discipline according to *all* the commandments. External idolatry, blasphemy, false oaths, untrue doctrine, and heresy are contrary to the First Table [of the Decalogue]. For this reason, earthly authority is obliged to prohibit, abolish, and punish these depravities [and] to accept the Holy Gospel, to believe, confess, and direct others to true divine service.

---

[71] Ibid., 617. Melanchthon hinted at this doctrine of religious establishment by civil law in his earlier writings (see, e.g., *CR* 2:710; *MW* 2:2, 21). But his first systematic articulation of the doctrine appears in his *Epitome of Moral Philosophy*, Book II published separately in 1539 and then as part of the full tract in 1540 (*CR* 16:85–105).

[72] *WA* 11:262.

[73] See esp. *LW* 47:99–119, 121–306 and further Mark U. Edwards, Jr., *Luther's Last Battles: Politics and Polemics, 1531–1546* (Ithaca/London, 1983).

[74] See, e.g., *LW* 49:378–90; and notes on subsequent letters in *LW* 50:85–92.

[75] *LC* (1555), 324; *CR* 11:918.

The political office "before all else should serve God, and should regulate and direct everything to the glory of God."[76]

With this teaching, Melanchthon helped to lay the theoretical basis for the welter of new religious establishment laws that were promulgated in Lutheran cities and territories, many of which contained comprehensive compendia of orthodox Lutheran confessions and doctrines, songs and prayers, and liturgies and rites.[77] The principle of *cuius regio eius religio* ("whose region, his religion"), set forth in the Religious Peace of Augsburg (1555) and expanded in the Peace of Westphalia (1648), rested ultimately on Melanchthon's theory that the magistrate's positive law was to use the First Table of the Decalogue to establish for his people proper Christian doctrine, liturgy, and spiritual morality.[78]

As custodians of the Second Table of the Decalogue, Melanchthon argued, magistrates are called to govern "the multiple relationships by which God has bound men together."[79] Melanchthon listed a whole series of positive laws that properly belong under each of the Commandments of the Second Table. On the basis of the Fourth Commandment ("Honor thy father and mother"), magistrates are obligated to prohibit and punish disobedience, disrespect, or disdain of authorities such as parents, political rulers, teachers, employers, masters, and others. On the basis of the Fifth Commandment ("Thou shalt not kill"), they are to punish unlawful killing, violence, assault, battery, wrath, hatred, mercilessness, and other offenses against one's neighbor. On the basis of the the Sixth Commandment ("Thou shalt not commit adultery"), they are to prohibit adultery, fornication, unchastity, incontinence, prostitution, pornography, obscenity, and other sexual offenses. On the basis of the Seventh Commandment ("Thou shalt not steal"), they are to outlaw theft, burglary, embezzlement, and similar offenses against another's property, as well as waste or noxious use or sumptuous use of one's own property. On the basis of the Eighth Commandment ("Thou shalt not bear false witness"), they are to punish all forms of perjury, dishonesty, fraud, defamation, and other violations of a person's reputation or status in the community. Finally, on the basis of the Ninth and Tenth Commandments ("Thou shalt not covet"), they are to punish all attempts to perform these or other offensive acts against another's person, property, reputation, or relationships.[80]

[76] *LC* (1555), 335–6 (rendering "weltliche" as "earthly" not "worldly").
[77] Collected in Sehling, Richter, and Kunkel and summarized below pp. 182–8.
[78] Ehler and Morall, *Church and State Through the Centuries*, 164–73, 189–93.
[79] *CR* 22:610.
[80] See *LC* (1521), 53ff.; *LC* (1555), 97ff.; *CR* 21:294ff., 387ff; *CR* 22:256ff.; *CR* 16:70ff.

Many of these aspects of social intercourse had traditionally been governed by the Church's canon law and organized in part by the seven sacraments. The sacrament of marriage, for example, supported the canon law of marriage and family life. The sacrament of penance supported the canon law of crimes against the persons, properties, and reputations of others. The sacraments of baptism and confirmation undergirded a constitutional law of natural rights and duties of Christian believers.[81]

Melanchthon used the Ten Commandments, instead of the seven sacraments, to organize the various systems of positive law. And he looked to the state, instead of the Church, to promulgate and enforce these positive laws on the basis of the Ten Commandments. Melanchthon's argument provided a further rationale, beyond Luther's, to support the abrupt transfer of legal power from the Church to the state upon the burning of the canon law books.[82] The magistrate was God's vice-regent, called to enforce God's law in the earthly kingdom through positive laws. God's law was most clearly summarized in the Ten Commandments. The magistrate therefore had to pass positive laws for each of these Commandments, superceding other laws that might have existed.

Melanchthon's argument also provided the reformers with an effective means to control the magistrate in the exercise of this newly augmented power. No positive law that violated the natural law was legitimate and binding. The natural law was best expressed in the Ten Commandments. The Ten Commandments were best interpreted by the Church and its theologians. Both traditional theological interpretations, reflected in part in the old canon law texts, and the new interpretations offered by Evangelical theologians should thus carry ample legal weight. Here was a sturdy rationale for the transplantation of old canon law rules into the new civil law that we already saw.[83] Here was also the start to a framework of theological checks and balances upon political authorities. This was institutionalized in sixteenth-century Germany in a number of ways that Melanchthon among others advocated. Evangelical churchmen and theology professors were both informally consulted by magistrates and formally appointed to the local *Obrigkeit* to participate in legislative and executive decisions. Court cases raising particularly difficult moral and theological issues were sent to both law faculties and theology faculties for resolution. This *Aktenversendung* process (literally the process of "sending the file"), which lasted in Germany until 1878, had a way of drawing

---

[81] See above pp. 37–8.   [82] See above pp. 53–4, 63–4, 97–9, 108–13.
[83] See above pp. 76–83.

together the best legal and theological learning of the day to address the hard moral and theological questions that came to the state for resolution by positive law.[84]

Compatability with the common good

Melanchthon's first criterion for "rational positive law" was that it should conform to natural law, especially as summarized in the Ten Commandments. His second criterion was that all positive law had to correspond with practical considerations of social utility and the common good. In elaborating this criterion, Melanchthon drew from the Ten Commandments as a whole a general duty of the state "to maintain external discipline, judgment, and peace in accordance with the divine commandments and the rational laws of the land."[85] Neither the divine commandments, however, nor the rational laws of the land based on them contained a systematic statement of the nature of the legal order required for the maintenance of "discipline, judgment, and peace." In laying the foundations for such a systematic statement, Melanchthon developed general theories of both criminal law and civil law.

In criminal law, Melanchthon urged magistrates to develop comprehensive codes that define and prohibit all manner of offense against the person, property, reputation, or relationships of another and to enforce these laws "swiftly and severely." He described three purposes of criminal law and punishment. First, criminal law and punishment served the goal of retribution. "God is a wise and righteous being, who out of His great and proper goodness created rational creatures to be like Him," Melanchthon wrote. "Therefore, if they strive against Him the order of justice [requires that] He destroy them." The magistrate, as God's vice-regent, was called to effectuate this divine end by defining the meaning of God's law through criminal laws, and punishing those who violated the same. Secondly, criminal law and punishment served the goal of deterrence, both special deterrence of the individual defendant and general deterrence of the broader community which witnesses his punishment. "When some are punished, others are reminded to take account of God's wrath and to fear His punishment and thus to reduce the causes of punishment." Thirdly, criminal punishment served the goal of rehabilitation – of allowing a person to learn again how to "distinguish between virtue and vice," and so come to better and fuller understanding of God's law, order, and justice.[86]

---

[84] See detailed sources in "Transformation."   [85] *CR* 22:615.   [86] Ibid., 224.

Melanchthon's theory of the three purposes of criminal law was part and product of his theology of the three uses of natural law. The *retributive* function of the criminal law ran closely parallel to the theological use of the natural law, though the emphases were different. Melanchthon the theologian emphasized the need to avenge violations of the natural law and to impel a sinner to seek grace. Melanchthon the jurist emphasized the need for the community to participate in such avenging of its law, and emphasized the responsibility of the magistrate to induce the sinner to seek forgiveness from God, the state, and the victim at once. The *deterrent* function of the criminal law ran closely parallel to the civil use of the natural law. Melanchthon the theologian stressed the "wrath of God against all unrighteousness" which coerced people against following their natural inclination to sin. He adduced ample biblical examples of the ill plight of the sinner to drive home his point. Melanchthon the jurist stressed the severity of the magistrate against all uncivil conduct. He pointed to many examples of the law's harsh public sanctions against criminals to deter people from all such uncivil conduct. The *rehabilitative* function of the criminal law ran closely parallel to the educational use of the natural law, though here, too, the emphases were different. Melanchthon the theologian emphasized the need for moral reeducation of justified believers alone. Melanchthon the jurist emphasized the need for moral reeducation of all individuals, especially those convicted criminals who had not yet been justified. This blending of the uses of natural law and the purposes of criminal law was an important bridge between theology and law.[87]

In civil law, as opposed to criminal law, Melanchthon postulated the duty of the ruler to facilitate and regulate the formation and function of various types of voluntary social relationships or associations. He focused on three such relationships: (1) private contract, (2) marriage and the family, and (3) the visible Church.

"God has ordained contracts of various kinds," Melanchthon wrote.[88] These include contracts of sale, lease, exchange of property, procurement of labor and employment, lending of money, extension of credit, and more.[89] All such contracts serve not only the utilitarian ends of exchanging goods and services but also the social ends of promoting equality and checking greed.[90] Accordingly, God has called the magistrate to

---

[87] See sources and discussion in Witte and Arthur, "Three Uses of the Law."
[88] *CR* 22:241.   [89] Ibid., 241–2.
[90] *CR* 16:128–52, 251–69, 494–508; *CR* 22:240; *MW* 2/2:802–3.

promulgate general contract laws that prescribe "fair, equal, and equitable" agreements, that invalidate contracts based on fraud, duress, mistake, or coercion, and that proscribe contracts that are unconscionable, immoral, or offensive to the public good.

Melanchthon was largely content to state these general principles of contract law in categorical form, although he occasionally applied them to specific cases. For example, he condemned with particular vehemence loan contracts that obliged debtors to pay usurious rates of interest – a subject on which Luther had also written at length, and which would become a regular feature of Evangelical ethics and legal theory.[91] He also condemned contracts or mortgages that entitled creditors to secure a loan with property whose value far exceeded the amount of the loan, unilateral labor and employment contracts that made a master's obligation to pay anything conditional on full performance from the servant, and contracts of purchase and sale that were based on inequality of exchange.[92] Such moral teachings on contract were quite consistent with prevailing teachings of the medieval canonists and theologians.[93] Melanchthon's articulation of them, however, was an important impetus for their transplantation and implementation in the new Protestant civil law of obligations.

Christian magistrates were also to promulgate positive laws to govern marriage and family relations. These laws must prescribe monogamous heterosexual marriages between two fit parties and proscribe homosexual, polygamous, bigamous, and other "unnatural" relations. They must ensure that each marriage was formed by voluntary consent of both parties and undo relationships based on fraud, mistake, coercion, or duress. They must promote the marital functions of procreation and childrearing and prohibit all forms of contraception, abortion, and infanticide. They must protect the authority of the *paterfamilias* over his wife and children but punish severely all forms of adultery, desertion, incest, and wife or child abuse by that *paterfamilias*. These teachings, together with those of Luther and other reformers, would have a formidable

---

[91] *CR* 16:128–52. See Luther's views in *LW* 45:231–310. On traditional views, see John T. Noonan, Jr., *The Scholastic Analysis of Usury* (Cambridge, MA, 1957).

[92] *CR* 16:251–69, 494–508.

[93] See Berman, *Faith and Order*, 197ff.; Helmholz, *The Spirit of the Classical Canon Law*, 229ff.; Stephan Kuttner, *Kanonistische Schuldlehre von Gratian bis auf die Dekretalen Gregors IX, systematisch auf Grund der handschriftlichen Quellen dargestellt* (Vatican City, 1935); Alfred Söllner, "Die causa in Konditionen- und Vertragsrecht des Mittelalters bei den Glossatoren, Kommentaren, und Kanonisten," *ZSS* (*Romanische Abteilung*) 77 (1960): 182.

influence on the reformation of marriage law, as we shall see in a later chapter.[94]

Finally, Christian magistrates were to regulate the visible Church by positive laws. These "ecclesiatical laws" were to govern not only doctrine, liturgy, and Sabbath observance, according to the First Table of the Decalogue, but also Church polity and property, according to the general principles of the Second Table of the Decalogue. "The prince is God's chief bishop (*summus episcopus*) in the Church," Melanchthon wrote.[95] He is to define the hierarchical polity of the Church – from local congregations to urban ecclesiastical circuits to the territorial council or synod. He is to decide the responsibilities and procedures of congregational consistories, circuit councils, and the territorial synod. He is to appoint ecclesiastical officials, pay them, supervise them, and, if necessary, admonish and discipline them. He is to ensure that the local universities and schools produce the pastors, teachers, and administrators needed to operate the Church. He is to furnish the land, the supplies, and the services necessary to erect and maintain each church building. He is to oversee the acquisition, use, maintenance, and alienation of Church property.[96] He is to send out his superintendents to ensure faithful compliance of the local church with both the Gospel of Christ and the law of the magistrate. Melanchthon subjected the local visible Church both to the rule and to the protection of the local magistrate.

Melanchthon described the duties not only of political officials but also of political subjects, that is, those who were subject to the magistrate's authority and law. Early in his career, Melanchthon taught that all subjects have the duty to obey, and no right to resist, political authority and positive law – even where such authority and law have become arbitrary and abusive. If the "magistrate commands anything with tyrannical caprice," he wrote in 1521, "we must bear with this magistrate because of love, where nothing can be changed without a public uprising or sedition."[97]

---

94 For Melanchthon's views of marriage and the family, see *CR* 16:509; *CR* 21:1051; *CR* 22:600; *CR* 23:667; *MW* 2/2:801–2 and further pp. 217–18, 223–5, 231–2 below.
95 Quoted by Emil Sehling, *Kirchenrecht* (Leipzig, 1908), 36–7; see similar views by Melanchthon in Sehling 1/1:149–52, 163–5.
96 *CR* 16:241 ff., 469ff., 570ff.; *CR* 22:227ff., 617ff. and further discussion in Peter Meinhold, *Philipp Melanchthon: Der Lehrer der Kirche* (Berlin, 1960), 40ff.; Liermann, *Deutsches evangelisches Kirchenrecht*, 150ff.; Maurer, *Die Kirche und ihr Recht*, 254ff.
97 *CR* 21:223–4. Melanchthon, however, did counsel those subject to tyrannical authority and law to escape if they could do so without tumult and uprising (ibid). This became an important predicate for the later guarantee of the Peace of Augsburg that a religious dissenter from a local regime must be given the right to emigrate peaceably from that regime.

Melanchthon based this theory of absolute civil obedience on various biblical texts, especially Romans 13: "the powers that be are ordained by God;" unswerving obedience to them is "mandated by conscience"; to defy them is to defy God and to incur God's wrath.[98]

As the power of German princes continued to grow, however, Melanchthon became deeply concerned to safeguard subjects from abuse and restrain princes from tyranny. At least by 1555, he joined those who recognized a right of resistance against tyrants based on natural law.[99] "Conscious disobedience to the secular *Obrigkeit* and against true and proper laws," he still maintained, "is deadly sin, that is, sin which God punishes with eternal damnation if one in conscious defiance finally persists in it."[100] However, if the positive law promulgated by the political official contradicts natural law, particularly the Ten Commandments, it is not binding in conscience and must be disobeyed. This was traditional medieval lore. It had radically different implications, however, in a unitary Protestant state in which there were no longer concurrent ecclesiastical and civil jurisdictions to challenge each other's legislation on the ground of violation of natural law. It was now left to the people – acting individually or collectively through territorial and imperial diets – to resist officials who had strayed beyond the authority of their office and to disobey laws that had defied the precepts of natural law.

Philip Melanchthon defined a good deal of the content and character of Lutheran theories of law, politics, and society. A whole generation of Germany's leading jurists in the sixteenth century came under his direct influence as students, colleagues, and correspondents.[101] Generations of students thereafter studied his legal, political, and moral writings, many

---

[98] Ibid. On Luther's comparable views, see Brecht 3:199–228; Gritsch, *Martin-God's Court Jaster*; id., "Martin Luther and Violence: A Reappraisal of the Neuralgic Theme," *Sixteenth Century Journal* 3 (1972):37.

[99] For detailed discussions of the rise of Lutheran resistance theory in the 1530s onward, see Heinz Scheible, *Das Widerstandsrecht als Problem der deutsche Protestanten 1523–1546* (Gütersloh, 1969); Eike Wolgast, *Die Religionsfrage als Problem des Widerstandsrechts im 16. Jahrhundert* (Heidelberg, 1980); David Whitford, "The Right of Resistance in the Theology of Martin Luther, With Specific Reference to the Magdeburg Confession of 1550" (Ph.D. Diss., Boston University, 1999); Richard Roy Benert, "Inferior Magistrates in Sixteenth-Century Political and Legal Thought" (Ph.D. Diss., University of Minnesota, 1967); Althaus, *The Ethics of Martin Luther*, 124ff. See texts in James M. Estes, ed., *Whether Secular Government Has the Right to Wield the Sword in Matters of Faith* (Toronto, 1994).

[100] *CR* 22:613.

[101] See Köhler, 125ff.; Guido Kisch, "Melanchthon und die Juristen seiner Zeit," in *Mélanges Philippe Meylan* (Paris, 1963), 2:135, and the detailed index in *Melanchthons Briefwechsel*, 10 vols., ed. Heinz Scheible (Stuttgart, 1977–1987).

of which were still being printed two centuries later and used as textbooks in universities throughout Germany and well beyond.[102]

Two of the most important of Melanchthon's later students who systematized and transmitted his legal teachings into seventeenth-century Germany and beyond were Martin Chemnitz and Nicolaus Hemming. Martin Chemnitz (1522–86) is well known today for his detailed and decisive Evangelical answer to the new Catholic teachings of the Council of Trent (1545–63).[103] He was well known in his own day for his brilliant commentary on Melanchthon's *Loci communes*, which included a lengthy exegesis of the Decalogue. Even more astutely than his teacher, Chemnitz drew from the Decalogue a whole volume of valuable "commandments and counsels," "principles and precepts," to govern earthly life. He grounded his readings and arguments with great philological and philosophical sophistication. While Melanchthon had often exegeted the Decalogue with an eye to parallels among classical moral authors, Chemnitz did so with an eye to Jewish legal authorities, which added further legal nuance and concreteness to his exegesis. Chemnitz's work had a shaping influence not only on Lutheran legal theory, but also on Lutheran ethics, homiletics, catechesis, and systematic theology.[104]

The same can be said of Melanchthon's student Nicolaus Hemming (1513–1600), a jurist, ethicist, and theologian, who transmitted Melanchthon's lore to his homeland of Denmark. Hemming was known in his day as the "teacher of Denmark" (*Praeceptor Daniae*), an honorary parallel to Melanchthon's title as the "teacher of Germany" (*Praeceptor Germaniae*).[105] Hemming was blessed with long life and a lively pen. He wrote at least two dozen major volumes, including a large work on Melanchthonian epistemology,[106] a volume on the reform of the canon law of marriage, annulment, and divorce,[107] and an important treatise on natural law.[108] Much of his writing was a faithful rendering

---

[102] See the editorial comments at the head of each of Melanchthon's works, as reprinted in the *CR* series. See also details on some of the main jurists' writings in Gisela Becker, *Deutsche Juristen und ihre Schriften auf den römischen Indices des 16. Jahrhunderts* (Berlin, 1970).

[103] See Jaroslav Pelikan, *Obedient Rebels: Catholic Substance and Protestant Principle in Luther's Reformation* (New York, 1964), 49ff.

[104] Martin Chemnitz, *Loci theologici* [1581], trans. J. A. O. Preus (St. Louis, MO, 1989), 2:331ff.; see further Thomas Kaufmann, "Martin Chemnitz (1522–1586): Zur Wirkungsgeschichte der theologischen Loci," in Scheible, ed., *Melanchthon in seinen Schülern*, 183–255.

[105] *Allgemeine Deutsche Biographie* (s.v. "Hemming, Nicolaus").

[106] Nicolaus Hemming, *De methodis libri duo* (Wittenberg, 1559).

[107] Id., *Libellus de conjugio, repudio, et divortio* (Leipzig, 1578).

[108] Id., *De lege naturae apodicta methodus* (Wittenberg, 1563). Fifteen of his tracts are in *D. Nicolai Hemming . . . Opuscula theologica* (Geneva, 1586).

and reshuffling of Luther's and Melanchthon's main themes and writings, though in later life Hemming tended toward some of John Calvin's theological views. Hemming made some modest amendments to Melanchthon's formulations on law. For example, he systematized more clearly than did Melanchthon the categories of divine law, natural law, and moral law. He argued that all three of these forms of laws have three uses in the earthly kingdom, which he labelled the "external, internal, and spiritual uses."[109] Most important, Hemming developed what he called a "demonstrative method of natural law." Using Melanchthon's notion of the *notitiae* (those inborn natural principles of practical reason), Hemming set out to demonstrate the natural universality and superiority of the Decalogue as a source and summary of natural law. He adduced hundreds of ancient Greek and Roman passages that, in his view, were consistent with conventional Evangelical interpretations of each of the Commandments. Particularly impressive were Hemming's lengthy arguments vindicating the natural qualities of the three domestic, ecclesiastical, and political orders that both Luther and Melanchthon had described for the earthly kingdom.[110]

JOHANNES EISERMANN ON LAW AND THE COMMON GOOD

Melanchthon and his many students defined what might be called the Wittenberg school of Lutheran jurisprudence. This school featured heavy reliance on Luther's theories of the two kingdoms and the three estates. It gave great emphasis to the Decalogue as a source and summary of natural law and positive law. And it offered a unique blend of teleology and utilitarianism in its account of the divinely sanctioned "uses" of the law.

A second school of Lutheran jurisprudence emerged in the middle third of the sixteenth century at the new Evangelical University of Marburg. Two of its new law professors, Johannes Eisermann and Johann Oldendorp, helped to define the content and accent of this Marburg school. Like their Wittenberg colleagues, these Marburg jurists built on Luther's theology, particularly as distilled in his two-kingdoms

---

[109] Id., *Opuscula*, 521–34, 850–912; id., *Enchiridion theologicum* (Leipzig, 1579), 132–72, 399–407.
[110] This is the central thesis of id., *De lege naturae apodicta methodus*, excerpted in Carl von Kaltenborn, *Die Vorläufer des Hugo Grotius auf dem Gebiete des ius naturae et gentium sowie der Politik im Reformationszeitalter* (Leipzig, 1848), Appendix, 27–44. See analysis in ibid., 237ff.; Otto W. Krause, *Naturrechtslehre des sechzehnten Jahrhunderts. Ihre Bedeutung für die Entwicklung eines natürliche Privatrechts* (Frankfurt am Main, 1982), 125ff. Fellow Lutheran Benedict Winkler pressed Hemming's principled method of natural law to even greater refinement in his massive *Principiorum iuris libri quinque* (Leipzig, 1615).

framework. But they gave new legal prominence to Luther's theories of the priesthood of all believers, the Christian vocation, and the role of Christian conscience in decision-making. And while the Wittenberg school tended to approach legal questions through theology and moral philosophy, the Marburg school tended to approach them through legal history and political theory. This led the latter to different legal and political accents and applications.

The founder of the Marburg school was Johannes Eisermann (ca. 1485–1558).[111] Born and raised near the city of Marburg, in the territory of Hesse, Eisermann studied theology and medicine at the University of Wittenberg, taking degrees in both subjects in 1514. In 1518, he began to read Plato, Aristotle, Cicero, and other classical authors under the tutelage of Philip Melanchthon. He also gave his own lectures at the University of Wittenberg on Pliny, Quintilian, and on biology and other aspects of natural philosophy. In this same period, Eisermann began a course of self-instruction in law, which he continued intermittently until finally becoming *doctor iuris* in 1532. He served briefly as rector of the University of Wittenberg in 1521 and 1522, but then returned to his homeland of Hesse, settling in Marburg, where the Reformation was also breaking out.

In 1523, Eisermann was appointed to serve on the Marburg city council. The following year, he became one of the lay judges (*Schöffen*) of the Marburg high court (*Hofgericht*).[112] These legal appointments came just as the territorial prince, Landgrave Philip of Hesse, was moving toward formal adoption of the Reformation. Eisermann worked with Melanchthon and others to craft Philip's lengthy reformation ordinance of 1526, which became a model law for other territories and cities that adopted the Reformation.[113] Eisermann also helped to draft and implement new urban and territorial laws on church administration and visitation, poor relief, and education, as well as a set of increasingly firm acts against the Anabaptists.[114] He helped Philip to draft his own last will and testament, a matter of state rendered doubly delicate by Philip's infamous bigamy.[115]

---

[111] Also known as Joannes Ferrarius Montanus, Joannes Hessus Montanus, and Johannes Hesse. Eisermann is not to be confused with Johannes Hesse of Breslau, a sturdy reformer with whom Luther corresponded; see *LW* 48:143, 166; *LW* 49:122, 175, 196–9, 216, 343. See details in *Allgemeine Deutsche Biographie* (s.v. "Ferrarius, Johannes").

[112] Walter Sohm *et al.*, eds., *Urkundliche Quellen zur hessischen Reformationsgeschichte*, 4 vols. (Marburg, 1957), 3:416. On the *Schöffen*, see Stölzel, *passim* and pp. 44–5 above.

[113] Richter, 1:56–69.

[114] See Sohm, *Urkundliche Quellen*, 1:95, 109, 144–9; 2:25–6, 78–9, 197–201, 413; 3:10–11, 136–9, 143–6; 4:98, 130–6, 211–14.

[115] Ibid., 2:242–4, 3:14–15. On Philip's bigamy, see Hasting Eells, *The Attitude of Martin Bucer Toward the Bigamy of Philip of Hesse* (New Haven, CT, 1924); and more generally, Hans J. Hillerbrand,

Eisermann also helped to resolve some of the legal questions surrounding the dissolution of the monasteries in Marburg and the conversion of their properties into new Evangelical schools – not least the University of Marburg that Philip proudly established in 1527.[116]

Later that same year of 1527, Philip appointed Eisermann as the first Professor of Civil Law at the University of Marburg, a post that he retained until shortly before his death in 1558. He also served periodically as rector and later as vice-chancellor of the University, and as legal counsel to Philip and as judge of the Marburg high court.[117] But Eisermann made his main mark as a distinguished teacher and scholar of law. He wrote several substantial tracts and commentaries on classical Roman law and feudal law, a stout handbook on domestic law, inheritance law, property law, and civil procedure, and two later tracts on the nature and procedure of adjudication.[118]

Eisermann's most original and enduring contribution to Lutheran legal theory came in his tract *On the Common Good*, later expanded and retitled *On the Good Ordering of a Commonwealth*.[119] This book was first published in German in 1533 and in several editions and languages thereafter. It was a popular text in Evangelical circles throughout the sixteenth century. In this tract, Eisermann repeated much of the new Evangelical theology of the day. He taught the doctrines of total human depravity and justification by faith alone. He drew familiar distinctions between the two kingdoms, two types of governments, two forms of righteousness and goodness. He endorsed strongly the reformers' favorite doctrines of

---

Landgrave Philip of Hesse (New York, 1967). I have found no evidence that Eisermann counseled Philip on the question of his bigamy. For Luther's counsel, see pp. 225–6 below.

[116] See, e.g., Johannes Eisermann (Johann Monatus Ferrarius), *Was...Philips Landtgraue zue Hessen...als ain Cristlicherfürst mit den Closterpersonen, pfarrherren, un abgötischen bildnissen, in seiner gnaden fürstenthumbe, auss Gottlicher geschrifft fürgenomemen hat* (Ausburg, 1528). See also Richter, 1:68 (cap. xxix).

[117] Sohm, *Urkundliche Quellen*, 2:32, 68.

[118] See, e.g., Johann Monatus Ferrarius, *Adnotationes in IIII. Institutionum Iustiniani* (Marburg, 1532); id., *Commentarius, omnibus qui in iure foro (que) iudicario versantur* (Marburg, 1542; Frankfurt am Main, 1600); id., *Ad titulum Pandectarum de regulis iuris commentarius* (Louvain, 1537; 1546); id., *Progymnasmata forensia sive processus iudiciarii recepti libri V* (Marburg, ca. 1542, 1556), revised as id., *Processus iudiciarii, ad mores nostros accommodati* (Hamburg, 1608); id., *Collectanea in usus feudorum*, in *Tractatus universi iuris* (Frankfurt am Main, 1554), vol. 10/2; id., *Tractatus de iudiciorum prae-exercitamentis, et iis, quae ad ius decentis officii atque etiam causas disceptantium modestius studium pertinent* (Frankfurt am Main, 1554, 1600).

[119] Id., *Von dem gemeinen Nutze* (Marburg, 1533), reprinted and revised as id., *De republica bene instituenda paraenesis* (Basel, 1556). The quotations that follow are adapted in part from an early English edition, *A Woorke of J. Ferrarius Monatus touchynge a Good Orderynge of a Common Weale* (London, 1559) (STC 10831). Because the pagination of both the 1533 and 1556 editions at my disposal was badly corrupted, I have cited to the book and chapter.

the priesthood of all believers and the calling of all Christians to a godly vocation. He embraced the natural primacy of the domestic, ecclesiastical, and political estates, and their complementary roles in teaching and enforcing the norms of natural law, particularly the Ten Commandments and the Golden Rule.[120] All these teachings were still very much in flux when Eisermann began writing his tract in the late 1520s. His distillation of them was itself influential in helping to systematize Evangelical theology in Marburg and beyond.

Eisermann's main concern in this tract, however, was how to construct a theory of the common good out of a theology of total depravity. If persons in the earthly kingdom are truly and utterly sinful and selfish by nature, how can they possibly be directed to doing any good for others or for the commonwealth altogether? If the earthly kingdom is truly the fallen realm of the Devil, how is it that we now live in a relatively decent German nation? Part of Eisermann's answer to these questions was the same as that of Luther and Melanchthon: God has allowed the natural law to continue to guide sinful persons in the earthly kingdom. Through its civil and theological uses, the law coerces all persons into a lower civil righteousness and induces some persons to a higher spiritual righteousness. Part of Eisermann's answer, however, was his own innovative theory of the origin, nature, and purpose of a Christian commonwealth.

Eisermann developed something of a Lutheran social contract theory. He adopted this theory in part from classical Greek and Roman authors. He also adapted it in part from St. Paul's image of the "body of Christ with its many members." This was a rich biological metaphor that Eisermann (a former student of medicine) translated into his theory of a Christian body politic.[121]

From nature to society

In Eisermann's view, the state of nature began as the perfect realm of Paradise. Adam and Eve were created in the image of God. They were the apex of creation, God's final and greatest creative act. They alone were given the power of reason and speech. They alone were given lordship "over all living things," and called to dress and keep the garden.

---

[120] I.1–4, II.1–2, III.2, IV.1, 4, VI.7, VIII.1, IX.2, 5.

[121] See, e.g., Romans 12:4; 1 Corinthians 12:12. On classical and medieval sources of social contract theory, see Otto von Gierke, *The Development of Political Theory*, trans. Bernard Freyd (New York, 1966), 91–142; J. W. Gough, *The Social Contract* (Oxford, 1963) and *Dictionary of the History of Ideas* (s.v. "Social Contract").

They were by their natures "civil and communal." They lived in perfect communion with God and perfect community with each other. They were created "to obey laws, to help each other, to use their goods without causing harm to others, to desire the just and the good, to favor honesty, and more."[122]

Through Satan's evil wiles, however, Adam and Eve fell into sin, and all humanity vicariously fell with them. After the Fall, all people lost their perfect communion with God. They lost their lordship over creation. They lost their natural community with each other. In this fallen state of nature, people were "greedy," "foul," and debased," "so lost and corrupt" that they were "inclined only to that which is forbidden and evil." "Questions began to arise about estates and dominions of things." "What is mine and what is thine began to breed disquietude," violence, and bloodshed. Rovers and robbers ravaged the properties and persons of others, setting off endless cycles of revenge and reprisal in subsequent generations. In the perfect state of nature in Paradise, human life had been lovely and long. In the sinful state of nature after the Fall, human life had become "brutish" and "short" ("ferus et brevis").[123]

Despite the fall into sin, however, God has allowed all people to retain a glimmer of those "inborn sparks" of honesty, virtue, and community with which they were created: an innate knowledge of a natural law of love of God, neighbor, and self, and a natural sense of equity by which these laws must be applied. These natural norms were "not entirely quenched" by sin, Eisermann insisted. They were "preserved in human reason." They could be quickly extinguished and forgotten through depraved and debased living. But they could also be ignited to give greater light if they were subject to "careful study."[124]

Throughout history, Eisermann argued, "God has always lifted up wise men" who have undertaken such "careful study" of these "inborn sparks" of natural law. Led by these wise men, the Egyptians, Greeks, Romans, and other ancient peoples of the West all saw that "man is by nature sociable and aspires to society and community of life, in order to curb vice and to embrace virtue, to help others, and to find a way to help himself and his community." Accordingly, each of these ancient peoples has formed "a covenant of human society (*foedus humanae societatis*) wherein men are trained by a discipline of laws and manners to do things for others and to live well."[125]

---

[122] I.1, 2.   [123] I.2–3; III.7.   [124] II.1; III.7; IV.2.   [125] I.3–5.

A commitment to the rule of law was the most essential provision of all these early social covenants. Indeed, said Eisermann, without law there could be no commonwealth.[126] Law was essential to curbing the depraved instincts of natural persons and driving them to greater orderliness, goodness, and even happiness. Eisermann cited various ancient Greek and Roman writers to the effect that "the good of citizens, the safety of cities, and the quietness and happiness of man's life is much advanced by the establishment of laws. Their virtue is to command, to control, to bid, and to forbid. For it is the law only which commands things that must be done, and not done. Thus the law is the ruler and leader of a civil life." In order to accomplish these objectives, the law must be written, clear, accessible, binding on both rulers and subjects, and enforced swiftly, surely, and equitably when trespassed.[127]

Certain types of laws have proved essential to realizing this commitment to the rule of law, Eisermann argued. Every ancient civilization adopted laws to protect the peace and order of the commonwealth, and to define the office and activities of its rulers. Their laws generally protected lives and properties. They encouraged charity and cared for others. They frowned on usury, price gouging, and fraud. They provided for the sojourner, the needy, and the immigrant. They insisted that words be honest, that promises be honored, that contracts be kept. They required that wrongs be righted, whether by criminal punishment or by civil redress. They mandated some form of common religious worship. And these ancient civilizations all required "the study of law," not just for students of the legal profession, but for all citizens, so that each generation might be committed anew to the rule of law and to the perpetuation of the social covenant. These are common provisions of the law of all nations (*ius gentium*), Eisermann argued with copious citations and illustrations. They reflect in part the cardinal commandments of the law of nature (*ius naturale*), preserved in those "inborn sparks" of human reason.[128]

Though they were united in their commitment to the rule of law, however, the first commonwealths were diverse in form and governance. They ranged from extended households to villages, towns, nations, whole empires. Some were monarchies, some oligarchies, some democracies, most some mixture of the same. Periodically, these societies fell apart by internal decay, external conquest, tyranny and riot, plague, or devastation, and the people returned to a more inchoate state of nature.

[126] I.3.   [127] III.7, 8; IX.2.   [128] I.4; see also VI.1–7, VII.1–8, IX.1, 3.

But aversion to the depravity of this state of nature and appetite for the law and order of a society has always driven peoples to form new social covenants – learning something, in each instance, from the failure of prior commonwealths.[129]

There is ample instruction in this story of the birth and growth of the commonwealth tradition, Eisermann insisted. One lesson is that we Christians today can and must learn from the experiences of prior civilizations. A modern Christian theorist would do especially well to absorb the social, legal, and political instruction of the advanced civilizations of Greece and Rome, both before and after the coming of Christ. Following humanist conventions of his day, Eisermann took this maxim to heart, peppering his tract with all manner of spicy references to Plato, Aristotle, Cicero, Seneca, and various early Roman jurists. He mixed these classical sources freely with citations of the Bible, the Church Fathers, and various medieval Christian jurists and theologians. Christians have no monopoly on the understanding of natural law and natural reason, Eisermann insisted, and a modern Evangelical jurist would be foolish to ignore the wisdom of these advanced classical traditions.

A second lesson of this history is that there is no single foreordained or natural system of society, politics, and law. Every people chooses its own social form, its own political structure, and its own system of law based on a "combination of nature, custom, and reason." Nature teaches the basic norms of love of God, neighbor, and self. Custom teaches the local circumstances in which those norms must be applied. Reason translates the general principles of natural law into the specific precepts that apply to local circumstances and concerns. "One shoe is not meant for every foot." It takes ample "political wisdom, experience, and foresight" to strike the right balance among the teachings of nature, custom, and reason.[130]

A third lesson of this history is that there is no single person – far less a single dynasty – in a commonwealth that naturally should rule. "A prince is every man, and every man is a prince," Eisermann wrote, citing classical sources. The choice of leadership in a commonwealth should turn upon a person's virtue and wisdom, not upon his connections or bloodline.[131] Eisermann did not develop this point into a more general theory of popular sovereignty, as later Protestant theorists would do.[132] But he did advert several times to the importance of periodic elections

---

[129] I.3; III.3, 7.   [130] III.3, 7; VIII.1; IX.2.   [131] II.2.
[132] On these later theories, see Gierke, *Development of Political Theory*, 143–240.

of officials as a means to ensure rule by the best rather than by the best connected.[133]

The Christian commonwealth

That said, Eisermann went on at great length to describe what he considered to be the best form and function of an overtly *Christian* commonwealth for his time and place in Marburg and Hesse, and perhaps for other German polities that had accepted Lutheranism. Any Christian commonwealth should build on the lessons of classical commonwealths. But these latter commonwealths are, by definition, incomplete. They can speak only to a "civil goodness," not to a "spiritual goodness"; an "outward conformity," not an inward renewal of their citizens. They can celebrate only the goods of the mind and the body, not the goods of the soul and the heart. For none of these classical civilizations had the full biblical revelation of the heavenly kingdom on which the earthly kingdom must be partly modeled. None of them had knowledge of "Christ, the fountain and source of all justice, the founder and governor" of any Christian commonwealth. Thus the architects of a Christian commonwealth must learn the first rules to live by "not out of the philosophers' writings, but out of the Word of truth," out of the teachings of the Bible.[134]

Each Christian commonwealth, Eisermann wrote, must be a reflection of the body of Christ on earth.[135] The best image of this comes from St. Paul:

For as in one body we have many members and all the members do not have the same function, so we though many are one body in Christ, and individually members one of another. Having gifts that differ according to the grace given to us, let us use them: if prophecy, in proportion to our faith; if service, in our serving; he who teaches, in his teaching; he who exhorts, in his exhortation; he who contributes, in his liberality; he who gives aid, with zeal; he who does acts of mercy, with cheerfulness.[136]

Historically, St. Paul's metaphor was used to describe everything from the local congregation to the whole of Western Christendom.[137] Eisermann used this metaphor of Christ's body to describe the form and function, the anatomy and physiology, of the Christian body politic.

---

[133] III.8; VIII.1.   [134] I.1, 4, 5; VI.7; IX.4.   [135] IV.1.

[136] Romans 12:4–8; see also 1 Corinthians 12:12. See Eisermann, *De republica*, 1.4; IV.1.

[137] See Ernst H. Kantorowicz, *The King's Two Bodies: A Study in Medieval Political Theology* (Princeton, 1957), 194ff.; O'Donovan, *Desire of the Nations*, 158ff.

The person

The core unit of the Christian commonwealth is the person, Eisermann argued, underscoring St. Paul's phrase "*individually* members one of another." Each person is created in the image of God. Each is required to be a priest to all peers. Each is called to a Christian vocation. "[E]very man counts with his own office." "[E]veryone does works that glorify God the creator and redeemer," and that render "special service for the commonwealth." Every person who directs "all his doings to his vocation, with a mind lightened inward, is a profitable citizen."[138]

This was a particularly robust application of Luther's teaching of the priesthood of all believers and the equality of all Christian vocations. Eisermann took this as an essential feature of a Christian commonwealth. He devoted nearly a quarter of his tract to outlining the core Christian duties of teachers, preachers, almsmen, shipmen, huntsmen, artisans, farmers, merchants, craftsmen, blacksmiths, mechanics, soldiers, husbands, wives, children, masters, servants, and many more. He argued further that each person must have fair access to education and a vocation, a just wage for his or her labor, fair markets in which to ply a trade, and a minimum level of subsistence and maintenance even in the harshest economic times. If all these vocations are properly "formed and reformed," he wrote, "the society will be united together and the honor of the commonwealth observed."[139]

Eisermann drew lessons of industry, privacy, and charity from this basic teaching about the Christian vocation and the priesthood of believers. First, in a Christian commonwealth, industry must be prized and idleness outlawed. All persons must be active in those vocations to which God has called them. Those who are idle "trouble the common good and the discipline of the commonwealth."[140] Most idlers are simply lazy, and must be pressed to greater diligence in their own vocation or put to corporal labor if they have none. Those blessed with time for leisure must be pressed to greater study and greater charity. Those who are idle because of sickness, age, or chronic infirmities must be cared for.[141]

Secondly, in a Christian commonwealth, privacy must be prized and officiousness barred. Persons should be active in the vocations to which God has called them. But they should not seek to overreach beyond their vocation into the private affairs of their neighbors. "Let not the shoemaker meddle above the latches of his shoes, or adventure to question that with which he has nothing to do," Eisermann wrote. Everyone

---

[138] I.4.   [139] III.5–6; V.1–8.   [140] I.5.   [141] I.5; IV.1; VI.4.

should know his or her own station in the commonwealth. It is good to be industrious and equip and enhance oneself so much as possible, but not at the cost of one's neighbors. "Everyone should continue to do his duty in peace with others – not intermeddling with others but being content with his own vocation."[142] This was a duty-based argument for privacy. It was the duty of each citizen to mind his or her own vocation, thereby ensuring the neighbor's privacy.

Eisermann also pressed a rights-based theory of privacy in arguing that each man should have his own private property. To be sure, Eisermann argued, Christ and his disciples held property in common, and this has been emulated by some monasteries and communes over the centuries. But to extend these examples of community property beyond these intimate societies is "absurd," Eisermann argued, good property lawyer that he was. "Private dominion in things" is essential to the survival and flourishing of a commonwealth, whether Christian or non-Christian. Without a concept of private property, people will return to the sinful habits of the state of nature, perennially fighting over material things. "Without certainty of his interest, no one would set plough to the ground," for fear of losing the fruits of his labor. Without assurance of protection, no one would dare start a family or a vocation. Private property is thus an essential part of every covenant of society. "It is most convenient that every man know his own, that title or ownership of things be distinguished, and that no property hang in uncertainty." A clear understanding and protection of private property will make people more diligent in the care and cultivation of what they have. It will also protect them against temptation. "Man's nature is easily corrupted, and will not stand still in one state. Every man will be led after his own fantasy" to take and to want more and more. Protection of private property sets a barrier to such depraved instincts – as is underscored in the Decalogue's Commandments "Thou shalt not steal" and "Thou shalt not covet."[143]

Thirdly, in a Christian commonwealth, charity must be prized and churlishness scorned. "Even though men are of private estate, they are not excused from helping others," Eisermann argued. This is the plain instruction not only of nature but especially of Scripture. We must "exhort delightfully in hospitality, rendering to none evil for evil, for we are commanded to feed [even] our enemies if they are hungry, to give them drink if they are thirsty, and thereby heap burning coals on their head and thus provoke them to do likewise."[144] In giving charity, "man is a veritable god to his fellow man."[145]

[142] I.5.   [143] VI.6, 7.   [144] IV.I; see also II.I.   [145] I.I.

Though saints and sinners alike deserve charity, a person of modest means must be discriminating in dispensing it. One's own family and dependents deserve closest care. Beyond that, only the worthy poor should be served – orphans, widows, the aged, the sick. The unworthy poor – the lazy beggar, the itinerant mendicant, the loitering vagabond – must work for their alms or be banished if they refuse.[146] Eisermann's insights were part of a whole industry of new Evangelical reflections on poverty and charity.[147]

The legal profession

While every person and every vocation "counted" in a Christian commonwealth, there were some natural divisions and hierarchies that gave priority to some persons and to some professions. Each human body has vital parts and lesser parts, Eisermann reasoned, and the Christian body politic is much the same. Eisermann described various social and political hierarchies of the Christian commonwealth without systematizing them too closely. He repeated the conventional Lutheran lore of the three natural orders of state, Church, and family, led by the prince, preacher, and *paterfamilias* and their respective assistants and charges. He described three classes (*Stände*) of citizens: the high estate of princes and preachers; the middle estate of counselors and nobles; and the lower estate of commoners. He endorsed enthusiastically the three classic professions of theology, law, and medicine (in all of which he had been trained), and their respective roles in caring for the spirit, mind, and body of individuals and of the commonwealth as a whole.[148] This part of Eisermann's argument was rather commonplace and parochial.

Eisermann did, however, argue much more forcefully than other early Evangelicals that a learned legal profession was essential to a Christian commonwealth. By the legal profession, he meant collectively the prince and other magistrates, the judges and counselors of the *Obrigkeit*, and the law professors and practicing lawyers. The general Christian calling of this whole legal profession was two-fold: first, to reform the commonwealth by law to be a better approximation of the heavenly kingdom; and secondly, to reform each individual in his or her preparation for heavenly citizenship. In a Christian commonwealth, Eisermann wrote:

God's laws must be joined with man's laws. The Ten Commandments must be kept. Idolatry and false worshipping must be rooted out. God's Word must be everywhere preached, in churches instituted for godly purposes. Moral discipline

---

[146] VII.5–7.   [147] See below pp. 191–5.   [148] II.1–6; III.8; IV.1–6.

must be heeded. Schools must be diligently attended so that the young are trained in good learning, knowledge of languages, for the understanding of God's Word, for the ruling and governing of the commonwealth, and especially for setting forth God's glory.

People must be cajoled, counseled, and if necessary coerced to "live justly in the world and keep the community among men, formed both by God's laws and man's law." By so doing, all citizens will be "prepared for a better life in heaven," and be "conveyed from these visible things to the invisible."[149]

The prince's and other high magistrate's role in all this was essential, and Eisermann described it at great length. Much like Luther and Melanchthon, he referred to the prince as "the vicar of Christ," "the father of the community," "the pastor of the people", "a veritable god on earth" – descriptions which Eisermann's patron, Landgrave Philip of Hesse, could only have appreciated (if not expected). The prince was to be a paragon of Christian virtue in his own life and a teacher of Christian virtue in his political office. He was to give light and life to those "sparkles of equity" within him and those injunctions to piety within the Bible. The prince was to be free from guile and graft, resistant to flattery, bribery, and currying of favor. He was to exemplify all the great virtues of clemency, wisdom, sobriety, frugality, and much more. Eisermann went on for several dozen pages describing and illustrating from the lives of sundry Christian emperors, kings, and princes what qualities and activities become a Christian prince or magistrate.[150]

The foremost activity of the Christian prince was to promulgate and to live under Christian laws. At minimum, these laws had to be consonant with those provisions of the law of nature and law of nations that we have already seen.[151] More fully conceived, these laws were to express the letter and spirit of the Ten Commandments and other biblical expressions of the law of God. For Eisermann, this meant that the law of the prince must coerce citizens to a "civil goodness," and also cultivate in them a "spiritual goodness." The prince was not only to protect citizens from each other, he was to care for them as if they were his own children. Eisermann was even more effusive about this than Luther and Melanchthon had been. He contemplated a very active Christian magistrate at the core of a very active Christian welfare state:

It is the duty of the magistrate to restore the decayed, gather the dispersed, recover the lost, reform the disordered, punish the evil, enlarge the common

---

[149] I.4; IX.2, 5.   [150] II.1–3; III.1, 4, 7.   [151] See above, p. 144–6.

good, relieve the poor, defend the orphan and the widow, promote virtue, administer justice, keep the law, demonstrate that he is the father of the country, hold the people's commitment to him as if they were his own children, embrace godliness faithfully and with his whole heart, perform all that is profitable or necessary among the people, according to his duty, no less than if God Himself were present.[152]

While the prince was to put the law on the books, his retinue or *Obrigkeit* was to put the law into action. Eisermann called the prince's *Obrigkeit* "the living law" of a Christian commonwealth. "The law is dead if it is not executed," he wrote, and it can be deadly if it is not executed in accordance with Christian justice and equity. Eisermann placed special emphasis on the duty of the learned judge to apply the law. "General laws are a preface to good governance," he wrote, but these laws will mean little unless they are equitably applied in particular cases. It is the great calling of the judge to "fetch equity and justice out of the bowels of the law." As such, the judge has "laid upon his shoulders the very charge of God, which he cannot escape, but of which he must give a sure accounting on the great day of the Lord," the Day of Final Judgment.[153]

Equally essential to the execution of the law was a corps of learned jurists and lawyers. Contrary to Luther's sentiments, Eisermann considered the law to be a "sacred vocation," and jurists to be veritable "oracles for the city." When properly trained and restrained, lawyers teach all citizens the true meaning of law, equity, and justice. They draft contracts, deeds, wills, and other essential documents that allow for the orderly transmission of property, the peaceful conduct of business, the licit association of groups, the proper discharge of one's duties to one's neighbors. They bring lawsuits to ensure an orderly restitution and retribution without the violence and chaos of the feud. They give opinions and counsel to resolve hard questions. They represent the indigent, the immigrant, the orphan and the widow. "God has not for naught so plentifully poured his grace upon them," Eisermann wrote of jurists, "but done so in order that they should serve mankind faithfully and fearfully, profit the same, and direct all the dispensation and ministry of the law and charge taken upon them to the profit of their neighbor and the glory of almighty God. Those who do this may well be called expounders of right and laws, and be made governors over commonwealths."

Eisermann was fully aware that the legal profession, even in the best of times, often defied these Christian ideals. Some princes were tyrants,

---

[152] II.3; III.1, 4, 7; VII.6; VIII.1.   [153] II.4; III.2; IV.5; IX.2.

thieves, and thugs. Some judges succumbed to bribery, prejudice, and abuse of process. Jurists and lawyers often "cared nothing about being true executioners of equity and justice, but only wanted to make a mark for their own advantage . . . to fill their pouches and to work their wiles, with vain talk." "It is an easy thing to stain this holy discipline" of law, Eisermann concluded. And thus many think that "the best commonwealth is that with the fewest lawyers." But the reality is that the commonwealth needs the legal profession – the prince, the judge, and the jurist alike. The solution to the corruption of this profession lies not in its gradual eradication but in its constant reformation.[154] About what that should entail, however, Eisermann had little to say beyond platitudes.

Eisermann's 1533 tract *On the Common Good* was the first detailed social contract theory of the Christian commonwealth to emerge in Evangelical Germany. It was by no means the last. By the middle of the sixteenth century, such Christian commonwealth theory had become increasingly commonplace and copious in Evangelical Germany and in many other Protestant polities. Martin Bucer, for example, the distinguished Strasbourg reformer, put the matter famously in his 1550 tract *On Christ's Kingdom*. Before composing this tract, which he dedicated to King Edward VI of England, Bucer had served as another advisor to Eisermann's patron, Landgrave Philip of Hesse. Whether in that context Bucer had encountered Eisermann's tract is not clear. But Bucer certainly followed a good bit of Eisermann's argument. Like Eisermann, Bucer saw close analogies between the heavenly kingdom and the earthly kingdom. Christ rules in both: directly in the heavenly kingdom, indirectly through the magistrates in the earthly kingdom. As Christ's representative, the magistrate is to establish proper Christian doctrine and worship, support churches, families, and schools, support each person in his or her vocation, and to punish those who violate the common good or offend the law of God. Bucer then put forth a whole series of laws of reform that would help Christian magistrates to reach this end: Children must be educated and catechized in Evangelical Christianity. The Sabbath Day must be kept holy. The Church must be made holier. Its ministries must be reformed. Its properties must be regulated and restricted. Marriage and divorce laws must be reformed. Poor relief must be enhanced. The idle and the able must be put to work. Honest vocations must be supported. Honest magistrates must be appointed. Fair trials

[154] IV.4–5.

must be guaranteed. Fit punishments must be assigned. Public sumptuousness, gambling, drunkenness, and prostitution must be punished. By
all these means, Bucer concluded, God's Word will be enhanced, God's
elect will be preserved, and God's children will "live well and happily
both here and in the time to come."[155] Bucer's was but one of a whole series of mid-sixteenth-century works on Christian commonwealth theory
that would come to impressive application over the next century both
on the Continent and in England.[156]

JOHANN OLDENDORP ON LAW AND EQUITY

Johannes Eisermann's theory of the Christian commonwealth and the
common good was one distinctive feature of what we have loosely called
the Marburg school of Lutheran jurisprudence. Eisermann's colleague
Johann Oldendorp added a second feature to this school: a thoroughly
Evangelical understanding of the sources of law and the nature of equity
and legal judgment.

Johann Oldendorp was described in his day as "the one person for
whom the maxim 'a jurist is a bad Christian' could never apply."[157]
He was a man of extraordinary piety and erudition, famous throughout Germany and beyond for his Christian humanity and legal learning. Ernst Troeltsch and Roderich von Stintzing both called him "the
most influential jurist" of the Reformation era.[158] He was also one of
the most prolific, the author of at least fifty-six separate volumes on
law. Eight volumes were decidedly jurisprudential, treating concepts of
law and equity, authority and liberty, justice and judgment. Most of
his other volumes dealt with legal issues of property, inheritance, civil
procedure, domestic relations, statutory interpretation, and conflict of
laws. He also published commentaries on several Roman law texts, an

[155] Bucer, *RC*, 225. See, e.g., Amy Burnett, *The Yoke of Christ: Martin Bucer and Christian Discipline* (Kirksville, MO, 1994); Martin Greschat, *Martin Bucer: Ein Reformator und seine Zeit* (Munich, 1990); Karl Kock, *Studium Pietas: Martin Bucer als Ethiker* (Neukirchen-Vluyn, 1962); Marijn de Kroon, *Studien zu Martin Bucers Obrigkeitsverständnis* (Gütersloh, 1984); D.F. Wright, ed., *Martin Bucer: Reforming Church and Community* (Cambridge, 1994).

[156] For continental developments, see Gierke, *Political Theory*, passim; for English developments, see my *From Sacrament to Contract: Marriage, Religion, and Law in the Western Tradition* (Louisville, KY, 1997), 165ff.

[157] Jacob Spiegel, *Lexicon iuris civilis* (Basel, 1554), col. 210, quoted by Friederich Merzbacher, "Johann Oldendorp und das kanonische Recht," in Siegfried Grundmann, ed., *Für Kirche und Recht: Festschrift für Joh. Heckel* (Cologne, 1959), 223n.

[158] Ernst Troeltsch, *Die Soziallehren der christlichen Kirchen und Gruppen* (Berlin, 1912), 1:545 n.253; Stintzing, 311.

encyclopedic legal dictionary, and several famous student handbooks and textbooks.[159]

Oldendorp was born in Hamburg about 1486.[160] He studied civil and canon law at the Universities of Rostock and Bologna. In 1516 he became a professor of Roman law and civil procedure at the University of Greifswald. In his early years he was steeped in legal humanism, with a particular interest in the styles of legal advocacy and judgment, and in the techniques of resolving conflicts between and among canon laws and civil laws.[161]

In the course of the early 1520s, Oldendorp was slowly drawn to the Evangelical cause. In 1526, he resolved to support the Reformation. He left Greifswald to become a city official (*Stadtsyndikus*) of Rostock, and he soon became a leader of the city's reformation party. He helped to draft the city's new reformation ordinance of 1530.[162] He also served as a superintendent for the new Evangelical churches, involving himself in the reforms of preaching, liturgy, and Church polity, in the reorganization of Church properties, and in the creation of a new Evangelical public school and almshouse. While in Rostock, Oldendorp also published two texts that adumbrated his legal theory: *What is Equitable and Right* (1529) and *A Statesman's Mirror of Good Policy* (1530).[163]

In 1534, the city council of Rostock retreated from the Reformation, and Oldendorp was forced to leave. He moved to Lübeck, an important commercial center that had just promulgated two lengthy reformation ordinances for the city and surrounding rural areas.[164] There, too, Oldendorp served as *Stadtsyndikus* and superintendent for the new

[159] See bibliographies in Hans-Helmut Dietze, *Oldendorp als Rechtsphilosoph und Protestant* (Königsberg, 1933), 18–21; Peter Macke, *Das Rechts- und Staatsdenken des Johannes Oldendorp* (Inaug. Diss., Cologne, 1966), viii–xi. A partial collection is provided in Oldendorp, *Opera omnia*.

[160] Wieacker, 283. Stintzing, 311, says 1480, which is repeated in Dietze, *Oldendorp*, 44; Erik Wolf, *Quellenbuch zur Geschichte der deutschen Rechtswissenschaft* (Frankfurt am Main, 1949), 98. But cf. Wolf, 141 (says 1488), 144 plate (says 1480). See biographical details in Dietze, *Oldendorp*, 44–63; Wolf, 138–76.

[161] See Johann Oldendorp, *Rationes sive argumenta, quibus in iure utimur* (Rostock, 1516) and his later publication, already begun in this early period, *Collatio juris civilis et canonici*.

[162] Richter, 1:144–5; see autobiographical reflections in Johann Oldendorp, *Wahrhafftige entschuldige Doct. Johann Oldendorp, Syndici tho Rostock, wedder de mortgirigen uprorschen schantdichter und falschen klegen* (Rostock, 1533); and further O. Pettke, "Zur Rolle Johann Oldendorps bei der offiziellen Durchführung der Reformation in Rostock," *ZSS KA* 101 (1984): 339.

[163] Johann Oldendorp, *Wat byllich und recht ist* (Rostock, 1529), reprinted in modern edition in Wolf, ed., *Quellenbuch*, 51–68 (hereafter *Billig und Recht*); id., *Van radtslagende, wo men gude Politie und ordenunge ynn Steden und landen erholden möghe* (Rostock, 1530), excerpted in modern edition as "Ratmannenspiegel," in Wolf, *Quellenbuch*, 69–98 (hereafter *Ratmannenspiegel*) and published separately as *Ein Ratmannenspiegel von Joh. Oldendorp* (Rostock, 1971).

[164] Richter, 1:141–54.

Evangelical churches. But there, too, Catholic opposition eventually forced him to leave. From 1536 to 1543, Oldendorp moved back and forth among the universities of Frankfurt an der Oder, Cologne, and Marburg, changing venues as local leaders in Frankfurt and Cologne changed their minds about Protestantism. Despite his itinerancy, he published a dozen volumes in this period, including *A Methodology of Natural, Common, and Civil Law* (1539), *Principles of the Decalogue* (1539), and *A Legal Disputation on Law and Equity* (1541).[165]

In 1539, Oldendorp came into personal contact with Melanchthon, a Christian theologian and philosopher of "the highest erudition," as he later called him.[166] Oldendorp was particularly taken with Melanchthon's topical method of systematic theology set out in his *Loci communes theologici* (1521). He dedicated one of his next works to Melanchthon,[167] and shortly thereafter published his own new legal synthesis, aptly titled *Loci communes iuris civilis*.[168]

In 1543, Oldendorp returned for good to the University of Marburg, where the Reformation had become firmly established under the rectorship of Johannes Eisermann. Oldendorp remained on the law faculty until his death in 1567. He accepted the call to Marburg on condition that he be freed from the usual requirement of lecturing on the Roman law texts and their medieval glosses.[169] He would come, he insisted, only if he could "teach the laws with special attention to their just consequences and their relationship to God's Word." "The study of law is the most important pursuit after God's Word," Oldendorp wrote. Accordingly, the study of law "should be organized not only in light of the Word, but

---

[165] Johann Oldendorp, *Iuris naturalis gentium et civilis isagoge* (Antwerp, 1539) [hereafter *Isagoge*]; id., *Divinae tabulae X. praeceptorum*, a title in *Isagoge*, Ciii–Div, later reprinted in Kaltenborn, *Die Vorläufer des Hugo Grotius*, Appendix, 1–25; Johann Oldendorp, *De iure et aequitate forensis disputatio* (Cologne, 1541) (hereafter *Disputatio*).

[166] Oldendorp, *Isagoge*, 6.

[167] Id., *Disputatio*, dedicatory letter, where Oldendorp lauds Melanchthon as one "who, by the method of reason, had collected in an epitome the whole of moral philosophy." See also id., *Responsio ad impiam delationem parochorum Coloniensium de communicatione sacramenti corporis et sanguinis Christi sub utraque specie, cum exemplo litterarum, quas Phil. Melanthon dedit ad Joh. Old.* (Marburg, 1543).

[168] Id., *Loci communes iuris civilis ex mendis tandem et barbarie in gratiam studiosorum utiliter restituti* (Louvain, 1545; rev. edn. Louvain, 1551). See also id., *Topicorum legalium . . . exactissima traditio*; id., *Loci iuris communes* (Frankfurt am Main, 1546). In all these tracts, Oldendorp drew heavily on Aristotle's and Cicero's and medieval topical methods as well. On these see generally Theodore Viehweg, *Topik und Jurisprudenz*, 2nd edn. (Munich, 1963); Hans Erich Troje, *Graeca Leguntur: Die Aneignung des byzantinischen Rechts und die Entstehung eines humanistichen Corpus iuris civilis in der Jurisprudenz des 16. Jahrhunderts* (Cologne/Vienna, 1971).

[169] On this traditional method of teaching, the *mos italicus*, see generally Kelley, *Foundations of Modern Historical Scholarship*.

in accordance with it in deed; the Word of God must be its starting point and its guide."[170]

Oldendorp took this maxim to heart both in teaching his courses and in devising his theory of law and equity. His textbooks and formal writings on legal philosophy are a dense blend of insights drawn from classical Greek and Roman jurists and philosophers, medieval civilians and canonists, and the new Evangelical theologians and jurists of his day. But it was the Bible, and conscientious meditation on the same, that provided the lynch pin for his theory of the sources of law and the relationship between law and equity.

Sources of law

Oldendorp's account of the sources of law effectively merged the overlapping hierarchies elaborated by the civil and canon lawyers of his day. Civil lawyers, building on various texts in the *Corpus iuris civilis* (565), generally distinguished among: (1) natural law (*ius naturale*), the set of immutable principles of reason and conscience, which are supreme in authority and divinity; (2) the law of nations (*ius gentium*), a relatively stable set of principles and customs common to several communities and often the basis for treaties and other diplomatic conventions; and (3) civil law (*ius civile*), both the statutes and the customs of political communities, whether imperial, royal, territorial, urban, manorial, feudal, or more local in character. Canon lawyers sometimes repeated this Roman law taxonomy. But, building especially on Gratian's *Decretum* (c. 1140), they also developed their own hierarchy of: (1) divine law (*ius divinum*), principally the norms of the Bible as interpreted by the Church and the Christian tradition; (2) natural law, the set of norms known through reason or intuition, and generally common among all peoples; and (3) civil law, the customs and statutes of local political communities.[171] Some canonists and philosophers superimposed on this trilogy a category of eternal law (*lex aeterna*), understood as the created order and wisdom of God Himself, which stands prior to and above the biblical revelation of divine law. Other canonists interposed a category of canon law (*ius canonicum*), understood as a separate source of positive law that elaborates and illustrates the norms of divine and natural law, and corrects

---

[170] Quoted by Stintzing, 323. See further Dietze, *Oldendorp*, 59; Köhler, 127.
[171] See, e.g., *Decretum*, Dist. I, with glosses, in Gratian, *The Treatise on Laws with the Ordinary Gloss*, trans. Augustine Thompson and James Gordley (Washington, DC, 1993).

and guides the provisions of civil law.[172] In this fuller iteration of the sources of law, the late medieval canonists thus distinguished: (1) eternal law; (2) divine law; (3) natural law; (4) canon law; and (5) civil law.

Oldendorp was conversant with these traditional accounts of the sources of law, and he rehearsed them sympathetically and repeatedly in his student textbooks and handbooks. In formulating his own hierarchy, however, Oldendorp focused on three sources or states of law: divine law, natural law, and civil law, each of which he defined in his own way.

Divine law

The highest source and state of law was divine law (*ius divina*), which for Oldendorp consisted exclusively of the laws of the Bible (*leges Bibliae*). Biblical laws were of three types, Oldendorp argued, following theological conventions. The *moral* laws of the Bible, particularly the Ten Commandments, were universal norms binding on all authorities and all subjects at all times. The *juridical* laws of the Bible – such as the Old Testament laws of tithing and sanctuary or the New Testament stories of ordering life in the apostolic Church – were probative of the meaning of the moral law, and useful for the governance of contemporary churches and states, but they were not per se binding. The *ceremonial* laws of the Pentateuch – laws respecting sacrifice, diet, ritual, temple life, and more – had been superceded by the new teachings of Christ and the apostles, and were no longer binding on anyone.[173]

Contrary to some traditional teachings, Oldendorp had little place in his system for an eternal law of the created order that stood prior to and superior to the divine law revealed in the Bible. To be sure, said Oldendorp, the creation order came prior to the Bible, and was indeed a perfect expression of God's being, will, and law in Paradise.[174] But though prior in time and perfect in genesis, the eternal law was no longer superior in authority as a source of law for life in the earthly kingdom. For owing to the fall into sin, the norms of the created order can be read "only through a glass darkly," leading to inevitable distortion and deception. Thus as a source of law for this earthly life, the eternal law of nature has effectively collapsed into the natural law of human nature. It is a useful, but ultimately a fallible, guide to proper human living.[175] Citing the

---

[172] The canon and civil law together were generally called the *ius commune*, with canon law generally regarded as superior to civil law in an instance of conflict. See pp. 33–50 above, and Helmholz, *The Spirit of the Classical Canon Law*, 1–20.

[173] Oldendorp, *Divinae Tabulae*, 17–18.

[174] See id., *Isagoge*, 6, and quotes from other sources in Macke, *Oldendorp*, 30–1.

[175] Id., *Isagoge*, 9–10.

reformers' doctrine of *sola Scriptura*, Oldendorp wrote: "What we know of God, His will, His law, His wisdom, His purposes, His being is most fully revealed in the Bible."[176] The laws of the Bible, particularly its moral commandments and counsels, are the clearest and most authoritative source of law in this world.

Also contrary to some traditional teachings, Oldendorp gave no power to the Church and its canon law to mediate the interpretation of biblical law. According to some variants of the medieval two-swords theory, the pope wielded the spiritual sword to interpret the Bible, and to establish its legal meaning by canon law rules. Such biblical interpretations were considered to be binding on all of Christendom; indeed, some medieval interpreters considered them to be "infallible."[177] The pope delegated the temporal sword to emperors, kings, and other civil magistrates. These civil authorities were to promulgate and enforce civil laws in a manner consistent with canon laws and the biblical interpretation reflected in the same.[178]

Oldendorp rejected this two-swords theory out of hand.[179] He embraced instead the familiar Protestant theory that the magistrate is the "vicar of God" directly called to interpret, apply, and enforce biblical law in the earthly kingdom.[180] Oldendorp considered the moral laws of the Bible to be the divine legal principles needed to guide various systems of positive law. Building on but revising Melanchthon's formulations, he traced public or constitutional laws for governing the earthly kingdom back to the principles of the Fourth Commandment ("Honor thy father and thy mother," the magistrate being the "father of the community"). He traced the ecclesiastical laws of the visible Church to the first Three Commandments on idolatry, false swearing, and Sabbath Day observance. He traced criminal laws to the principles of the Fifth, Sixth, and Seventh Commandments ("Thou shalt not kill, steal, or commit adultery"), the private law of property and contracts to the principles of the Seventh Commandment ("Thou shalt not steal"), the laws of procedure and evidence to the principles of the Eighth Commandment ("Thou shalt not bear false witness"), and family law to the principles of the Fourth and Sixth Commandments as well as the Tenth Commandment

---

[176] Johann Oldendorp, *De copia verborum et rerum in iure civili* (Cologne, 1542), 233.

[177] See Tierney, *Origins of Papal Infallibility*.

[178] See sources and discussion above, pp. 108–9.

[179] A detailed critique of the two-swords theory, which Oldendorp cited, was Schwarzenberg, *Beschwerung der alten teüfelischen Schlangen*, (Zwickau, 1527), xiv–lv.

[180] See, e.g., Oldendorp, *Collatio*, 46; id., *Lexicon juris* (pagination missing) (s.v. "magistratus"); id., *Isagoge*, 19; id., *De copia verborum*, 260.

("Thou shalt not covet . . . thy neighbor's wife"). He traced the laws of taxation and social welfare to the general summary of the law ("Thou shalt love thy neighbor as thyself"), echoing the theory of the common good expounded by his colleague Johannes Eisermann.[181]

Natural law

Though superior in clarity and authority, the divine law did not eclipse the natural law (*ius naturale*), Oldendorp argued. Natural law for Oldendorp was the law of the human heart or conscience. Oldendorp called this variously the "law inside people" ("lex in hominibus"), the "law inscribed" on the heart ("ius insculptum"), and the "instruction of conscience" ("instructio conscientiae").[182] Following Melanchthon, Oldendorp believed that "God has implanted in us natural elements (*notitiae*) of knowledge by which we distinguish equity from iniquity."[183] "The source of [these] natural norms . . . is the heart and conscience of man, on which God has inscribed them."[184] Even independent of their knowledge of the divine law of the Bible, all individuals are thus by nature inclined toward the general moral principles taught by the Bible: love of God, neighbor, and self; love for one's spouse, child, and kin; love of peace, order, and stability; a predisposition toward the Golden Rule; an inclination to speak the truth, to honor one's promises, to respect another's person, property, and reputation.[185] Many of these natural norms were thus held in common among all peoples of the world, regardless of their direct access to biblical law. They formed a common law, or law of nations (*ius gentium*).

The teachings of natural law and biblical law are ultimately the same, Oldendorp believed. But "the natural elements of knowledge in persons have been obscured because of original sin." Thus "a merciful God has restored and inscribed them on tables of stone so that there would be a sure testimony that these laws of nature are confirmed by the word of God, which He has also inscribed on the souls of men."[186] Neither

---

[181] See esp. Oldendorp, *Divinae Tabulae*, 15–25; id., *Billig und Recht*, 60–62; id., *De copia verborum*, 170ff., 253ff., with analysis in Dietze, *Oldendorp*, 114–121; Krause, *Naturrechtslehre*, 118–22; Macke, *Oldendorp*, 39–46. Oldendorp urged citizens "to enhance the common good (*gemeyne nütticheyt*) as the highest ideal. For by serving the common good, you not only help one person but many": *Billig und Recht*, 60. See above pp. 143–54 on Eisermann.

[182] Oldendorp, *Isagoge*, 15; id., *Actionum iuris civilis loci communes, ad usum forensem secundum aequissimas Legislatorum sententias bona fide accommodati* (Cologne, 1539), 11; id., *De copia verborum*, 259.

[183] Id., *Isagoge*, 6.   [184] Ibid., 15.

[185] Ibid., 15, 17; Oldendorp, *Billig und Recht*, 58–65; id., *Actionum iuris civilis loci communes*, 9–10.

[186] Oldendorp, *Disputatio*, 15. See also id., *Isagoge*, 9–10: "the nature of man has been corrupted through the fall of Adam; so that just elements (*notitiae*) remain, by which nevertheless it is possible to recognize the magnificent bounty of divine and natural law."

the biblical law nor the natural law, however, provides a comprehensive code of human conduct that covers every contingency of human action and interaction. Accordingly, the moral laws of the Bible gave rise to various forms of juridicial and ceremonial laws that were specific to the biblical time and place of the Hebrew people. Likewise, the moral principles of natural law must give rise to multiple forms of statutory and customary laws that are specific to the current time and place of the German people. In biblical times, God often directly guided the elaboration and application of moral law: through his personal interventions in Paradise and on Mt. Sinai and through the later teachings of Moses and the prophets, of Christ and the apostles. In our times, God's guidance in the application and elaboration of moral principles comes less personally but more pervasively – through the perennial teachings of every human conscience on which God has inscribed his natural law.[187]

Conscience, for Oldendorp, was a form of reason. It was not just ordinary human reason or civil reason (*ratio civilis*). It was a God-given reason or natural reason (*ratio naturalis*). Thus the natural law implanted by God in human conscience "does not depend on the power of the person but stands free, unchangeable. God has written it into your reason. Therefore you must apply your unbiased mind and read [its teachings] diligently."[188] When consulted and followed in its purest form, "conscience is an infallible guide."[189] To be sure, Oldendorp acknowledged, no sinful person is fully capable of an unbiased consultation of his or her conscience. Hence there is a perennial need for the Bible, for prayer, for the intervention of the Holy Spirit to come to a better understanding of God's law. But, even independently of invocation of these spiritual aids, the God-given conscience provides ample instruction on the meaning and measure of the natural law.[190] In effect, conscience was, for Oldendorp, a form of practical reason.

Civil law

Civil law (*ius civile*) consists simply of all the laws of a commonwealth or republic (*leges rei publicae*). "In its ultimate sense," Oldendorp wrote capaciously, "the category of law" consists of all legal norms that command, prohibit, permit, or punish human conduct.[191] Such legal norms may be written or unwritten, general or particular, universal or local, positive or customary, public or private, criminal or civil, legislative or

---

[187] Ibid., 3, 11.   [188] Oldendorp, *Billig und Recht*, 57.   [189] Quoted by Dietze, *Oldendorp*, 81.
[190] Oldendorp, *Lexicon juris*, 101 (s.v. "conscientia").   [191] Id., *Disputatio*, 72ff.

judicial.[192] All these, in their own way, are legitimate forms and norms of civil law, Oldendorp believed. A dialectical presentation of these laws – a taxonomy that presses them into ever more refined sets of binary opposites – is the best way for students and practitioners to come to terms with the category of law. In his legal textbooks, handbooks, and dictionary, Oldendorp spelled out these contrasts in great detail, grounded them in the writings of medieval canonists and civilians, and demonstrated their utility for legal advocacy and decision-making.[193] Such dialectical legal writing was of a piece with that of many other Protestant jurists in the sixteenth century: Konrad Lagus and Christoph Hegendorf of Wittenberg, Francis Duaren and Francis Hotman of France, Nicolaus Everardus and Johannes Althusius of the Netherlands, and many others who worked under the direct inspiration of Protestant theology and theologians.[194]

All such civil laws, Oldendorp insisted, depend for their authority and legitimacy on their conformity with natural law and ultimately with divine law. "A civil law that departs *in toto*" from these higher laws "is not binding," Oldendorp insisted.[195] He listed a number of civil laws of his day that he considered to be per se illegitimate. He condemned, as directly contrary to divine law, human laws permitting the sale of Church benefices, allowing for divorce and remarriage, and tolerating usurious rates of interest on loans. He condemned, as contrary to natural law, human laws permitting bad-faith possession of property, allowing disinheritance of family members, causing undue delay in administering justice, rendering judgment in a case in which one has an interest, and instituting slavery and other strict forms of servitude.[196] More generally, he argued that natural law requires an owner to use private property for social ends and not, for example, to exclude others from use of it in instances where such use does the owner no harm.[197]

It was the magistrate's duty to institute "good policy" through the promulgation and enforcement of positive civil laws.[198] Much of what

---

[192] See esp. sources cited in notes 162, 167, 184 above. See also Oldendorp, *Billig und Recht*, 57–8; id., *Lexicon juris* (s.v. "ius").

[193] See sources in notes 160, 164, 167, 175, 184.

[194] Stintzing, 114–53, 251–65, 282–310; Coing, *Handbuch*, 2:615–795; Kisch, *Erasmus und die Jurisprudenz seiner Zeit*; Harold J. Berman and Charles J. Reid, Jr., "Roman Law in Europe and the *Jus Commune*: A Historical Overview with Emphasis on the New Legal Science of the Sixteenth Century," *Syracuse Journal of International Law and Commerce* 20 (Spring, 1994): 12ff.

[195] Oldendorp, *Isagoge*, 13.

[196] Ibid., 12–13. See further quotations in Macke, *Oldendorp*, 49–50.

[197] Oldendorp, *Billig und Recht*, 60–2.

[198] The most comprehensive formulation of the nature and function of the state and politics appears in id., *Ratmannenspiegel*. See analysis of this and other writings in Dietze, *Oldendorp*, 90–111; Macke, *Oldendorp*, 73–105. Oldendorp used various terms to describe the state (*der Staat*): the secular

Oldendorp considered to be "good policy" in a Christian common-wealth was rather conventional. But he described this in the Evangel-ical language of the "civil, theological, and educational uses" of law which enable us to "peacefully pass through this shadowy life and be led to Christ and to eternal life."[199] With Melanchthon, he emphasized the "educational use" of the law, "our teacher in the path to Christ" (*paedagogus noster ad Christum*), and the corresponding paternal and peda-gogical role of the magistrate, the "father of the community."[200] More-over, specific to his Evangelical sympathies, Oldendorp insisted that the magistrate must support the true faith by seeing to it (among other things) that there are enough well-qualified and well-paid preachers, so that they may "combat unbelief among the people."[201] The mag-istrate must also prohibit and punish acts of greed, idleness, sump-tuousness of dress, and other immoral conduct that had traditionally been within the jurisdiction of the Church.[202] And the magistrate must institute and support good public schools and public charities – poli-cies that Oldendorp had himself pursued in Rostock and Lübeck, and which other reformers pressed relentlessly as part of the reformation program.[203]

The magistrate must also seek to maintain peace with other civil polities. Despite the divisions born of the Reformation, Oldendorp ar-gued, the people of all republics still form the body of Christ on earth (*corpus Christianum*) and should live "next to each other, not against each other."[204] War is justified only for defense against an unjust attack. Even when attacked, Oldendorp wrote, a civil polity should seek to settle the conflict peaceably. If that proves impossible, a polity should leave three days before defending itself in order to give the intending attackers a chance to change their minds – a rather startling, some might say sui-cidal, application of the biblical principle of "turning the other cheek." Moreover, defense should be limited to that which is necessary, because its only purpose is to restore peace.[205]

It was also the magistrate's duty to abide by the law: not only the divine and natural laws that empowered his office, but also the civil laws that he and his predecessors promulgated. "It is an old question," Oldendorp wrote, "whether the magistrates are superior to the law or whether the

regime (*weltliches Regiment*), the worldly regime (*weltliches Regiment*) the republic (*res publica*), the civil order (*ordo civilis*), the magistracy (*Oberkeit*), and the corporation of citizens (*universitas civium*). See detailed sources in Dietze, *Oldendorp*, 94ff.

[199] Oldendorp, *Lexicon juris*, 249.   [200] Ibid.   [201] Id., *Ratmannenspiegel*, 90–2.
[202] Ibid., 92–4.   [203] Ibid., 94–7. See chapters 5, and 7 below.   [204] Id., *Lexicon juris*, 407.
[205] Id., *Ratmannenspiegel*, 92–94.

law binds the magistrates." His answer was that "the magistrates are ministers, that is, servants of the laws."[206] "It is false and simplistic," he wrote, "to assert that the prince has power to go against the law. For it is proper to such majesty . . . to serve the laws" – whether divine, natural, or civil.[207]

Theory of equity

There remained, for Oldendorp, a crucial question that neither Luther nor Melanchthon had adequately addressed, namely, by what criteria are legal norms, whether biblical, natural, or civil, to be applied in individual cases? The very generality of a legal norm or rule, Oldendorp wrote citing Eisermann, presupposes that it is applicable in a wide variety of different situations, each with its own unique circumstances. Yet the rule itself contains no indication of how the multiplicity of differences is to be taken into account. Two centuries after Oldendorp, Immanuel Kant expressed this point succinctly in his dictum that "there is no rule for applying a rule."[208]

Luther had spoken cryptically but provocatively to the issue. "The strictest law [can do] the greatest wrong," he wrote, citing Cicero. Thus "equity is necessary" in the application of rules of all sorts, whether in the state or the Church, in the household or the classroom.[209] Any ruler, whatever his office, "who does not know how to dissemble does not know how to rule," Luther said pithily. "This is what is meant by [doing] equity (*epiekeia*)."[210] To apply a rule equitably, Luther insisted "is not rashly to relax laws and discipline." It is rather to balance firmness and fairness and to recognize circumstances that might militate against literal application of the rule or that might raise questions that the rule does not and perhaps should not reach. In such instances, "equity will weigh for or against" strict application of the rule, and a wise ruler will know the juster course. "But the weighing must be of such kind that the law is not undermined, for no undermining of natural law or divine law must be allowed."[211]

---

[206] Id., *Lexicon juris*, 272; see also id., *Divinae Tabulae*, 19; id., *Ratmannenspiegel*, 73–77.

[207] Quoted by Macke, *Oldendorp*, 79–80.

[208] Immanuel Kant, *Critique of Pure Reason*, A/32–B/71–A/34–B/74.

[209] *WA TR* 3, No. 4178; *LW* 54:325, citing Cicero, *De officiis*, 1.10.

[210] *WA TR* 1, No. 315; *LW* 54:43–4. See further *WA* 14:667ff. on judges.

[211] *WA TR* 3, No. 4178; *LW* 54:325. See also Luther's discussion of the equitable application of the rules of war and soldiers in *LW* 46:100: "[I]t is impossible to establish hard and fast rules and laws in this matter. There are so many cases and so many exceptions to any rule that it is

Melanchthon had addressed the problem at greater length, but had largely followed the teachings of Aristotle[212] and the Roman law, and the ample medieval glosses and elaborations on the same.[213] Rulers were required, he wrote, to "tailor" the general principles of natural law "to fit the circumstances."[214] If a "generally just law works injustice in a particular case," it is the responsibility of a judge to apply the law as "equitably and benevolently" as possible, so as to mitigate or remove the injustice.[215] But a "generally just law" must be maintained even if in a particular case it results in injustice, for "pious persons may not be left in uncertainty" about the requirements of the law.[216] Even the highest judges, Melanchthon insisted, "must decide cases according to the law that is written. Otherwise what use would it be to enact laws, if judges were allowed to invent equities out of their heads just as spiders spin webs?"[217]

Oldendorp took a very different approach by insisting that every application of a legal rule required a judge to apply equity (*Billigkeit, aequitas, epiekeia*). Luther and Melanchthon, following tradition, had contrasted equity with strict law. Equity, they believed, corrected defects in a strict rule or its application. But equity was for the exceptional case. To use it indiscriminately, they believed, would erode the rule of law – of both natural law and civil law. Oldendorp contrasted equity with all law, not just strict law. Every law, he believed, was a strict law, because every law by its nature is general and abstract.[218] No lawmaker can anticipate perfectly the circumstances in which the rule will be applied. Thus every application of every rule has to be governed by equity. For Oldendorp,

very difficult or even impossible to decide everything accurately and equitably. This is true of all laws; they can never be formulated so certainly and so justly that cases do not arise which deserve to be made exceptions. If we do not make exceptions and strictly follow the law we do the greatest injustice of all."

[212] See Aristotle, *Ethics*, bk. 5, ch. 1.10; id., *The Art of Rhetoric*, bk. 1, ch. 12:13–19.

[213] See esp. *CR* 11:218–23, 551–5, 669–75; *CR* 16:66–72. See above pp. 77–8 and W. W. Buckland, *Equity in Roman Law* (London, 1911); Norbert Horn, *Aequitas in den Lehren des Baldus* (Cologne, 1968); Pier Giovanni Caron, "Aequitas et interpretatio dans la doctrine canonique aux xiiie et xive siècles," *Monumenta Iuris Canonici Series C* 4 (1971): 131; Hermann Lange, "*Ius aequum* und *ius strictum* bei den Glossatoren," in E. J. H. Schrage, ed., *Das römische Recht im Mittelalter* (Darmstadt, 1987), 89–115. For more recent literature, see Christoph Strohm, "Die Voraussetzungen reformatorischer Naturrechtslehre in der humanistischen Jurisprudenz," *ZSS KA* 86 (2000): 398–413.

[214] *CR* 16:72–81; *CR* 21:1090.

[215] *CR* 16:66–72, 245–7. See also *MW* 2/1: 159; *LC* (1555), 332–3; *CR* 11:218–23, 262ff.

[216] *CR* 22:612.   [217] *CR* 11:671–2.

[218] See Oldendorp, *Disputatio*, 72: "[T]he highest law is sometimes simply Law, other times is the apex of law, inflexible Law, general definition, subtlety of words, firm Law, strict Law [all of which are contrasted with] equity, the good and equitable, epiekeia, or suitability, good faith, natural Justice, etc."

therefore, equity is to be used in every case. And not to use it would erode the rule of law. In Oldendorp's formulation, law and equity, *Recht und Billigkeit, ius et aequitas,* stood opposite each other and completed each other, becoming a single thing.[219]

Equity, for Oldendorp, was the capacity or faculty of a judge to make a reasoned and conscientious judgment in each particular case. Equity was an exercise of both civil reason and natural reason, of both the mind and soul, of the judge. On the one hand, equity required careful examination of the concrete circumstances of the particular case, enabling the judge properly to apply the general rule to those particular circumstances. It included earnest study, analysis, and comparison of comparable cases and legal authorities, as any good jurist and judge is trained to do. This was an exercise of civil reason, which was essential to every legal judgment. On the other hand, equity also required what Oldendorp called "a judgment of the soul" (*iudicium animi*).[220] It required consultation and application of the natural law of conscience, the God-given law inside people.[221] This was effectively an exercise of natural reason, which was essential to making every judgment of law (*Rechtsentscheidung*) a judgment of conscience (*Gewissensentscheidung*) as well.

To retrieve equity from one's conscience and ensure that one's judgment was an exercise of both reason and conscience, Oldendorp argued, required a combination of refined professional craftmanship and simple Christian piety.[222] "A judgment cannot be made in conscience," Oldendorp wrote, "without some formula of law which indicates in the heart of man that what he does is just or unjust. Therefore, law, that is, the law of Holy Scripture, is in the person."[223] In order to discern what is equitable, the individual jurist, having exercised his legally trained civil reason to the maximum degree, must then study the Bible, pray to God, and search his conscience for instruction. This pious method was to be used not only for the hard case – whether to execute a felon convicted for a capital crime on slender evidence or to separate a young child dependent on its loving mother in a case of disputed custody. This method

---

[219] Oldendorp writes: "Natural law and equity are one thing" (*Billig und Recht,* 59). See discussion in Wolf, 161; Kisch, *Erasmus und die Jurisprudenz,* 228ff.; Dietze, *Oldendorp,* 88–89.

[220] Oldendorp, *Lexicon juris,* 28–9 (s.v. "aequitas"), 238–40 (s.v. "iudicium"); id., *Topicarum legalium . . . exactissima traditio,* 194–6. See also id., *Disputatio,* 13: "Equity is the judgment of the soul, sought from true reason, concerning the circumstances of things which pertain to moral character, since [these circumstances] indicate what ought or ought not to be done."

[221] See esp. Macke, *Oldendorp,* 151ff.

[222] See Oldendorp, *Disputatio,* 14; id., *Billig und Recht,* 66–8.

[223] Oldendorp, *Disputatio,* 145–6. See discussion in Dietze, *Oldendorp,* 78–89, 126–31; Macke, *Oldendorp,* 67–72.

was to be used in every legal case, since every case required the equitable application of a rule. In some cases, this equitable method would yield a strict application of the rule. In other cases, it would compel the judge to suspend a legal rule, to interpret it favorably towards one of the parties, to give special solicitude to a civil litigant or criminal defendant who was poor, orphaned, widowed, or abused, or to reform and improve the rule and thus create a basis for its future equitable application in a comparable case. When applied in the courtroom, Oldendorp's theory of equity was a unique form of Christian practical reasoning, on the one hand, and pious judicial activism on the other.

Oldendorp's theory of equity built squarely on Luther's belief in the Christian conscience as the ultimate source of moral decisions. Luther had justified his own defiance of Emperor Charles V at the Diet of Worms in 1521 as acts "for God and in my conscience." As he reputedly put it: "I am bound by the scriptures . . . and my conscience is captive to the Word of God. I cannot and will not retract anything, since it is neither safe nor right to go against conscience. I cannot do otherwise, here I stand, may God help me, Amen."[224] In his later writings, Luther had also urged every magistrate not only to "have the law as firmly in hand as the sword," but also, Solomon-like, to "cling solely to God, and to be at him constantly, praying for a right understanding [of the law] beyond that of all the law books and teachers, to rule his subjects." With such an attitude, "God will certainly accord him the ability to implement all laws, counsels, and actions in a proper and godly way."[225]

Oldendorp developed Luther's emphasis on a biblically and prayerfully informed conscience into a constituent element of his theory of law and equity. Every legal decision, for Oldendorp, was ultimately a moral decision. Every such decision, therefore, required consultation of conscience, and conscientious invocation of Scripture, prayer, and reflection. While such consultation of conscience was a general duty for every law-abiding citizen, it was a special duty for the judge in the interpretation and application of legal rules. Just as Luther, a learned theologian of the Church, could ultimately break a positive law that violated conscience, so the judge, a learned counselor of the state, could ultimately waive a positive law that trespassed these same transcendent norms.

Oldendorp also built on the traditional teaching that the traditional Catholic Church's canon law was the "the mother of exceptions," "the

[224] *WA* 7:838.   [225] *WA* 11:272–3.

epitome of the law of love," and "the mother of justice." These equitable qualities, we saw, had traditionally rendered the canon laws applied in the Church courts an attractive alternative to the civil laws applied in secular courts.[226] Oldendorp's theory sought to render these equitable qualities endemic to all laws and to all courts in a Christian commonwealth. Law and equity, he believed, were fundamentally conjoined, whatever the source of the law, and whatever the forum for its implementation. It was the duty of the Christian legislator to promulgate civil laws consistent with the moral teachings of divine and natural law. It was the duty of the Christian judge to interpret these laws with the equitable methods of both civil and natural reason.

SUMMARY AND CONCLUSIONS

The foregoing pages have sought to take the measure of the emerging theories of law, society, and politics among sixteenth-century Evangelical jurists. To illustrate the range of new theories, I have offered close studies of (1) Philip Melanchthon, the great moralist of the University of Wittenberg; (2) Johannes Eisermann, a student of Melanchthon and the first law professor of the new Evangelical University of Marburg; and (3) Johann Oldendorp, a distinguished and prolific jurist, who joined the Marburg law faculty a few years after Eisermann. It must be emphasized that there were dozens of other Evangelical moralists and jurists in the first half of the sixteenth century who wrote on law, politics, and society. Sometimes their views echoed those of Melanchthon, Eisermann, or Oldendorp. Sometimes, they adhered more closely to the traditional teachings of medieval canonists and civilians. The Lutheran Reformation did not produce a single or uniform jurisprudence. But it did produce a series of direct and dramatic legal applications of several cardinal teachings of Lutheran theology.

Melanchthon, Eisermann, and Oldendorp all began their theories with a basic understanding of Luther's two-kingdoms framework. While Luther tended to emphasize the distinctions between these two kingdoms, however, Lutheran jurists tended to emphasize their cooperation. While Luther tended to view the domestic, ecclesiastical, and political orders as natural and equal in their governance of the earthly kingdom, the jurists gave new emphasis and power to the political order of the magistrate, the *Obrigkeit*, and the legal profession.

---

[226] See above pp. 39–40. See also Oldendorp, *Collatio*, 32–3.

First, the Evangelical jurists emphasized more than did Luther that the Bible was an essential source of earthly law. Luther was all for using the Bible to guide life in the earthly kingdom. But he touched only intermittently and ambivalently on the Gospel's precise legal role. He tended to use the Bible as a convenient trope and trump in arguing for certain legal reforms, without spelling out a systematic theological jurisprudence. By contrast, Melanchthon, Eisermann, and Oldendorp all viewed the Bible as the highest source of law for life in the earthly kingdom. For them, it was the fullest statement of the divine law. It contained the best summary of the natural law. It provided the surest guide for positive law. With human reason distorted by sin, the jurists argued, faith in the Gospel was essential to rational apprehension and application of law in the earthly kingdom. The Gospel was the best fuel to bring to light and life what the jurists called the "inborn sparks" of natural knowledge of good and evil that God has allowed us to retain in our reason and conscience despite the fall into sin.

The jurists laid special emphasis on the Ten Commandments, and the Gospel's summary of its basic command to love God, neighbor, and self. The First Table of the Ten Commandments, they believed, laid out the cardinal principles of spiritual law and morality that governed the relationship between persons and God. The Second Table laid out the cardinal principles of civil law and morality that governed the basic relationships among persons. This division of principles was useful not only for preaching, catechesis, and theological ethics, as Luther and the theologians had argued. For the jurists, the Ten Commandments also proved useful to systematizing the positive law of the earthly kingdom. The First Table undergirded the positive laws of religious establishment and ecclesiastical order. The Second Table undergirded the positive laws governing crime, property, family, civil procedure, evidence, and more.

The Ten Commandments came to play a role in Lutheran jurisprudence akin to the role that the seven sacraments had played in Catholic jurisprudence. Medieval Catholic canonists and moralists had drawn whole systems of law around each of the sacraments. Thus the sacrament of ordination supported a detailed law of the clergy and Church life. The sacraments of baptism and the Eucharist supported a rich law of liturgy, religious doctrine, catechesis, and discipline. The sacrament of marriage supported the law of sex, marriage, and family life. The sacrament of penance supported a detailed law of crime, tort, and moral obligation. The sacrament of extreme unction undergirded the law of wills, inheritance, and trusts. Not all positive canon law, of course, fit under the sacraments. But the sacraments provided the canonists with a useful framework for organizing some of the legal institutions of the Church.

The Ten Commandments played a comparable role in Lutheran jurisprudence. The Commandments against idolatry, blasphemy, and Sabbath-breaking undergirded the new religious laws of Lutheran communities – laws governing orthodox doctrine and liturgy, ecclesiastical polity and property, local clergy and Church administrators. The Commandment "Thou shalt not steal" was the source of the law of property, as well as a source of criminal law alongside the Commandment "Thou shalt not kill." The Commandments requiring one to honor parents and to forgo adultery and coveting another's wife were the source of a new civil law of sex, marriage, and family. "Thou shalt not bear false witness" was the organizing principle of the law of civil procedure, evidence, and defamation. "Thou shalt not covet" undergirded a whole battery of inchoate crimes and civil offenses. Not all positive law fit under the Ten Commandments. And the actual positive laws that were placed under each Commandment or Table could be of fresh Evangelical promulgation, or could just as well be of biblical, Roman, or canonical origin. But the Ten Commandments provided the Evangelical jurists with a useful framework for organizing some of the legal institutions of the state.

Secondly, the Evangelical jurists emphasized, more than did Luther, the three uses of law in the governance of the earthly kingdom. Luther had developed the "uses of the law" doctrine as part of his theology of salvation, and part of his answer to the antinomians. Legal works played no role in the drama of salvation. Yet, the law itself was useful in the earthly kingdom to restrain sin and to drive sinners to the repentance that was necessary for faith in Christ and thus entrance into the heavenly kingdom. Melanchthon, Eisermann, and Oldendorp all concurred in this understanding of the civil and theological uses of law. But, unlike Luther, they also emphasized the educational use of the law in the earthly kingdom. When properly understood and applied, the law not only coerced sinners, it also educated saints. It yielded not only a basic civil morality, but also a higher spiritual morality. This was a further argument that the jurists used to insist on positive laws that established religious doctrine, liturgy, and morality in each polity. The positive law was to teach not only the civil morality of the Second Table of the Decalogue, but also the spiritual morality of the First Table. It was to teach citizens not only the letter of the moral law, but also its spirit. The law thereby was useful in defining and enforcing not only a "morality of duty" but also a "morality of aspiration."[227]

Each of our three writers pressed the uses doctrine to further specific applications. Melanchthon applied the three uses of the law to differentiate and define the three purposes of criminal law and punishment. In his view, the civil use of the law corresponded to criminal deterrence. The theological use of the law corresponded to criminal retribution. The educational use of the law corresponded to criminal rehabilitation. This argument had obvious implications for the exercise of ecclesiastical and parental discipline as well. Indeed, political, ecclesiastical, and parental authority alike had to be exercised with an eye to balancing the civil, theological, and educational uses of the law. More specifically, the prince, the preacher, and the *paterfamilias* had to strive to balance the concurrent concerns for the deterrence, retribution, and reformation of their subjects.

Johann Oldendorp applied this uses doctrine in part to develop his theory of Christian equity. The task of the Christian judge was not only to apply the letter of the law using the tools of civil legal reasoning. It was also to apply the spirit of the law, using the tools of prayer, conscientious meditation, and reading of Scripture. Civil legal reasoning would only yield a civil understanding and application of positive law. Spiritual legal reasoning would yield a higher spiritual understanding and application. Oldendorp did not put his theory of Christian equity in quite these terms. But his theory depended upon a distinction that was central to the uses doctrine: that between a lower civil use and a higher spiritual use of the law.

Johannes Eisermann applied this uses doctrine to emphasize the distinction between the civil goodness and justice of any commonwealth and the spiritual goodness and justice of the Christian commonwealth. Any commonwealth worthy of its name abides by the civil use of the law, holding its citizens and subjects to the basic duties of civil morality and punishing those who violate the same. A true Christian commonwealth, however, also cultivates the pedagogical use of the law, driving its citizens to the spiritual morality of the Gospel and so preparing them for a better life in the heavenly kingdom.

Thirdly, building on this last point, the jurists emphasized the need to establish an overtly Evangelical order of law, society, and politics in the earthly kingdom. Luther certainly had something of the same aspiration.

---

[227] These terms are from Fuller, *Morality of Law*.

But Melanchthon, Eisermann, and Oldendorp were less reserved than Luther about building bridges between the two kingdoms. It might well be, the jurists admitted with Luther, that Western Christendom in general was depraved and deprived of divine order and revelation. But this did not mean that an individual Lutheran polity could not itself be organized as an overtly Christian body politic.

Eisermann provided the most expansive argument for the creation of an Evangelical Christian commonwealth. He emphasized that the precise form and function of every such Christian commonwealth will differ, for each community will strike its own unique balance between the norms of "nature, custom, and reason" and have its own unique interpretation of the Commandments of Scripture and tradition. But certain features of a Christian commonwealth will be inevitable. Eisermann repeated the notion that the positive law of each such polity must reflect and project the natural law, particularly as summarized in the Decalogue and the Gospel. He also repeated the notion that the positive law was to support a higher spiritual morality, through establishment by law of the right doctrine, liturgy, confession, canon, and Church structure that should prevail in that polity. But Eisermann went further. A true Christian commonwealth should seek to be the very body of Christ on earth – a miniature *corpus Christianum*. It should seek to follow St. Paul's image that all are "individual members one of another." This meant that each person and each vocation must count and must be supported in a Christian commonwealth. Each person must respect the dignity, property, and privacy of the other, and discharge the charity, care, and priestly service that become the Christian faith. A true Christian commonwealth should also follow St. Paul's image that some members of the body are greater and some are lesser. This, for Eisermann, supported an intricate hierarchy of estates, orders, and professions within the local polity, each with their own vocations in serving the common good and reforming the commonwealth.

Fourthly, the jurists developed an intricate theory of both political power and limitations on political power. Luther had endorsed a robust theory of political authority, labeling the magistrate the vicar of Christ, the father of the community, and the only true lawmaking authority of the earthly kingdom. But Luther had limited political power with his emphasis on the inherent limitation of its jurisdiction to earthly matters, the internal checks provided by the *Obrigkeit*, and the external checks provided by the concurrent orders of the family and the Church that God had appointed to the earthly kingdom.

The jurists often repeated Luther's teachings, but they also undercut them. By granting the magistrate power over religious doctrine and liturgy, they effectively extended his power at least partly into the heavenly kingdom. By glorifying the prince as the highest legal authority within the earthly kingdom, they severely compromised the checks and balances of the lower *Obrigkeit*. By giving the magistrate exclusive power to define the legal form and function of the Church and the family, they jeopardized the institutional checks and balances the ecclesiastical and domestic orders might have imposed on the political order. Here now was the Christian magistrate, directly appointed by God, wielding plenary legal authority within his own polity, and without serious institutional rivals. Luther's theory had provided ample incentive to shift lawmaking authority from the Church to the state. The jurists' theory seemed to provide the magistrates with all that was needed for absolute power and tyranny.

But this was only one side of the Lutheran jurists' theory of the Christian magistrate. Lutheran jurists also placed a number of safeguards against tyranny. Some of these were familiar to the Roman law and canon law traditions. Melanchthon, Eisermann, and Oldendorp alike emphasized that the magistrate was bound to obey his own laws, since they derive from the natural law that binds him and his subjects. They emphasized the importance of written, published laws, which served in part to restrain wicked and capricious rulers. They declared Roman law to be a written embodiment of legal reason, to be used as something of a template for new positive law and a check against untoward application of new laws. They emphasized the responsibility of the clergy to preach and prophesy against injustice and tyranny, and the duty of parents to teach their children and dependants the priority of divine law over human law, conscience over commandment. They emphasized the right of the Christian believer to disobey laws that openly violated the Bible and the Christian conscience. These were mostly traditional teachings, which the Lutheran jurists endorsed and glossed freely.

The Lutheran jurists' arguments for enhancing the power and prestige of the political office also paradoxically put additional safeguards on it. One safeguard lay in their theory of the Ten Commandments as the source of positive law. This enhanced the magistrate's power to reach both civil and spiritual matters. But it also restrained the magistrate in the use of his power. For the Ten Commandments, both the First and the Second Table, were best interpreted by the Church and its theologians, not by the state and the *Obrigkeit*. The magistrate was thus obligated to draw on theologians and clergy is order to understand the moral and religious dimensions of the law. He was to appoint them to the legislature. He was to request their opinions on discrete questions. He was to consult the theology faculties on difficult cases. The local clergy and the local theology faculties thus served as important safeguards against political abuse, even though they held no formal legal power.

A second safeguard lay in the jurists' flattering descriptions of the magistrate as the paragon of Christian virtue, the vicar of Christ, and the father of the community. This enhanced the splendor and glory of the political office. But it also held its occupant to a very high moral and Christian standard. Those officials who defied this description, by the very nature of the office, should not and could not serve, and risked resistance or all-out revolt if they persisted. When this view of high moral standards for political office was coupled with a theory of election to office, which became increasingly common in some later sixteenth-century cities and duchies, it provided a critical restriction on tyranny.

A third safeguard lay in the intense pluralism of Germany, with its 300-plus separate and often very small polities. The small size of these polities did allow for the easier local realization of a unitary Lutheran commonwealth under the plenary legal authority of the Lutheran magistrate. But the small size of these polities also made it easier for people to leave – taking with them their labor, their expertise, their taxes, their services, and other essential contributions to the local commonwealth. The sterner the tyranny, the smaller the population, was the theory. This right of a person to leave a polity and policy that he or she found odious or onerous was eventually guaranteed by the Religious Peace of Augsburg of 1555, and was enforceable against a local polity ultimately by the emperor. This, too, was an ample restraint on tyranny, at least in theory.

Finally, the jurists developed an exquisite new theory that Christian equity was endemic to all law and judgment. Luther had touched on this in his maxim that a judge must learn to "dissemble" in applying a rule. Eisermann had touched on it in his injunction that a judge must constantly "fetch equity from the bowels of the law." It was Oldendorp, however, who developed it into a full theory of judicial equity. Every law was by its nature a strict law, he argued, and every law, by definition, therefore required equitable application. To do equity was an exercise of both the mind and the soul of the judge. It required the judge to apply civil reason, to separate salient from superficial fact, to reason from precedent and analogy. It also, however, required the judge to use natural reason, to consult the natural law inscribed on his conscience, to meditate prayerfully on Scripture, and so decide on the right application or reformation of the rule. Such conscientious application of rules was required not only in exceptional cases but in all cases. It was concerned not only with being just and merciful to the party in the particular case, but also with serving the letter and the spirit of the law itself.

Traditionally, equity was considered to be a unique quality of the canon law and a unique ability of the ecclesiastical judge. Thus in medieval Germany cases that required formal equity were removed to the Church courts for resolution. Likewise in medieval England, equity was administered in the court of the Chancellor, staffed by a ranking ecclesiastic trained in the canon law.[228] Oldendorp's theory effectively merged law and equity. All law required equity to be just, and all equity required law to be applied justly. Law and equity belonged together and completed each other. It was the general responsibility of the legislator to "build equity into the law," in passing new laws. But it was the special calling of every judge to do equity in every case. Oldendorp's theory had direct implications for legal reform in Evangelical Germany. It helped to support the merger of Church courts and state courts in Evangelical Germany; separate courts of equity were no longer required. It helped to support the convergence of canon law and civil law in Evangelical Germany. And it helped to support the growing professionalization of the German judiciary in the sixteenth century, and the requirement that judges be educated both in law and in theology, in civil and in canon law.[229]

In a 1531 oration at the University of Wittenberg, Philip Melanchthon declared: "It is impossible to uphold civil discipline without religion, and jurisprudence is shaped most by religious doctrine." Indeed, only when "religion adds its voice to civil precepts" does law have the authority to govern and the power to reform.[230] These early sentiments were the watchwords of sixteenth-century Lutheran jurisprudence. For the early Evangelical jurists, law and Gospel, justice and mercy, rule and equity, discipline and love, order and faith, structure and spirit, all properly belonged in the governance of the earthly kingdom. To separate one dimension from the other was to serve the Devil and to get a foretaste of hell. To hold them in tension was to serve the Divine and to see a glimmer of heaven.

---

[228] On Germany, see above pp. 36–40. On England, see Berman, *Faith and Order*, 55–82.
[229] See generally Burmeister, *Das Studium der Rechte*.   [230] *CR* 11:210.

5. Cover Page of Johannes Bugenhagen, *Der Erbarn Stadt Braunschwyg Christenliche Ordenung: zu dienst dem heiligen Euangelio, Christlicher lieb, zucht, fride, vnd eynigkeit: Auch darunter vil Christlicher lere für die Bürger* (Nuremberg, 1531)

Crucifixion of Jesus Christ, with two thieves.

5

From Gospel to Law: The Lutheran reformation laws

The Lutheran Reformation did not create the reformation ordinance. The reformation ordinance, in fact, helped to create the Lutheran Reformation. But the Lutheran Reformation did reform the reformation ordinance, eventually rendering it a formidable instrument for the implementation and institutionalization of cardinal Evangelical ideas of theology and law. The task of this brief chapter is to show (1) how the "legal reformation" movement of the fifteenth century led into the Lutheran Reformation; and (2) how the Lutheran Reformation, in turn, yielded a new legal reformation movement.

THE EARLY LEGAL REFORMATIONS

The Western tradition has long recognized the value of periodic reform, renewal, and regeneration of a person or a community. The term *reformatio* in this sense appears already in several classical Greek and Roman writings, and these came in for endless glosses and commentary among the Church Fathers and medieval writers. Furthermore, the Western Christian tradition has long recognized that periodic reform of the Church's doctrine, liturgy, clergy, polity, and law are essential to the survival and flourishing of the faith. The term *reformatio* in this sense recurred repeatedly in Christian writings during the Christianization of the Roman Empire in the fourth and fifth centuries and the "renaissance" of Emperor Charlemagne at the turn of the ninth century. It recurred again in the medieval revival of the Church led by Pope Gregory VII, variously called the "Gregorian Reform," the "twelfth-century Renaissance," and the "Papal Revolution."[1] The language of "reformation" came to

---

[1] See Gerhard Ladner, *The Idea of Reform: Its Impact on Christian Thought and Action in the Age of the Fathers* (Cambridge, MA, 1959); Lewis W. Spitz, "Reformation," in *Dictionary of the History of Ideas*, ed. Philip P. Wiener (New York, 1973), 4:60–69; Lewis W. Spitz, ed., *The Reformation – Material or Spiritual?* (Boston, 1962); Berman, *Law and Revolution*, 85ff., 574ff.; Karl Frederick Morrison,

powerful expression yet again during the conciliar movement of the Church in the early fifteenth century, which, in the words of the Council of Constance (1415), sought a "reformation of the Church of God in its head and in its members."[2] Indeed, the whole period from the twelfth century forward has been aptly called a perpetual "age of reform."[3]

Concrete talk of a *legal* reformation of the political order was of more recent vintage. In the early fifteenth century, as we saw in chapter one, jurists in Germany and beyond began to call for the reformation of the doctrines, structures, and methods of private and criminal law within the various imperial, territorial, urban, and other orders that comprised the German state. The most prominent early expression of this came in Emperor Sigismund's famous *Reformatio Sigismundi* of 1438 that set out a whole series of reforms of spiritual and secular life, lore, and law in Germany and elsewhere in the Holy Roman Empire. These imperial reform measures were intermittently echoed and elaborated in the grievances filed at later imperial diets, and in some of the peace statutes (*Landfriede*) to emerge from the same. Rather little came of these imperial legal reforms, however, until the sixteenth century, with the establishment of the general imperial court (*Reichskammergericht*) in Germany in 1495, and the gradual implementation of a streamlined system of lower courts.[4]

More immediately effective were the legal reformations in some of the German cities and territories of the Empire in the fifteenth and early sixteenth centuries. These local legal reformations aimed, in part, to reform abuses of the Church's law, polity, and property – particularly the adventuresome extension of ecclesiastical jurisdiction and Church property holdings in some German polities.[5] But equally important, these legal reformations aimed to routinize and reform the civil laws and procedures of these local polities. Eventually this legal reformation movement yielded impressive new codes of private law and criminal law. They also revamped criminal and civil procedure, eventually replacing the lay *Schöffen* courts that applied local civil law by new learned courts that used formal written forms of procedure and new rules of pleading,

---

The Mimetic Tradition of Reform in the West (Princeton, 1982); id., *The Two Kingdoms: Ecclesiology in Carolingian Political Thought* (Princeton, 1964); Robert L. Benson and Giles Constable, eds., *Renaissance and Renewal in the Twelfth Century* (Cambridge, MA, 1982).

[2] Henry Bettenson and Chris Maunder, eds., *Documents of the Christian Church*, 3rd edn. (Oxford, 1999), 149; see Tierney, *Foundations of the Conciliar Theory*.

[3] Ozment, *Age of Reform*; Eike Wolgast, "Reform, Reformation," in Otto Brunner *et al.*, eds., *Geschichtliche Grundbegriffe. Historisches Lexicon zur politisch-sozialen Sprache in Deutschland* (Stuttgart, 1984), 5:313–60.

[4] See above pp. 42–3.   [5] See above pp. 43–9.

evidence, adversarial argument, appeal, and more. Increasingly at the turn of the sixteenth century, professional lawyers came to represent clients in adversarial proceedings in local courts in accordance with written rules and procedures. Increasingly, professional judges issued formal opinions, at least in major cases, with an eye to interpreting local legal reformation laws, adducing Roman law and canon law authorities in support of their positions, and being consistent with precedents of the local courts. Increasingly, the learned opinions of professorial jurists, and sometimes of whole law faculties of German universities, were solicited in important cases, both by litigants and by courts, and these juridical opinions became important sources of law in their own right.

From one perspective, this legal reformation movement of the fifteenth century had rather little to do with the theological reformation movement introduced in the next century by Luther and others. After all, reforms of court structure, procedural rules, or individual doctrines of private or criminal law seem a world away from theological debates over the niceties of justification by faith alone, the priesthood of all believers, or the distinctions between the two kingdoms. Moreover, this traditional legal reformation movement simply continued, almost without interruption, throughout the sixteenth and seventeenth centuries. German cities, principalities, and territories, both Protestant and Catholic, continued to promulgate all manner of (what they still sometimes called) "legal reformations," many times with only passing mention of any change in the prevailing theology and Church life of the local polity.

From another perspective, however, this fifteenth-century legal reformation movement was a critical precursor to the sixteenth-century theological reformation movement of Luther and his followers. First, these fifteenth-century legal reformations laid important groundwork for the massive shift of jurisdiction from the Church to the state in the sixteenth century. One of the cardinal teachings of the early Lutheran Reformation was that law was the province of the state not of the Church. This Evangelical teaching built squarely on the fifteenth-century legal reformations that had already truncated the Church's temporal jurisdiction and policed closely the Church's spiritual jurisdiction. The Lutheran Reformation embraced and accelerated this trend, often shifting to the local magistrate principal legal authority over the clergy, polity, and property of the local church, as well as over marriage, education, poor relief, and other subjects traditionally governed by the Church and its canon law.

Second, the Lutheran Reformation built squarely on the new emphasis and methods of learned law that the legal reformation movement had introduced into Germany. The Lutheran Reformation was, in no small part, born in the German university – in Luther's early lectures on the Psalms and St. Paul, in his prerogative as a professor to challenge the Church to reform itself, in his acts of burning the canon law books before members of his faculty.[6] Thereafter, the Lutheran Reformation found some of its strongest leaders among the learned theologians and learned jurists in the Evangelical German universities. Lutheran theologians, several themselves trained in law, joined with Lutheran jurists to work out the legal dimensions and consequences of their theological reforms. At the University of Wittenberg, for example, Luther, Melanchthon, Johannes Bugenhagen, Justus Jonas, and several other theologians worked hand in hand (and sometimes hand to hand) with such jurists as Melchior Kling, Konrad Lagus, Johann Apel, Nicolaus Hemming, Jerome Schürpf, Johannes Schneidewin, and several others. By 1555, the Wittenberg theology and law professors together had published well over one hundred major tracts on law, disseminating their ideas throughout Germany and beyond. Law professors and theology professors at other Evangelical universities in Marburg, Tübingen, Leipzig, Greifswald, Frankfurt an der Oder, and Köningsberg were likewise active in developing a new learned law based, in part, on Evangelical theology.

This learned law did not remain confined to the lectern or to books. The methods born of the legal reformation movement allowed for their rapid dissemination and implementation in Evangelical Germany.[7] A number of professionally trained jurists who had joined the Evangelical movement sat on local courts as judges and notaries, or on local councils as secretaries and legal advisors, and thereby took a direct hand in shaping the new laws.[8] Furthermore, a number of Evangelical jurists and theologians issued formal legal opinions (*consilia*) on request from courts, councils, or individual litigants. The most coveted *consilia* were those of Luther, Melanchthon, Bugenhagen, Brenz, and Bucer, among theologians, and those of Oldendorp, Eisermann, Apel, Kling, Schneidewin, and Schürpf, among jurists. Many of these *consilia* were later collected and published and became important legal texts. There were more than forty such collections in circulation in Germany by the end of the sixteenth century; those of Schürpf and Oldendorp remained in print

---

[6] See Oberman, "University and Society on the Threshold of Modern Times."

[7] See Steven Rowan, "Jurists and the Printing Press in Germany: The First Century," in Gerald P. Tyson and Sylvia S. Wagonheim, eds., *Print and Culture in the Renaissance: Essays on the Advent of Printing in Germany* (Newark, NJ, 1986), 74.

[8] See pp. 73–4, 78, 141–2, 155–7 on the roles of Lazarus Spengler, Johannes Eisermann, and Johann Oldendorp. See many other examples of influential local jurists in Köhler, 25ff.

for more than two centuries thereafter.[9] Still further, civil courts regularly consulted the law faculties (and sometimes the theology faculties) of local Evangelical universities by using what was called the "file-sending" (*Aktenversendung*) procedure. The courts sent the written records of cases raising difficult legal and moral issues to the faculties, who would discuss the case and submit judgments and opinions which were often taken by the courts as binding. Studies of several German cities that accepted the Reformation have demonstrated the important influence of this *Aktenversendung* procedure on shaping the substantive law of the local polities in accordance with Evangelical norms and forms.[10]

The most direct and dramatic legal method for communicating the new Evangelical learning, however, was in the promulgation of new "legal reformations" or "reformation laws." Following the legal reformers of the fifteenth century, the theological reformers of the sixteenth century used local law as an instrument and indicator of reform. The Lutheran Reformation was a broadly pluralistic movement at the start, led by scores of theologians and jurists scattered throughout Germany. Part of what gave this theological movement rapid definition and cohesion was the ability of these scattered Evangelical leaders, particularly those who were university theologians and jurists, to translate their new theological ideas into new laws for local cities, duchies, and territories. This built squarely on the practice of fifteenth-century local polities and communities of using local laws to reform traditional norms and define new ideals, particularly during periods of political unrest or instability.[11] Eventually, the Lutheran reformers consolidated and systematized their theological reformation and revised the local laws accordingly, just as the legal reformers eventually moved toward more general codes of legal doctrine and procedures triggering a whole series of new and more refined legal reformations. But, in the early years of the Lutheran Reformation, the use of local law reform was of signal importance to defining and enforcing the basics of the new theological movement.

What thus emerged in early sixteenth-century Germany was two types of legal reformations. The first *traditional* types were the century-old legal

---

[9] See Guido Kisch, *Consilia: Eine Bibliographie der juristischen Konsiliensammlungen* (Basel, 1970); Heinrich Gehrke, *Die Rechtsprechung- und Konsilienliteratur Deutschlands bis zum Ende des alten Reichs* (Frankfurt am Main, Univ. Fachber. Rechtwissen. Diss., 1972).

[10] See examples in Kock, *Studium Pietatis*, 139ff.; W. Haalk, "Die Rostocker Juristenfakultät als Spruchskollegium," *Wissenschaftliche Zeitschrift der Universität Rostock* 3 (1958): 401, 414ff.; Wilhelm Ebel, *Studie über einem Goslarer Ratsurteilsbuch des 16. Jahrhunderts nebst einem Urkundenanhang* (Göttingen, 1961); Stölzel, 1:388ff.; Dawson, *Oracles of the Law*, 198ff.

[11] See Bob Scribner, "Germany," in Bob Scribner *et al.*, eds., *The Reformation in National Context* (Cambridge, 1994), 4–29, at 18ff.

reformations of private law and criminal law and of the methods, procedures, and forums of legislation and adjudication. The second *Lutheran*
types were the brand new legal reformations that followed on the acceptance of the Lutheran Reformation by a local German polity. In the later
sixteenth and seventeenth centuries, these traditional and Lutheran types
of legal reformations increasingly converged, particularly in the massive
new codes and public policy ordinances issued by the major territories
and cities of early modern Germany. In the first half of the sixteenth
century, however, these two types of legal reformations remained quite
distinct. The Lutheran legal reformations did build on some of the methods and momentum of the traditional legal reformation movement. But
in the early decades of the sixteenth century, they went their own way to
consolidate and routinize the Lutheran Reformation.

THE LUTHERAN REFORMATION LAWS

The phrase "Lutheran reformation laws" embraces a wide array of written laws that governed religious and ecclesiastical life in Evangelical
Germany. These laws were usually promulgated or commissioned by
magistrates in the cities, duchies, or territories. Sometimes they came
forth from synods or special gatherings of Evangelical Church leaders.
Not infrequently, they were formal *consilia* or informal letters issued by
leading reformers and faculties that carried the authority of their authors
and influenced later statutes and court opinions.

These written pronouncements on sixteenth-century religious and ecclesiastical life came in sundry legal forms. They were variously labeled
as reformations, ordinances, acts, statutes, mandates, articles, edicts, decrees, instructions, and even occasionally as decretals (*Decreten*).[12] The
differences in form and authority among these legal genres were important in cases that raised issues of conflict of laws, and in later efforts
to systematize and codify the religious laws of Germany.[13] But in the
first half of the sixteenth century, these various kinds of legal pronouncements were often jumbled indiscriminately together. They varied greatly
in length, formality, and legal sophistication – ranging from a few legal
sentences scrawled out by a local notary to detailed legal codes of over
one hundred dense folio pages. The huge sixteen-volume collection by

---

[12] On the multiple forms of the reformation ordinance, see Wilhelm Ebel, *Geschichte der Gesetzgebung in Deutschland* (Göttingen, 1958), 58ff.; Marc Raeff, *The Well-Ordered Police State: Social and Institutional Change through Law in the Germanies and Russia, 1600–1800* (New Haven, CT, 1983), 46ff.; Burkhard von Bonin, *Die praktische Bedeutung des ius reformandi: Eine rechtsgeschichtliche Studie* (Stuttgart, 1902).

[13] See, e.g., sources and discussion in Stephen Buchholz, "Justus Henning Böhmer (1674–1749) und das Kirchenrecht," *Ius Commune* 18 (1991): 37.

Emil Sehling and others holds more than a thousand of these Lutheran reformation laws.[14] There are untold hundreds more of them in the German archives.

These Lutheran reformation laws were sometimes called just that: *Reformationen, Rechtsreformationen,* or *Reformationsordnungen.* But they were just as often called church ordinances (*Kirchenordnungen*) or Church laws (*Kirchenrechte*), even though they dealt with many other legal subjects besides formal Church life. Many of these general reformation laws had separate sections on worship, baptism, liturgy, preaching, marriage, poor relief, education, and other subjects. Not infrequently, these separate sections of bigger ordinances had a legal life of their own. These sections were sometimes issued individually both before and after the bigger ordinance, and then labeled as such. So a local polity might have in circulation not only a big reformation law with multiple sections, but also all manner of more discrete worship ordinances (*Gottesdienstordnungen*), baptismal ordinances (*Taufordnungen*), marriage ordinances (*Eheordnungen*), school ordinances (*Schulordnungen*), poor relief ordinances (*Armenordnungen*), and many others.

It was very common in early Evangelical Germany for one influential city or territory (often called "the mother city" or "mother Land") to send out its new reformation ordinance as a prototype to surrounding towns and villages, each of which would adopt their own variants of the big ordinance, and the excerpted smaller sections of the same. And, then inevitably, these locally transplanted ordinances and sections would go through their own revisions, reproductions, and eventual transplantations.[15]

To render matters even more complicated, many times these reformation or Church ordinances – and the excerpted sections of the same – were incorporated into, or echoed by, the religion clauses of new territorial ordinances (*Landesordnungen*) or "public policy" ordinances (*Polizeiordnungen*).[16] These were generally major pieces of formal

---

[14] Richter includes 172 of the major reformation ordinances of the sixteenth century, more than 100 of them published before 1555.
[15] See Wieacker, 183ff.; Berman, *Law and Revolution,* 482ff.
[16] On the rendering of "Polizeiordnung" (literally "police ordinance") as "policy ordinance," see R. W. Scribner, "Police and the Territorial State in Sixteenth Century Württemberg," in Kouri and Scott, eds., *Politics and Society in Reformation Europe,* 103ff.; Karl Härter, "Entwicklung und Funktion der Polizeigesetzgebung des Heiligen Römischen Reiches Deutscher Nation im 16. Jahrhundert," *Ius Commune* 20 (1993): 61; Franz Ludwig Knemeyer, "Polizei," in Brunner *et al.,* eds., *Geschichtliche Grundbegriffe,* 875–97. The term *Polizei* came to mean more narrowly "police" only in the eighteenth century. The more typical sixteenth-century rendering of "polizei" as "policy" is reflected in Oldendorp, *Van radtslangende, wo men gude Politie und ordenunge ynn Steden und Landen enholden möghe,* discussed above pp. 162–4.

legislation issued by territorial princes and dukes as well as by the emperor. They covered a wide array of subjects beyond religion, but they often included ample provisions on religion and public morality. These ordinances, in turn, were amply amended and then reissued, particularly upon the succession of a new duke, prince, or emperor. The ensuing problems of conflict of laws must have been a dream for sixteenth-century jurists eager to find loopholes to help their clients or torment their students. But they are a nightmare for historians trying to summarize the new reformation laws – particularly given that sixteenth-century Germany had more than 300 polities, many featuring very lively legislative pens.

A whole industry of important writing on these Lutheran reformation laws is now available for the stout of heart to read.[17] A good bit of this literature is still marked by classic debates among German historians and churchmen at the turn of the twentieth century: Are these "reformation laws" a product or a betrayal of the original Lutheran message? Are they actually forms of law or simply standards of discipline? Are they a reversion to or a revision of prevailing canon laws? My argument, in this and succeeding chapters, is that these "reformation laws" were continuous with the original Lutheran message, that they were an integral part of sixteenth-century German law, and that they are neither simply a revision of nor a reversion to canon law, but rather a skillful blend of Catholic and Evangelical theology and canonical and civilian legal learning.

The example of Wittenberg

A brief look at the new reformation laws that governed the small town of Wittenberg provides a good illustration of the complex network of law to govern religious and ecclesiastical life in early Evangelical Germany. Wittenberg, with its population of some 2,500, issued more than a dozen of its own reformation laws in the first generation of the Lutheran Reformation. It issued its first "Church Ordinance" as early as 1522, which in reality was largely a set of instructions on poor relief and the community chest.[18] In 1523, three new laws revised the liturgy and procedure of religious worship, the eucharist, and baptism in Wittenberg. A 1525 order

---

[17] Among classics, see Sehling, *Kirchenrecht*; Johannes Friedrich von Schulte, *Lehrbuch des katholischen und evangelischen Kirchenrechts* (Kieken, 1886); Emil Friedberg, *Lehrbuch des katholischen und evangelischen Kirchenrechts* (Leipzig, 1909); Rudolph Sohm, *Kirchenrecht* (Leipzig, 1892). For more recent writing, see sources and discussion in Schwanhäusser, *Gesetzgebungsrecht*; Sichelschmidt, *Recht aus christlicher Liebe*; Gerhard Rau *et al.*, eds., *Das Recht der Kirche*, 3 vols. (Gütersloh, 1994–97); and authoritative articles in *Zeitschrift für evangelisches Kirchenrecht*.
[18] Sehling 1/1, 696–700.

made cosmetic changes to religious ceremonies and the religious calendar. In 1526, Luther issued a comprehensive new German mass as well as a liturgy book for baptism; these were prescribed for use in the local Wittenberg churches and incorporated by reference into several later local statutes. In 1530 and 1531, respectively, the Augsburg Confession and its Apology began to circulate locally as the preferred statement of Evangelical teaching. In 1533, Wittenberg issued a more detailed "Church Ordinance" than that of 1522, collecting and amending some of the existing laws and confessional statements on religious worship, singing, the sacraments, and Church offices and adding more detailed provisions on schools, hospitals, poor relief centers, and Church diaconal work. That same year, Wittenberg also issued a brief ordinance on marriage ceremonies. In 1535 and 1539, it promulgated successive ordinances on the ordination of ministers and other Church officers.[19]

Many of these early piecemeal laws came together in revised and expanded form in a comprehensive "Constitution of the Consistory of Wittenberg" in 1542, and the "Wittenberg Reformation" of 1545. The 1542 Constitution established a "consistory court" in Wittenberg and in several surrounding towns. The Wittenberg version of the consistory court was to be staffed by two theologians and two jurists from the local University as well as a professionally trained notary and treasurer. The consistory was empowered to hear and adjudicate disputes that arose under prevailing religious laws. It enforced those laws using censure, fines, the ban, and excommunication in extreme cases – referring cases to the civil authorities if criminal prosecution or civil litigation was also warranted. The 1545 "Wittenberg Reformation" – a substantial and influential law drafted by Luther, Melanchthon, Bugenhagen, and others – set out the established doctrine, liturgy, and the sacraments for the local churches, with further substantial entries on preaching and ecclesiastical authority, on marriage, and on education in local schools.[20]

Superimposed somewhat tenuously on these local religious laws of Wittenberg were various territorial laws issued by the princes and courts of Albertine and Ernestine Saxony. Ironically, the most important early territorial law was in fact a theological document drafted by Melanchthon – *Instructions for the Visitors of Parish Pastors*, issued first in 1527, more fully in 1528, and then in several revised versions thereafter. The *Instructions* were a crisp primer of twenty-five large folio pages, adorned with a robust preface by Luther. Luther had pressed for the

---

[19] Ibid., 1/1:1–28, 697–710.　　[20] Ibid., 1/1:200–22.

early preparation of this document in order to define clearly the basics of Evangelical doctrine, liturgy, and morality for the preachers, teachers, and congregants in Wittenberg and cities throughout the territory of Saxony. The 1528 version of the *Instructions* included meaty entries on the Decalogue, prayer, tribulation, baptism, eucharist, penance, sin, confession, Church organization, marriage, free will, Christian freedom, the Turks, daily worship, the ban, superintendents, and schools.[21] After 1530, these *Instructions* often circulated together with Luther's new *Small Catechism* and *Large Catechism* (1529), as well as the Augsburg Confession (1530).[22]

The *Instructions* were intended to be something of a checklist for territorial visitors and superintendents to judge the Evangelical coherence and adherence of local churches and communities that had converted to the Reformation. The *Instructions*, however, soon became the core of a model religious law for Wittenberg as well as for many other local polities within the territory of Saxony. By 1538, a mere decade after the *Instructions* were first issued, some four dozen villages and towns surrounding Wittenberg, as well as the influential cities of Leipzig and Dresden, had adopted a version of these *Instructions* as the foundation for their own reformation ordinances. Each of these local ordinances, in turn, went through several amendments and revisions in the next decades, often thereby triggering ripple changes in the local laws of their neighboring towns and cities, including Wittenberg.[23] In 1539, the prince of Albertine Saxony issued a general "Church Ordinance for Saxony," adopting and adapting several of the same provisions of the 1528 *Instructions*. This big territorial church ordinance went through several iterations and amendments in the ensuing five decades.[24] In 1580, the Saxon prince issued a massive new territorial "Church Ordinance of Saxony" to bring all these local legal variations on religious and Church life into uniformity.[25]

The *Instructions* were not the only territorial laws to govern local religious and ecclesiastical life in Wittenberg and other Saxon towns. A long series of increasingly detailed territorial ordinances (*Landesordnungen*) and public policy ordinances (*Polizeiordnungen*) also came into play. These Saxon territorial laws had provisions to govern the religious education

---

[21] Ibid., 1/1:142–75, with updates ibid., 183–6, 222–28, 305–16. The 1528 *Instruction* is also in *WA* 26:195–240; *LW* 40:263–320.

[22] Reprinted in *TC* 37–95, 530–733.

[23] See Sichelschmidt, *Recht aus christlicher Liebe*, 1–10; Sehling 1/1:33–142, with samples ibid., 1/1:183–99, 524–724.

[24] Ibid., 1/1: 264–81.   [25] Ibid., 1/1: 359–457.

and catechesis of children, the schedule of tithes, Church rates, and religious taxes, the acquisition, use, and maintenance of religious properties, pews, cemeteries, parsonages, and more. These territorial laws also dwelt at increasing length with the education, ordination, supervision, and regulation of the preachers and teachers in villages and towns throughout the territory. They insisted on proper observance ("without papalism") of religious holidays, public liturgies, and ceremonies – all to be enjoyed without drunkenness, sumptuousness, and other such excesses. They prescribed severe penalties for "misuse of God's Word," through blasphemy, sacrilege, false oath-swearing, superstition, alchemy, witchcraft, false teaching, and other religious crimes. They included detailed regulations of schools, marriage, and poor relief. In an instance of conflict, these territorial laws presumptively preempted the local laws of Wittenberg and other towns and cities. Such cases were generally to be heard by territorial high courts (*Hofgerichte*) rather than by local courts or consistories.[26]

Some of these Saxon territorial laws on religion had parallels in, and (until 1555) competition from, the imperial laws of the Holy Roman Empire. The emperor had already begun to pass and to enforce "reformation ordinances" in the fifteenth century, as noted above. This imperial legislation on religion continued throughout the sixteenth and early seventeenth centuries – in Protestant and Catholic polities of Germany alike.[27] Particularly important were the new imperial public policy ordinances (*Reichspolizeiordnungen*) of 1530, 1548, and 1577, as well as the comprehensive new criminal code for the Empire, the *Carolina* of 1532, named for Emperor Charles V and substantially drafted by the Lutheran jurist Johann Schwarzenberg.[28] These imperial laws on religion included

---

[26] Ibid., 1 / 1: 178–83, 229–30, 336–42; Arthur Kern, *Deutsche Hofordnungen des 16. und 17. Jahrhunderts*, 2 vols. (Berlin, 1905–7), 2:44ff. See further Heiner Lück, "Wittenberg als Zentrum kursächsischer Rechtspflege: Hofgericht – Juristenfakultät – Schöffenstuhl – Konsistorium," in Stefan Oehmig, ed., *700 Jahre Wittenberg* (Weimar, 1995), 213–48; Carl Wolfgang Huismann Schoss *Die rechtliche Stellung, Struktur und Funktion der frühen evangelischen Konsistorien nach den evangelischen Kirchenordnungen des 16 Jahrhunderts* (Inaug., Diss.; Heidelberg, 1980).

[27] See Wilfred Enderle, "Die katholischen Reichsstädte im Zeitalter der Reformation und der Konfessionsbildung," *ZSS KA* 106 (1989): 228–69; Heinrich Richard Schmidt, *Reichsstädte, Reich, und Reformation: Korporative Religionspolitik 1521–1529/30* (Stuttgart, 1986).

[28] The 1530 and 1548 *Reichspolizeiordnungen* are in C. Cau *et al.*, *Groot Placaetboeck*, 11 vols. (Louvain, 1658–1797), vol. 1; the 1577 version is in Kunkel, 2/1:57. The *Constitutio Criminalis Carolina* (1532) is in Josef Kohler and Willy Scheel, eds., *Die peinliche Gerichtsordnung Kaiser Karls V. Constitutio Criminalis Carolina*, repr. (Aalen, 1968). For a tabular summary of the subject matter of these earlier *Reichspolizeiordnungen*, see Kunkel, 1:21. For analysis of their religious laws, see Härter, "Entwicklung und Funktion der Polizeigesetzgebung," 93ff; Raeff, *The Well-Ordered Police State*, 56ff.

stern prohibitions on blasphemy, false swearing, superstition, witchcraft, alchemy, and other "false beliefs" – provisions that were enforced with great alacrity in some of the imperial cities of the Empire, both Protestant and Catholic.[29] The imperial laws also included general provisions on observance of the Sabbath and holy days, faithful attendance at worship, faithful payment of tithes for local ministers and churches, and more. The 1530 and 1548 *Reichspolizeiordnungen* and other imperial laws on religion in the 1530s and 1540s dealt harshly with some of the budding Evangelical communities of Germany in an effort to stamp them out. At the time of the Peace of Augsburg (1555), imperial laws continued to insist on faithful religious observance and adherence to public Christian morality, but they left the precise confessional identity of each polity to local officials to define and enforce.[30]

Patterns of reform

This pattern of overlapping and shifting urban and territorial reformation laws that prevailed in Wittenberg and Saxony was quite common in other parts of sixteenth-century Germany. Local acceptance of the Lutheran Reformation was almost always signaled by promulgation of a preliminary reformation law. This early law, in turn, usually went through multiple amendments and iterations in succeeding decades.

Of the roughly eighty-five "free" cities in the German sections of the Empire in 1521, some fifty ultimately accepted the Protestant Reformation. Twenty additional cities experimented with the Reformation and eventually came to tolerate the co-existence of Evangelical and Catholic communities. Most of these cities that joined the Reformation – some thirty of them by 1535 – promulgated new reformation laws, often triggering the promulgation of parallel reformation laws for the villages and rural areas around these cities.[31] While some of the urban and territorial councils could call on prototypes for this legislation reaching back more than a century, a number of the territories and duchies had to begin with a *tabula rasa*. Yet territorial reformation laws also began to appear rather

---

[29] *Carolina*, art. 106; 1530, 1548, 1577 RPO, tit. 1–4. See Gerd Schwerhoff, "Blasphemie vor den Schranken der städtischen Justiz: Basel, Köln, und Nürnberg im Vergleich (14. bis. 17. Jahrhundert)," *Ius Commune* 25 (1998): 39–120.

[30] See sources and discussion in Peter Moraw *et al.*, "Reich," in Brunner *et al.*, eds., *Geschichtliche Grundbegriffe*, 5:423–508, at 446ff.

[31] Moeller, *Imperial Cities and the Reformation*, 41–2, citing the imperial registers of the 1521 Diet of Worms from A. Wrede, *Reichsakten unter Kaiser Karl V* (Gotha, 1896), 2:440ff. See further Brecht, "Gemeinsame Politik," 180–263; Ernst-Wilhelm Kohls, "Evangelische Bewegung und Kirchenordnungen in oberdeutschen Reichsstädten," *ZSS KA* 53 (1967): 110–34.

early in the course of the Lutheran Reformation, often adopted and adapted from neighboring polities and then amply amended in response to local concerns. Prussia had a preliminary reformation law in place in 1525, which was greatly expanded in 1540 and again in 1544. Hesse had a major reformation ordinance in 1526 with revised and expanded versions issued in 1533, 1537, and 1566. Brandenburg-Ansbach had its first reformation ordinance in place by 1526; it was heavily revised in the ordinance of Brandenburg-Nürnberg of 1533 and the Brandenburg Ordinance of 1540. Lünenburg had its first reformation law in 1527, until revised by the Brunswick-Lünenburg ordinance of 1542/43. This pattern continued in a number of territories, principalities, and duchies in the 1530s to 1550s.[32]

The reformers did not leave the promulgation of these new reformation laws to the vagaries of the political process. Many of the leading Evangelical theologians and jurists negotiated and drafted these new laws, and often also helped to implement them in the local consistories and courts. Luther himself helped to draft the new laws of Leisnig (1523) and Wittenberg (1533 and 1545), and also influenced the reformation ordinances of Göttingen (1530) and Herzberg (1538). Melanchthon's ideas dominated the new reformation laws of Nuremberg (1526), Wittenberg (1533), Herzberg (1538), Cologne (1543), and Mecklenburg (1552) and also lay at the heart of the territorial laws of Hesse (1526) and Saxony (1533).[33] Melanchthon also had a considerable influence on legal reforms in Tübingen, Frankfurt an der Oder, Leipzig, Rostock, Heidelberg, Marburg, and Jena.[34] Johannes Brenz helped to draft the early reformation laws of Schwäbisch-Hall (1526 and 1543) and Brandenburg-Nürnberg (1533), and was the principal draftsman of the massive reformation ordinances of Württemberg (1536, 1537, 1553, 1556, 1559).[35] Justus Jonas had a strong influence on the reformation ordinances of Wittenberg (1533, 1545), Saxony (1538), and Halle (1541). Andreas Osiander played a critical role in negotiating and promulgating the reformation laws of Brandenburg (1533) and Pfalzneuburg (1543). Johann Oldendorp helped to shape the reformation laws of Rostock (1530) and several revisions of the laws of Lübeck, Marburg, and Hesse. Martin Bucer had a strong hand in drafting the new laws of Strasbourg

---

[32] See Franz Lau and Ernst Bizer, *A History of the Reformation in Germany to 1555*, trans. Brian A. Hardy (London, 1969), 55ff.

[33] See Brecht, 3:287–332.

[34] Hartfelder, *Melanchthon als Praeceptor Germaniae* (Berlin, 1899), esp. 498ff.

[35] See James M. Estes, *Christian Magistrate and State Church: The Reforming Career of Johannes Brenz* (Toronto, 1982), 16ff.

(1524) and Ulm (1531) and also influenced the new reformation laws of Augsburg (1537), Kassel (1539), and Cologne (1543).

By far the most fertile legislative pen among the early reformers was that of the Wittenberg theologian, pastor, and schoolmaster Johannes Bugenhagen. Bugenhagen drafted the city reformation laws of Brunswick (1528 and 1543), Hamburg (1529), Lübeck (1531), Bremen (1534), and Hildesheim (1544). He also had a strong hand in drafting the laws for the territories of Pomerania (1535), Schleswig-Holstein (1542), Brunswick-Wolfenbüttel (1543), and the Kingdoms of Norway and Denmark (1537) (later revised by Melanchthon's famous Danish student Nicolaus Hemming). Through correspondence and consultation, Bugenhagen also worked his ideas into the reformation laws of several other cities and territories in Germany and abroad, including East Friesland (1529), Mindener (1530), Göttingen (1530), Herforder (1532 and 1534), Soester (1533), Brandenburg-Nürnberg (1540), and Osnabrück (1543).[36]

The reformers made ample use of scissors and paste in crafting these reformation laws. They regularly duplicated their own formulations and those of their closest co-religionists in drafting new laws. They corresponded with each other about the laws, and frequently circulated draft laws among their inner circle for comment and critique.[37] They referred to and paraphrased liberally the writings of the leading reformers, particularly those of Luther and Melanchthon, in crafting the provisions of religious doctrine, worship, and the sacraments. This close collaboration led to considerable uniformity among the new ordinances, and considerable legal appropriation of the reformers' cardinal theological ideas.

While these Lutheran reformation laws were very wide-ranging in subject matter, sophistication, and detail, they typically had lengthy provisions on: (1) religious doctrine, liturgy, and worship, and local forms of Church administration and supervision; (2) public religious morality – laws on blasphemy, Sabbath observance, false swearing, sumptuousness, public drunkenness, and the like; (3) poor relief and other forms of social welfare; (4) sex, marriage, and family life; and (5) education and public schools.

The first set of provisions featured a rather simple interplay between new Protestant theological doctrines and traditional legal forms, both

---

[36] See Kurd Schulz, "Bugenhagen als Schöpfer der Kirchenordnung," in Werner Rautenberg, ed., *Johann Bugenhagen: Beiträge zu seinem 400. Todestag* (Berlin, 1958), 51; Anneliese Sprengler-Ruppenthal, "Bugenhagen und das kanonische Recht," *ZSS KA* 75 (1989): 375. See also Melanchthon's funeral oration for Bugenhagen in *CR* 12:295.

[37] See, e.g., the detailed commentary by Luther, Jonas, Bugenhagen, and Melanchthon on the draft church ordinance of Brandenburg-Ansbach and the city of Nuremberg in *LW* 50:61–67.

canonist and Romanist.[38] The Reformation brought many important changes to spiritual life in the new Evangelical polities of Germany and these are reflected flatly in the new reformation laws: the resystematization of dogma; the truncation of the sacraments; the reforms of liturgy, devotional life, and the religious calendar; the vernacularization of the Bible and the distribution of the sermon; the expansion of catechesis and religious instruction; the revamping of corporate worship, congregational music, religious symbolism, Church art and architecture; the radical reforms of ecclesiastical discipline and local Church administration, and much more. But the actual civil law documents used to define and enforce these new theological and ecclesiastical changes were very much like the traditional canon law documents that they replaced. Moreover, some of these reformation ordinances retained a good deal of the traditional canon law in its local division of parishes and bishoprics, in the local commissioning of synods and councils, in the local laws of tithing, burial, advowson, benefices, and more.

A similar conversion and convergence of canon law into civil law is evident in the new Lutheran civil laws of morality. New Sabbath-day laws, issued by Evangelical princes and city councils, prohibited all forms of unnecessary labor and uncouth leisure on Sundays and holy days, and required faithful attendance at services, much in the style of the old canon law, but now to be enforced principally by civil courts. Other new civil laws prohibited blasphemy, sacrilege, witchcraft, sorcery, magic, alchemy, false oaths, and similar offenses. Sumptuary laws proscribed immodest apparel, wasteful living, and extravagant feasts and funerals. Entertainment laws placed strict limits on public drunkenness, boisterous celebration, gambling, and other games that involved fate, luck, and magic. Neither the Lutheran magistrates' emphasis on these moral offenses, nor their definition of them strayed far from the formulations of the medieval canon law. What was new was that these new subjects now fell primarily under civil law rather than under canon law, and were to be enforced primarily by state courts rather than Church courts.[39]

The third set of provisions, reforming the lore and law of social welfare, was a considerably more eclectic combination of canon law and civil law

---

[38] See, e.g., Sichelschmidt, *Recht aus christlicher Liebe*; Sprengler-Ruppenthal, "Das kanonische Recht"; Wolter, *Ius canonicum in iure civili*; Rau et al., eds., *Das Recht der Kirche*; Harold J. Berman, "The Interaction of Spiritual Law and Secular Law: An Historical Overview with Special Reference to Sixteenth-Century Lutheran Germany," in Michael Hoeflich, ed., *Lex et Romanitas: Essays for Alan Watson* (Berkeley, CA, 2000), 149–80.

[39] See sources and discussion in Grünberger, "Institutionalisierung"; id., "Die Institutionalisierung des Sittendiskurses durch Humanismus und Reformation im 15. und 16. Jahrhundert" (unpublished ms.).

norms, on the one hand, and of humanist and Evangelical learning, on the other. Prior to the sixteenth century, the Catholic Church taught that both poverty and charity were spiritually edifying. Voluntary poverty was a form of Christian sacrifice and self-denial that conferred spiritual benefits upon its practitioners and provided spiritual opportunities for others to accord them their charity. Itinerant monks and mendicants in search of alms were the most worthy exemplars of this ideal, but many other deserving poor were at hand as well. Voluntary charity, in turn, conferred spiritual benefits upon its practitioner, particularly when pursued as a work of penance and purgation in the context of the sacraments of penance or extreme unction. To be charitable to others was to serve Christ, who had said, "Inasmuch as ye have done it unto one of the least of these my brethren, ye have done it unto me" (Matthew 25:40).

These teachings helped to render the medieval Church, at least in theory, the primary object and subject of charity and social welfare. To give to the Church was the best way to give to Christ, since the Church was the body of Christ on earth. The Church thus received alms through the collections of its mendicant monks, the charitable offerings from its many pilgrims, the penitential offerings assigned to cancel sins, the final bequests designed to expedite purgation in the life hereafter, and much more. The Church also distributed alms through the diaconal work of the parishes, the hospitality of the monasteries, and the welfare services of the many Church-run almshouses, hospices, schools, chantries, and ecclesiastical guilds. A rich latticework of canonical and confessional rules calibrated these obligations and opportunities of individual and ecclesiastical charity, and governed the many charitable corporations, trusts, and foundations under the Church's general auspices.[40]

Already in the fourteenth and fifteenth centuries, however, a number of German cities and territories became active in the administration of social welfare, especially where local clergy did not or could not discharge

---

[40] For overviews, from various perspectives, see Brian Tierney, *Medieval Poor Law: A Sketch of Canonical Theory and its Application in England* (Berkeley/Los Angeles, 1959); Gilles Couvreur, *Les pauvres ont-ils des droits?* (Rome, 1961); Lindberg, *Beyond Charity*; Michel Mollatt, ed., *Etudes sur l'histoire de la pauvreté* (Sorbonne, 1974); Franz Ehrle, *Beiträge zur Geschichte und Reform der Armenpflege* (Freiburg im Breisgau, 1881); Wilhelm Liese, *Geschichte der Caritas* (Freiburg im Breisgau, 1922); Hans Liermann, *Handbuch des Stiftungsrechts* (Tübingen, 1963); Georg Ratzinger, *Geschichte der kirchlichen Armenpflege*, 2nd edn. (Freiburg im Breisgau, 1884); Carl R. Steinbecker, *Poor Relief in the Sixteenth Century* (Washington, DC, 1937), 1–17, 44–56; G. W. Uhlhorn, *Die christliche Liebestätigkeit in der alten Kirche* (Stuttgart, 1882–1890). For a sampling of primary sources, see Couvreur, *Les pauvres*, appendix, 285–320; Lindberg, *Beyond Charity*, 173ff.; Rudolf Weigand, *Die Naturrechtslehre der Legisten und Dekretisten von Irnerius bis Accursius und von Gratian bis Johannes Teutonicus* (Munich, 1967), 85ff. 307ff.; Jean-Claude Schmitt, *Les citations bibliques et canoniques dans les traités médiévaux sur la pauvreté (XIVe– XVe siècles)*, 2 vols. (Paris, 1994), 2:547ff.

their charitable services. In several locales, civil authorities placed firm limits on mendicant begging and on monastic property holdings. In others, they supervised and sometimes even took over the local clergy's collections and distributions of tithes and other funds for the poor. Wealthier German cities and territories began to establish and regulate their own chartered almshouses, hospitals, orphanages, and charitable guilds, sometimes in direct competition with local Church institutions.[41]

Moreover, an increasing number of local Church properties in Germany came to be held in a form of tenure called *frankelmoigne* ("free alms"). Lay donors would alienate property to a local diocese, parish, monastery, guild, or other unit by gift or testament. The donor, however, would sometimes also stipulate the charitable and related uses to which that property could be devoted – often on pain of forfeiture of the property to the estate of the donor in the event of its misuse, and often under the condition that such property be regulated by civil not ecclesiastical courts and authorities.[42] These instances of laicization and local regulation of social welfare were important prototypes and foundations for the Lutheran reformation of social welfare.

The Lutheran reformers rejected traditional teachings of both the spiritual idealization of poverty and the spiritual efficaciousness of charity. All persons were called to work the work of God in the world, they argued. They were not to be idle or to impoverish themselves voluntarily. Voluntary poverty was a form of social parasitism to be punished, not a symbol of spiritual sacrifice to be rewarded. Only the worthy local poor deserved charity, and only if they could not be helped by their immediate family members, the family being the "first school of charity." Charity, in turn, was not a form of spiritual self-enhancement. It was a vocation of the priesthood of believers. Charity brought no immediate spiritual reward to the giver. Instead, it brought spiritual opportunity to the receiver. The Evangelical doctrine of justification by faith alone undercut the spiritual efficacy of charity for the giver. Salvation came through faith in Christ, not through charity to one's neighbor. But the Evangelical doctrine of the priesthood of all believers enhanced the spiritual efficacy of charity for the receiver. Those who were already saved by faith became members of the priesthood of all believers. They were called to love and serve their neighbors charitably in imitation of Christ. Those who

---

[41] See sources and discussion in Robert Jütte, *Obrigkeitliche Armenfürsorge in den deutschen Reichsstädten der frühen Neuzeit* (Cologne/Vienna, 1984); Thomas Fischer, *Städtische Armut und Armenfürsorge im 15. und 16. Jahrhundert* (Göttingen, 1979); Knobler, "Luther and the Legal Concept of the Poor," 77ff.

[42] Berman, *Law and Revolution*, 237ff.; Liermann, *Handbuch des Stiftungsrechts*, 1:126ff.

received the charity of their neighbors would see in this personal sacrificial act the good works brought by faith, and so be moved to have faith themselves.[43]

Such Evangelical teachings accorded well with some of the anti-begging sentiments and laws of late medieval German cities and territories. The Lutheran reformers adopted and expanded these anti-begging laws with alacrity in the early 1520s and thereafter, often adorning these laws with ample discussion of their belief that it was every Christian's duty to work in a vocation and to avoid idle parasitism.[44] Such Evangelical teachings also accorded somewhat with traditional understandings of what Brian Pullan has aptly called "redemptive charity" – charity as a means of bringing the receiver into salvation.[45]

The reformers, however, also went beyond these late medieval teachings. They broadened their critique of itinerant mendicant monks into a full campaign to outlaw monasticism altogether and to confiscate monastic properties. They translated their belief in the spiritual efficacy of the direct personal relationship between giver and receiver into a new emphasis on local charity for the local poor, without dense administrative bureaucracies. Particularly the complex tangle of ecclesiastical guilds, endowments, foundations, and other charitable institutions of the Church was, for the early reformers, not only economically inefficient but spiritually inefficacious. The "redemptive charity" that the reformers had in mind came more in the direct personal encounter between the faithful giver and the grateful receiver, not so much in the conventional notion that the receiver should experience and receive charity within a Church institution.

The Lutheran reformers also rejected the traditional belief that the Church was to be the primary object and subject of charity. The Church,

---

43 See esp. Bucer, *DS*, 7:261 ff.; *LW* 31:29, 204; *LW* 35:46; *LW* 44:193; *LW* 49:27; and further on these and other reformers, Carter, *Beyond Charity*; Frank Peter Lane, "Poverty and Poor Relief in the German Church Orders of Johann Bugenhagen, 1485–1558" (PhD Diss., Ohio State University, 1974); Edward Lloyd Rice, "The Influence of the Reformation in Nuremberg's Provisions for Social Welfare, 1521–1528" (PhD Diss., Ohio State University, 1974); Robert Jütte, "Andreas Hyperius (1511–1564) und die Reform des frühneuzeitlichen Armenswesens," *AFR* 75 (1984): 113.

44 The relative influence of Evangelical versus Catholic and humanist teachings on these reforms is the subject of ample debate. See summary in Lindberg, *Beyond Charity*, 9ff. For good case studies of early Evangelical influence, see ibid., 128ff.; Otto Winckelmann, *Das Fürsorgewesen der Stadt Strassburg vor und nach der Reformation bis zum Ausgang des sechzehnten Jahrhunderts*, repr. (New York, 1971); id., "Die Armenordnungen von Nürnberg (1522), Kitzingen (1523), Regensburg (1523), und Ypern (1525)," *AFR* 11 (1914): 1.

45 Brian Pullan, "Support and Redeem: Charity and Poor Relief in Italian Cities from the Fourteenth to the Seventeenth Centuries," *Continuity and Change* 3 (1988): 177, 188. See further id., *Rich and Poor in Renaissance Florence: The Social Institutions of a Catholic State to 1620* (Oxford, 1971).

they argued, was called to preach the Word, to administer the sacraments, and to discipline the saints. For the local church to receive and administer charity beyond its immediate congregation distracted from its primary ministry. For the Church to run monasteries, almshouses, charities, hospices, orphanages, and more detracted from its essential mission. The local parish church should continue to receive the tithes of its members, as biblical laws taught. It should continue to tend to the immediate needs of its local members, as the apostolic Church had done. But most other gifts to the Church and the clergy were, in the reformers' view, misdirected. Most other forms of ecclesiastical charity, particularly those surrounding pilgrimages, penance, and purgation, were, for the reformers, types of "spiritual bribery," predicated on the fabricated sacraments of penance and extreme unction and on the false teachings of purgatory and works righteousness.[46]

In place of traditional ecclesiastical charities, the reformers instituted a series of local civil institutions of welfare, usually administered directly by local townsfolk. Built on late medieval prototypes, these local welfare systems were centered on the community chest, administered by the local magistrate, and directed to the local, worthy poor and needy. The community chest was, at first, comprised of the Church's monastic properties and endowments that had been confiscated in the early years of the Reformation. These community chests were eventually supplemented by local taxation and private donation. In larger cities and territories, several such community chests were established, and the poor were closely monitored in the use of their services. At minimum, this system provided food, clothing, and shelter for the poor, and emergency relief in times of war, disaster, or pestilence. In larger and wealthier communities, the community chest eventually supported the development of a more comprehensive local welfare system featuring public orphanages, workhouses, boarding schools, vocational centers, hospices, and more, administered or supervised by the local magistrate. These more generous forms of social welfare the Lutheran reformers considered to be an essential service of the Christian magistrate, the father of the community called to care for his political children.[47]

---

[46] See esp. *LW* 35:45–73; *LW* 45:273–310.

[47] The best early example is the Leisnig "Ordinance of a Common Chest" (1523), influenced and prefaced by Luther and a model for several later evangelical polities. See *LW* 45:159. See further Knobler, "Luther's Concept of the Poor," 193ff.; Harold J. Grimm, "Luther's Contribution to the Sixteenth-Century Organization of Poor Relief," *AFR* 61 (1970): 222; William J. Wright, "Reformation Contributions to the Development of Public Welfare Policy in Hesse," *Journal of Modern History* 49 (1977): D1145; id., *Capitalism, the State, and the Lutheran Reformation: Sixteenth-Century Hesse* (Athens, OH, 1988).

The last two sets of provisions in the sixteenth-century reformation ordinances – on marriage and education – will occupy us at greater length in the next two chapters. Each of these legal subjects had been at the heart of medieval theology and canon law. Each was at the heart of the new Lutheran theology and jurisprudence, and among the first difficult subjects that early Lutherans sought to reform. The reforms that the early Lutherans advocated for these subjects, often on explicitly theological grounds, were translated quickly into new legal norms and forms.

6. Woodcut from Johannes Cogelerus, *Imagines elegantissimae: quae multum lucis ad intelligendos doctrinae Christianae locos adferre possunt, Collectae, partim ex praelectionibus Domini Philippi Melanthonis, partim ex scriptis Patrum a Iohanne Cogelero, Verbi diuini ministro Stetini cum praefatione D. Georgij Maioris* (Wittenberg, 1558)

Inside a church building, a Protestant preacher joins the hands of a man (with one attendant) and a woman (with three attendants) together in a public marriage ceremony.

6

The mother of all earthly laws: The reformation of marriage law

Questions of sex, marriage, and family life occupied Lutheran theologians and jurists from the very beginning of the Reformation. The leading theological lights – Martin Luther, Philip Melanchthon, Martin Bucer, Johannes Bugenhagen, and Johannes Brenz – all prepared lengthy tracts on the subject in the 1520s. A score of leading jurists took up legal questions of marriage in their legal opinions and commentaries, often working under the direct inspiration of Evangelical theology and theologians. Virtually every German polity that converted to the Evangelical cause had new marriage laws on the books within a decade of its acceptance of the Reformation, which was then heavily revised in subsequent generations.

The reformers' early preoccupation with marriage was driven in part by their theology. Many of the core issues of the Reformation were affected by the prevailing Catholic theology and canon law of marriage. The Church's jurisdiction over marriage was, for the reformers, a particularly flagrant example of the Church's usurpation of the magistrate's authority. The Catholic sacramental concept of marriage, on which the Church predicated its jurisdiction, raised deep questions of sacramental theology and biblical interpretation. The canonical prohibition on the marriage of clergy and monastics stood sharply juxtaposed to Evangelical doctrines of the priesthood and of the Christian vocation. The canon law impediments to marriage, its prohibitions on complete divorce and remarriage, and its close regulations of sexuality, parenting, and education all stood in considerable tension with the reformers' interpretation of biblical teaching. That a child could enter marriage without parental permission or Church consecration betrayed, in the reformers' views, basic responsibilities of family, Church, and state to children. Issues of marriage doctrine and law thus involved and epitomized many of the cardinal theological issues of the Lutheran Reformation.

The reformers' early preoccupation with marriage was driven, in part, by their jurisprudence. The starting assumption of the budding Lutheran theories of law, society, and politics was that the earthly kingdom was governed by the three natural estates of household, Church, and state. *Hausvater, Gottesvater,* and *Landesvater; paterfamilias, patertheologicus,* and *paterpoliticus* – these were the three natural offices through which God revealed Himself and reflected His authority in the world. These three offices and orders stood equal before God and before each other. Each was called to discharge essential tasks in the earthly kingdom without impediment or interference from the other. The reform of marriage, therefore, was as important as the reform of the Church and the state. Indeed, marital reform was even more urgent, for the marital household was, in the reformers' view, the "oldest," "most primal," and "most essential" of the three estates, yet the most deprecated and subordinated of the three. Marriage is the "mother of all earthly laws," Luther wrote, and the source from which the Church, the state, and other earthly institutions flowed. "God has most richly blessed this estate above all others, and in addition, has bestowed on it and wrapped up in it everything in the world, to the end that this estate might be well and richly provided for. Married life therefore is no jest or presumption; it is an excellent thing and a matter of divine seriousness."[1]

The reformers' early preoccupation with marriage was driven, in part, by their politics. A number of early leaders of the Reformation faced aggressive prosecution by the Catholic Church and its political allies for violation of the canon law of marriage and celibacy.[2] Among the earliest Protestant leaders were ex-priests and ex-monastics who had forsaken their orders and vows, and often married shortly thereafter.[3] Indeed, one of the acts of solidarity with the new Protestant cause was to marry or

---

[1] *TC* 639–41 and *WA* 30/1:152. See *WA TR* 3, No. 3528, *LW* 54:222–3: marriage is "a divine institution from which everything proceeds and without which the whole world would have remained empty, and all creatures would have been meaningless." See similar views in *TC* 611ff.; *WA* 49:297ff.; *WA* 2:734; *LW* 44:81ff.; *LC* (1555), 323; *TC* 363–83; and further sources above pp. 92–4, 100–01, 109–10 and below pp. 217, 230–2 and in Reinhard Schwarz, "*Ecclesia, oeconomia, politia:* Sozialgeschichte und fundamentalethische Aspekte der protestantischen Drei-Stände Lehre," in Horst Renz and Friedrich-Wilhelm Graf, eds., *Protestantismus und Neuzeit* (Gütersloh, 1984), 3: 78.

[2] See several examples in Brecht, 2:91–2.

[3] One of the earliest examples was the Wittenberg wedding of ex-monk Wenzeslaus Linck in April, 1523, a lavish ceremony which Luther and several other early reformers attended and celebrated. See Bernd Moeller, "Wenzel Lincks Hochzeit: Ueber Sexualität, Keuscheit und Ehe in der frühen Reformation," *Zeitschrift für Theologie und Kirche* 97 (2000): 317. The wedding two years later of ex-monk Luther to ex-nun Katherine von Bora was considerably more modest. See Brecht, 2:195ff. One of the four witnesses at Luther's wedding was the distinguished Wittenberg jurist Johann Apel, an ex-priest and canonist who had been defrocked and excommunicated from the Catholic Church two years before for his secret wedding to an ex-nun and had thereafter joined the Evangelical cause. See Apel, *Defensio,* with preface by Luther.

divorce in open violation of the canon law and in defiance of a bishop's instructions. This was not just an instance of crime and disobedience. It was an outright scandal, particularly when an ex-monk such as Brother Martin Luther married an ex-nun such as Sister Katherine von Bora – a *prima facie* case of spiritual incest.[4] As Catholic Church courts began to prosecute these canon law offenses, Protestant theologians and jurists rose to the defense of their co-religionists, producing a welter of briefs, letters, sermons, and pamphlets that denounced traditional norms and pronounced a new theology of marriage.

Evangelical theologians treated marriage not as a sacramental institution of the heavenly kingdom, but as a social estate of the earthly kingdom. Marriage was a natural institution that served the goods and goals of mutual love and support of husband and wife, procreation and nurture of children, and mutual protection of spouses from sexual sin. All adults, preachers and others alike, should pursue the calling of marriage, for all were in need of the comforts of marital love and of protection from sexual sin. When properly structured and governed, the marital household served as a model of authority, charity, and pedagogy in the earthly kingdom and as a vital instrument for the reform of Church, state, and society. Parents served as "bishops" to their children. Siblings served as priests to each other. The household altogether – particularly the Christian household of the married minister – was a source of "evangelical impulses" in society.[5]

Though divinely created and spiritually edifying, however, marriage and the family remained a social estate of the earthly kingdom. All parties could partake of this institution, regardless of their faith. Though subject to divine law and clerical counseling, marriage and family life came within the jurisdiction of the magistrate, not the cleric; of the civil law, not the canon law. The magistrate, as God's vice-regent of the earthly kingdom, was to set the laws for marriage formation, maintenance, and dissolution; child custody, care, and control; family property, inheritance, and commerce.

Political leaders rapidly translated this new Protestant gospel into civil law.[6] Just as the civil act of marriage often came to signal a person's

---

[4] See Carter Lindberg, "The Future of a Tradition: Luther and the Family," in Dean O. Wenthe *et al.*, eds., *All Theology is Christology: Essays in Honor of David P. Scaer* (Fort Wayne, IN, 2000), 133–151, at 134.

[5] See Gustav M. Bruce, *Luther as an Educator* (Westport, CT, 1979), 123; Gerald Strauss, *Luther's House of Learning: Indoctrination of the Young in the German Reformation* (Baltimore, MD, 1978), 112 and more generally William Lazareth, *Luther on the Christian Home* (Philadelphia, 1960).

[6] There is an ample debate among historians over whether magistrates embraced Protestantism out of convenience, to seize the Catholic Church's ample jurisdiction and wealth, or out of the

conversion to Protestantism, so the Civil Marriage Act came to symbolize a political community's acceptance of the new Evangelical theology. Political leaders were quick to establish comprehensive new marriage laws for their polities, sometimes building on late medieval civil laws that had already controlled some aspects of this institution. The first reformation ordinances on marriage and family life were promulgated in 1522. More than sixty such laws were on the books by the time of Luther's death in 1546. The number of new marriage laws more than doubled again in the second half of the sixteenth century in Evangelical portions of Germany. Collectively, these new Evangelical marriage laws: (1) shifted primary marital jurisdiction from the Church to the state; (2) strongly encouraged the marriage of clergy; (3) denied that celibacy, virginity, and monasticism were superior callings to marriage; (4) denied the sacramentality of marriage and the religious tests and impediments traditionally imposed on its participants; (5) modified the doctrine of consent to betrothal and marriage, and required the participation of parents, peers, priests, and political officials in the process of marriage formation; (6) sharply curtailed the number of impediments to betrothal and putative marriages; and (7) introduced divorce, in the modern sense, on proof of adultery, malicious desertion, and other faults, with a subsequent right to remarriage at least for the innocent party. These changes eventually brought profound and permanent change to the life, lore, and law of marriage in Evangelical Germany.[7]

THE INHERITANCE

Marriage and family life had been a central concern of the Christian Church from the very beginning, and the Lutheran reformers rehearsed

conviction that it was their task to reform and rule the earthly kingdom along new confessional lines. For diverse views see, e.g., Ozment, *Protestants*, esp. 67ff.; R. Po-Chia Hsia, *Social Discipline in the Reformation: Central Europe 1550–1750* (London and New York, 1989); Heinrich Richard Schmidt, *Konfessionalisierung im 16. Jahrhundert* (Munich, 1992); O'Malley, *Trent and all That*.

[7] This chapter is, in part, a distillation and update of my *From Sacrament to Contract*, chaps. 1–2, which includes extensive citations to the primary and secondary literature (hereafter *FSC*). Several important studies have emerged since I wrote those chapters, many with extensive bibliographies: Steven Ozment, *Ancestors: The Loving Family in Old Europe* (Cambridge, MA, 2001); id., *Flesh and Spirit: Private Life in Early Modern Europe* (New York, 1999); id., *The Bürgermeister's Daughter: Scandal in a Sixteenth-Century German Town* (New York, 1996); Susan C. Karant-Nunn, *The Reformation of Ritual: An Interpretation of Early Modern Germany* (London and New York, 1997), 6–42; Harrington, *Reordering Marriage and Society*; Uwe Sibeth, *Eherecht und Staatsbildung: Ehegesetzgebung und Eherechtsprechung in der Landgrafschaft Hessen(-Kassel) in der frühen Neuzeit* (Darmstadt, 1994); H. Selderjhuis, *Marriage and Divorce in the Thought of Martin Bucer*, trans. John Vriend and Lyle D. Biersma (Kirksville, MO, 1999); Lindberg, "Luther and the Family"; Helmar Junghaus, "Die evangelische Ehe," in Martin Treu, ed., *Katherina von Bora, die Lutherin* (Wittenberg, 1999):1; Scott Hendrix, "Luther on Marriage," *Lutheran Quarterly* 14/3 (2000): 335.

this tradition at length in grounding and situating their theology and law of marriage. It is worth our rehearsing this history at some length, too, to see precisely the continuity and discontinuity between traditional and Evangelical lore and law.

Theology of marriage

The earliest Church Fathers and apostolic canons taught that the institution of marriage was created and ordered by God. Already in Paradise, God had brought the first man and the first woman together, and commanded them to "be fruitful and multiply" (Genesis 1:28). God had created them as social creatures, naturally inclined and attracted to each other. God had given them the physical capacity to join together and to beget children. God had commanded them to love, help, and nurture each other and to inculcate in each other and in their children the love of God, neighbor, and self. These duties and qualities of marriage continued after the fall into sin. After the Fall, however, marriage also became a remedy for lust, a balm to incontinence. Rather than allowing sinful persons to burn with lust, God provided the remedy of marriage, in order for parties to direct their natural drives and passions to the service and love of the spouse, the child, and the broader community.

On this foundation, Augustine, Bishop of Hippo (354–430), had developed his famous theory that marriage has three inherent goods (*bona*).[8] Marriage "is the ordained means of procreation (*proles*), the guarantee of chastity (*fides*), and the bond of permanent union (*sacramentum*)."[9] As a created, natural means of procreation, Christian marriage rendered sexual intercourse licit. As a contract of fidelity, marriage gave husband and wife an equal power over the other's body, an equal right to demand that the other spouse avoid adultery, and an equal claim to the "service, in a certain measure, of sustaining each other's weakness, for the avoidance of illicit intercourse."[10] As a "certain sacramental bond," marriage was a source and symbol of permanent union between Christians.[11] "[M]arriage bears a kind of sacred bond," Augustine wrote; "it can be dissolved in no way except by the death of one of the parties."[12]

---

[8] Augustine, *The City of God Against the Pagans*, trans. and ed. R. W. Dyson (New York/Cambridge, 1998), XIV.10, 21, 22; XV.16; XIX.7, 14.

[9] Id., *On Original Sin*, chap. 39, in Philip Schaff and Henry Wace, eds., *A Second Library of Nicene and Post-Nicene Fathers of the Christian Church*, 2nd. ser., repr., 15 vols. (Grand Rapids, MI, 1952), 5:251.

[10] Id., "Adulterous Marriage," in Augustine, *Treatises on Marriage and other Subjects*, trans. R. J. Wilcox et al., ed. Roy J. Deferrari (New York, 1955), chaps. 4–7.

[11] Id., *On Marriage and Concupiscence*, chaps. 11, 19, in *Fathers Library*, 5:261, 271.

[12] Id., "Adulterous Marriage," chap. 15.

Procreation, fidelity, and sacrament: These were the three goods of marriage, in Augustine's view. They were the reason why the institution of marriage was good. They were why participation in marriage was good. They were the goods that a person could hope and expect to realize upon marrying. Augustine usually listed the goods of marriage in this order, giving first place to the good of procreation.[13] Augustine, however, did not call procreation the primary good of marriage, and the others secondary. He sometimes changed the order of his list of marital goods to "fidelity, procreation, and sacrament."[14] Even when he listed procreation as the first marital good, Augustine made clear that spousal fidelity and sacramental stability were essential for a marriage to be good – and sufficient when married couples were childless or their children had left the household.[15]

While this patristic teaching on marriage was subject to endless variation and amendment in subsequent centuries, the most critical transformation came during the Papal Revolution of ca. 1075–1300. This was the era when the Catholic clergy, led by Pope Gregory VII (1073–85), threw off their royal and civil rulers and established the Roman Catholic Church as an autonomous legal and political corporation within Western Christendom. The Church's revolutionary rise to power triggered an enormous transformation of Western society, politics, and culture. The first modern Western universities were established in Italy, France, and England, with their core faculties of law, theology, and medicine devoted to the study of the rediscovered ancient texts of Greek philosophy, Roman law, and patristic theology.[16]

It was in this revolutionary context that the Church developed a detailed systematic theology and law of marriage. From the twelfth century forward, the Church's doctrine of marriage was categorized, systematized, and refined, notably in the works of Hugh of St. Victor, Peter Lombard, and Thomas Aquinas, and the scores of thick glosses and commentaries on their texts published in subsequent centuries.[17] From

---

[13] Id., *De incompetentibus nuptiis*, II.12, in Deferrari, ed., *St. Augustine*, 116 (emphasized added). See also id., *Contra Faustum Manichaeum*, in Sancti Aureli Augustini, *De utilitate credendi . . . Contra Faustum* (Vindoboani, 1891), chap. 19, n. 26.

[14] Id., *Commentary on the Literal Meaning of Genesis*, bk. 2, chap. 7, n.12.

[15] Id., "Adulterous Marriage," chap. 3. See further John J. Hugo, *St. Augustine on Nature, Sex, and Marriage* (Chicago, 1969), 126ff.; Augustine Regan, "The Perennial Value of Augustine's Theology of the Goods of Marriage," *Studia Moralia* 21 (1983): 351–78.

[16] See Berman, *Law and Revolution*.

[17] See esp. Hugh of St. Victor, *On the Sacraments of the Christian Faith*, Part II, trans. R. Deferrari (Cambridge, MA, 1951); Petrus Lombardus, *Libri IV sententiarum* (1150), 2nd rev. edn. (Florence,

the twelfth century forward, the Church's canon law of marriage was also systematized, first in Gratian's *Decretum* (c. 1140), then in a welter of later legal commentaries and new papal and conciliar laws that eventually would form the *Corpus iuris canonici*.[18]

Medieval theologians and canonists treated marriage in a three-fold manner: (1) as a created, natural association, subject to the laws of nature; (2) as a consensual contract, subject to the general laws of contract; and (3) as a sacrament of faith, subject to the spiritual laws of the Church.

First, marriage was regarded as a created natural association, which served, in Augustine's phrase, both as "a duty for the sound and a remedy for the sick."[19] As a created, natural institution, marriage was subject to the law of nature, communicated in reason and conscience, and often confirmed in the Bible. This natural law, medieval writers taught, communicated God's will that fit persons marry when they reach the age of puberty, that they conceive children and nurture and educate them, and that they remain naturally bonded to their blood and kin, serving them in times of need, frailty, and old age. It prescribed heterosexual, life-long unions between couples, featuring mutual support and faithfulness. It required love for one's spouse and children.[20] It proscribed bigamy, incest, bestiality, buggery, polygamy, sodomy, and other unnatural relations.[21]

Many medieval writers, however – following St. Paul's teachings in 1 Corinthians 7 – subordinated the duty of propagation to that of celibate contemplation, the natural drive for sexual union to the spiritual drive for beatitude.[22] For, as Peter Lombard put it: "The first institution [of marriage in Paradise] was commanded, the second permitted . . . to the human race for the purpose of preventing fornication. But this permission, because it does not select better things, is a remedy not a reward; if anyone rejects it, he will deserve judgment of death. An act which is

---

1916), bk. 4, dist. 26–42; Aquinas, *Comm. Sent.*, Sent. IV, Dist. 26ff., revised in *ST* III Supp., qq. 41–68; *SCG* bk. III, Pt. II, chs. 122–6.

[18] See collection in Emil Friedberg, ed., *Corpus iuris canonici*, 2 vols. (Leipzig, 1879–81). See list of later canon law titles in Coing, 1:1011 ff., with excerpts in Weigand, ed., *Naturrechtslehre*, 283ff. and detailed analysis in James A. Brundage, *Law, Sex, and Christian Society in Medieval Europe* (Chicago, 1987), 176–550.

[19] Lombardus, *Libri sententiarum*, bk. 4, dist. 26.2; Aquinas, *ST*, II–II, qq. 151–6; III, q. 41, art. 1; Hugh of St. Victor, *Sacraments*, 325–9.

[20] See John T. Noonan, "Marital Affection in the Canonists," *Studia Gratiana* 12 (1967): 489; Jean Leclercq, *Monks on Marriage: A Twelfth-Century View* (New York, 1982), 12–39, 72–81; Alan MacFarlane, *Marriage and Love in England, 1300–1840* (Oxford, 1986), 124ff., 321ff.

[21] See texts in Weigand, *Naturrechtslehre*, 283–98.

[22] Lombardus, *Libri sententiarum*, bk. 4, dist. 26.3–4; Aquinas, *ST* III Supp., q. 41, art. 2. See further sources and texts in Joseph Friesen, *Geschichte des kanonischen Eherechts bis zum Verfall der Glossenliteratur*, 2nd edn., repr. (Aalen, 1963), 25ff.

allowed by permission, however, is voluntary, not necessary."[23] After the fall into sin, marriage remained a duty, but only for those tempted by sexual sin. For those not so tempted, marriage was an inferior option. It was better and more virtuous to pursue the spiritual life of celibacy and contemplation than the temporal life of marriage and family. For marriage was regarded as an institution of the natural sphere, not the supernatural sphere. Though ordained by God and good, it served primarily for the protection of the human community, not for the perfection of the individual. Participation in it merely kept a person free from sin and vice. It did not contribute directly to his or her virtue. The celibate, contemplative life, by contrast, was a calling of the supernatural sphere. Participation in it increased a person's virtue and aided the pursuit of beatitude.[24] To this pursuit, Thomas Aquinas put it, "marriage is a very great obstacle," for it forces a person to dwell on the carnal and natural rather than the spiritual and supernatural aspects of life.[25]

Secondly, marriage was also a contractual relation subject to general rules of contract. Marriage required the mutual consent of the parties if it was to be legitimate and binding. "What makes a marriage is not the consent to cohabitation or the carnal copula," Peter Lombard wrote; "it is the consent to conjugal society that does."[26] The form and function of this conjugal society, and the requirements for entrance into it, were set by the laws of nature. But the choice of whether to enter this society lay with the parties. "Marriage, therefore," said Peter Lombard, "is the marital union between persons legitimate according to the [natural] law, who persevere in a single sharing of life."[27]

As a contract, marriage was subject to the general moral principles of contract that prevailed in medieval canon law and civil law.[28] One such principle was freedom of contract, and this applied equally to marriage contracts.[29] Marriage contracts entered into by force, fear, or fraud, or through inducement of parents, masters, or feudal or manorial lords, were thus not binding.[30] A second general principle of contract was that consensual agreements, entered into with or without formalities, were

---

[23] Lombardus, *Libri sententiarum*, bk. 4, dist. 26.3.

[24] Christopher N. L. Brooke, *The Medieval Idea of Marriage* (Oxford/New York, 1991), 61–92.

[25] Aquinas, *ST* III Supp., q. 41, art. 2.

[26] Lombardus, *Libri sententiarum*, bk. 4, dist. 28.4. For earlier views, see Brundage, *Law, Sex, and Christian Society*, 235–42, 260–78.

[27] Lombardus, *Libri sententiarum*, bk. 4, dist. 27.2.   [28] See Berman, *Faith and Order*, 190–6.

[29] John T. Noonan, *Canons and Canonists in Context* (Goldbach, 1997), 173–98.

[30] See Charles J. Reid, "The Canonistic Contribution to the Western Rights Tradition," *Boston College Law Review* 33 (1991): 37, 73–80.

legally binding. Absent proof of mistake or frustration, or some condition that would render the contract unjust, either party could petition a court to enforce its terms. This general principle also applied to marriage contracts. Both husband and wife had an equal right to sue in court for enforcement even of a naked promise of marriage, for discharge of an essential and licit condition to marriage, or for vindication of their conjugal rights to the body of their spouse.[31]

Thirdly, marriage was also raised by Christ to the dignity of a sacrament and was thus subject to the Church's spiritual laws.[32] Unlike the other six sacraments, however, marriage required no formalities and no clerical or lay instruction, witness, or participation. The two parties were themselves "ministers of the sacrament." Their consciences instructed them in the taking of the sacrament, and their own testimony was considered sufficient evidence to validate their marriages in a case of dispute. Although the Fourth Lateran Council of 1215 and later canon laws strongly encouraged the couple to seek the consent of their parents, to publish their banns for marriage in the church, to solemnize their union with the blessing of the priest, to invite witnesses to the wedding, and to comply with the marital customs of their domicile, none of these steps was an absolute requirement.

Like the other six sacraments, marriage was conceived to be an instrument of sanctification that, when contracted between Christians, caused and conferred grace upon those who put no obstacle in its way. Marriage sanctified the Christian couple by allowing them to comply with God's law for marriage, and by reminding them that Christ the bridegroom took the Church as His bride and accorded it His highest love and devotion, even to death. It sanctified the Christian community by enlarging the Church and by educating its children as people of God. The natural marital functions of propagation and education were thus given spiritual significance when performed by Christians within the extended Christian Church.

When performed as a Christian sacrament, marriage transformed the relationship of a husband and wife, much as baptism transformed the character of the baptized. In baptism, the seemingly simple ritual act

---

[31] See Rudolf Weigand, *Die bedingte Eheschliessung im kanonischen Recht* (Munich, 1963); Reid, "The Canonistic Contribution," 80–91.

[32] Jaroslav Pelikan, *Reformation of Church and Dogma (1300–1700)* (Chicago, 1984), 51 ff.; Brundage, *Law, Sex, and Christian Society*, 430ff. Luther's teacher, Gabriel Biel, referred to the sacrament of marriage as "the most excellent and first of all by the moment and place of its institution and by the signification and efficacy of its end": *Sermones dominicales* (Hagenau, 1510), XIX, quoting translation by Harrington in *Reordering Marriage*, 60.

of sprinkling water on the forehead spiritually transformed the baptized party, canceling the original sin of Adam, promising the baptized party divine aid and protection in life, and welcoming the baptized believer into the sanctuary of the Church, the spiritual care of parents and godparents, and the community and communion of the congregation. Similarly in marriage, the simple ritual act of a Christian man and woman coming together consensually in marriage spiritually transformed their relationship, removing the sin of sexual intercourse, promising divine help in fulfilling their marital and parental duties, welcoming them into the hierarchy of institutions that comprised the Church universal.[33]

It was the simple exchange of present promises between Christian parties that rendered this union sacramental, and triggered God's sanctifying grace. Neither consecration of the marriage through a church wedding nor consummation of the marriage through sexual intercourse were critical in the sacramental process. Even a secretly contracted, unconsummated marriage between a man and a woman capable of entering conjugal society in accordance with natural law could be an instrument of sacramental grace. It was the mutual exchange of wills, the genuine union of mind to be married, that triggered the conferral of sacramental grace. The fruits of that sacramental grace pervaded the institution from that time forward.[34]

Once this channel of sacramental grace was properly opened, it could not be closed. A marriage properly contracted between Christians, in accordance with the laws of nature, was thus an indissoluble union, a permanently open channel of grace. Thomas Aquinas captured this in a critical passage on the indissolubility of marriage:

[S]ince the sacraments effect what they figure, it is to be believed that grace is conferred through this sacrament on the spouses, whereby they might belong to the union of Christ and the Church. And this is very necessary to them so that as they concern themselves with carnal and earthly matters, they do not become detached from Christ and the Church. Now since the union of husband and wife designates the union of Christ and the Church, the figure must correspond with that which it signifies. Now the union of Christ and the Church is a union of one to another, and it is to last in perpetuity. For there is only one Church . . . and Christ will never be separated from His Church. As he himself says in the last chapter of Matthew, "Behold I am with you even unto the end of the world. . . ." It follows necessarily then that a marriage, in so far as it is a sacrament of the Church, must be one holding to another indivisibly.[35]

---

[33] See esp. Theodore Mackin, *What is Marriage?* (New York, 1982), 20–2, 31–3, 332–3.
[34] *ST* II–II, q. 100, art. 2; X.4.1.14.   [35] *SCG* IV.78.

Aquinas went on to integrate this medieval understanding of marriage as a natural, contractual, and sacramental institution with the traditional Augustinian understanding of the marital goods of procreation, faith, and sacrament.[36] If marriage is viewed as a natural institution, Aquinas argued, procreation (*proles*) is the primary good. Building on Augustine and other early writers, Aquinas argued that man and woman are naturally inclined to come together for the sake of having children, and that nature teaches the licit means of doing so is through a voluntary act of marriage.[37] Procreation, however, means more than just conceiving children. It also means rearing and educating them for spiritual and temporal living. The good of procreation cannot be achieved in this fuller sense simply through the licit union of husband and wife in sexual intercourse. It also requires maintenance of a faithful, stable, and permanent union of husband and wife, so that both mother and father may participate in the education and rearing of their children. In this natural sense, the primary good of marriage is procreation; the secondary goods are faith and sacramental stability.[38]

If marriage is viewed as a contractual association, faith (*fides*) is the primary good. Marital faith is not a spiritual faith, but a faith of justice, Aquinas argued. It means keeping faith, being faithful, holding faithfully to one's promises made in the contract of marriage. Marital faith requires, as Augustine had said, forgoing sexual intercourse with another and honoring the "connubial debt" (that is, yielding to the reasonable sexual advances of one's spouse). But marital faith also involves the commitment to be indissolubly united with one's spouse in body and mind, to be the "greatest of friends," to be willing to share fully and equally in the person, property, lineage, and reputation – indeed, in the "whole life" – of one's spouse. It is to be and bear with each other in youth and in old age, in sickness and in health, in prosperity and adversity. Marital faith, in this richer understanding, is a good in itself, Aquinas insisted. It need not necessarily be expected or intended for the procreation of children; indeed, a marriage promise need not even be consummated to be valid and binding.[39] In this contractual sense, the primary good of marriage is faith (*fides*); the secondary goods are sacrament and procreation.[40]

---

[36] Comm. Sent. IV. Dist. 26ff.; see also in *ST* III Supp., q. 49; *SCG*, Bk. III, Pt. II, ch. 122–6.

[37] *Comm. Sent.* IV. Dist. 26, q. 1; Dist. 33, q. 1.

[38] Ibid. *Comm. Sent.* IV. Dist. 26, q. 1; *ST* III Supp., q. 49, art. 2–3, 5; *SCG*, III.II.123.1–10; ibid., 124.3.

[39] *Comm. Sent.* IV. Dist. 26, q. 2; 27, q. 1; 31, q. 1; 33, q. 1; 41, q. 1; *ST* III Supp., qq. 42, 47, 49; SCG III.II.123.3,4, 8; 124.4–5; 125.6; 126.1–6. See further John Finnis, *Aquinas: Moral, Political, and Legal Theory* (Oxford, 1998), 143–148.

[40] *ST* III Supp. q. 29, art. 2.

If marriage is viewed as a spiritual institution, Aquinas wrote, "sacrament is in every way the most important of the three marriage goods, since it belongs to marriage considered as a sacrament of grace; while the other two belong to it as an office of nature; and a perfection of grace is more excellent than a perfection of nature."[41]

Aquinas' understanding of the good of *sacramentum* went well beyond the formulations of Augustine. Augustine called marriage a sacrament to demonstrate its symbolic stability. Aquinas called marriage a sacrament to demonstrate its spiritual efficacy. Augustine said that marriage as a perennial symbol of Christ's bond to the Church should not be dissolved. Aquinas said that marriage as a permanent channel of sacramental grace could not be dissolved. Augustine called marriage a sacrament because it was indissoluble. Aquinas called marriage indissoluble because it was a sacrament.

Thomas Aquinas' elegant integration of the three goods of marriage found a growing team of champions in the fourteenth through sixteenth centuries. Luther, Melanchthon, and other early Evangelical reformers knew Aquinas' and Augustine's theories in depth, and they started many of their criticisms and many of their reforms of the tradition with their teachings, rather than those of later medieval writers, primarily in mind.

The canon law of marriage [42]

The medieval Church built a complex and comprehensive canon law of marriage upon this theological foundation that was enforced throughout much of Germany by the Church courts.

The canon law distinguished three stages of consent in marriage: (1) the betrothal or promise to marry in the future ("I, Jack, promise to take you, Jill, to be my wife"); (2) the promise to be married in the present, which constitutes a true and valid union even without sexual intercourse ("I, Jill, now take you, Jack, as my husband"); and (3) the consummation of the marriage by voluntary sexual intercourse. None of these stages in the formation of marriage required much formality to be valid and enforceable. The first two steps required only the oral exchange of words,

---

[41] *Comm. Sent.* IV. Dist. 31, q. 2; *ST* III Supp., q. 49, art. 3.

[42] On the medieval canon law of marriage, see esp. Brundage, *Sex, Marriage, and Christian Society*, 229–550; R. H. Helmholz, *Marriage Litigation in Medieval England* (Cambridge, 1974), 25–111; Rudolph Sohm, *Das Recht der Eheschliessung aus dem deutschen und kanonischen Recht geschichtlich entwickelt*, repr. (Aalen, 1966), 107–86 and other sources listed in *FSC*, 223–6.

or (where parties were mute, deaf, or incapable of *de facto* exchange) some symbolic equivalent thereof. Parties could add much more to either stage – attaching legitimate conditions to the betrothal, swearing public oaths, or formalizing their wedding in a church followed by a public celebration, for example. But none of this was mandatory, even if preferred by the Church. No formal documents or witnesses were required for the betrothal. No authorities (whether parental, feudal, political, or ecclesiastical) were required to approve or to preside at the marriage. The consummation of marriage through intercourse also required little beyond voluntary participation by both parties. Forced intercourse, even within marriage, was a sin, and in aggravated cases also a crime.

The canon law recognized a variety of lawful impediments to the first stage of betrothal – that is, conditions under which either of the parties could break off their engagement without sin. A faithful party could spurn a fiancé(e) who had become a heretic or pagan, had abducted another (particularly a relative of the fiancé(e)), had been raped, had become impotent or severely deformed or deranged after betrothal, had deserted him or her for more than two years, or had failed to make a present promise within the time of engagement agreed upon by the parties. In all these cases, the innocent party was advised to petition a Church court to annul the betrothal. A religious vow of chastity or entry by either party into a religious order automatically nullified the agreement. A betrothal could also be dissolved by mutual consent of the parties.

A future promise to marry, followed by sexual intercourse, was viewed as a consummated marriage at canon law, and was considered valid, even if not licit. Intercourse after betrothal raised the presumption that the parties had implicitly consented to be truly married and to consummate their marriage. This presumption could be defeated if one of the parties proved that he or she had been forcibly abducted by the other. Even then the marriage was generally considered valid, though the abducting party was guilty of grave sin.

The canon law also recognized several impediments to the second stage of marital consent, that of contracting marriage in the present. These were of two types: (1) prohibitive impediments which rendered the contracting of marriage unlawful and sinful, but whose violation did not necessarily render the marriage invalid; and (2) diriment (or absolute) impediments which proscribed the contracting of marriage, and, if it was contracted, nullified and dissolved it completely, regardless of what the parties wished.

Prohibitive impediments dealt largely with cases of remarriage. They were captured in a medieval Latin rhyme used by the jurists in teaching the canon law to their students:

> Incestus, raptus, sponsatae mors uxoris
> Susceptus propriae sobolis, mors presbyteralis
> Vel si poeniteat solemniter, aut monialem
> Accipiat, prohibent haec coniugium sociandum.[43]

Incestus prevented a party from marrying a blood relative within the prohibited degrees. *Raptus* prevented marriage by a man who had raped or violently abducted his would-be spouse or her relative. *Spontanae mors uxoris* precluded remarriage to a man who had killed his prior wife, unless such killing was excused at law and the man fully exonerated. *Susceptus propriae sobolis* prevented remarriage to a person who had fraudulently or in bad faith become a godparent of his prior step-child in order to prevent his wife's remarriage in the event of his death. *Mors presbyteralis* prohibited marriage to a party who had killed an ordained priest or monastic. *Si poeniteat solemniter* precluded marriage to a party who had been assigned public and solemn penance for a mortal sin. *Si monialem accipiat* was an impediment that precluded marriage to a professed nun or monk.

Diriment impediments nullified even fully consummated putative marriages, leaving parties free to remarry, but often saddled with charges of serious and sometimes mortal sin. These impediments, too, were captured in a little Latin jingle for law students:

> Error, conditio, votum, cognatio, crimen
> Cultus disparitas, vis, ordo, ligamen, honestas,
> Dissensus, et affinis, si forte coire nequitis,
> Haec facienda vetant connubia, facta retractant.[44]

One set of diriment impediments sought to preserve the freedom of consent of both parties. Lack of consent by either party (*dissensus*) voided the marriage. Thus proof of extreme duress, fear, compulsion, or fraud (*vis*) – by a parent, putative spouse, or third party – impinged on consent and could invalidate a marriage contract, particularly if the action was brought soon after the union. A mistake (*error*) about the identity of the

---

43 Hostiensis, *Summa de Matrimonio*, quoted and discussed in James D. Scanlan, "Husband and Wife: Pre-Reformation Canon Law on Marriages of the Officials' Courts," in *An Introduction to Scottish Legal History* (Edinburgh, 1958), 69–81, at 74.
44 Ibid., 75.

other party, and in some cases of the virginity of the woman prior to marriage, was also a ground for nullification of a marriage.

A second set of diriment impediments defined which parties were free to give their consent. Parties who had, prior to the putative marriage, made religious vows of celibacy (*votum*) in one of the sacred orders of the Church (*ordo*) were eternally bound to God and thus could not bind themselves to another in marriage. Their marriage was thus automatically void. Christians could not contract marriage with infidels, Jews, or pagans (*cultus disparitas*), since the sacrament of baptism was a prerequisite for marriage. Such marriages could not symbolize the union of Christ with his faithful Church, and they were automatically annulled on discovery. Moreover, if a party departed from the faith after consummation and remained incorrigible, a Church court could declare the marriage void, particularly if the couple had children who would be forced to choose between their parents' faiths. Persons related up to the fourth degree either to a common ancestor or to a couple (whether married or not) who had engaged in sexual relations were prohibited from marrying. These were the impediments of consanguinity and affinity set out in Leviticus. They were grouped under the general topic of *cognatio*: Parents could not marry their adopted children or grandchildren, nor the spouses of their adopted children. One who baptized or confirmed a party or who became his or her godparent could not marry him or her; for these persons were considered to be the "spiritual fathers or mothers" of the party who received the sacrament. One could not marry the relative up to the fourth degree of a now-deceased fiancé(e) (*iustitia publicae honestae*). And a once adulterous spouse could not, upon becoming free to remarry, enter into marriage with his or her former paramour if he or she contributed in any way to the former spouse's death (*crimen*).

A third set of diriment impediments protected the ultimate sanctity and sanctifying function of the sacrament of marriage. Conditions attached to marriage promises that were illegal or repugnant to the sacrament, or harmful to the offspring, automatically rendered the marriage contract void. Thus a promise with the condition "that we abstain for a season" was valid. But a condition "that we engage in contraception," "that we abort our offspring" or "that we permit each other sexual liberty with others" nullified the marriage contract. Such conditions vitiated the spiritual purpose of marriage – to unite together in love and to raise children in the service of God. Likewise, permanent impotence, insanity, or bewitchment of either party were generally grounds for nullification, provided that such a condition was latent before marriage, and unknown to the parties.

A fourth set of impediments (*ligamen*) annulled all bigamous and polyg-amous relations as contrary to the biblical command, even if the parties had children. Annulment for such an impediment required proof of one's spouse's prior marriage contract, and that it was not dissolved by the former spouse's death or by a formal annulment.

Absolute divorce, with a subsequent right to remarry, was not permit-ted at canon law. The sacramental bond, once consummated, remained indissoluble at least till the physical or civil death of one of the parties. Divorce (*divortio*) at canon law meant only separation from bed and board (*a mensa et thoro*). Both husband and wife were given standing in Church courts to sue for separation. During pendency of the case, a Church court could order a husband to pay his wife temporary alimony to sus-tain her, particularly if she had already moved out of the marital home out of fear of or under pressure from her husband. If a Church court found adequate grounds for divorce – on evidence of adultery, deser-tion, or cruelty – it would order the estranged parties to live separately, and sometimes make further orders respecting custody and support of the children.[45] A separated spouse, though freed from the physical bond of marriage, was not freed from the spiritual bond. A subsequent mar-riage contracted before the death of one's estranged spouse was an act of bigamy – a mortal sin at canon law and a capital crime at civil law.

THE NEW EVANGELICAL THEOLOGY OF MARRIAGE

Luther's attack

In his early writings, Martin Luther attacked the traditional Catholic the-ology and canon law of marriage repeatedly. "[T]he estate of marriage has fallen into awful disrepute," he declared in a sermon of 1522:

There are many pagan books which treat of nothing but the depravity of woman kind and the unhappiness of the estate of marriage. . . . Every day one encounters parents who forget their former misery because, like the mouse, they have now had their fill. They deter their children from marriage and entice them into priesthood and nunnery, citing the trials and troubles of married life. Thus do they bring their own children home to the devil, as we daily observe; they provide them with ease for the body and hell for the soul. . . . [Furthermore,] the shameful confusion wrought by the accursed papal law has occasioned so much distress, and the lax authority of both the spiritual and the temporal swords has given rise to so many dreadful abuses and false situations that I would much

---

45 See good examples in Helmholz, *Marriage Litigation*, 74–111.

prefer neither to look into the matter nor to hear of it. But timidity is no help in an emergency.[46]

According to Luther, evidence for the decrepit estate of marriage and marriage law was all around.[47] Germany, he charged, had suffered through more than a century of sexual immorality brought on by the neglect and corruption of Church and state officials alike. Prostitution was rampant. Clergy and laity regularly kept concubines, sired illegitimate children, and then abandoned them. The small fines imposed by the bishops on sexually active clerics and monks – the so-called "whore tax" (*Hurenzins*) and "cradle tax" (*Wigenzins*) – provided little deterrence to such clerical misconduct and ample income to the bishops' coffers.[48] The stern laws against adultery, fornication, sodomy, and other sexual crimes had become largely dead letters. Lewd pamphlets and books exalting sexual liberty and license were published with virtual impunity. Writings extolling celibacy and deprecating marriage and sex dissuaded many couples from marriage and persuaded many parents to send their children to monasteries and cloisters. The numbers of single men and women, of monasteries and cloisters, of monks and nuns, have reached new heights, Luther charged. Within the marital household itself, mass confusion reigned over the laws of marital formation, maintenance, and dissolution, and over the laws of care of parents, children, and spouses.

Luther's lengthy indictment of prevailing German patterns of sex, marriage, and family life, while hyperbolic, was neither without precedent nor without merit. Already in the previous century, a host of theologians and canonists had issued similar attacks, and had already inspired a good number of reforms at canon law and increasingly at civil law as well.[49] Luther and his followers went beyond these conventional critics, however, in attributing much of the decay of marriage not only to the negligence of authority and the laxness of society but also to the paradoxes in the traditional canon law and theology of marriage.

According to Luther and other Evangelical reformers, the canon law purported to govern in accordance with natural law and Scripture. Yet

---

[46] *LW* 45:36–7.
[47] *LW* 44:3ff., 153ff., 176ff., 184, 215; *LW* 45:141ff., 243ff., 385ff.; *LW* 36:99ff.; see further Steven Ozment, *When Fathers Ruled: Family Life in Reformation Europe* (Cambridge, MA, 1983), 3–24; id., *Protestants*, 151–8; Scott Hendrix, "Masculinity and Patriarchy in Reformation Germany," *Journal of the History of Ideas* 56 (1995): 177.
[48] *LW* 39:290–1; see further Lindberg, "Luther and the Family," 135–6 and id., *The European Reformations* (Oxford, 1996), 172ff.
[49] See sources above pp. 46–9, 61–3.

it was filled with provisions not prefigured in natural law or Scripture. The canon law discouraged or prevented mature persons from marrying by its celebration of celibacy, its proscription against breach of vows of celibacy and chastity, its permission to breach oaths of betrothal, and its numerous impediments that led to marital annulment. Yet it encouraged marriages between the immature by declaring valid secret unions consummated without parental permission as well as oaths of betrothal followed by sexual intercourse. The canon law highlighted the sanctity and solemnity of marriage by deeming it a sacrament. Yet it permitted a couple to enter this holy union without clerical or parental witness, instruction, or participation. Celibate and impeded persons were thus driven by their sinful passion to incontinence and all manner of sexual deviance. Married couples, not taught the biblical norms for marriage, adopted numerous immoral practices.[50]

Such paradoxes of the canon law of marriage, Luther and other Evangelical reformers argued, were rooted in tensions within the Catholic theology of marriage. Although Catholic theologians emphasized the sanctity and sanctifying purpose of the marriage sacrament, they nevertheless subordinated it to celibacy and monasticism. Although they taught that marriage was a duty mandated for all persons by natural law, they excused many from this duty through the restrictions of canon law. A true reformation of the law of marriage, therefore, required a new theological foundation. Accordingly, Luther and several other theologians worked assiduously in the early years of the Reformation to lay this new theological foundation, often working in direct collaboration with like-minded jurists.[51]

---

[50] See Albert Stein, "Luther über Eherecht und Juristen," in Junghaus, ed., *Leben und Werk Martin Luthers*, 1:171ff.; Köhler, 38ff. An interesting example of the depth of Luther's understanding of the canon law of marriage is his 1531 letter to Robert Barnes on Henry VIII's complex marriage and annulment case *LW* 50:27–40.

[51] For detailed lists of these theological and legal writings, see *FSC*, 227–231. For discussion of the new Evangelical theology of marriage, see, e.g., Emil Friedberg, *Das Recht der Eheschliessung in seiner geschichtlichen Entwicklung*, repr. (Aalen, 1968), 153–240; Walter Köhler, "Luther als Eherichter," *Beiträge zur sächsischen Kirchengeschichte* 47 (1947): 18; Hans Liermann, "Evangelisches Kirchenrecht und staatliches Eherecht in Deutschland, Rechtsgeschichtliches-Gegenwartsprobleme," in Thomas Wurtenberger, ed., *Existenz und Ordnung: Festschrift für Erik Wolf* (Frankfurt am Main, 1962), 43; Karl Michaelis, "Ueber Luthers eherechtliche Anschauungen und deren Verhältnis zum mittelalterlichen und neuzeitlichen Eherecht," in *Festschrift für Erich Ruppel zum 65. Geburtstag* (Hanover, 1968), 43; Reinhard Seeberg, "Luthers Anschauung von dem Geschlechtsleben der Ehe und ihre geschichtliche Stellung," *Luther-Jahrbuch* 7 (1925): 77; Klaus Suppan, *Die Ehelehre Martin Luthers. Theologische und rechtshistorische Aspekte des reformatorischen Eheverständnisses* (Salzburg, 1971).

Traditional foundations

Following tradition, the Lutheran reformers viewed marriage as at once a natural, contractual, and spiritual estate. Marriage was created and ordered by God as a monogamous union between a fit man and a fit woman, presumptively for life. Marriage depended in its essence on the voluntary consent of both parties. Marriage brought spiritual comfort and edification to its faithful participants.

Moreover, according to the reformers, marriage was, as Augustine had said, both a duty for the sound and a remedy for the sick. God had created Adam and Eve to be naturally inclined and attracted to each other.[52] He had commanded them to be "fruitful and multiply" and to fill the earth with their kind and to teach their children the meaning and measure of God's faith, law, and order. This commandment to join together in marriage became doubly imperative after the fall into sin, lest people succumb to the evil temptations of lust and lasciviousness. Luther put this traditional lore strongly in his *Large Catechism* (1529):

How gloriously God honors and extols this estate, inasmuch as by his commandments, He both sanctions and guards it. . . . He also wishes us to honor it, and to maintain and conduct it as a divine and blessed estate; because, in the first place, He has instituted it before all others, and therefore created man and woman separately (as is evident), not for lewdness, but that they should live together, be fruitful, beget children, and nourish and train them to the honor of God. Therefore God has also most richly blessed this estate above all others, and, in addition, has bestowed on it and wrapped up in it everything in the world, to the end that this estate might be well and richly provided for. Married life therefore is no jest or presumption; but it is an excellent thing and a matter of divine seriousness. For it is of the utmost importance to Him that persons be raised who may serve the world and promote the knowledge of God, godly living, and all virtues, to fight against wickedness and the devil.[53]

Philip Melanchthon echoed these sentiments in a lengthy article on marriage in his *Apology to the Augsburg Confession* (1531), adding that marriage was not only a natural duty and remedy but also a natural facility and right that no human ordinance should discourage or impede:

Genesis 1:28 teaches that people were created to be fruitful, and that one sex in a proper way should desire another. For we are speaking not of concupiscence,

---

[52] See *LW* 45:18: "For it is not a matter of free choice or decision, but a natural and necessary thing, that whatever is a man must have a woman and whatever is a woman must have a man."

[53] *TC* 639; see also *LW* 21:89ff.; *LW* 45:17ff.; *LW* 43ff.; Althaus, *Ethics*, 83ff.

which is sin, but of the appetite which would have existed in nature even if it had remained uncorrupted, which they call physical love. And this love of one sex for the other is truly a divine ordinance. . . .

Because this creation or divine ordinance is a natural right (*ius naturale*), jurists have accordingly said wisely and correctly that the union of male and female belongs to the [order of] natural laws (*iuris naturalis*). But since natural law is immutable, the right to contract marriage (*ius contrahendi conjugi*) must always remain. For where nature does not change, that ordinance with which God has endowed nature does not change, and cannot be removed. . . . Moreover a natural right is truly a divine right (*ius divinum*), because it is an ordinance divinely impressed upon nature. But inasmuch as this right cannot be changed without an extraordinary work of God, it is necessary that the right to contract marriage remains, because the natural desire of [one] sex for [the other] sex is an ordinance of God (*ordinatio Dei*) in nature, and for this reason is a right.[54]

These catechetical and confessional statements on marriage were widely known in the Evangelical world, and echoed repeatedly in the more specialized writings of theologians and jurists.

Following tradition further, the Lutheran reformers taught that marriage has three inherent goods. They, too, echoing Augustine and Aquinas, put these marital goods in varying orders of priority depending on what dimension of marriage they were emphasizing. The reformers' preferred formula for these marital goods, however, was not the Augustinian trilogy of children, faith and sacrament (*proles, fides, sacramentum*). Most of the reformers preferred to speak instead of the three marital goods of (1) mutual love and support of husband and wife; (2) procreation and nurture of children; and (3) mutual protection of both spouses from sexual sin.[55]

This trilogy of love, procreation, and protection was no invention of the Reformation. It had already appeared more than a millennium before in late patristic and Roman law texts, ably distilled by St. Isidore of Seville in his *Etymologies* (ca. 633).[56] Some medieval moralists had adopted this trilogy to describe the reasons (*causae*) for a person to marry, as distinguished from the inherent goods (*bona*) of the institution of marriage itself. The reformers rejected this medieval distinction. From God's point of view, they argued, marriage has built-in purposes or reasons that God wishes to see achieved among his human creatures. From humanity's point of view, these are the created goods that we need to realize. To

---

[54] *TC* 366–7.   [55] *WA* 34:52; *FSC*, 96–108, 143–50.
[56] *Etymologiae*, 9.7.27. See discussion in Germain Grisez, *The Way of the Lord Jesus: Living a Christian Life*, 2 vols. (Quincy, IL, 1993), 2:558ff.

make fine distinctions between the goods and purposes or the causes and effects of marriage was ultimately to engage in idle casuistry, most reformers believed. Love, procreation, and protection was the essential formula.

This Evangelical formula of the marital goods of love, procreation, and protection overlapped with Augustine's formula of faith, children, and sacramentality, but it also amended and emended it in critical ways.

Marital love

Like Augustine, Evangelical reformers emphasized the good of marital faithfulness (*fides*). Parties were to be faithful to their marital promises, and loyal to their spouses. A marriage once properly contracted was presumptively binding on both parties for life. Infidelity to the marriage contract – whether sexual, physical, spiritual, or emotional – was a sin against this good of fidelity. The breakup of a marriage was also a sin against this good, even if sometimes justified as the lesser of two evils.

Unlike Augustine, however, the reformers often cast this good of *fides* in overt terms of marital love, intimacy, friendship, and companionship – adducing passages from Aristotle, the Roman Stoics, and Thomas Aquinas to drive home their point.[57] Luther was among the strongest such proponents of the good of marital love:

Over and above all [other loves] is marital love. Marital love drives husband and wife to say to each other, "It is you whom I want, not what is yours. I want neither your silver nor your gold. I want neither. I want only you. I want you in your entirety, or nor at all." All other kinds of love seek something other than the loved one: this kind wants only to have the beloved's own self completely. If Adam had not fallen, the love of bride and groom would have been the loveliest thing.[58]

"There's more to [marriage] than a union of the flesh," Luther wrote, although he considered sexual intimacy and warmth to be essential to the flourishing of marriage.[59] "There must [also] be harmony with respect to patterns of life and ways of thinking":[60]

---

[57] See sources in *FSC*, 96–108, 143–50 and my "The Goods and Goals of Marriage," *Notre Dame Law Review*, 76 (2001), 1022–38.

[58] *WA* 2:167; see also *WA* 13:11; *WA* 17/2:350ff.; Althaus, *Ethics*, 84ff.; Lindberg, "Luther and the Family," 142ff.

[59] Luther distinguished "the first love" of marriage, which is "passionate," "ardent," and "intoxicated," from a "deeper connubial love" that grows with time and experience between husband and wife: *WA TR* 3, No. 3530; *LW* 54:223. See further Olavi Lähteenmäki, *Sexus und Ehe bei Luther* (Turku, 1955).

[60] *WA TR* 5, No. 5524, *LW* 54:444.

The chief virtue of marriage [is] that spouses can rely upon each other and with confidence entrust everything they have on earth to each other, so that it is as safe with one's spouse as with oneself. . . . God's Word is actually inscribed on one's spouse. When a man looks at his wife as if she were the only woman on earth, and when a woman looks at her husband if he were the only man on earth; yes, if no king or queen, not even the sun itself sparkles any more brightly and lights up your eyes more than your own husband or wife, then right there you are face to face with God speaking. God promises to you your wife or husband, actually gives your spouse to you, saying: "The man shall be yours; the woman shall be yours. I am pleased beyond measure! Creatures earthly and heavenly are jumping for joy." For there is no jewelry more precious than God's Word; through it you come to regard your spouse as a gift of God and, as long as you do that, you will have no regrets.[61]

Luther did not press these warm sentiments to the point of denying the traditional headship of husband to wife and the traditional leadership of the *paterfamilias* within the marital household. Luther had no modern egalitarian theory of marriage. But Luther also did not betray these warm sentiments to the point of becoming the grim prophet of patriarchy, paternalism, and procreation *über alles* that some modern critics make him out to be. For Luther, love was a necessary and sufficient good of marriage. He supported marriages between loving couples, even those between young men and older women beyond child-bearing years or between couples who knew full well that they could have no children.[62] He stressed repeatedly that husband and wife were spiritual, intellectual, and emotional "partners," each to have regard and respect for the strengths of the other. He called his own wife Katherine respectfully "Mr. Kathy" and said more than once of her: "I am an inferior lord, she the superior; I am Aaron, she is my Moses."[63] He repeatedly told husbands and wives alike to tend to each other's spiritual, emotional, and sexual needs and to share in all aspects of child-rearing and household maintenance – from changing their children's diapers to helping their children establish their own new homes when they had grown up.[64]

Several other German reformers wrote with equal flourish about the good of marital love and fidelity. The Zurich reformer Heinrich Bullinger for example, who was influential both in Germany and in England, wrote similarly that God planted in a married man and woman "the love, the heart, the inclination and natural affection that is right to have

---

[61] *WA* 34:52.5–9, 12–21 quoting translation from Hendrix, "Luther on Marriage." See also *LW* 31:351ff.

[62] See, e.g., *WA TR* 4, No. 5212; *LW* 2:301ff.   [63] Quoted by Ozment, *Ancestors*, 36–7.

[64] *LW* 45:39ff.

with the other. . . . Marital love ought to be (next unto God) above all loves," with couples rendering to each other "the most excellent and unstinting service, diligence and earnest labor . . . one doing for another, one loving, depending, helping, and forbearing another, always rejoicing and suffering one with another."[65] The Strasbourg reformer Martin Bucer, who was also influential on both sides of the English Channel, wrote effusively about marital love. Marital couples must be

> united not only in body but in mind also, with such an affection as none may be dearer and more ardent among all the relations of mankind, nor of more efficacy to the mutual offices of love, and of loyalty. They must communicate and consent in all things both divine and human, which have any moment to well and happy living. The wife must honor and obey her husband, as the Church honors and obeys Christ her head. The husband must love and cherish his wife, as Christ his Church. Thus they must be to each other, if they will be true man and wife in the sight of God, whom certainly churches must follow in their judgment. Now the proper and ultimate end of marriage is not copulation, or children, for then there was no true matrimony between Joseph and Mary the mother of Christ, nor between many holy persons more, but the full and proper and main end of marriage is the communicating of all duties, both divine and human, each to the other, with utmost benevolence and affection.[66]

Children

Like Augustine, the reformers emphasized the good of children (*proles*), if such a blessing were naturally possible and divinely granted. But the reformers amended Augustine's account with Aquinas' gloss that the good of procreation included the Christian nurture and education of children, a responsibility that fell on husband and wife alike.[67] They underscored this amendment by insisting on the creation of schools for the religious and civic education of all children, and by producing a welter of catechisms, textbooks, and household manuals to assist in the same.[68]

The reformers did sometimes describe this good of procreation in strong terms. They also sometimes referred misogynistically to women's "private parts" as simple relief stations for randy husbands and simple vessels for bearing children.[69] But these inflammatory passages must be

---

[65] Heinrich Bullinger, *Der christlich Ehestand* (Zürich, 1540), translated by Myles Coverdale as *The Christen State of Marriage* (London, 1541), folios iii.b–iiii (spelling modernized).

[66] Bucer, *RC*, bk. II, chap. 38.   [67] *WA TR* 5:5513; *LW* 54:441–2.   [68] See chap. 7 below.

[69] Quoting *WA TR* 4:3921; see detailed sources and discussion in Harrington, *Reordering Marriage*, 71ff.; Susan C. Karant-Nunn, "The Transmission of Luther's Teachings on Women and Matrimony: The Case of Zwickau," *AFR* 77 (1986): 31–46.

balanced against those elegies on marital love already quoted, as well as the many softer and more typical descriptions of the good of procreation. As Luther put it:

"[T]he true definition of marriage is a divine and legitimate union of a husband and woman in the hope of offspring or at least the avoidance of fornication and sin for the sake of the glory of God. The greatest end is to obey God and avoid sin, to invoke God, pray, love, educate offspring to the glory of God, live with one's wife in fear of the Lord, and bear the cross.[70]

Luther wished for himself and Kathy, as well as for all other married couples, the joy of having children, not only for their own sakes but for the sake of God as well. Indeed, for a pious couple, procreation was effectively a work of creation and salvation at once, Luther believed. Child-rearing, he wrote,

is the noblest and most precious work, because to God there can be nothing dearer than the salvation of souls. . . . [Y]ou can see how rich the estate of marriage is in good works. God has entrusted to its bosom souls begotten of its own body on whom it can lavish all manner of Christian works. Most certainly, father and mother are apostles, bishops, [and] priests to their children, for it is they who make them acquainted with the gospel. See therefore how good and great is God's work and ordinance.[71]

Protection from sin

Unlike Augustine, the early Protestant reformers emphasized protection from sexual sin as a marital good in itself, not just a function of *fides*. Since the fall into sin, lust has pervaded the conscience of every person, the reformers insisted. Marriage has become not only an option but a necessity for sinful humanity. For without it, a person's distorted sexuality becomes a force capable of overthrowing the most devout conscience. A person is enticed by his or her own nature to prostitution, masturbation, voyeurism, and sundry other sinful acts. "You can't be without a wife and remain without sin," Luther declared.[72] Anyone who chooses to "live alone undertakes an impossible task . . . counter to God's word and the nature that God has given and preserves in him."[73] The calling of marriage, Luther wrote, should be declined only by those who have received God's gift of continence. "Such persons are rare, not one in a thousand [later he said "a hundred thousand"], for they are a special

---

[70] *WA* 2:168–9; *WA* 43:310.   [71] *LW* 45:46.   [72] *WA TR* 1, No. 233; *LW* 54:31.
[73] *WA* 18:276; see further Althaus, *Ethics*, 87ff.

miracle of God." The Apostle Paul has identified this group as the permanently impotent and the eunuchs; few others can claim such a unique gift.[74]

This understanding of the protective good of marriage undergirded the reformers' bitter attack on the traditional canon law rules of mandatory celibacy.[75] To require celibacy of clerics, monks, and nuns, the reformers believed, was beyond the authority of the Church and ultimately a source of great sin. Celibacy was for God to give, not for the Church to require. It was for each individual, not for the Church, to decide whether he or she had received this gift.[76] By demanding monastic vows of chastity and clerical vows of celibacy, the Church was seen to be intruding on Christian freedom and violating Scripture, nature, and common sense.[77] By institutionalizing and encouraging celibacy the Church was seen to prey on the immature and the uncertain. By holding out food, shelter, security, and opportunity, the monasteries enticed poor and needy parents to condemn their children to celibate monasticism. Mandatory celibacy, Luther taught, was hardly a prerequisite for the true service of God. Instead it led to "great whoredom and all manner of fleshly impurity and ... hearts filled with thoughts of women day and night."[78] For the consciences of Christians and non-Christians alike are infused with lust, and a life of celibacy and monasticism only heightens the temptation.[79]

Furthermore, the imputation of superior spirituality and holier virtue to the celibate contemplative life was, for the reformers, contradicted by the Bible. The Bible teaches that each person must perform his or her calling with the gifts that God provides. The gifts of continence and contemplation are but two among many, and are by no means superior to the gifts of marriage and child-rearing. Each calling plays an equally important, holy, and virtuous role in the drama of redemption, and its

---

[74] *LW* 45:18–22; *LW* 28:9–12, 27–31. See also *CR* (1555), 112ff., 137ff.; Inge Mager, " 'Es is nicht gut dass der Mensch allein sei' (Gen 2, 18): Zum Familienleben Philipp Melanchthons," *AFR* 81 (1990): 120–37.

[75] *LW* 44:243–400; *LW* 46:139ff.; *LC* (1521), 59ff.; Johannes Bugenhagen, *Von dem ehelichen Stände der Bischoffe vnd Daiken* (Wittenberg, 1525); id., *Was man vom Closter leben halten sol*; *TC*, 363ff. 419ff.; Heinrich Schatt, *Das priester ee nit wider des Gottlich, gaystlich, unnd weltlich recht sey* (Augsburg, 1523), and further sources pp. 61–4 above. See generally Bernard Lohse, *Mönchtum und Reformation: Luthers Auseinandersetzung mit dem Mönchsideal des Mittelalters* (Göttingen, 1963).

[76] *TC*, 499, 501.

[77] This is the heart of Luther's 1521 diatribe against monastic vows in *LW* 44:243, *LW* 46:139. See also Melanchthon, *CR* 1:195; Apel, *Defensio*, folios A11–12.

[78] *WA* 12:98; see further Seeberg, "Luthers Anschauung," 94ff.; August Franzen, *Zölibat und Priesterehe in der Auseinandersetzung der Reformationszeit und der katholischen Reform des 16. Jahrhundert* (Münster, 1969).

[79] Ibid. See also Apel, *Defensio*, A11–A12.

fulfillment is a service to God.[80] Luther concurred with the Apostle Paul that the celibate person "may better be able to preach and care for God's word." But, he immediately added: "It is God's word and the preaching which makes celibacy – such as that of Christ and of Paul – better than the estate of marriage. In itself, however, the celibate life is far inferior."[81]

This understanding of the good of marriage as a protection against sexual sin also undergirded the reformers' repeated counsel that widows and widowers, as well as divorcees, could and sometimes should remarry, after a suitable period of grieving. Medieval writers, building on St. Paul and some of the Church Fathers, had discouraged all such remarriages, arguing that these were forms of "digamy" or "serial polygamy." The reformers taught the opposite. A grieving and lonely widow, widower, or divorcee often benefits from a new spouse, especially if he or she still has children to care for. Even more important, this now-single party who has known the pleasures and warmth of sexual intimacy will be doubly tempted to sexual sin in its sudden absence. St. Paul's instruction that "it is better to marry than to burn," becomes doubly imperative for them. Luther wrote:

I'm astonished that the lawyers, and especially the canonists, are so deeply offended by digamy. Lawyers interpret digamy in an astonishing way if somebody marries a widow, etc. Oh, how vast is the ignorance of God in man's heart that he can't distinguish between a commandment of God and a tradition of men. To have one, two, three, or four wives in succession is [in every case] a marriage and isn't contrary to God, but what's to prevent fornication and adultery, which are against God's command?[82]

Luther, Bucer, and Melanchthon sometimes pressed this counsel to even more adventuresome, if not scandalous, ends of condoning private bigamy as a lesser sin than public adultery or concubinage.[83] Luther hinted at this in several entries in his letters and *Table Talk*.[84] A 1532 case in his *Table Talk* reads thus:

A certain man took a wife, and after bearing several children, she contracted syphilis and was unable to fulfill her marital obligation. Thereupon her husband, troubled by the flesh, denied himself beyond his ability to sustain the burden

---

[80] *LC* (1521), 60–1; *TC*, 501.   [81] *LW* 45:47.

[82] *WA TR* 3, No. 3609B; *LW* 54:243–4. See Bucer, *RC*, bk. 2, chaps. 23, 24, 34, 41, 44; Georg May, *Die Stellung des deutschen Protestantismus zu Ehescheidung, Wiederverheiratung und kirchlicher Trauung Geschiedener* (Paderborn, 1965).

[83] See Luther on the concubinage of Lamech and Abraham in *WA* 29:144ff., 303ff.

[84] See, e.g., *WA TR* 1, No. 611; *WA TR* 2, No. 1461; *LW* 50:33.

of chastity. It is asked, Ought he be allowed a second wife? I reply that one or another of two things must happen: either he commits adultery or he takes another wife. It is my advice that he take a second wife; however, he should not abandon his first wife but should provide for her sufficiently to enable her to support her life. There are many cases of this kind, from which it ought to be clearly seen and recognized that this is the law and that is the gospel.[85]

This might be read as a case of digamy rather than bigamy. It might be understood that the "second wife" was to be taken after divorce from the first wife, who was still to be cared for despite the divorce. Divorce, as we shall see in a moment, would presumably be warranted in this case on account of the wife's adultery that led to her condition of syphilis.

Luther and his colleagues went further in their advice to Landgrave Philip of Hesse, patron of the Marburg jurist Johannes Eisermann.[86] Landgrave Philip had been diplomatically married at the age of nineteen to Christina, the daughter of Duke George of Albertine Saxony. He claimed that "he had never any love or desire for her on account of her form, fragrance, and manner," though this did not prevent him from siring seven children with her. Throughout his married life, and especially when his wife grew frigid in later life, Philip admitted to robust engagement with prostitutes and paramours of all sorts, and was rewarded with a rash of syphilis. He was now deeply ashamed of his conduct, confessed it fully, and sought to do better. He insisted that he still needed a sexual outlet, or he would again be driven to resort to consorting with his maids and prostitutes. He had taken a single concubine and wanted to marry her, thinking that contracting such a second marriage would be better than breaking the first. Philip asked Martin Bucer for his advice and blessing on this bigamous arrangement. Bucer instead counseled divorce from his first wife, with remarriage to his concubine. Divorce was licit, if for no other reason than Philip's own repeated and fully confessed adultery. But Philip apparently did not want to risk public confession of such conduct. He preferred to keep and support his first wife, and to marry and support the second as well, in the tradition of David, Solomon, and the other patriarchs of Israel. A troubled Bucer took the case to Luther and Melanchthon for their counsel. Luther reports what happened thereafter:

Martin Bucer brought [us] a certified statement which set forth that the landgrave was unable to remain chaste on account of certain defects in his wife. Accordingly, he had lived so and so, which was not good, especially for an

---

[85] *WA TR* 1, No. 414; *LW* 54:65–6. [86] See above pp. 141–2.

Evangelical, and indeed one of the most prominent Evangelical princes. He swore before God and on his conscience that he was unable to avoid such vice unless he was permitted to take another wife. The account of his life and purpose shocked us in view of the vicious scandal that would follow and we begged His Grace not to do it. We were then told he was unable to refrain and would carry out his intention in spite of us by appealing to the emperor or pope. To prevent this, we humbly requested him, if he insisted on doing it or (as he said) was unable to do otherwise before God and his conscience, at least to do it secretly because he was constrained by his need, for it could not be defended in public and under imperial law. We were promised that he would do so. Afterward we made an effort to help as much as we could to justify it before God with examples of [the relative virtues of bigamy over concubinage evident in the story of] Abraham, etc. All this took place and was negotiated under seal of confession, and we cannot be charged with having done this willingly, gladly, or with pleasure. It was exceedingly difficult for us to do, but because we could not prevent it, we thought that we ought at least to ease his conscience as much as possible.[87]

Philip apparently shared the reformers' counsel with others, and publicly celebrated his second wedding in open defiance of his own and more general imperial laws of bigamy. This caused a great scandal in Germany. Both the emperor and the pope eventually weighed in to condemn Philip for his actions and Luther and his colleagues for their counsel. In defense of Luther and his colleagues, this was supposed to have been quiet private pastoral counsel reluctantly given to an obviously troubled soul, who could keep neither his continence nor his confidence. But it must also be said that this advice was of a (long) piece with the reformers' broader insistence that one of the fundamental goods and goals of marriage was to protect parties from sexual sin.

Not a sacrament

While the reformers endorsed, with ample amendment, Augustine's two goods of *fides* and *proles*, they had no place for the good of *sacramentum* – either in the medieval sense of a permanent channel of sanctifying grace, or even in the Augustine's own sense of symbolic stability. For the reformers, marriage was neither a sacrament of the Church, of the order of baptism or the eucharist, nor a permanent union dissolvable only upon the death of one of the parties.

---

[87] Letter to Elector John of Saxony (June 10, 1540), *WA Br* 9:131–135, quoting from translation in Luther, *Letters of Spiritual Counsel*, ed. Theodore G. Tappert (Philadelphia, 1955), 288–91. See further *WA Br* 8:631ff.; *WA TR* 4:5038, 5046, 5096.

For the reformers, marriage was a social institution of the earthly kingdom, not a sacrament of the heavenly kingdom. Though divinely ordained to serve a holy purpose, marriage remained, in Luther's words, "a natural order," "an earthly institution," "a secular and outward thing."[88] "No one can deny that marriage is an external, worldly matter, like clothing and food, house and property, subject to temporal authority, as the many imperial laws enacted on the subject prove."[89] To be sure, Luther agreed, marriage can symbolize the union of Christ with His Church, as St. Paul wrote in Ephesians 5:32. The sacrifices that husband and wife make for each other and for their children can express the sacrificial love of Christ on the cross. A "blessed marriage and home" can be "a true church, a chosen cloister, yes, a paradise" on earth.[90] But these analogies and metaphors do not make marriage a sacrament of the order of baptism and the Eucharist. Sacraments are God's gifts and signs of grace, ensuring Christians of the promise of redemption which is available only to those who have faith.[91] Marriage carries no such promise and demands no such faith. "[N]owhere in Scripture," writes Luther, "do we read that anyone would receive the grace of God by getting married; nor does the rite of matrimony contain any hint that the ceremony is of divine institution."[92] Scripture teaches that only baptism and the Eucharist (and perhaps penance) confer this promise of grace. All other so-called sacraments are "mere human artifices" that the Church has created to augment its legal powers and fill its coffers with court fees and fines.[93]

Because marriage was not a sacrament, the reformers argued, there should be no formal religious tests for marriage. Parties would certainly do well to marry within the faith for the sake of themselves and their children, but nothing compels this. Religious differences should not be viewed as an impediment to a valid marriage, but a challenge to be more faithful within marriage and to induce proper faith in each other. Luther wrote:

[M]arriage is an outward, bodily thing, like any other worldly undertaking. Just as I may eat, drink, sleep, walk, ride with, buy from, speak to, and deal with a heathen, Jew, Turk, or heretic, so I may also marry and continue in wedlock with him. Pay no attention to the precepts of those fools who forbid it. You will

[88] *LW* 21:93.
[89] *LW* 46:265. See further Hartwig Dieterich, *Das protestantische Eherecht in Deutschland bis zur Mitte des 17. Jahrhunderts* (Munich, 1970), 8off.; Walter Köhler, *Zürcher Ehegericht und Genfer Konsistorium*, 2 vols. (Leipzig, 1942), 2:427ff.
[90] *LW* 44:85.   [91] See *LW* 36:11; *TC* 310ff.; Pelikan, *Spirit Versus Structure*, 17–31, 113–38.
[92] *LW* 36:92–3.   [93] Ibid., 97ff.

find plenty of Christians – and indeed the greater part of them – who are worse in their secret unbelief than any Jew, heathen, Turk, or heretic. A heathen is just as much a person – God's good creation – as St. Peter, St. Paul, and St. Lucy, not to speak of slack or spurious Christians.[94]

Because marriage was not a sacrament, divorce and remarriage were licit, and sometimes even necessary. To be sure, the reformers, like their Catholic brethren, insisted that marriages should be stable and presumptively indissoluble. But this presumption could be overcome if one of the essential marital goods were chronically betrayed or frustrated. If there were a breach of marital love by one of the parties – by reason of adultery, desertion, or cruelty – the marriage was broken. The innocent spouse who could not forgive this breach could sue for divorce and remarry. If there were a failure of procreation – by reason of sterility, incapacity, or disease discovered shortly after the wedding – the marriage was also broken. Those spouses who could not reconcile themselves to this condition could seek an annulment and at least the healthy spouse could marry another. And if there were a failure of protection from sin – by reason of frigidity, separation, desertion, or cruelty – the marriage was again broken. If the parties could not be reconciled to regular cohabitation and consortium, they could divorce and seek another marriage.[95] In every instance, divorce was painful, sinful, and sad, and it was a step to be taken only after ample forethought and counsel. But it was a licit, and sometimes an essential, step to take.

Martin Bucer put the Evangelical case for divorce and remarriage more flatly than most, but his argument signals the striking changes born of the rejection of marriage as a sacrament. Marriage has

four necessary properties: 1. That the [couple] should live together. . . . 2. That they should love one another in the height of dearness. . . . 3. That the husband bear himself as the head and preserver of the wife instructing her to all godliness and integrity of life; that the wife also be to her husband a help, according to her place, especially furthering him in the true worship of God, and next in all the occasions of civil life. 4. That they not defraud each other of conjugal benevolence.

Marriages that exhibit these four properties must be maintained and celebrated. But even "where only one [property] be wanting in both or either party . . . it cannot then be said that the covenant of matrimony holds good between such." To perpetuate the formal structure of

---

94 *LW* 45:25.
95 *WA Br* 3:288–90; *WA* 15:558ff.; Brecht 2:93–4.

marriage after a necessary property is lost, Bucer argued, is not only a destructive custom, but an unbiblical practice. "[T]he Lord did not only permit, but also expressly and earnestly commanded his people, by whom he would that all holiness and faith of the marriage covenant be observed, that he could not induce his mind to love his wife with a true conjugal love, might dismiss her that she might marry another" who is more meet and good.[96]

Because marriage was not a sacrament, it also did not belong primarily within the jurisdiction of the Church, that is, within the law-making authority of the clergy, consistory, and congregation. Luther underscored this several times in his sermons and instructions to fellow pastors:

First, we [pastors] have enough work to do in our proper office. Second, marriage is outside the church, is a civil matter, and therefore should belong to the government. Third, these cases [of marital dispute] have no limits, extend to the height, the breadth, and the depth, and produce many offenses that bring disgrace to the gospel. . . . [W]e prefer to leave this business to civil officials. The responsibility rests on them. Only in cases of conscience should pastors give counsel to godly people. Controversies and court cases [respecting marriage] we leave to the lawyers. [97]

This did not mean that marriage was beyond the pale of God's authority and law, nor that it should be beyond the influence and concern of the Church. "It is sheer folly," Luther opined, to treat marriage as "nothing more than a purely human and secular state, with which God has nothing to do."[98] The civil magistrate holds his authority of God. His will is to reflect God's will. His law is to reflect God's law. His rule is to respect God's creation ordinances and institutions. His civil calling is no less spiritual than that of the Church. Marriage is thus still completely subject to godly law, but this law is now to be administered by a magistrate, not a cleric.[99]

Moreover, questions of the formation, maintenance, and dissolution of marriage remain important public concerns, in which Church officials and members must still play a key role. First, Luther and other reformers took seriously the duty of pastoral counseling in marriage disputes that raised matters of conscience. As pastors themselves, many of the reformers issued scores of private letters to parishioners who came to them for counsel. Secondly, theologians and preachers were to communicate to magistrates and their subjects God's law and will for marriage and the

---

[96] Bucer, *RC*, bk. 2, chaps. 26, 38, 39.
[97] *WA TR* 3, No. 4716; *LW* 54:363–4. See also *WA TR* 2, No. 3267; *LW* 54:194.
[98] *LW* 21:95.
[99] See Dieterich, *Das protestantische Eherecht*, 44ff., 81ff.; Seeberg, "Luthers Anschauung," 93ff.

family, and press for reforms when prevailing marital laws violated God's law. As a theologian, Luther published an ample series of pamphlets and sermons on questions of marriage and marriage law, sometimes wincing about how often his interventions were still needed. Thirdly, to aid church members in their instruction and care, and to give notice to all members of society of a couple's marriage, the local parish church clerk was to develop a publicly available marriage registry which all married couples would be required to sign. Fourthly, the pastors and teachers of the local church were to instruct and discipline the marriages of its members by pronouncing the public banns of betrothal, by blessing and instructing the couple at their public church wedding ceremony, and by punishing sexual turpitude or egregious violations of marriage law with public reprimands, bans, or, in serious cases, excommunication. Fifth, it was incumbent upon all members of the Church to participate in the spiritual upbringing and counsel of all new children, as their collective baptismal vows required.[100]

Marriage as social estate

The lynchpin of prevailing Catholic teaching was that marriage was a sacrament of the Church. This understanding both integrated and elevated the natural and contractual dimensions of marriage, and placed marriage in the hierarchy of Church orders as something of an institution and instrument of grace. The lynchpin of the budding Evangelical teaching was that marriage was the founding social estate of the earthly kingdom, the first order of creation in which God revealed His law and authority, His love and charity. This Evangelical understanding rendered marriage both a private and a public institution, whose proper formation and maintenance were essential to the just and orderly instruction and operation of Church, state, and other earthly institutions. Marriage is "the mother of all earthly laws," Luther wrote. "The estate of marriage is the spring from which all authority originates and flows," George Spalatin echoed.[101] Marriage "is not only placed on an equality with other estates, but it precedes and surpasses them all, whether they be that of emperor, princes, bishops, or whoever you please. For both

---

[100] See Dieterich, *Das protestantische Eherecht*, 47, 86; Roland Kirstein, *Die Entwicklung der Sponsalienlehre und der Lehre vom Eheschluss in der deutschen protestantischen Eherechtslehre bis zu J. H. Böhmer* (Bonn, 1966), 39ff.; Walter Köhler, "Die Anfänge des protestantischen Eherechtes," 278ff.

[101] *Vierzehen ursachen die billich yederman bewegen sollen den Ehestand lieb und hoch zuhaben und achten* (Erfurt, 1531), 2a, translated in Harrington, *Reordering Marriage*, 25.

ecclesiastical and civil estates must humble themselves and all be found in this estate."[102]

Evangelical moralists and jurists alike concurred in this. Philip Melanchthon wrote:

The earthly life has orders (*Stände*) and works (*Werke*) which serve to keep the human race, and are ordained by God, within certain limits and means. Matrimony is first, for God does not want human nature simply to run its course as animals do. Therefore, God has ordained marriage, Genesis 2 and Matthew 19 and 1 Corinthians 7, as an eternal inseparable fellowship of one husband and one wife. . . . [M]atrimony is a very lovely, beautiful fellowship and church of God if two people in true faith and obedience toward God live together, together invoke God, and rear children in the knowledge of God and virtue.[103]

"All orders of human society," the Frankfurt jurist Justin Göbler concurred, "derive from the first estate, matrimony, which was instituted by God himself. On this origin and foundation stand all other estates, communities, and associations of men. . . . From the administration of the household, which we call *oeconomia*, comes the administration of a government, a state being nothing more than the proliferation of households."[104]

The social estate of the family was to teach all people, particularly children, Christian values, morals, and mores. It was to exemplify for a sinful society a community of love and cooperation, meditation and discussion, song and prayer. It was to hold out for the Church and the state an example of firm but benign parental discipline, rule, and authority. It was to take in and care for wayfarers, widows, and destitute persons – a responsibility previously assumed largely by monasteries and cloisters. The social estate of marriage was thus as indispensable an agent in God's redemption plan as the Church had been for the Catholics. It no longer stood within the orders of the Church but alongside it. Moreover, the social estate of marriage was as indispensable an agent of social order and communal cohesion as the state should be. It was not simply a creation of the civil law, but a godly creation designed to aid the state in discharging its divine mandate. Thus marriage should be viewed not an inferior option but as a divine calling and a social status desirable for all people.[105]

The best example of such an idealized marital household was the local parsonage, the home of the married Lutheran minister. The reformers

---

[102] *TC* 639–41.   [103] *LC* (1555), 323–4.
[104] Justin Göbler, *Der Rechten Spiegel* (Frankfurt am Main, 1550), translated in Strauss, *Law, Resistance, and the State*, 118.
[105] *WA* 34:73; *WA* 50:651–2; *LW* 41:176–7; *TC*, 393.

had already argued that pastors, like everyone else, should be married – lest they be tempted by sexual sin, deprived of the joys of marital love, and precluded from the great act of divine and human creativity in having children. Such arguments, coupled with a theology of the priesthood of all believers and the equality of clergy and laity, proved strong enough for the early reformers to institute and encourage clerical marriage, even in the face of a millennium of canon law to the contrary. Here was an even stronger argument for clerical marriage. The clergy were to be exemplars of marriage. The minister's household was to be a source and model for the right order and government of the local church, state, and broader community. As Adolf von Harnack put it a century ago: "The Evangelical parsonage, founded by Luther, became the model and blessing of the entire German nation, a nursery of piety and education, a place of social welfare and social equality. Without the German parsonage, the history of Germany since the sixteenth century is inconceivable."[106]

THE NEW CIVIL LAW OF MARRIAGE

The reformers' new theology of marriage helped to transform prevailing German marriage law. The new marital theology was something of a self-executing program of action. It required civil authorities to divest the Catholic Church of its jurisdiction over marriage and assured them that this was a mandate of Scripture, not a sin against the Church. It called for new civil marriage laws that were consonant with God's Word but required that the Church (and thus the reformers themselves) advise the civil authorities on what God's Word commands. Both the magistrates' seizure of jurisdiction over marriage and the reformers' active development of new marriage laws were thus seen as divine tasks.

Although the new Lutheran marriage laws were wideranging, three fundamental changes in the traditional canon law of marriage were common.[107] The new civil law of marriage: (1) modified the traditional

---

[106] Quoted by Lindberg, "Luther and the Family," 141. See further Harrington, *Reordering Marriage*, 83ff.

[107] The best collections are in Sehling and Richter. Within the vast literature on the promulgation and enforcement of this new legislation, see, besides sources already cited, Martin Brecht, "Anfänge reformatorischen Kirchenordnungen bei Johannes Brenz," *ZSS KA* 96 (1969): 322; B. Gesschen, *Zur ältesten Geschichte und ehegerichtslichen Praxis des Leipziger Konsistoriums* (Leipzig, 1894); Ernst-Wilhelm Kohls, "Martin Bucers Anteil und Anleigen bei der Auffassung der Ulmer Kirchenordnung in Jahre 1531," *Zeitschrift für evangelischen Kirchenrecht* 15 (1970): 333; Thomas Max Safley, *Let No Man Put Asunder: The Control of Marriage in the German Southwest, A Comparative Study, 1550–1600* (Kirksville, MO, 1984), 41ff.; Gottfried Seebass, *Das reformatorische Werk des Andreas Osiander* (Nuremberg, 1967), 184ff.; A. Sprengler-Ruppenthal, "Zur Rezeption des römischen Rechts in Eherecht der Reformation," *ZSS KA* 112 (1978): 392ff.; Gerold Tietz, *Verlobung, Trauung,*

consent doctrine, and required the participation of others in the process of marriage formation; (2) sharply curtailed the number of impediments to betrothal and to marriage; and (3) introduced absolute divorce on proof of cause, with a right of remarriage. Such changes, taken together, simplified the laws of marriage formation and dissolution, provided for broader public participation in this marriage process, and protected the social functions of marriage and the family.

The law of consent to marriage

As in canon law, so in the new civil law, the marriage bond was to be formed by a free consensual union between two parties. Many of the reformers, however, accepted the traditional consent doctrine only after: (1) modifying the canonists' distinctions among the betrothal or future promise to marry, the present promise to marry, and the consent to consummate the marriage through sexual intercourse; (2) requiring that parents and witnesses participate in the marriage process; and (3) enlarging the task of the Church in the process of marital formation.

Luther was the most ardent advocate of these reforms. For Luther, the three forms of consent accepted at canon law were scripturally unwarranted, semantically confusing, and a source of public mischief. The Bible, said Luther, makes no distinction between a present and future promise of marriage. Any promise to marry, freely given in good faith, creates a valid, indissoluble marriage before God and the world; this marriage is consummated through sexual intercourse. Even before consummation, however, Scripture makes clear that breach of this promise through sexual relations with, or a subsequent marriage promise to, another is adultery.

Furthermore, the distinction between present and future promises of marriage depends upon "a scoundrelly game" ("ein lauter Narrenspiel") in Latin words that have no equivalent in German and thus confuse the average person. The Catholic Church courts usually interpreted the words "Ich will Dich zum Weibe haben" or "Ich will Dich nehmen; Ich will Dich haben; Du sollst mein sein" as a future promise, though in common German parlance these were usually intended to be present promises.[108] A present promise, traditional Church courts insisted, must

---

und Hochzeit in den evangelischen Kirchenordnungen des 16. Jahrhunderts (PhD Diss., Tübingen, 1969); François Wendel, *Le mariage à Strasbourg à l'époque de la réforme 1520–1692* (Strasbourg, 1928), 77ff.

[108] *LW* 45:11ff., 274ff. See also Johannes Brenz, *Wie in Eesachen vnnd den fellen so sich derhalben zutragen nach Götlichem billichem rechten christenlich zu handeln* (Nuremberg, 1529), chap. 2; Sohm, *Das Recht der Eheschliessung*, 138–9, 197–198; Kirstein, *Die Entwicklung*, 28ff. The promises are ambiguous

use the Latin phrase *"Accipio te in uxorem"* or the German phrase *"Ich nehme Dich zu meinem Weibe,"* though neither phrase was popular in lay circles. Such a post hoc interpretation of promises, Luther charged, exploited the ignorance of the common people, disregarded the intent of the couple, and betrayed the presumption of the Church courts against marriage. By interpreting many promises to be betrothals, Church courts had availed themselves of the much more liberal rules for dissolving betrothals and thus had been able to dissolve numerous marriages. Through their combined doctrines of construing marriage promises as betrothals and of permitting the religious vow to dissolve betrothals, the canon lawyers had thus covertly subsidized celibacy and monasticism.

To allay the confusion and reverse the presumption against marriage, Luther at first proposed that all promises to become married in the future (*sponsalia de futuro*) be viewed as binding marriage vows in the present (*sponsalia de praesenti*) unless either party had expressly stipulated some future condition or event. A promise in any language with a verb in the future tense was not enough to defeat the presumption. An expressly stated condition was required to preclude the merger of betrothal and marriage. Luther later retreated a bit from this position. He recognized the validity of distinctions between betrothal and marriage promises, but he insisted that the interval between the two promises be very short (as had been the case in his own marriage with Katherine) and that a high burden of proof of cause be placed on either party wishing to break their engagement.[109]

Luther and his followers did not attach such solemnity and finality to the marriage promise without safeguards. First, they insisted that, before any such promise, the couple seek the consent of their parents on both sides, or, if they were dead or missing, of their next of kin or guardian. Such consent, they argued, was mandated by Scripture (in the Commandment to honor one's parents) as well as by natural law, Roman law, and early canon law, but had been lost in the Catholic Church through the current toleration of secret marriages. The parents played an essential role in the process of marriage formation, Luther argued. They judged the maturity of the couple and the harmony and legality of their prospective relationship. More importantly, their will was to reflect the will of God for the couple. Like the priest and the prince,

---

because the verb forms "will" and "sollst," though commonly understood to be in the present tense, can also be interpreted as future.

[109] *WA TR* 2, No. 3179a. See also *WA TR* 3, No. 3921; *LW* 54:294–5.

the parent had been given authority as God's agent to perform a specific calling in the institution of marriage. Parents are "apostles, bishops, and priests to their children."[110] By giving their consent to the couple, parents were giving God's consent.

Marriages contracted without parental consent were, in the view of Luther and other reformers, presumptively void.[111] But where parents withheld their consent unreasonably, ordered their child to lead a celibate life, or used their authority to coerce a child to enter marriage unwillingly, they no longer performed a godly task. In such cases Luther urged the child to petition a minister or a magistrate for approval, and thereafter to be married despite a parent's objection.[112] If the magistrate or minister, too, was unreasonable or coercive, Luther urged the child to seek refuge in another place or simply to marry without such permission.

Luther stressed his teaching on parental consent and its limitations many times in his sermons, letters, consilia, and formal writings. An interesting example can be found in Luther's intervention in the case of a young Wittenberg law student, Johannes Schneidewin, who later would become a distinguished law professor at the University of Wittenberg and a strong supporter of Luther's reforms of marriage law. While studying at Wittenberg, Schneidewin was a tenant in Luther's home, and with Luther's blessing had fallen in love with a local woman, Anna Dürer. Johannes had sought his widowed mother's permission to marry Anna in his home town of Stollberg, but his mother had ignored his repeated queries. Luther then wrote thrice to Mrs. Schneidewin, asking her permission, and assuring her that the parties were fit and ready to be married and very much in love:

Some time ago, I wrote to you that your son John is attached by a great love to an honorable girl here. . . . I hoped to receive a favorable reply from you. I too have become impatient with your obstructing your son's marriage, and this has moved me to write to you once again. Because I too am fond of your son, I am unwilling to see his hope turned to ashes. The girl pleases him very much, her station in life is not unlike his, and she is, besides, a pious girl of an honorable family. Accordingly, I believe you have reason to be satisfied, especially because your son has submitted to you in filial obedience. . . . It therefore behooves you, as a loving mother, to give your consent . . . I pray you not to delay your consent any longer. Let the good fellow have peace of mind. And I cannot wait much longer. I shall have to act as my office requires.[113]

---

[110] *LW* 45:46.   [111] *LW* 46:205ff.; see Dieterich, *Das protestantische Eherecht*, 93–6.
[112] *WA TR* 5, No. 5441; *LW* 54:424.
[113] *WA Br* 8:453–455, Luther, *Letters of Spiritual Counsel*, 287–288. See also *WA Br* 8:492–3, 499.

Luther did not wait long to exercise his ministerial office. He married the couple less than two months later. An appreciative Professor Schneidewin later dedicated his first book on the law of marriage "to the memory of the honorable Dr. Martin Luther."[114]

Secondly, in addition to parental consent, Luther insisted that the promise to marry be made publicly, in the presence of at least two good and honorable witnesses. These witnesses could, if necessary, attest to the event of the marriage or to the intent of the parties and could also help instruct the couple on the solemnity and responsibility of their relationship – a function tied to Luther's doctrine of the priesthood of all believers.[115]

Thirdly, Luther and his followers insisted that, before consummating their marriage, the couple repeat their vows publicly in the church, seek the blessing and instruction of the pastor, and register in the public marriage directory kept in the church. Luther saw the further publicizing of marriage as an invitation for others to aid and support the couple, a warning for them to avoid sexual relations with either party, and a safeguard against false or insincere marriage promises made for the purpose of seducing the other party. Just as the parental consent was to reflect God's will that the couple be married, so the pastor's blessing and instruction was to reflect God's will for the marriage – that it remain an indissoluble bond of love and mutual service.[116]

With these requirements of parental consent, witnesses, and church registration and solemnization, Luther deliberately discouraged the secret marriages that the canon law had recognized (though not encouraged). He made marriage "a public institution," advocating the involvement of specific third parties throughout the process of marriage formation. Luther did, however, insist that private vows followed by sexual intercourse should constitute a valid marriage if the woman was impregnated or if the intercourse became publicly known. This was to be a case-by-case exception to the usual rule that a private promise was not an adequate basis for a valid marriage. Luther made the exception to protect the legitimacy and life of the child and to prevent the woman from falling victim to "the strong prejudice [against] marrying a despoiled woman."[117]

---

[114] Johannes Schneidewin, *In institutionum imperialium titulum X. De nuptiis. . . .* (Frankfurt am Main, 1562), prooemium.

[115] *LW* 46:268ff.

[116] *LW* 53:110ff. See discussion in Kirstein, *Die Entwicklung*, 734; Köhler, "Die Anfänge," 292.

[117] Ibid. See further Michaelis, "Ueber Luthers eherechtliche Anschauungen," 51ff.

The jurists worked out the legal implications of these reforms of the law of marital consent. Luther's conflation of future and present marriage promises found support only among later jurists who had joined the Evangelical cause. Earlier jurists, such as Kling, Schürpf, and Lagus, despite Luther's heated arguments with them, retained the traditional canon law distinction between present and future promises to marry and insisted on a separate group of impediments for each promise. Although they urged courts to interpret promises in accordance with the common German language, they silently rejected Luther's other recommendations.[118] Only in the second half of the sixteenth century were Luther's teachings made, in Rudolph Sohm's words, "the general Protestant doctrine and praxis which lasted into the eighteenth century."[119] Beust, Schneidewin, Goden, Hemming, Monner, Mauser, and other later Evangelical jurists rejected or severely diminished the distinction between the present promise to marry and the public unconditional betrothal, and shortened the time between the formal engagement and the wedding. Like Luther they inveighed against the secret marriage, and many affirmed, for the same reason as Luther, the exception for private marriages whose consummation became publicly known or which resulted in pregnancy.[120]

Luther's reforms of the law of marital consent also came to expression in the new civil law. Many statutes used the terms "betrothal" (*Verlöbnis*) and "marriage" (*Ehe*) interchangeably and deemed the public betrothal to be a completed (*geschlossen*) marriage.[121] Several other statutes, while retaining the traditional distinction between promises of betrothal and marriage, attached far greater importance and finality to public unconditioned betrothals, providing (1) that these promises take precedence over all secret betrothals (even those made subsequently); (2) that promiscuity by either betrothed party is punishable as adultery; and (3) that these promises can be dissolved only on grounds also permitted for divorce.[122] The functional distinction between future and present

---

[118] Dieterich, *Das protestantische Eherecht*, 121. [119] Sohm, *Das Recht der Eheschliessung*, 198.

[120] See ibid., 233ff. and a good contemporary catalogue of views in von Beust, *Tractatus connubiorum*, vol. 1, folios 5a–5b.

[121] See the church ordinances of Zürich (1529), Brandenburg-Nürnberg (1533), Württemberg (1536), Kassell (1539), Schwabisch-Hall (1543), Cologne (1543), and Tecklenburg (1588) as well as the consistory ordinance of Brandenberg (1573) in Richter, 1:135ff., 209ff., 270ff., 304ff.; 2:16ff., 47ff., 476ff., and 381ff.

[122] See the Goslar consistory ordinance (1555) and the declaration of the Synod of Emden (1571) in Richter, 2:166ff., 340. See also the Opinions of the Wittenberg Court quoted in Sohm, *Das Recht der Eheschliessung*, 199–200.

promises was thus considerably narrowed at law in a number of German polities.[123]

The requirement of parental consent to marriages, particularly for children who had not yet reached the age of majority, won virtually unanimous acceptance in sixteenth-century Germany among jurists and legislators alike. Parental consent was a particularly prominent topic of discussion among the jurists. They adduced evidence in support of this change from Roman, early canon, and Germanic law. For several of the early jurists, like Kling and Schürpf, who advocated closer allegiance to canon law, parental consent was highly commendable but not absolutely necessary. Couples who married without parental consent should be fined by the state and disciplined by the Church, but neither the parents nor either one of the parties should be able to annul the marriage because of this omission. Several later jurists, such as Monner, Mauser, and Schneidewin, argued that such secret marriages should be annulled, unless the parties had consummated their private vows; post hoc consent by the parties should have no effect. Virtually all the jurists urged that the couple seek the approval of both fathers and mothers. Where the parents were dead or missing, they assiduously listed in the order of priority the next of kin, tutors, guardians, and others whose consent should be sought. Finally, the jurists discussed in detail the conditions which parents could attach to their consent. Reasonable conditions of time ("You may marry my daughter but only after a year"), of place ("... only in the church of Wittenberg"), or of support ("... only when you secure a job") were generally accepted by the jurists. But they carefully denied parents the opportunity to use the consent doctrine to place coercive demands or unreasonable restrictions on the couple. Monner and Mauser, in fact, argued that parents or guardians who abused their consensual authority should be fined, even imprisoned in cases of serious abuse.[124]

Given the prominent attention to parental consent by theologians and jurists, it is not surprising that most of the new civil statutes required such consent. Very few statutes, however, ordered that all marriages contracted without parental consent be nullified.[125] The presence of witnesses or the public declaration of betrothal in a church was usually accepted as an adequate substitute, though several statutes ordered

---

[123] See overview in Tietz, *Verlobung, Trauung, und Hochzeit.*

[124] See Dieterich, *Das protestantische Eherecht,* 123–27.

[125] See Marriage Ordinance of Württemberg (1537) in Richter, 1:280. The Wittenberg marriage court apparently also took this rigid stance, though absolute parental consent was not prescribed in the Wittenberg statute. See Dieterich, *Das protestantischen Eherecht,* 156–57.

stern penalties for parties who failed to gain parental consent.[126] The ambit of the parents' authority in the marriage process was also carefully circumscribed in the new statutes. Courts were to prohibit parents from entering their unwilling children in cloisters or monasteries or from obstructing children who wished to leave their sacred orders. Children saddled with severe conditions or restrictions on their prospective marriages were granted rights of appeal to the local court; where the court found for the child, the parents (or guardians) were subject to fines and other penalties.[127] In most jurisdictions, parental consent was no longer required once the child reached the age of majority.[128]

The requirement of at least two good and honorable witnesses to the marriage promise was accepted by virtually all jurists and legislative draftsmen. A few early statutes denied outright the validity of an unwitnessed marriage promise, but, in most jurisdictions, the validity of these promises was left to the discretion of the court.[129] At first, unwitnessed marriages were rarely dissolved. But as the scandal of pre-marital sex and pregnancy grew and courts were faced with time-consuming evidentiary inquiries into the relationship of litigating couples, these private promises were increasingly struck down. Parties who consummated their private promises were fined, imprisoned, and, in some jurisdictions, banished. In the later sixteenth century, a number of territories also began to require either that the couple invite a government official as one witness to their promises or that they announce their promises before the city hall or other specified civic building.[130]

---

[126] See, e.g., the church ordinances of Basel (1529) and Brandenburg (1573) and the declarations of the Synod of Emden (1571) in Richter, 1:125; 2:376, 340. See also the reformation ordinance of Hessen (1526), marriage ordinance of Württemberg (1553), and the Schauenburg policy ordinance (1615), quoted in Gustav Schmelzeisen, *Polizeiordnung und Privatrecht* (Münster/Cologne, 1955), 33–34.

[127] See the constitution of the Wittenberg consistory ordinance (1542), the church ordinance of Celle (1545), the marriage ordinance of Dresden (1556), the territorial ordinance of Prussia (1577), the marriage ordinance of Kurpf (1582) and the Schauenburg policy ordinance (1615) in Sehling, 1:20ff., 292ff., 343ff. and Schmelzeisen, *Polizeiordnung und Privatrecht*, 36. See also illustrative cases in Beust, *Tractatus de iure connubiorum*, folios 82b–86a.

[128] See, e.g., the church ordinance of Goslar (1555) in Richter, 2:165. The age of majority in that jurisdiction was twenty for men, eighteen for women; in some jurisdictions, the age of majority was as high as twenty-seven for men and twenty-five for women; see Schmelzeisen, *Polizeiordnung und Privatrecht*, 35.

[129] The marriage ordinance of Zurich (1525), copied in several south German cities, was the first to declare void *ab initio* all unwitnessed marriages. See Köhler, "Die Anfänge," 74ff. The more typical early statutes are the church ordinance of Ulm (1531) and the marriage ordinance of Württemberg (1537) in Richter, 1:158, 280.

[130] Marriage ordinance of Württemberg (1553) and church ordinance of Goslar (1555) in Richter, 2:129, 165. See discussion in Köhler, "Die Anfänge," 292.

In many jurisdictions, the Church was assigned an indispensable role in the process of marriage formation. Couples were required, on pain of stiff penalties, to register their marriage with local church officials.[131] The public church celebration of the marriage and the pastor's instruction and blessing were made mandatory even for couples who had earlier announced their betrothal and received parental consent.[132] Several ordinances explicitly ordered punishment for betrothed couples who consummated their marriages before participating in the church ceremony.[133] By the 1550s, this "anticipatory sex" was grounds for imprisonment or banishment from the community as well as excommunication from the Church.[134]

These four interrelated reforms introduced into the German civil law of marriage – the growing conflation of unconditioned future and present promises to marry, along with the requirements of parental consent, witnesses, and church registration and celebration for marriage – remained standard provisions in the next three centuries, not only in Germany but also in many other Western nations. These reforms were based, in part, on the new theology of the Lutheran social model of marriage. But they were also based on earlier Roman law and canon law provisions, which had fallen into desuetude by the eve of the Reformation.

Indeed, the Council of Trent made comparable changes to the canon law of marital formation, appealing to many of the same early canon law and Roman law precedents adduced by the reformers, but grounding these reforms in the distinctive sacramental theology of the Catholic tradition. In the Decree *Tametsi* in 1563, the Council decreed that (1) to contract a valid marriage, parties had to exchange present promises in the company of a priest and witnesses; (2) all betrothals had to be announced publicly three times before celebration of the marriage; and (3) each parish was required to keep an updated public registry of marriage. The Council further encouraged (but did not require) parents to counsel their children in choosing compatible spouses.[135]

---

[131] See, e.g., church ordinance of Ulm (1531) in Richter, 1:159.

[132] See the Zurich Chorgericht ordinance (1525) and the church ordinances of Basel (1530), Kassel (1530), Ulm (1531), Strasbourg (1534), and the numerous later statutes quoted and discussed in Friedberg, *Der Eheschliessung*, 213–17, and Schmelzeisen, *Polizeiordnung und Privatrecht*, 45–46.

[133] See the ordinances of Nürnberg (1537), Augsburg (1553), and Ulm (1557), described in Ozment, *When Fathers Ruled*, 36ff.; Köhler, "Die Anfänge," 296ff.

[134] See the marriage ordinance of Württemberg (1553) in Richter, 2:128 and the church ordinances of Palatine on the Rhine (1563), in Sehling, 6:133.

[135] See above chapter 1.

The law of impediments to marriage

Lutheran theologians and jurists strove with equal vigor to reform the canon law of impediments. For the reformers, a number of these reasons for annulment of betrothals and marriage were biblically groundless. Several others, though grounded in the Bible, had become a source of corruption and confusion.

According to the Bible, as the reformers understood it, marriage is a duty prescribed by the law of creation and a right of persons protected by the law of Christ. No human law could impinge on this divine duty or infringe on this "divine right" without the warrant of divine law.[136] No human authority could impede or annul a marriage without divine authorization.[137] As Melanchthon put it: "the union of male and female belongs to [the order of] natural laws. Since natural law is immutable, the right to contract marriage (*ius contrahendi conjugi*) must always remain."[138] Impediments to marriage, therefore, that were not clear commands of God and nature could not be countenanced. Thus the impediments protecting the sanctity of the marriage sacrament were untenable, for the Bible (as the reformers understood it) does not teach that marriage is a sacrament. Impediments protecting religious vows of celibacy or chastity were unnecessary, for Scripture subordinates such vows to the vows of marriage.

Even the biblically based impediments of the canon law had, in the reformers' view, become sources of corruption and confusion. It had long been the official practice of the Church to relax certain impediments (such as consanguinity and affinity) where they worked injustice to the parties or to their children. Parties could receive a dispensation from these impediments and be excused from the legal strictures. This "equitable" practice met with little criticism, and indeed was continued by the reformers, as we just saw in the infamous case of Philip of Hesse. The reformers' concern was with the abuse of this practice in certain bishoprics in Germany. Certain corrupt clerics, in the reformers' judgment, had turned their "equitable" authority to their own financial gain by relaxing any number of impediments if the dispensation payment was high enough. This clerical bribery and trafficking in dispensations from impediments evoked caustic attacks from the reformers. "[T]here

---

[136] *LW* 36:100.
[137] See ibid., 96ff and *LW* 45:22ff. criticizing the eighteen impediments set out in Angelo Carletti di Chivasso's famous confessional book, *Summa angelica de casibus conscientiae* (1486), one of the books which Luther burned, along with the canon law books, in 1520. See above p. 53.
[138] *TC* 366–7.

is no impediment to marriage nowadays," Luther charged, "which they cannot legitimize for money. These man-made regulations seem to have come into existence for no other reason than raking in money and netting in souls. . . . "[139] Such abuses not only desecrated the priestly office, but resulted in a liberal law of impediments for the rich and a constrictive law for the poor. Furthermore, the reformers averred, the impediments had become so intricate that they were confusing to the common person. The confession manuals were filled with ornate legalistic discussions of the impediments, incomprehensible to the uninitiated and frequently not in the language of the common people.[140]

Acting on these general criticisms, the reformers developed a simplified and, in their view, more biblical law of impediments. They (1) adopted most of the physical impediments; (2) accepted, with some qualification, the impediments protecting the parties' consent; (3) adopted a severely truncated law of personal impediments; and (4) discarded the spiritual impediments protecting the sanctity of the sacrament.

Given the importance attached by the reformers to the physical and sexual union of husband and wife, they readily accepted the canonists' physical impediments of permanent impotence and bigamy, on the strength of the same favorite passages in Moses, the Gospels, and St. Paul.[141]

By accepting the consensual theory of marriage, the reformers also accepted the traditional impediments that guaranteed free consent. Thus a man and a woman who had been joined under duress, coercion, or fear were seen as "unmarried before God" and thus free to dissolve their union. Both Lutheran theologians and jurists, however, unlike the canonists, required that the pressure exerted on the couple be particularly pervasive and malicious – a requirement which they based on patristic authority. The reformers, like the canonists, accepted errors of person as grounds for annulment. Luther, Bucer, and Brenz, however, urged Christian couples to follow the example of Jacob and Leah and accept such unions as a challenge placed before them by God – a recommendation which is repeated in some of the statutes. A number of reformers also permitted annulment of marriage based on errors of quality, the mistaken assumption that one's spouse was a virgin. For, as the Mosaic and Pauline law made clear, one's prior commitment to marriage, whether through a promise or through sexual intercourse, prevented him or her

---

[139] *LW* 36:96–106; *LW* 45:7–9.
[140] Ibid. See also *LW* 45:22–30; Bucer, *RC*, chap. 17; and discussion of other views in Dieterich, *Das protestantische Eherecht*, 97–8.
[141] Ibid.

from entering any true marriage thereafter. Thus the second putative marriage was void from the start.[142]

In developing the civil law of personal impediments the reformers were far less faithful to the canon law tradition. They rejected several of these impediments and liberalized others in an attempt to remove as many obstacles to marriage and as many obfuscations of Scripture as possible.

First, the reformers rejected impediments designed to protect the celibate and the chaste. The canon laws prohibiting marriage to clerics, monks, and nuns were unanimously rejected as unscriptural.[143] Several statutes explicitly condoned clerical marriage and enjoined subjects to accept their offspring as legitimate children and heirs.[144] Canon laws forbidding remarriage to those who had initially married a cleric, monk, or nun had no parallel in the new civil law. The traditional assumption that vows of chastity and celibacy automatically dissolved betrothals and unconsummated marriages found acceptance only among the early conservative jurists, such as Kling and Schürpf.[145]

Secondly, the reformers rejected or simplified the intricate restrictions on those related by blood, family, spiritual, or legal ties. Only early Lutheran jurists and legislators accepted the canon law formulation of the impediment of consanguinity which permitted annulment of marriages between parties related by blood to the fourth degree.[146]

---

[142] See generally, ibid., *LW* 45:22ff., 66ff., 102ff., 128ff. and discussion in Friedberg, *Die Eheschliessung*, 212ff.; Kirstein, *Die Entwicklung*, 28ff., 57ff.; Köhler, "Die Anfänge," 375ff. For statutory examples, see, e.g., the consistory ordinances of Brandenburg (1573) and Prussia (1584) in Richter, 2:383ff., 466ff. (on impediments to protect free consent); Kurbrandenburg church ordinance (1540), ibid., 1:323ff. (on the impediment respecting errors of quality).

[143] See, e.g., *LW* 35:138, 45:28; *Common Places of Martin Bucer*, trans. and ed. D. F. Wright (Aberdeen, 1972), 406ff. and discussion of other reformers' views in Dieterich, *Das protestantishe Eherecht*, 78ff., 110ff. Conservative jurists, such as Kling and Schürpf, however, rejected this impediment with great hesitation; Schürpf, in fact, by 1536, considered the children of clerics to be illegitimate and recommended that legacies and inheritances not be bequeathed to them. See Stintzing, 275.

[144] Church ordinances of Northeim (1539), Kurbrandenburg (1540), Braunschweig-Wolfenbüttel (1543) as well as the consistory ordinance of Wittenberg (1542) in Richter, 1:287ff., 323ff., 367ff., and 2:56ff.

[145] *LW* 36:97–9.

[146] The early writers who adopted this position – Brenz, Kling, Clammer, Mauser, and Monner – accepted the traditional doctrine as a restriction on marriage; they advocated annulment of consummated marriages only if the parties were related by blood to the second degree. To support their position, these early writers cited Scripture (Leviticus 18:6–13) for the first degree; Roman law (*Digest* 23, 2, 53, 68) and Scripture for the second; canon law and Germanic law for the third; and canon law for the fourth. See Dieterich, *Das protestantischen Eherecht*, 131–5. It should be noted that strict enforcement of the impediment of consanguinity to the fourth degree eliminated for any one person several hundred people as prospective marriage partners – a significant restriction for those who lived in small, isolated communities. See Rudolf Weigand, "Ehe- und Familienrecht in der mittelalterlichen Stadt," in Alfred Haverkamp, ed., *Haus und Familie in der spätmittelalterlichen Stadt* (Tübingen, 1984), 173; Richard Köbner, "Die Eheauffassung des ausgehenden deutschen Mittelalters," *Archiv für Kulturgeschichte* 9 (1911): 136.

Several reformers permitted restrictions on parties related by blood only to the third or to the second degree, and both positions found statutory expression.[147] Luther's repeated arguments for adopting only the slender group of impediments of consanguinity set forth in Leviticus were routinely rejected.[148] Similarly, the canon law impediments of affinity and public decorum, which annulled marriage between a person and the blood relative of his or her deceased spouse or fiancé(e) to the fourth degree, were accepted in qualified form only by early Lutheran jurists and legislators.[149] The arguments by theologians to reduce these restrictions to "in-laws" in the third, second, or even first degrees all came to legislative expression.[150]

Thirdly, the spiritual impediments, prohibiting marriages between godparents and their children, were rejected by virtually all the reformers and legislators.[151]

Fourthly, the legal impediments, proscribing marriages between a variety of parties related by adoption, were liberalized, and in some jurisdictions abandoned altogether.[152]

Fifthly, a number of jurisdictions that had accepted Luther's conflation of future and present marriage promises rejected the canon law impediment of multiple relationships. The canonists had maintained that any betrothal was dissolved if one of the parties made a subsequent marriage promise to, or had sexual relations with, another. This rule

---

[147] See a convenient table in Melanchthon, *De arbore consanguinitatis et affinitatis, sive de gradibus* (Wittenberg, 1540), folios aii–bii. For Osiander's position, see the summary in Judith W. Harvey, "The Influence of the Reformation on Nürnberg Marriage Laws, 1520–1535" (PhD Diss., Ohio State University, 1972), 250. Impediments of consanguinity to the third degree were accepted by the Württemberg marriage ordinance (1537), the church ordinance of Celle (1545), the Mecklenburg church ordinance (1557), the Hessen reformation ordinance (1572), the Mecklenburg policy ordinance (1572), the Lübeck ordinance (1581) respectively in Richter, 1:280; Sehling, 1:296; 5:212; Schmelzeisen, *Polizeiordnung und Privatrecht*, 50ff. Impediments of consanguinity to the second degree were accepted by the Saxon General Articles (1557): Richter, 2:178ff.

[148] See *LW* 45:3ff., 23ff. and corrections in *WA Br* 7:152–3. See esp. *LW* 45:3ff., 23ff.; Bucer, *Common Places*, 410ff. The Levitical law of impediments of consanguinity was adopted by later statutes, e.g., the Brandenburg ordinance (1694) and the Prussian cabinet order (1740), quoted and discussed in Schmelzeisen, *Polizeiordnung und Privatrecht*, 51–52.

[149] See Dieterich, *Das protestantische Eherecht*, 135–6.

[150] Ibid., 100, 161.

[151] Ibid., 100, 136. Though most statutes silently ignored the spiritual impediments, a few later statutes explicitly denied their validity. See, e.g., the church ordinance of Lower Saxony (1585) and the Braunschweiger policy ordinance (1618), quoted and discussed in Schmelzeisen, *Polizeiordnung und Privatrecht*, 53.

[152] This impediment was retained by a few early reformers such as Kling, Schürpf, and Brenz. Many later jurists who rejected the impediment still insisted that the adopted child be granted the full rights of protection and inheritance accorded the natural child. See Dieterich, *Das protestantische Eherecht*, 101, 137.

was adopted by the reformers only for conditional betrothal promises. They regarded unconditional public promises of betrothal as indissoluble and thus superior to any subsequent physical or verbal commitments of marriage to each other.[153]

The reformers rejected the spiritual impediments of unbelief and crime which had been designed to protect the sanctity of the marriage sacrament. The canon law had prohibited marriage between Christians and non-Christians and permitted annulment where one party had permanently left the Church. Only those couples who had been sanctified by baptism and who remained true to the faith could symbolize the union of Christ and His Church. To the reformers, marriage had no such symbolic Christian function and thus no prerequisites of baptism or unanimity of faith.[154] The canonists had also prohibited marriage to the person who had done public penance (for mortal sin) or who was guilty of certain sexual crimes. For his or her marital union would be constantly perverted by this grave former sin, and thus neither the mortal sinner nor the spouse could receive the sanctifying grace of the sacrament. To the reformers, marriage imparted no such sanctifying grace and thus required no such prerequisite purity. To be sure, Luther writes, "sins and crimes should be punished, but with other penalties, not by forbidding marriage. David committed adultery with Bathsheba, Uriah's wife, and had her husband killed besides. He was guilty of both crimes, still he [could take] her to be his wife."[155] A number of jurists and legislators concurred.

The law of divorce and remarriage

The reformers' attack on the canon law of impediments was closely allied with their attack on the canon law of divorce. Just as they discarded many impediments, as infringements of the right to enter marriage, they rejected the canon law of divorce as an abridgment of the right to end one marriage and enter another.

Since the twelfth century, the Church had consistently taught that (1) divorce meant only separation of the couple from bed and board; (2) such separation had to be ordered by a Church court on proof of adultery, desertion, or cruelty; divorce could not be undertaken voluntarily; and (3) despite the divorce, the sacramental bond between the parties

---

[153] See the church ordinance of Celle (1545), the consistory ordinance of Goslar (1555), and the marriage ordinance of Dresden (1556) in Sehling, 1:295; Richter, 2:166; Sehling, 1:343.
[154] Dieterich, *Das protestantische Eherecht*, 68, 102.   [155] *LW* 45:26.

remained intact, and thus neither party was free to remarry until the death of the estranged spouse. Once properly established, the marriage bond could not be severed, even if the parties became bitter enemies.

In practice, the canon law of divorce was partly mitigated by the law of impediments, which allowed parties to dissolve putative marriages and enter others. But the declaration of annulment simply meant that the marriage never existed because it had been contracted improperly, and it required proof in a Church court of an absolute (diriment) impediment. A declaration of annulment often also meant that the parties had sinned gravely in joining together and were subject to penitential (and, at times, also legal) discipline. Such annulments were not nearly so easy to come by as some sixteenth-century Protestants seemed to imagine. They were particularly difficult to procure if the parties had consummated their marriages and had children.[156]

The Lutheran reformers rejected this traditional doctrine with arguments from Scripture, history, and utility. Scripture teaches, the reformers insisted, that marriage is a natural institution of the earthly kingdom, not a sacramental institution of the heavenly kingdom. The essence of marriage is the community of husband and wife in this life, not their sacramental union in the life to come.[157] For a couple to establish "a true marriage" in this earthly life, wrote Martin Bucer, "God requires them to live together and be united in body and mind. . . . The proper end of marriage is . . . the communicating of all duties, both divine and human, each to the other with the utmost benevolence and affection."[158] Irreconcilable separation of the parties was tantamount to dissolution of the marriage, for the requisite benevolent communion of marriage could no longer be carried out. The traditional teaching that permanently separated couples were still bound in marriage rested on the unbiblical assumption that marriage is a binding sacrament.

Furthermore, the reformers charged, for the Church to equate divorce with judicial separation and to prohibit divorcees from remarrying had

---

[156] See Helmholz, *The Spirit of the Classical Canon Law*, 240–1.

[157] *LW* 46:276ff.; *CR* 7:487; 21:1079ff.; Johannes Bugenhagen, *Vom ehebruch und weglauffen* (Wittenberg, 1539, 1541), folios 171ff.; Brenz, *Wie in Ehesachen*, folio 185ff.; Schneidewin, *De nuptiis* . . . , 484ff.; Konrad Mauser, *Explicatio erudita et utilis X. tituli inst. de nuptiis* (Jena, 1569), 335ff.; Basilius Monner, *Tractatus duo. I. De matrimonio. II. De clandestinis conjugiis*, 2nd. edn. (Jena, 1604), 203ff. See further Hans Hesse, *Evangelisches Ehescheidungsrecht in Deutschland* (Bonn, 1960); F. Albrecht, *Verbrechen und Strafen als Ehescheidungsgrund nach evangelischem Kirchenrecht* (PhD Diss., Munich, 1903); J. Grabner, *Ueber Desertion und Quasi-desertion als Scheidungsgrund nach dem evangelischen Kirchenrecht* (PhD Diss. Leipzig, 1882); Aemilius Richter, *Beiträge zur Geschichte des Ehescheidungsrechts in der evangelischen Kirche* (Aalen, 1958).

[158] Bucer, *Common Places*, 465.

no basis in Scripture. The term *divortium*, as used in Scripture, means dissolution of marriage, not simply separation. No philological evidence from biblical or early patristic times suggests otherwise. Medieval writers had improperly introduced their interpretation of the term in order to support their sacramental concept of marriage.[159] Where Scripture permits divorce, the reformers believed, it also permits remarriage. "In the case of adultery," for example, Luther wrote, "Christ permits divorce of husband and wife so that the innocent person may remarry."[160] Other reformers considered the sentence of divorce and the right of remarriage to be "one and the same."[161] For the divorcee, like any single person, had to heed God's duty to form families and to accept God's remedy against incontinence and other sexual sins. To deprive the divorcee of the spiritual and physical benefits of marriage, as the Church traditionally had done, could not be countenanced. It was unbiblical and led to all manner of sexual sin.

The reformers bolstered these Scriptural arguments for divorce and remarriage with arguments from history. They adduced support for their biblical exegesis from the commentaries of the Church Fathers. They found a wealth of precedents for laws of divorce and remarriage in the Mosaic law based on Deuteronomy 24:1 (permitting divorce for "uncleanness") and the many decrees of the Christian Roman emperors, particularly the Theodosian Code (438) and Justinian's Code and *Novellae* (565).[162]

These historical laws of divorce, however, were hardly commensurate with the teachings of the Gospel. Christ had permitted divorce only on grounds of adultery and only as a special exception to the general command "What God has joined together let not man put asunder" (Mark 10:2–12; Luke 16:18; Matthew 5:31–2, 19:3–19). St. Paul had hinted further in 1 Corinthians 7:15 that divorce might be permitted on grounds of desertion: "if the unbelieving [spouse] depart, let him depart. A brother or sister is not under bondage in such cases, but God hath called us to

---

[159] Ibid., 416–17; *LW* 46:275–81. [160] *LW* 45:30–31.

[161] Quoted by Ozment, *When Fathers Ruled*, 84.

[162] Luther touched on an additional argument that when a Christian magistrate "puts asunder" a marriage, he is in fact operating as God, since he is God's vice-regent. See, e.g., *WA TR* 1, No. 414; *LW* 54:65–6: "I feel that judgments about marriage belong to the jurists. Since they make judgments concerning fathers, mothers, children, and servants, why shouldn't they make decisions about the life of married people? When the papists oppose the imperial law concerning divorce, I reply that this doesn't follow from what is written, 'What God has joined together, let no man put asunder', for the emperor [who is God's vice-regent] puts asunder with his laws; it's not man who puts asunder, but God [in the person of his vice-regent], for here 'man' signifies a private person."

peace." The laws of Moses and of the Roman Empire, however, had put marriages asunder for many other reasons besides adultery and desertion. The Mosaic law had permitted divorce for "uncleanness," indecency, and incompatibility of all kinds. At Roman law, a person could divorce a spouse who was guilty of treason or iconoclasm, who had committed one of many felonies or fraudulent acts against third parties, or who had abused, deserted, threatened, or in other ways maltreated members of their family. Divorce was also permitted if a husband wrongly accused his wife of adultery or if a wife was guilty of shameful or immoral acts (such as abortion, bigamy or exhibitionism), or if the husband became delinquent, insolent, or impotent or persistently refused to have sexual relations. In the later Roman Empire, divorce was even permitted by mutual consent of the parties. The innocent party was, in most instances, permitted to remarry another.[163] Such liberal laws remained in constant tension with the New Testament command that all but the unchaste and unfaithful must remain indissolubly bound.

The reformers resolved this tension by distinguishing between moral laws designed for Christians in the heavenly kingdom and civil laws designed for all persons in the earthly kingdom. Christ's command, the reformers taught, is an absolute moral standard for Christians. It demands of them love, patience, forgiveness, and a conciliatory spirit. It sets out what is absolutely right, what the true law would be if the earthly kingdom were free from sin and populated only by perfect Christians. The earthly kingdom, however, is fallen, and many of its sinful citizens disregard the moral law. Thus it becomes necessary for civil authorities to promulgate laws that both facilitate and protect marriage and its social functions as well as maintain peace and order in sinful society. The positive laws of the German magistrates, like those of Moses and the Roman emperors, therefore, must inevitably compromise moral ideals for marriage. They must allow for divorce and remarriage.[164]

It might be advisable nowadays that certain queer, stubborn, and obstinate people, who have no capacity for toleration and are not suited for married life at all, should be permitted to get a divorce, since people are as evil as they are, any other way of governing is impossible. Frequently something must be

---

[163] Theodosian Code 3.16.1,2; Justinian Code 5.17.8,9,10. Divorce by mutual consent, permitted by Emperor Anastasius in 497, was rejected some forty years later in Justinian's *Novella* 117.8–14. See, generally, Susan Treggiari, *Roman Marriage: Iusti Coniuges from the Time of Cicero to the Time of Ulpian* (Oxford, 1991), 435ff.; Judith Evans Grubb, *Law and Family in Late Antiquity: The Emperor Constantine's Marriage Legislation* (Oxford, 1995), 203ff.

[164] *LW* 21:94ff.; Bucer, *Common Places*, 411ff.; and the views of Brenz and Bugenhagen discussed by Ozment, *When Fathers Ruled*, 89ff.; Sprengler-Ruppenthal, "Zur Rezeption," 395ff.

tolerated, even though it is not a good thing to do, to prevent something even worse from happening.[165]

"The reality is that some households become broken beyond repair," Bugenhagen continued. This is "an eyesore to both the Church and the state" and is better removed lest "it cause further evil."[166] The law of divorce and remarriage, like other positive laws, must thus be inspired by the moral norms of Scripture as well as by pragmatic concerns of utility and good governance.

By conjoining these arguments from Scripture, utility, and history, the reformers concluded that (1) absolute divorce with a subsequent right to marry had been instituted by Moses and Christ; (2) the expansion of divorce was a result of sin and a remedy against greater sin; and (3) God had revealed the expanded grounds for divorce in history. On this basis, the reformers advocated a new civil law of divorce and remarriage. They specified the proper grounds for divorce and the procedures which estranged couples had to follow.

The Lutheran reformers and legislators of Germany unanimously accepted adultery as a ground for divorce on the stated authority of Scripture and frequently also of Roman law and early canon law.[167] Theologians such as Luther and Bugenhagen, however, advocated that the couple first be given time to resolve the matter privately. They instructed adulterers to seek forgiveness and innocent spouses to be forgiving. They further urged pastors and friends to sponsor the mending of this torn marriage in any way they could. These recommendations found statutory support. A number of marriage ordinances repeated the reformers' prescriptions.[168] Criminal statutes provided that punishment of the adulterer could not commence until the innocent party sued for divorce. Absent such suits, a judge could begin criminal proceedings

---

[165] *LW* 21:94; see also Bucer, *Common Places*, 411–12, and discussion of other reformers in Richter, *Beiträge* 32ff.; Ozment, *When Fathers Ruled*, 89.

[166] Bugenhagen, *Vom Ehebruch und weglauffen*, folios miii–oiii.

[167] See the numerous church ordinances and other statutes quoted and discussed by Hans Dietrich, *Evangelisches Ehescheidungsrecht nach den Bestimmungen der deutschen Kirchenordnungen des 16. Jahrhunderts* (Berlin, 1892), 12–14, 164; Hesse, *Evangelisches Ehescheidungsrecht*, 31–33; Albrecht, *Verbrechen und Strafen*, 43–6. The church ordinance of Lübeck (1531) and marriage ordinance of Württemberg (1537), drafted by Brenz, as well as the marriage ordinance of Pfalz (1563) and church ordinance of Huttenberg (1555) cite Roman law prominently alongside Scripture in support of this ground for divorce. See Sehling, 5:356; Richter, 1:280; 2:257, 163. Melanchthon and Kling refer several times to earlier canonical and patristic writings in their discussions of adultery: *CR* 21:103 and Kling, *Matrimonialium causarum tractatus* (1553), folio 101v. See also Richter, *Beiträge*, 29–30, on Kling's views.

[168] *LW* 45:32. See discussion in Ozment, *When Fathers Ruled*, 85ff.; Hesse, *Evangelische Ehescheidungsrecht*, 32.

against an adulterer only if his or her violation was "open, undoubted, and scandalous."[169] Even in such cases, authorities preferred less severe penalties (not banishment or imprisonment) that would still allow the couple to rejoin. Where efforts of private reconciliation failed, and continued cohabitation of the parties yielded only misery and threats to the safety of the parties and their children, the innocent spouse could sue for divorce.

Husbands and wives had equal rights to sue for divorce. Thereafter, the innocent party was permitted to remarry, after a time of healing – usually a few months or a year. The adulterer faced stern criminal sanctions scaled to the egregiousness of the offense. These ranged from fines or short imprisonment to exile or execution in the case of repeat adulterers. The call by many reformers to execute all divorced adulterers found little acceptance among the authorities, though many jurisdictions, in response, stiffened their penalties for adultery.[170] Only the egregious repeat offender was subject to execution.[171]

Though a few theologians and early legislators accepted adultery as the only ground for divorce, many others defended a more expansive divorce law.[172] Desertion or abandonment was a widely accepted ground for divorce among the reformers. A party who deserted his or her spouse and family destroyed the bond of communal love, service, and support needed for the marriage to survive and for children to be properly nourished and reared. Not every absence of a spouse, however, could be considered a form of desertion. Theologians such as Bugenhagen

---

[169] Bambergensis Halsgericht und rechtliche Ordnung, art. 145 (1507), repeated with revisions in Constitutio Criminalis Carolina, art. 120 (1532), in Josef Kohler and Willy Scheel, eds., *Die peinliche Gerichtsordnung Kaiser Karls V. Constitutio Criminalis Carolina*, repr. (Aalen, 1968), 63.

[170] See, e.g., Bugenhagen, *Vom Ehebruch und Weglauffen*, folios oiii–piii.

[171] See, e.g., Bucer, *Common Places*, 410–11. On the reaction of the civil authorities thereto, see Dieterich, *Das protestantische Eherecht*, 105ff.; Harvey, *The Influence*, 113ff.; Kock, *Studium Pietatis*, 141ff.; Köhler, *Das Ehe*, 109ff. The *Bambergensis* and *Carolina*, however, ordered "death by the sword" as criminal punishment for adultery; these statutes further provided that innocent spouses who, on discovery of the philandering parties, immediately killed one or both of them were not subject to penalty. Such provisions, which had been part of German law for centuries, were only rarely enforced by the end of the sixteenth century. Even where the adulterer was spared, however, he or she was denied the right to remarry and was subject to severe penalty when prosecuted for subsequent acts of prostitution, homosexuality, or other sexual crimes. See Schmelzeisen, *Polizeiordnung und Privatrecht*, 53–4.

[172] This was the view of, e.g., Ambrosius Blaurer and Johannes Oecolampadius, among theologians, and Schürpf, Schneidewin, Kling, and the draftsmen of the church ordinances of Schwabisch-Hall (1531) and of Lower Saxony (1585), among jurists. Johannes Brenz initially permitted divorce only on this ground, but later expanded the grounds for divorce. Even in this later period, however, Brenz permitted remarriage only to victims of adultery, and exacted ecclesiastical penalties against Church members who divorced for reasons other than adultery. See Köhler, "Die Anfänge," 302; Hesse, *Evangelisches Ehescheidungsrecht*, 32–33; Albrecht, *Verbrechen und Strafen*, 14–16; Schmelzeisen, *Polizeiordnung und Privatrecht*, 61.

and jurists such as Schneidewin insisted that the abandonment be notoriously willful and malicious, a requirement that was repeated in several statutes.[173] No divorce was thus permitted if the absent partner was serving in the prince's army, engaged in study or business abroad, or visiting a foreign place. Divorce for desertion was permitted only where the partner's absence was completely inexcusable and inequitable, left the spouse and family in grave danger, or was so unreasonably prolonged that the party had presumably died or fallen into delinquency or adultery. The deserted spouse was in such cases free to remarry. If the long-lost deserter returned, he or she was presumed guilty of adultery until proven innocent.[174] If the deserter never returned, the spouse could, after a designated period of time, petition for an *ex parte* divorce and for the right to marry another. No legislature accepted Luther's recommendation that a deserted party of good reputation need wait only a year before bringing such an action, but few went so far as to require the full seven to ten years stipulated at Roman law.[175] Waiting periods of three years after desertion were the statutory norm.

Quasi-desertion, the unjustifiable abstention from sexual intercourse, found limited acceptance as a ground for divorce. Luther, Brenz, Bucer, and the jurist Clammer argued that voluntary abandonment of such an essential aspect of marriage was tantamount to abandonment of the marriage itself. Furthermore, it violated St. Paul's injunction in 1 Corinthians 7 that spouses abstain from sex only by mutual consent. Luther counseled the deprived spouse to warn the other spouse of his or her discontent, and to invite the pastor or friends to speak with the spouse. If the spouse remained abstinent, Luther permitted the deprived spouse to sue for divorce and remarry.[176] Only a few statutes adopted this teaching.[177]

At the urging of several more liberal reformers, most notably Martin Bucer, numerous other grounds for divorce sporadically gained acceptance in German territories. Already in the 1520s, Zürich and Basel under Ulrich Zwingli's inspiration recognized, alongside adultery and desertion, impotence, grave incompatibility, sexually incapacitating

---

[173] Bugenhagen, *Vom Ehebruch und Weglauffen*, folios oiii–piii. See church ordinances of Pomerania (1535) and Lippische (1538), in Richter, 1:25off.; 2:499ff. and other statutes quoted and discussed in Hesse, *Evangelisches Ehescheidungsrecht*, 33–5; Dietrich, *Evangelisches Ehescheidungsrecht*, 17–25; Grabner, *Ueber Desertion*, 63ff.; Schmelzeisen, *Polizeiordnung und Privatrecht*, 60–61.

[174] See, e.g., the church ordinances of Goslar (1531) and Celle (1545) and the Consistory Ordinance of Mecklenberg (1571) in Richter, 1:156; Sehling, 1:295ff.; 5: 239ff.

[175] See *WA TR* 3, No. 4499; *WA TR* 5, No. 5569.

[176] *LW* 45:33–4. See also Dietrich, *Evangelisches Ehescheidungsrecht*, 25–31.

[177] Church ordinances of Lippe (1538), Göttingen (1542), and Mecklenberg (1552); the Württemberg marriage ordinance (1553) and the consistory ordinance of Prussia (1584) in Richter, 1:365; 2:120, 130, 466, 499.

illnesses, felonies, deception, and serious threats by one spouse against the life of the other spouse as grounds for divorce.[178] By the 1550s, confessional differences between the couple, defamation of a spouse's moral character, abuse and maltreatment, conspiracies or plots against a spouse, acts of incest and bigamy, delinquent frequenting of "public games" or places of ill repute, and acts of treason or sacrilege all came to legislative expression as grounds for divorce.[179] Though no single marriage statute in this period explicitly adopted all these grounds for divorce, a few statutes did permit divorce "on any grounds recognized by Scripture and the Roman law of Justinian."[180]

The reformers insisted that divorce, like marriage, be a public act. Just as a couple could not form the marriage bond in secret, so they could not sever it in secret. They had to inform the community and Church of their intentions and petition a civil judge to order the divorce.[181] This requirement of publicity was a formidable obstacle to divorce. Couples who publicized their intent to divorce invited not only the counsel and comfort of friends and pastors but frequently also the derision of the community and the discipline of the Church. Furthermore, judges had great discretion to deny or delay petitions for divorce and to grant interim remedies short of this irreversible remedy. Particularly in conservative courts, the petitioner had a heavy burden of proof to show that the divorce was mandated by statute, that all efforts at reconciliation had proved fruitless, and that no alternative remedy was available.[182]

SUMMARY AND CONCLUSIONS

Like Catholics, the Lutheran reformers taught that marriage was a natural, contractual, and spiritual institution subject to godly law. They also

---

[178] Ozment, *When Fathers Ruled*, 93.

[179] See statutes in Dietrich, *Evangelisches Ehescheidungsrecht*, 31ff.; Hesse, *Evangelisches Ehescheidungsrecht*, 35ff.; Köhler, "Die Anfänge," 303ff. See a contemporary catalogue in von Beust, *Tractatus de iure connubiorum* (1591 edn.), folios 54b–59.

[180] See the church ordinances of Hanover (1536) and Huttenberg (1555), and the marriage ordinance of Pfalz (1563), quoted in Dietrich, *Evangelisches Ehescheidungsrecht*, 31–2. A similar provision is recommended by Basilius [Erasmus] Sarcerius, *Corpus juris matrimonialis. Vom Ursprung, Anfang und Herkomen des Heyligen Ehestandts* (Frankfurt am Main, 1569), folio 216.

[181] See, e.g., *LW* 36:102ff.; *LW* 45:30ff.; *LW* 46:311ff. See comparable practices in Switzerland described in Thomas Max Safley, "Canon Law and Swiss Reform: Legal Theory and Practice in the Marital Courts of Zurich, Bern, Basel, and St. Gall," in Helmholz, ed., *Canon Law in Protestant Lands*, 187.

[182] Witness the conservative practices of the courts of Nuremberg, Zurich, and Basel as described in Harvey, *The Influence*, 153ff.; Ozment, *When Fathers Ruled*; Adrian Staehelin, *Die Einführung der Ehescheidung in Basel zur Zeit der Reformation* (Basel, 1957), 101ff.

taught that marriage had inherent goods of mutual faith and love of husband, mutual protection of both parties from sexual sin, and mutual procreation and nurture of children.

Unlike Catholics, however, the Lutheran reformers rejected that subordination of marriage to celibacy, and the prohibition against marriage of clergy. The individual was too tempted by sinful passion to forgo marriage. The family was too vital a social institution in God's redemption plan to be hindered. The celibate life had no superior virtue and no inherent superiority to marriage and was no prerequisite for ecclesiastical service. On the contrary, the pious Lutheran parsonage was a source and a model of authority and liberty, faithfulness and charity, for the entire community to emulate.

Also unlike Catholics, the Lutheran reformers rejected the notion that marriage was a sacrament. Marriage, they taught, was an estate of the earthly kingdom, not an order of the heavenly kingdom. Though a holy institution of God, marriage required no prerequisite faith or purity and conferred no sanctifying grace, as did true sacraments. Rather, it had distinctive uses in the life of the individual and of society, much like the three uses of the law. It restricted prostitution, promiscuity, and other public sexual sins: its civil use. It revealed to humanity its sinfulness and its need for God's marital gift: its theological use. It taught love, restraint, and other public virtues and morals: its educational use. All fit men and women were free to enter such unions, provided they complied with the laws of marriage formation.

As an estate of the earthly kingdom, marriage was subject to the prince not the pope. Civil law, not canon law, was to govern marriage. Marital disputes were to be brought before civil courts, not Church courts. Marriage was still subject to God's law, but this law was now to be administered by the civil authorities who had been called as God's vice-regents to govern the earthly kingdom. Church officials were required to counsel the magistrate about God's law and to cooperate with him in publicizing and disciplining marriage. Theologians were to give instruction and admonition on the meaning of God's law for sex, marriage, and family life. All Church members, as priests, were required to counsel those who contemplated marriage and to admonish those who sought annulment or divorce, and to participate in the spiritual nurture of all baptized children. But the Church no longer had formal legal authority over marriage.

The reforms of German marriage law introduced during the Lutheran Reformation reflected this reconceptualization of marriage. Civil marriage courts replaced Church courts in numerous Lutheran polities, frequently at the instigation of the reformers. New civil marriage statutes were promulgated, many replete with Evangelical marriage doctrines. Lutheran jurists throughout Germany published treatises on marriage law, affirming and embellishing the basic marriage doctrine set forth by the theologians.

This new civil law of marriage had a number of important innovations that can be directly traced to the theology and advocacy of Luther, Melanchthon, Bucer, Brenz, Bugenhagen, and their many Evangelical colleagues. Because the reformers rejected the subordination of marriage to celibacy, they rejected laws that forbade clerical and monastic marriage, that denied remarriage to those who had married a cleric or monastic, and that permitted vows of chastity to annul vows of marriage. Because they rejected the sacramental nature of marriage, the reformers rejected impediments of crime and heresy and prohibitions against divorce in the modern sense. Marriage was for them the community of the couple in the present, not their sacramental union in the life to come. Where that community was broken, for one of a number of specific reasons (such as adultery or desertion), the couple could sue for divorce. Because people by their lustful natures were in need of God's remedy of marriage, the reformers removed numerous legal, spiritual, and consanguineous impediments to marriage not countenanced by Scripture. Because of their emphasis on the godly responsibility of the prince, the pedagogical role of the Church and the family, and the priestly calling of all believers, the reformers insisted that both marriage and divorce be public. The validity of marriage promises depended upon parental consent, witnesses, Church consecration and registration, and priestly instruction. Couples who wished to divorce had to announce their intentions in the Church and community and to petition a civil judge to dissolve the bond. In the process of marriage formation and dissolution, therefore, the couple was subject to God's law, as appropriated in the civil law, and to God's will, as revealed in the admonitions of parents, peers, and pastors. Such reforms, taken together, transformed the life, lore, and law of marriage and family in Evangelical Germany.

It must also be stressed, however, that the Lutheran reformers appropriated a great deal of the canon law in their formation of the civil law of marriage. Canon law doctrines that grounded marriage in the mutual consent of the parties continued with only minor changes. Canon law prohibitions against unnatural relations, and against infringement of natural marital functions, remained in effect. Canon law impediments that protected free consent, that implemented Scriptural prohibitions against marriage of relatives, and that governed the couple's physical relations were largely retained. Such canon laws were as consistent with Catholic as with Lutheran concepts of marriage, and they continued largely uninterrupted.

Moreover, Lutheran jurists and judges turned readily to canon law texts and authorities in formulating their doctrines of marriage law. The opinions of judges and jurists in the later sixteenth century on cases of disputed betrothals, wife abuse, incest, child custody, desertion, adultery, divorce, annulment, and the like are chock-full of citations to the *Decretum*, *Decretales* and various canonists.[183] Legal dictionary and handbook entries on marriage, prepared by Lutheran jurists, cite Catholic theological and canon law sources with great frequency and authority.[184] Learned tracts on marriage law, prepared by Lutheran jurists, often made greater use of canon law and Roman law authorities than the new Protestant texts. The Lutheran reformers worked within the Western tradition of marriage. Their new theology of marriage, though filled with bold revisions, preserved a good deal of the teaching of the Roman Catholic tradition. Their new civil law of marriage was heavily indebted to the canon law which it replaced.

[183] See, e.g., cases collected in von Beust, *Tractatus de iure connubiorum*. In the cases and commentaries, von Beust draws eclectically from Protestant, Catholic, and Roman authorities. In instances of conflict of laws, authorities are generally listed side by side, with Protestant sources generally preferred to Catholic, and legal opinions preferred to theological opinions. A catalogue of authorities lists more than twenty canonists, including such leading lights as Gratian, Hostiensis, Innocent III, Innocent IV, Jason de Maino, Johannes Andreae, Joannes de Imola, Panormitanus, and Paulus de Castro.

[184] See, e.g., Oldendorp, *Lexicon iuris*, 138–139; id., *Collatio iuris civilis et canonici* (s.v. "Matrimonium"). See further discussion on Oldendorp above pp. 78–81, 154–68.

Eine Predigt /
Marti. Luther /
das man Kin=
der zur Schu=
len halten
solle.

Wittemberg.

MDXXX.

7. Cover page of Martin Luther, *Eine Predigt Marti. Luther das man Kinder zur Schulen halten solle* (Wittenberg, 1530)

At the top, God; Jesus Christ; Holy Spirit as a dove. At the bottom, a nativity scene with baby Jesus, Mary, and Joseph. The nativity scene is flanked by Martin Luther's coat of arms on the left and Philipp Melanhcthon's coat of arms on the right.

The civic seminary: The reformation of education law

The Lutheran Reformation was not only a fundamental reform of Church, state, and family, the three institutional pillars of the earthly kingdom. It was also a fundamental reform of the school and other institutions of education. Luther had already signaled the importance of educational reform in his revolutionary manifestos of 1520.[1] By the end of the sixteenth century, a rich collection of Evangelical sermons, pamphlets, and monographs on education lay at hand together with more than a hundred new Evangelical school ordinances.

The Lutheran reformers' early preoccupation with educational reform was driven by both theological and practical concerns. The new Evangelical theology assumed at least a minimal level of education in the community. The doctrines of *sola Scriptura* and lay participation in the vernacular liturgy assumed literacy and popular familiarity with Bibles, catechisms, and liturgical documents. The doctrines of the priesthood of all believers and the calling of all persons to a God-given vocation depended on the ready access of everyone to an educational program that suited their particular calling and character. The doctrine of the civil, theological, and educational uses of law in the earthly kingdom presumed widespread understanding of both the moral laws of conscience and the civil laws of the state. Germany's traditional pedagogical beliefs and structures, the reformers believed, could not readily accommodate this new theology.

Moreover, swift educational reform was critical to resolving some of the most pressing practical problems to beset the Lutheran Reformation in its early years. Evangelical Church leaders desperately needed right-minded pastors and teachers to staff the new Evangelical churches and charities. Evangelical magistrates needed civil jurists and counselors to replace the many canonists who had traditionally staffed the

---

[1] See esp. *LW* 44:200–7.

civil bureaucracy. The rapid destruction of cathedrals, cloisters, and chantries in the early years of the Reformation left Germany without its principal organs of lower education. The rapid dissolution of traditional forms of endowments, tithing, and penitential gifts deprived German students of critical sources of funding. The rapid disappearance of available positions within the Church bureaucracy rendered many parents hesitant to send their children to the schools that were left. Questions of education, therefore, demanded the reformers' immediate attention.

The reformers' resolution of these questions helped to render the Lutheran Reformation a quintessentially educational movement. The Lutheran Reformation was born in the university – in Luther's lectures on the Psalms and St. Paul, in his prerogative as a professor to challenge the Church to reform itself, in his acts of burning the canon law and confessional books before the law faculty of the University of Wittenberg. The Lutheran Reformation found its leaders among the learned theologians and jurists of the German universities, whose rectors and senators steadfastly protected them, despite threats of excommunication, interdict, and financial hardship.[2]

The leading reformers of the 1520s to 1550s laid the foundation for a comprehensive system of public education in Germany, under the law and governance of the civil magistrate. The new educational system featured hundreds of new Latin schools, boys' schools, and girls' schools, which offered mandatory instruction in the traditional liberal arts and the new Protestant faith. It also featured a massive outpouring of popular tracts and public lectures designed to teach persons of all walks of life all that was needed for body and soul. The new printing industry poured out pamphlets and tracts on commerce, geography, history, law, medicine, economy, husbandry, family life, and other civil subjects, together with sundry Bibles, catechisms, prayer books, and other guides for daily Christian living.[3] In the apt phrase of Philip Melanchthon, "the teacher of Germany," this new German educational system was

---

[2] See Oberman, "University and Society on the Threshold of Modern Times," 19; Lewis W. Spitz, "The Importance of the Reformation for the Universities: Culture and Confessions in the Critical Years," in Kittelson and Transue, eds., *Rebirth, Reform, and Resilience*, 42.

[3] See generally Edwards, *Printing, Propaganda, and Martin Luther*; Carmen Luke, *Pedagogy, Printing, and Protestantism: The Discourse on Childhood* (Albany, NY, 1989); Robert W. Scribner, *For the Sake of Simple Folk: Popular Propaganda for the German Reformation* (Cambridge, 1981); Miriam Chrisman, *Conflicting Visions of Reform: German Lay Propaganda Pamphlets, 1519–1530* (Atlantic Highlands, NJ, 1996); ead., *Lay Culture, Learned Culture: Books and Social Change in Strasbourg, 1480–1599* (New Haven, CT, 1982).

a "civic seminary" designed to inculcate both right religion and broad erudition in the populace.[4]

THE INHERITANCE

In the centuries before the Lutheran Reformation, the Church had dominated German education. The Church regarded "teaching" as a special apostolic calling of its clergy, alongside preaching and sacramental administration. Christ's last recorded words to his apostles had been: "Go ye therefore, and *teach* all nations, baptizing them in the name of the Father, and of the Son, and of the Holy Ghost: *teaching* them to observe all that I have commanded you: and lo, I am with you always, even unto the end of the world."[5] This calling to teach, the Church believed, had passed, through apostolic succession, to the pope and his prelates. It obligated them both to guard the faith set forth in the Bible and to elaborate its meaning for daily life. The Bible would thereby be transmitted faithfully to each new generation, and the meaning of the Bible elaborated through a living Christian tradition.[6]

The Church discharged its teaching authority through multiple media. The Bible was preserved through the transcriptions of monks and papal scribes, and later through the publications of authorized printers. The religious tradition was elaborated through sundry papal decretals and encyclicals, conciliar decrees and judgments, diocesan instructions and injunctions, and all manner of official rites, prayers, canons, creeds, and catechisms, as well as theological books.[7]

Formal schooling was one important means by which the Church exercised its teaching authority. School teaching, like all other forms of teaching offered by the Church, was fundamentally religious in character,

---

[4] For the phrase *seminarium civitatis* (literally "seminary of the city"), see Philip Melanchthon, *In laudem novae scholae* (1526), *MW* 3:69. For broader use of the term and concept, see Gerhard Müller, "Philipp Melanchthon zwischen Pädagogik und Theologie," in Wolfgang Reinhard, ed., *Humanismus im Bildungswesen des 15. und 16. Jahrhundert* (Weinheim, 1984), 95–106, at 97–9. On Melanchthon's title, see Hartfelder, *Philipp Melanchthon als Praeceptor Germaniae*; Scheible, *Melanchthon: Eine Biographie*.

[5] Matthew 28:18–20 (emphasis added). See papers in John M. Todd, ed., *Problems of Authority* (Baltimore, MD, 1962); Yves Congar and Bernard D. Dupuy, eds., *L'Episcopat et l'église universelle* (Paris, 1962).

[6] Introduction to John A. McHugh and Charles J. Callan, trans. and ed., *Catechism of the Council of Trent* (1982), xi–xiv; Yves Congar, *Tradition and the Life of the Church*, trans. A. N. Woodrow (London, 1964).

[7] Frederick Eby and Charles F. Arrowood, *The History and Philosophy of Education, Ancient and Medieval* (New York, 1940), 758–61.

designed to teach the precepts and practices of the Christian faith for all walks of life. The Church had established its first schools in Germany by the later seventh century. By 1500, a vast network of Church schools was in place governed by general canon law principles and the tailored rules of local bishops and synods.[8]

Cathedral, monastic, and parish schools delivered much of the formal lower education in Germany. These schools offered both humanistic and religious instruction, principally to budding spiritual and secular clergy. The youngest students were taught to read, write, and sing. Intermediate students were versed in the *trivium* (grammar, rhetoric, and dialectic) and the *quadrivium* (arithmetic, geometry, music, and astronomy), using primarily Greek and Roman texts. Advanced students were trained in biblical and theological studies in preparation for their clerical vocations. Clerical schoolmasters (*scholastici*), trained in scholastic theology and philosophy, guided children through these programs under the supervision and employ of bishops and monastic superiors.[9] Many of the larger cathedral and monastic schools were supported by substantial endowments that helped to defray the costs of teachers, texts, and tuition fees. Though the bulk of students in these schools were of noble or magisterial stock, precocious youngsters of all classes found their way into the classroom as well, through the recommendations and support of parishes, orphanages, and monasteries.[10]

The Church also provided a number of less formal means of lower education. The largest monasteries and cathedrals sometimes held "external" or "college" schools for training choir members, acolytes, and clerks in the rudiments of reading and music. Ecclesiastical chantries and guilds were regularly commissioned by benefactors to provide education for youth. Cloisters provided both domestic and humanistic training for some of the young girls in the community. Parish priests provided

---

[8] Among countless older studies, see ibid., 715–836; Friedrich Paulsen, *Geschichte des gelehrten Unterrichts auf den deutschen Schulen und Universitäten vom Ausgang des Mittelalters bis zur Gegenwart*, 3rd. edn. (Leipzig, 1919), 7–52; Johannes Janssen, *History of the German People at the Close of the Middle Ages*, 15th Germ. edn., 2nd rev. Engl. edn. trans. M. A. Mitchell and A. M. Christie, 14 vols. (London, 1905), 1:25–60. For more recent studies, see sources and discussion in Ernst Ralf Hintz, *Learning and Persuasion in the German Middle Ages* (New York/London, 1997); Nikolaus Henkel, *Deutsche Übersetzungen Lateinischer Schultexte: Ihre Verbreitung und Funktion im Mittelalter und in der frühen Neuzeit* (Munich, 1988); Klaus Petzold, *Die Grundlagen der Erziehungslehre im Spätmittelalter und bei Luther* (Heidelberg, 1969).

[9] See William S. Learned, *The Oberlehrer: A Study of the Social and Professional Evolution of the German Schoolmaster*, repr. (Cambridge, MA, 1986), with sample sources in Henkel, *Deutsche Übersetzungen*.

[10] Per Third Lateran Council (1179), canon 18 and the Fourth Lateran Council (1215), canon 11, in H. J. Schroeder, *Disciplinary Decrees of the General Councils: Text, Translation, and Commentary* (New York, 1937), 229–230, 252–253.

rudimentary reading and writing skills to their catechumens and general moral and religious instruction to their congregants.[11] Several fifteenth-century decrees issued by German synods and councils enjoined clerics to use their pulpits and confessionals to educate their flocks in the teachings of the Gospel, Decalogue, and catechism.[12]

A dozen German universities established between 1348 and 1506 provided advanced training in theology, medicine, law, and the arts.[13] Though these universities were independent corporations formally outside of the Church's jurisdiction, they generally remained under strong Church influence. The Church issued the charters that established the universities and the licenses that allowed their professors to teach.[14] Clerics and monks comprised the majority of the teaching staff. Monasteries provided fraternities and foundations to house and support students, particularly foreigners. Parish priests and cathedral canons served as university chaplains. General councils and local synods passed regulations to control the curriculum, teaching staff, and student body of the universities. Local bishops and Church courts adjudicated the majority of disputes between and among students, professors, and the Church hierarchy, with Church courts holding plenary personal jurisdiction over students.[15]

Despite its vast institutions and influence, however, the Church held no monopoly on late medieval German education. By 1500, dozens of independent private boarding or day schools, run by one or more lay teachers paid through private fees, could be found in the cities. Large craft and mercantile guilds maintained their own schools, both to train apprentices and to educate members of their families.[16] The Brethren of the Common Life, a lay religious movement originating in the Lowlands, was the most famous of a whole series of lay religious orders for men and women that offered a refined education in humane letters and the classics and that came to attract a substantial number of German students.

Also by 1500, a number of German cities (particularly those in the Hanseatic League) had established, often over clerical objection, their

---

[11] Paulsen, *Geschichte*, 13ff.   [12] Janssen, *History*, 1:34ff.; *Catechism of the Council*, xiii–xx.

[13] Hastings Rashdall, *The Universities of Europe in the Middle Ages*, rev. edn., 3 vols., ed. F. M. Powicke and A. B. Enden (London/Oxford, 1936), 2:211–88; Muther, *Aus dem Universitäts- und Gelehrtenleben* (Graz, 1966).

[14] The University of Wittenberg, however, was not chartered by the Church on its founding in 1502. See Oberman, "University and Society," 28.

[15] Eby and Arrowood, *History*, 761–9; Paulsen, *Geschichte*, 28–9.

[16] Paulsen, *Geschichte*, 17–21.

own systems of city schools (*Ratschulen*) – Latin schools, vernacular reading and writing schools, and a handful of girls' schools – that competed with the Church schools for students and sponsors.[17] These city schools were staffed by local city clerks and syndics and supported by local tax funds and private donations. They were designed primarily to train new generations of civil bureaucrats, businessmen, and administrators. Although the vernacular boys' schools and girls' schools could not match the curriculum or prestige of their Church rivals, the Latin schools could. They offered a robust training in the seven liberal arts, which provided the foundation for either further vocational instruction or advanced university study. In older, well-endowed bishoprics, such as Cologne, Worms, and Mainz, the Church was able to increase the number of monastic and cathedral schools to keep the rival city schools in check. (In 1500, for example, Cologne alone maintained eleven cathedral schools and fifteen monastic schools.[18]) Where the bishop wielded less influence, however, as in Nuremberg, Hamburg, and Lübeck, city schools came to dominate local education.

Likewise, several of the German universities, though chartered and accredited by the Church, were supported by large princely endowments, and structured to produce not only clerics and theologians, but also councilors, judges, ambassadors, lawyers, and other civil servants to serve in the territorial estates. The universities in Wittenberg, Tübingen, Ingolstadt, and Frankfurt an der Oder, in fact, allowed students to matriculate at minimal cost if they would agree to serve in the prince's retinue, rather than the bishop's, upon graduation.[19] These early encroachments on the Church's magisterium were important signposts along the way to the Protestant reformers' creation of a new system of civil education in Germany.

THE NEW LUTHERAN THEOLOGY OF EDUCATION

Critique

In his early writings, Luther attacked the Church's educational tradition with vehemence. The lower schools were, in his experience and

---

[17] On vernacular schools, see esp. Cornelia Niekus Moore, *The Maiden's Mirror: Reading Materials for Girls in the Sixteenth and Seventeenth Centuries* (Wiesbaden, 1987); on Latin schools, Henkel, *Deutsche Übersetzungen*. For a list of city schools, some founded in the thirteenth and early fourteenth centuries, see Eby and Arrowood, *History*, 821–5.

[18] Learned, *The Oberlehrer*, 4.

[19] Oberman, "University and Society," 28–29: Spitz, "The Importance," 47–8.

judgment, "a hell and purgatory in which we were tormented with [Latin] cases and tenses, and yet learned less than nothing despite all the flogging, trembling, anguish, and misery."[20] The curriculum offered only a spare diet of Latin grammar and Greek verse and consisted principally of rote memorization of the Church calendar, Decalogue, Creed, Lord's Prayer, and selected hymns and confessional rhymes. A graduate of these schools "remained a poor, illiterate man all of his days."[21]

Some of the universities, too, in Luther's view, were "dens of murderers," "temples of Moloch," and "synagogues of corruption." Even some of the best universities in Germany had become edifices of prurience and "loose living." Their administrators often converted their endowments to personal use. Their teachers lived in luxury and flouted their responsibilities with impunity. Their faculties offered too little instruction in religion and morality and betrayed too great an appetite for rationalism and scholasticism. "[T]he blind, heathen teacher Aristotle rules far more than Christ" in the universities, Luther charged. Aristotle's *Physics, Metaphysics*, and *Ethics* distort the Gospel and "oppose divine grace and all Christian virtues." Therefore, "[t]he universities, too, need a good, thorough reformation."[22] Indeed, Luther wrote, "I believe that it is simply impossible to reform the Church, if the canons, the decretals, scholastic theology, philosophy, logic, as they are now taught, are not eliminated from the ground up and other studies established."[23] For "what have men been learning till now . . . except to become asses, blockheads, and numbskulls?"[24]

Luther was hardly alone in these criticisms. Since the early fifteenth century, eminent German humanists such as Rudolf Agricola, Johannes Reuchlin, Jakob Wimpfeling, and many others had railed against the Church schools and universities for their barbarization of the pure Latin, Greek, and Hebrew languages, their distortions of classical and patristic texts, and their manipulation of all students and studies to the service and aggrandizement of the Church.[25] Early converts to the Lutheran cause offered similar sentiments. The young Martin Bucer was

---

[20] *LW* 45:369; see also *LW* 26:345–6 on unsuitable schoolmasters.

[21] Quoted by Frederick Eby, *The Development of Modern Education in Theory, Organization, and Practice*, 2nd. edn. (New York, 1952), 63.

[22] *LW* 44:115, 200–1. See also *LW* 48:37, 42, 59.

[23] Letter to Trutvetter, May 9, 1518, quoting translation in Spitz, "The Importance," 52.

[24] *LW* 45:351–2.

[25] See Reinhard, *Humanismus im Bildungswesen*; Lewis W. Spitz, *The Religious Renaissance of the German Humanists* (Cambridge, MA, 1963), 20–80; Moeller, *Imperial Cities and the Reformation*, 19–40; id., ed., *Studien zum städtischen Bildungswesen des späten Mittelalters und der frühen Neuzeit* (Göttingen, 1983).

appalled by the "astonishing absence" of Bibles and catechisms in the vernacular and Latin schools of Strasbourg, and urged teachers and preachers alike to help restore true religious instruction as the cornerstone of their pedagogy.[26] The Wittenberg jurist Johann Apel complained bitterly that "among the thirty jurists [he encountered] not one of them could write a proper Latin brief," far less "teach a proper course."[27]

Philip Melanchthon called the Latin schools of his day "swamps of depravity" specializing in "property, pride, and pretense," and run by "barbarians who have vulgarly and by means of force and fear arrogated to themselves titles and rewards and retained men by means of malicious devices."[28] He was particularly outraged at the "barbarization" of the ancient languages of Greek and Latin, the ignorance of classical and early Church history, and the extraordinary levels of ignorance that marked the legal, theological, and medical professions of his day.[29] Like Luther, Melanchthon blamed the universities – those "synagogues of Satan," as he put it, bent on perpetuating "papal hegemony" and "the theological hallucinations of those who have offered us the subtleties of Aristotle instead of the teachings of Christ."[30] Nowadays, Melanchthon wrote, no one can learn the arts or theology without becoming steeped in the arid scholastic philosophy favored by Rome. No one can learn the law without being drilled incessantly in the "tyrannical canon law." "But an ambitious young man is trapped," for no one can ascend to any sort of "distinguished public office" without a university education.[31]

It must be said that the very presence of Luther, Melanchthon, and other reformers in "distinguished public offices" belied some of the hyperbole of these early attacks on the educational tradition of Germany. After all, Luther, Melanchthon, and many other reformers had been educated exclusively in German Church schools and universities. Yet, from the start of their careers, they demonstrated an extraordinary erudition

---

[26] Moeller, *Imperial Cities*, 43–72; Amy Nelson Burnett, "Church Discipline and Moral Reformation in the Thought of Martin Bucer," *Sixteenth Century Journal* 22 (1991), 440–5; William J. Wright, "The Impact of the Reformation on Hessian Education," *Church History* 44 (1975), 186ff. On Bucer's later efforts at educational reform, see Bucer, *DS*, 7:509ff.; Wilhelm Diehl, "Martin Bucers Bedeutung für das kirchliche Leben in Hessen," *Schriften des Vereins für Reformationsgeschichte* 22 (1904): 39.

[27] Quoted by Theodore Muther, *Doctor Johann Apell. Ein Beitrag zur Geschichte der deutschen Jurisprudenz* (Königsberg, 1861), 6.

[28] *MW* 3:29, 30; see further Hartfelder, *Melanchthon*, 413–16.

[29] *MW* 3:29–42; *CR* 11:231–9. See further Kusukawa, *The Transformation of Natural Philosophy*, 37ff.

[30] *LC* (1521), 19.   [31] *CR* 1:286, 342–3; *CR* 11:108, 617.

and theological imagination that would have been impossible had their caricature of German education been true. Moreover, while Luther remained skeptical of the utility of much classical and scholastic learning in lower and higher education, Melanchthon eventually became a great teacher of the ethics, politics, and philosophy of Aristotle, Cicero, the Roman jurists, and the medieval scholastics – a pattern which a number of his students emulated.[32]

Reconstruction

Luther and his followers grounded their educational reforms in their signature doctrine of the two kingdoms. Luther and Melanchthon, in particular, stressed that education was essential to the maintenance of the heavenly kingdom – "second only to the Church in importance," as Luther once put it.[33] Education is essential to the constant preservation of the Gospel. The ancient languages of Hebrew, Greek, and Latin "are the scabbard in which the sword of the spirit is contained," and they must be transmitted faithfully to each generation. The ancient arts of rhetoric, logic, and dialectic are essential to the proper preaching and rational disputation of Scripture.[34] "[T]he light of the Gospel will be extinguished without erudition," Melanchthon wrote.[35] "It is a great mistake to imagine that ministers can be carved from any wood, and that the teaching of religion can be grasped without erudition, and without long training" in proper schools and universities.[36] Education is equally essential to the spiritual flourishing of each Christian believer. Each person, as an individual accountable to God, must be educated enough to read the Bible daily, to master its contents, and to make choices rooted in its teachings.

---

[32] See esp. Heinz Scheible, "Philip Melanchthon," in Carter Lindberg, ed., The *Reformation Theologians* (Oxford, 2001); Heinz Scheible, ed., *Melanchthon in seinen Schülern* (Wiesbaden, 1997).

[33] *LW* 41:176. See also *WA TR* 4, No. 5247; *LW* 54:403–4: "In a city as much depends on a schoolmaster as on a minister. We can get along without burgomasters, princes, and noblemen, but we can't do without schools, for they must rule the world."

[34] *LW* 44:201. For Melanchthon's views, see esp. *MW* 3:41, 111; *CR* 11:231–9, with English translation "On the Study of Languages," in *Orations on Philosophy and Education*, ed. Kusukawa, 29–37. For similar sentiments by humanists sympathetic to the Evangelical cause, see especially the work of Johannes Sturm (1507–1589), a co-worker (of sorts) with Martin Bucer in Strassburg, and crafter of the famous ten-class lower school in Strasbourg that won widespread acclaim in Germany, Switzerland, and France. According to Sturm: "Knowledge and purity and elegance of diction should become the aim of scholarship and teaching, and both teachers and students should assiduously bend their efforts to this end." See *Joannis Sturmii de institutione scholastica opuscula selecta*, in Reinhold Vormbaum, ed., *Die evangelischen Schulordnungen des sechzehnten Jahrhunderts*, 3 vols. (Gütersloh, 1860), 1:653–745.

[35] *CR* 11:612.   [36] *CR* 11:613–14, quoting translation in *Orations*, ed. Kusukawa, 16.

Each believer, as a member of the priesthood of believers, must be taught the habits of Christian discipline and discipleship and the skills necessary to pursue the distinctive vocation to which God has called him or her. Scripture thus repeatedly enjoins persons to educate themselves and their children, so that God and the Gospel will be well served.[37]

The reformers likewise considered education to be essential to the maintenance of the earthly kingdom. Indeed, Luther wrote, "Were there neither soul, nor heaven, nor hell, it would still be necessary to have schools for the sake of things here below."[38] For education enhances the common good. A community's "best and greatest welfare, safety, and strength" lies not in wealth of arms and allies, but "rather in its having many able, learned, wise, honorable, and well-educated citizens."[39] Contrary to conventional German folklore that the educated are absentminded and useless to daily life ("die Gelehrten, die Verkehrten"), the reformers insisted that educated citizens are essential to the success of the community.[40] They are better able to apprehend and appropriate the moral and civil law in their own lives.[41] They tend to be more sober in judgment, temperate in character, ethical in their dealings. They tend to run better businesses. They have the cultural and linguistic learning necessary to deal effectively with foreign merchants and governments.[42] They generate great wealth and foster charity and good will for the community.[43] As Melanchthon put it, "better letters bring better morals; better morals bring better communities."[44] Therefore "simple necessity has forced men, even among the heathen, to maintain

---

[37] *CR* 11:353.

[38] Quoted by P. R. Cole, *A History of Educational Thought* (London, 1931), 193.

[39] *LW* 45:356. See also *MW* 3:65, where Melanchthon argues: "No art, no work, no fruit . . . is as valuable as learning. For without laws and judgments, and without religion, the state cannot be held together, nor the human community be assembled and governed. People would wander wildly and kill each other."

[40] See Heiko A. Oberman, "*Die Gelehrten die Verkehrten*: Popular Response to Learned Culture in the Renaissance and Reformation," in id., *The Impact of the Reformation* (Grand Rapids, MI, 1994), 201–24.

[41] Luther, somewhat obliquely, ties the school's education to the educational use of the law. See *LW* 45:356: "[S]imple necessity has forced men, even among the heathen, to maintain pedagogues and schoolmasters if their nation was to be brought to a high standard. Hence, the word 'schoolmaster' is used by Paul in Galatians [3:24] as a word taken from the common usage and practice of mankind, where he says, 'The law was our schoolmaster'." See also *LW* 26:345–7. Melanchthon makes this connection between school education and the educational use of the law explicit in his *Catechesis puerilis* (1532/1558), *CR* 23: 103, 176–7. See discussion in Müller, "Melanchthon," 103. On the three uses of the law doctrine, see pp. 102–5, 127–9, 134–5, above.

[42] *LW* 46:243.   [43] Ibid., 234; see also *LW* 45:355–6.

[44] *CR* 1:70–3 and discussion in Müller, "Melanchthon," 96–8.

pedagogues and schoolmasters if their nation was to be brought to a high standard."[45]

A system of education also serves, and is served by, the three great estates of family, Church, and state – that "pedagogical triangle" in Melanchthon's apt phrase.[46] It teaches parents and children alike the basic skills of domestic economy and husbandry, and the meaning and measure of being a true Christian child, mother, wife, father, or husband. It prepares theologians, pastors, teachers, sextons, and others who will effectively carry on the work of the visible Church. It prepares jurists, councilors, clerks, and other members of a new civil bureaucracy to replace the clerical bureaucracy on which the German magistrates had traditionally relied.[47] The reformers laid special emphasis on the value of education for the preservation and perpetuation of the visible Church. "God has preserved the Church through schools," Luther wrote. "When schools flourish, things go well and the Church is secure."[48] When they fail, the Church flounders. The reformers also stressed the need for an educated religious and civic leadership.[49] "We theologians and jurists must remain or everything else will go down to destruction with us," Luther declared. "When the theologians disappear, God's word also disappears, and nothing but heathens remain, indeed, nothing but devils. When the jurists disappear, then the law disappears, and peace with it; and nothing but robbery, murder, crime, and violence remain, indeed, nothing but wild beasts."[50]

On the strength of these arguments, the reformers set forth a number of principles of education that eventually won widespread acceptance in the Evangelical communities of Germany and beyond.

First, the local magistrate bears the principal responsibility for formal schooling. To be sure, parents must continue to rear and instruct their children in a Christian manner, to teach them the prayers and

[45] *LW* 45:356.
[46] Quoted by W. Wiater, " 'The Church and the School Should Have the Same Doctrine': State, Church and School According to Philip Melanchthon," in Reinhard Golz and Wolfgang Mayrhofer, eds., *Luther and Melanchthon in the Educational Thought of Central and Eastern Europe*, trans. Arista Da Silva and Alan Maimon (Rutgers, NJ, 1999), 59. See further *CR* 11:107, 127, 214, 445, 617; 26:90; Huschke, *Melanchthons Lehre vom Ordo politicus*, 61ff. For comparable views by Luther, see *LW* 41:176–7; F. M. Schiele, "Luther und das Luthertum in ihrer Bedeutung für die Geschichte der Schule und der Erziehung," *Preussisches Jahrbuch* 31 (1908): 383; F. Falk, "Luthers Schrift an die Ratsherren der deutschen Städte und ihre geschichtliche Wirkung auf die deutschen, Schulen," *Luther-Jahrbuch* 19 (1937), 67–71, who stress that for Luther education is critical to the *ordo economicus, ordo ecclesiasticus,* and *ordo politicus.*
[47] *LW* 40:314; *LW* 46:236–45.   [48] *LW* 54:452.
[49] See esp. *CR* 11:78–82.   [50] *LW* 46:251–2.

the catechisms, to offer them examples of love and discipline.[51] Guilds and mercantile leagues must continue to cultivate apprentices in their crafts and commercial arts. But the civil magistrates – emperors, princes, dukes, and city counselors – are "the fathers of the community," and "the supreme guardians of youth," and they bear primary institutional responsibility for formal education.[52] They must establish and maintain schools, just as readily as they build castles, raise armies, and promulgate laws. If magistrates already have state schools in place, they must retain and enhance them. If they have church schools within their jurisdictions, they must confiscate them and convert them to state institutions.[53]

The reformers' consignment of school education to the jurisdiction of the magistrate did not absolve the visible Church from all teaching responsibility or deprive education of its religious character.[54] Local churches, they insisted, must continue daily to teach their members the Scriptures, the liturgies, and the prayers. The local church parish must still teach children the Bible, catechisms, hymns, psalms, liturgies, and prayers – not just on Sunday, but also, in Johannes Bugenhagen's words, "before and after each school day."[55] Church leaders must still instruct magistrates on the commandments of God's Word and "urge magistrates and parents to rule wisely and to send their children to school...."[56] But the Church's teaching authority is too limited in scope and content to render it the primary custodian of the schools, the reformers argued. The Church's teaching is directed primarily at its own parishioners, not the entire citizenry. It dwells primarily with the spiritual matters of the heavenly kingdom, not the temporal matters of the earthly kingdom. To saddle the Church with jurisdiction over all schooling, therefore, would

---

[51] See, e.g., *TC*, 575; Bruce, *Luther as an Educator*, 213–19. See also *MW* 3:70; Bucer, *DS* 7:509ff. and quotations from Johannes Bugenhagen in Julius Robert Rost, *Die pädagogische Bedeutung Bugenhagens* (Inaug. Diss., Leipzig, 1890), 14–16.

[52] 1526 letter of Luther to Elector John of Saxony, in *Luther's Correspondence and Other Contemporary Letters*, trans. and ed. Preserved Smith and Charles M. Jacobs (Philadelphia, 1918), 2:384.

[53] *LW* 45:175–6; *LW* 46:256–7. More than a decade after issuing his *Ninety-Five Theses*, Luther still entertained the notion of simply retaining the old monasteries as schools (*LW* 37:161, 364). Johannes Brenz long advocated simply converting the cloisters into Lutheran seminaries, an idea finally realized in his cloister ordinance of Württemberg (1556). See discussion below pp. 284–90.

[54] See esp. *CR* 11:606–18.

[55] See [Johannes Bugenhagen,] "Schulordnung aus der Braunschweig'schen Kirchenordnung" (1543), in Vormbaum, *Schulordnungen*, 1:44, 46ff. and discussion in Rost, *Bugenhagen*, 40–2. Bugenhagen was more insistent than some of the other reformers on Church participation in religious instruction of children. Indeed, at one point, he charged that pastors who did not help in the establishment of schools and the teaching of Bible and religion were "soft and not worth much" (quoted ibid., 13).

[56] *TC*, 536–37.

compromise its divine message and mission. Only the magistrate, as "father of the entire community," has sufficiently universal authority to govern the schools.[57]

The magistrate must continue to preserve the religious mission and ministry of the school. For the magistrate is God's vice-regent in the world, called to appropriate and cultivate God's word and will throughout the earthly kingdom. "God has created human society so that some might teach others about religion," Melanchthon writes. "Since princes are the custodians of human society, it belongs to them to bring about, to the extent they are capable, that which God has rightly required."[58] Indeed, "magistrates are called gods by the Holy Spirit, so that they would preserve and retain the divine gifts on earth – religion, civil order, and all the honorable arts. Because of that responsibility for divine things, they bear the solemn title [of gods on earth], and the magistrates have no greater and more venerable distinction than that."[59]

Secondly, magistrates must provide parents and children alike with various opportunities to educate themselves. Public libraries should be available in each community to foster self-education and preservation of knowledge. Schoolmasters and professors should hold periodic public lectures on matters of medicine, commerce, agriculture, geography, and law.[60] Magistrates should educate their citizens on the requirements of moral and civil laws, by posting the laws in public places, disseminating them through pamphlets and handbooks, declaring them from the pulpit and the town hall.[61] The reformers' ideal was a generally educated citizenry, each person being further trained for his or her special calling.

Thirdly, magistrates must make at least a rudimentary formal education compulsory for all children. The reformers reached this principle reluctantly, for it stood in considerable tension with their cherished doctrines of Christian freedom and family responsibility. Their reluctance fell away, however, when they began to discover the dramatic drop in student enrollment in the middle of the 1520s. German city schools were complaining bitterly of the dearth of available, let alone able, students, and a number of them simply closed their doors in frustration. The number of private tutors and private boarding schools was dropping

---

[57] See, e.g., *MW* 3:111.   [58] Ibid.

[59] *CR* 11:209–14, quoting translation in Kusukawa, ed., *Orations*, 6–7. See further discussion in Scheible, "Philip Melanchthon."

[60] See [Martin Bucer,] Ulm church ordinance, in Richter, 1:157–8, with discussion of the law in action in Kohls, "Martin Bucers Anteil," 356; id., *Die Schule bei Martin Bucer in ihrem Verhältnis zu Kirche und Obrigkeit* (Heidelberg, 1963), 33ff.

[61] See Bucer's views in ibid. and Melanchthon's in *CR* 1:706–8; *CR* 21:127, 132; *CR* 23:176–7.

precipitously. German universities were losing students in record numbers. The University of Cologne went from 370 students in 1516 to 54 in 1524. Luther's alma mater at Erfurt plummeted from 311 students in 1520 to 14 in 1527. The University of Vienna matriculated 661 students in 1519, only 12 in 1532. The University of Rostock had 300 students in 1500, none at all in 1529. Even the University of Wittenberg, for all its reformist zeal, dipped from 245 students in 1521 to only 73 in 1527.[62] "[T]he common people appear to be quite indifferent to the matter of maintaining the schools," Luther noted with alarm. "I see them withdrawing their children from instruction and training them to the making of a living and to caring for their bellies. . . . [N]early all the municipal authorities let the schools go to ruin as though they had absolution from all responsibilities."[63]

In retrospect, it can be seen that a number of factors contributed to this dramatic decline in schools and students: three generations of humanistic attacks on traditional German education; the dissolution of the monastic and chantry endowments that had traditionally supported students; foot-dragging by civil authorities asked to convert confiscated Church properties into public schools; the social unsettlement born of the knights' uprising, the peasants' revolt, and their aftermath; the rash of plagues and poor crops in the mid- and late 1520s; the fresh rise of popular skepticism about learning as a whole, among other factors. Whatever the actual reasons, Luther's contemporaries put the blame squarely on him and his followers. In Erasmus' famous quip: "Wherever Lutheranism prevails, there learning and literature disappear."[64]

The reformers, therefore, began to insist on compulsory school attendance. Since the *paterfamilias* did not seem to appreciate the value and validity of education of his children, the *paterpoliticus* would have to intervene, for the sake of the children and the community. "[I]t is the duty of the temporal authority to compel its subjects to keep their children in school, especially the promising ones," Luther declared. "For it is truly the duty of government to maintain the offices and estates . . . so that there will always be preachers, jurists, pastors, writers, physicians, schoolmasters, and the like, for we cannot do without them. If the government can compel such of its subjects as are fit for military service to carry pike and musket, man the ramparts, and do other kinds of work

---

[62] Eby, *Development*, 64.
[63] *WA*, 30/2:62; see further *MW* 3:70–82; Strauss, *Luther's House of Learning*, 268–99.
[64] Quoted by Eby, *Development*, 64.

in time of war, how much more can it and should it compel its subjects to keep their children in school."[65]

Fourthly, children must begin their schooling at the earliest age possible. To restore Christendom, Luther wrote, "we must make a new beginning with children." Likewise Justus Menius wrote in an educational book for which Luther wrote a preface: "Men who are to serve their country must be raised to it from earliest childhood; in no other way can an impression be made on them."[66] The reformers predicated this recommendation directly on their theology of sin. According to Bugenhagen, "baptized children live in the grace of God and know nothing of good and evil. Yet they still are born with a sinful nature.... The moment they begin to become rational, then the Devil appears also to teach them all manner of mischief. This is the moment to seize them."[67] For proper religious instruction, from an early age, will help to inoculate them against these temptations.

Fifthly, schools must be readily available and accessible to all children.[68] Both boys and girls should have their own schools, within a reasonable distance of their homes.[69] Both rich and poor should be allowed to attend them. Public and private money should be gathered to support an endowment for poor students – either confiscated from the large monastic holdings and endowments, or saved from household money that had traditionally been spent on indulgences, masses, vigils, pilgrimages, and sundry other forms of compulsory religious giving.[70]

Sixthly, schools must serve as "civic seminaries,"[71] inculcating both right religion and broad erudition in their students. "[T]he foremost reading for everybody, both in the universities and in the schools, should be the Holy Scripture," Luther declared in 1520, sounding his great theme of *sola Scriptura*.[72] Indeed, "I would advise no one to send his child where the Holy Scriptures are not supreme."[73] Melanchthon,

---

[65] *LW* 46:256–7; see also *Luther's Correspondence*, 2:384.
[66] Quoted by Strauss, *Luther's House of Learning*, 35.
[67] [Johannes Bugenhagen,] Schulordnung aus der Braunschweigen Kirchenordnung (1528), in Vormbaum, *Schulordnungen*, 1:9.
[68] *WA* 30/2:545; *WA* 30/2:60–3. See also Philip Melanchthon, "Letter to the Mayor and Council of Halle," in *Der Briefwechsel des Justus Jonas*, ed. Kaweru, 2:158. On the importance of girls' schools among the reformers, see Moore, *The Maiden's Mirror*.
[69] *LW* 44:206; see further Susan C. Karant-Nunn, "The Reality of Early Lutheran Education: The Electoral District of Saxony – A Case Study," *Luther-Jahrbuch* 57 (1990): 128; Rost, *Bugenhagen*, 23–5; Justus Menius, "Preface to Luther's Catechism (1529)," in Gustav L. Schmidt, *Justus Menius, Der Reformator Thüringens nach archivalischen und andern Quellen* (Gotha, 1867), 2:189–90
[70] *LW* 45:350–1; *LW* 46:25, 229.   [71] *MW* 3:69.
[72] *LW* 44:205–6.   [73] Ibid., 207.

too, impressed repeatedly on his readers that "all the knowledge in the world of history, geography, arithmetic, the calendar, languages, and medicine . . . is useless and meaningless without the prior knowledge of God . . . taught in the Bible."[74] But, despite their strong adherence to the theme of *sola Scriptura*, the Evangelical reformers regarded biblical instruction alone as insufficient for any curriculum. Education, after all, was as much a matter of the earthly kingdom as the heavenly kingdom; it depended upon the texts of both reason and revelation to be successful. The reformers thus outlined new curricula for private tutoring, vernacular schools, Latin schools, and the universities alike, curricula that balanced the twin commands of piety and erudition.

For private tutorial instruction, which often was the only formal instruction available in rural areas and small towns, Melanchthon took the lead, developing a *Handbook for How Children Must be Taught to Read and Write* (1524),[75] *A Catechism for Youngsters* (1532/1558),[76] and, for more advanced students, a text on *Common Topics in Theology* (1521).[77] The youngest students were to learn the alphabet and grammar, using various learning techniques that Melanchthon had included in his earlier textbooks on Latin and Greek grammar.[78] Students were then to be taught to memorize and to understand sundry religious texts: the Lord's Prayer, the Ave Maria, the ecumenical creeds, Psalm 66, the Ten Commandments, the Beatitudes, and various chapters from the Gospels and St. Paul. Advanced students were to be schooled in the seven liberal arts, supplemented by a careful instruction in such theological topics as sin, grace, law, love, the sacraments, and others. Upon completing their tutorials, the best students were to be sent to the universities for advanced training.

For the Latin schools, Melanchthon, together with Luther and Bugenhagen, devised a more carefully stratified curriculum. Students

---

[74] *CR* 5:130.

[75] Philip Melanchthon, *Handtbuchlein wie man die Kinder zu der geschrifft vnd lere halten soll* (Wittenberg, 1521/1524/1530).

[76] *CR* 23:103, 117.

[77] *LC* (1521), 82. Though this work is usually regarded as the first Protestant work of systematic theology, Melanchthon's dedicatory epistle makes clear its pedagogical aim: "This study was prepared for the sole purpose of indicating as cogently as possible to my private students the issues at stake in Paul's theology . . . in this book, the principal topics of Christian teaching are pointed out so that youth may arrive at a twofold understanding: (1) what one must chiefly look for in Scripture; and (2) how corrupt are the theological hallucinations of those who have offered us the subtleties of Aristotle instead of the teachings of Christ" (ibid., 18–19). Melanchthon used many of the topics of his *Loci communes* to devise the ordination examination for advanced theology schools in Wittenberg: *CR* 23:xxxv.

[78] *CR* 20:3, 193, 391.

were to be divided into groups and allowed to excel in accordance with their abilities and interests.[79] A first-level group of students was to be instructed in the alphabet, various prayers and creeds, and in the Latin grammar of Donatus and Cato's *Moral Distichs*. A second-level group of students was to receive further grammatical instruction from various classical and humanist authors, religious instruction from the Psalms and the Gospels, the Lord's Prayer, the Decalogue, and the Creed, and moral instruction from the comedies of Terence and Plautus, the verses of Erasmus, and most importantly *Aesop's Fables* (which Luther translated into German). A third, advanced group of students was to be steeped in the works of Ovid, Cicero, and Virgil, and then learn dialectic, rhetoric, and poetics. All three groups of students, the reformers said, must be trained in Latin as their primary language, taught to memorize important religious and humane passages, constantly instructed in music and hymnology, and periodically schooled in physical education, mathematics, science, and history, as time allowed. All three groups were to be spared the assignment of too many useless books. Careful reading and understanding of a few critical texts was far more useful than superficial reading in a large library. To facilitate this, Melanchthon prepared new texts on Latin and Greek grammar, rhetoric, dialectic, moral philosophy, and natural philosophy, and endorsed with enthusiastic forewords several other new texts for use in the schools.[80]

Most students, the reformers believed, will be unable to complete the entire Latin school curriculum and will not be expected to do so. A few children will do better, by reason of handicap or temperament, to forgo formal schooling altogether. Many students will, upon acquisition of certain basic skills, wish to pursue further vocational training in their homes, guilds, or the vernacular schools. Only the most highly qualified students should be encouraged and supported to complete this program and to pursue university studies in preparation for a life of ecclesiastical or civil service.[81] A student need not be ashamed about, or discouraged from, departing the Latin academy *in medias res*. "[I]t is not necessary that all boys become pastors, preachers, and schoolmasters," doctors,

---

[79] *Instructions for the Visitors of Parish Pastors in Electoral Saxony* (1528/1538), *LW* 40:263–320, at 314–20. A similar structure appears in the 1528 Brunswick school ordinance drafted by Johannes Bugenhagen. In the Article "Von dem arbyde in den Scholen," Bugenhagen indicates: "With regard to the work and exercises in the school, generally it shall be as Philip Melanchthon has prescribed in ... *Instructions to the Visitors in the Parishes*, etc.": Vormbaum, *Schulordnungen*, 1:14.

[80] See Kusukawa, ed., *Orations*; Hans-Ruediger Schwab, *Philipp Melanchthon, Der Lehrer Deutschlands: Ein biographisches Lesebuch* (Munich, 1997).

[81] *LW* 44:206–7.

magistrates, or lawyers.[82] Every person has a place in God's kingdom, and every vocation dutifully pursued is equally noble and worthy in God's sight.

For the German vernacular boys' and girls' schools, Johannes Bugenhagen offered the most refined and sustained recommendations. In comparison with the Latin schools, the vernacular schools were to offer a less differentiated and more flexible curriculum. Students were to be taught the rudiments of reading, writing, and arithmetic using whatever texts were at hand. They were to memorize the Decalogue, the Lord's Prayer, and the Apostles' Creed, and to read Psalms, sing hymns, and learn biblical history. But, once this rudimentary training was completed, the students were to learn the practical skills of agriculture, commerce, household duties, and the like that would equip them to pursue honest vocations in the local community. Instruction was to be principally in German, following the local dialect, though students with special aptitudes or interests might also be trained in Greek, Latin, and Hebrew.[83]

In his later years, Luther stressed the importance of the catechism in the religious training of students in the Latin and vernacular schools – even hinting, in a few passages, that catechetical instruction might be more important than untutored Bible reading. Luther increased his emphasis on the catechism to combat the growing spiritual laxness of his followers and the growing spiritual license of the antinomians that he encountered in the later 1520s.[84] Exasperated by the distorted doctrines he encountered in sermons and letters, Luther wrote: "Nowadays everyone thinks he is a master of Scripture, and every Tom, Dick, and Harry imagines that he understands the Bible and knows it inside out."[85] As an antidote, Luther offered his famous *Short Catechism* and *Large Catechism*. Both catechisms set out the texts of the Decalogue, Apostles' Creed, and Lord's Prayer, together with explanations; the *Large Catechism* offered more detailed explanations of each text, together with disquisitions on the sacraments of baptism and the eucharist.[86]

Luther did not craft his catechisms either to canonize immutably his theological formulations or to shelter students from a broad biblical and

---

[82] *LW* 46:231.
[83] See "Der Erbaren Stadt Hamborg Christliche Ordeninge" (1529), art. 6 ("Van deudeschen Schryffschole") and art. 7 ("Van der Jungkfruwen Schole"), in Richter, 1:127, 128 and further discussion in Rost, *Bugenhagen*, 20–30.
[84] See, e.g., *WA TR* 6, No. 6288.   [85] Ibid., 6008.
[86] Originals and translations in *TC*, 530–773. See detailed commentary in Albrecht Peters, *Kommentar zu Luthers Katechismen*, 5 vols. to date (Göttingen, 1990–).

humanistic training.[87] Luther's catechisms were not canonical Protestant confessions or creeds. They were simple, pithy, ecumenical statements of the rudiments of the Christian faith, painted in predominantly pastoral and practical tones. Luther offered them, as he put it, to replace the "many confusing kinds of texts and forms of the Decalogue, the Lord's Prayer, the Creed, and the sacraments" to which students were being exposed. He urged teachers either to adopt his catechisms or to "choose whatever form [of instruction] you please, and stick to it," so that students will not be confused. Only for those teachers and pastors "who cannot do better" and who are "so unskilled that [they] have absolutely no knowledge" did he insist on close adherence to his catechetical formulations.[88]

Luther suggested many times that a teacher might also wish to turn for guidance to any number of other catechisms and religious handbooks that antedated his – that of the Catholic theologian Jean Gerson,[89] those of fellow theologians like Melanchthon, Bucer, or Brenz,[90] or even those of Lutheran jurists like Christoph Hegendorf.[91] Luther was not nearly so jealous of his catechetical formulations as some recent writers have insisted. Moreover, neither Luther's catechisms nor those of any of his co-religionists were intended to overshadow the curriculum of either the Latin schools or the vernacular schools. They were designed simply to enhance the Bible reading that the student would hear daily at home and at church and to enlighten the sundry other humane texts in the curriculum.

The reformers' educational principles were calculated both to resonate with German experience and to break the Catholic Church's

---

[87] Per contra Strauss, *Luther's House of Learning*, 155ff.; Richard Gawthrop and Gerald Strauss, "Protestantism and Literacy in Early Modern Germany," *Past and Present* 104 (1984), 35ff.

[88] Preface to the Small Catechism (1529), *TC*, 532–3.

[89] Jean Gerson, *Opusculum tripartitum de praeceptis decalogi, de confessione, et de arte moriendi* (Paris, 1487) with discussion in Harold J. Grimm, "Luther's Catechisms as Textbooks," in Harold J. Grimm and Theodore Hoelty-Nickel, eds., *Luther and Culture* (Columbus, OH, 1960), 121. On the profusion of fifteenth-century Catholic catechisms, and the reformers' eventual dependence on them, see Ferdinand Cohrs, *Die evangelischen Katechismusversuche vor Luthers Enchiridion*, 4 vols. (Berlin, 1900–2), with updates and corrections in Timothy J. Wengert, *Law and Gospel: Philip Melanchthon's Debate with John Agricola of Eisleben over Poenitentia* (Carlisle, 1997).

[90] See Melanchthon, *Catechesis puerilis* (1532/1558), *CR* 20:100. On Bucer's catechisms, see Burnett, "Church Discipline," 441; August Ernst and Johann Adam, *Katechetische Geschichte des Elsasses bis zur Revolution* (Strasbourg, 1897), 115ff. For Brenz's 1527 catechism, see Julius Hartmann and Karl Jäger, *Johann Brenz: nach gedruckten und ungedruckten Quellen* (Hamburg, 1840), 1:123–131; for his 1533 Catechism or Children's Sermons, see Ozment, *Protestants: The Birth of a Revolution*, 104–17.

[91] See the collection in Kohls, *Evangelische Katechismen*; Gustav Kawerau, ed., *Zwei älteste Katechismen der lutherischen Reformation von P. Shultz und Chr. Hegendorf* (Halle, 1890), 3–17. The catechism of the Evangelical jurist and theologian Christoph Hegendorf, a friend of Melanchthon and the Lutheran schoolmaster Hermann Tulichius, circulated broadly both in Latin and in its German translation *Die zehen Gepot der glaub, und das Vater unser, für die kinder ausgelegt* (Wittenberg, 1527).

traditional dominance of education. On the one hand, the reformers retained a good deal of Germany's pedagogical tradition. The system of state-run public education built squarely on the existence and experience of the Latin schools and vernacular schools in the large cities. The tripartite division of the classes paralleled the structure of the monastic and cathedral schools. The system of state-run charities to support poor students built on the practice of princes, guilds, and monasteries to maintain educational endowments. The curricula of the lower schools kept religion at their core, and retained the seven liberal arts as well as a number of texts prescribed by the canon law. The Protestant universities retained their traditional charters, faculty divisions, and degree programs.

On the other hand, the reformers cast these traditional pedagogical practices into their own distinctive ensemble, rooted in the two-kingdoms theory. In their view, the Christian magistrate was to replace the Church cleric as the chief protector and cultivator of the public school and university. The civil law was to replace the canon law as the chief law governing education. The school was to replace the Church and the home as the chief organ of education. The Bible was to replace the scholastic text as the first book of the curriculum. The general callings of all Christians were to replace the special calling of the clergy as the *raison d'être* of education. In the reformers' view, education was to remain fundamentally religious in character, but subject to broader political control and directed to broader civic ends.

These startling new principles of education did not win easy acceptance in the young Evangelical communities of Germany. Luther, in particular, spent a good deal of time defending them, both in private letters and in his oft-reprinted sermons *To The Councilmen of all Cities in Germany That They Establish and Maintain Christian Schools* (1524) and *A Sermon on Keeping Children in School* (1530). Luther laced his advocacy with both cajolery and threats.

On the one hand, Luther, the pastor, sought to entice reticent parents and students to see the value and validity of education:

Just look, emperors and kings must have chancellors and clerks, counselors, jurists, and scholars. . . . All the counts, lords, cities, and castles must have syndics, city clerks, and other scholars. There is not a nobleman who does not need a clerk. And to speak also about men of ordinary education, there are also the miners, merchants, and businessmen. . . . Think, too, how many parishes, pulpits, schools, and sacristanships there are. Most of them are sufficiently provided for [by endowments], and vacancies are occurring every day.

If students do not enroll in schools, "I would like to know where we are going to get pastors, schoolmasters, and sacristans three years from now." If his readers were still not convinced, Luther held forth "about the pure pleasure a man gets from having studied, even though he never holds an office of any kind, how at home by himself he can read all kinds of things, talk and associate with educated people, and travel and do business in foreign lands."[92]

On the other hand, Luther, the prophet, charged would-be dissenters from these educational principles with blasphemy and treason:

If God has given you a child who has the ability and the talent for his office, and you do not train him . . . you are doing all in your power to oppose worldly authority . . . [and] you are depriving God of an angel, a servant, and king and prince in his kingdom; a savior and comforter of men in matters that pertain to body and soul, property and honor; a captain and a knight to fight against the devil. Thus you are making a place for the devil and advancing his kingdom so that he brings more souls into sin, death, and hell every day and keeps them there.[93]

THE NEW CIVIL LAW OF PUBLIC EDUCATION

The German magistrates proved considerably more receptive than the German masses to the reformers' educational principles. Traditional Church teachings had given the magistrates little responsibility for education, and little control over the sizeable Church schools and endowments within their domains. Most civil encroachments on the Church's magisterium were viewed as sins, punishable by the interdict and the ban. The new Protestant teachings, by contrast, declared the magistrates to be the chief custodians of education, called by God to seize the failing Church schools and their endowments and shepherd them toward their divine mandates. Both conscientious and covetous magistrates found inspiration in such teachings, and they quickly cast the reformers' pedagogical principles into civil law. They issued a torrent of new school laws in the first two generations of the Lutheran Reformation: some as free-standing school ordinances (*Schulordnungen*), most as provisions subsumed within the broader Church ordinances (*Kirchenordnungen*) and public policy ordinances (*Polizeiordnungen*) issued by urban or territorial rulers.[94]

---

[92] *LW* 46:234, 243–4. [93] Ibid., 229, 242.
[94] The best collections are in Kunkel; Richter; Sehling; Vormbaum, *Schulordnungen*; Johann M. Reu, *Quellen zur Geschichte des kirchlichen Unterrichts in der evangelischen Kirche Deutschlands zwischen 1530 und 1600* (Gütersloh, 1904–1935); Goebel, *Luther in der Schule*.

The Lutheran Reformation had its most direct and dramatic influence on lower education in Germany.[95] Viewed as a whole, the new school ordinances created a two-track system of lower schools. First, Latin and vernacular city schools (*Ratschulen*), either inherited from pre-Reformation times or established in place of the cathedral or monastic schools that were confiscated, formed the core of the new school system. As in pre-Reformation times, these schools were established and maintained principally by the local city councils and supervised by city clerks, superintendents, and on occasion local judges vested with principal educational authority. Also as in pre-Reformation times, the city Latin schools attracted the greatest tax support and best teachers, and provided the richest curriculum in religion and the liberal arts. The vernacular boys' schools and girls' schools (also called reading and writing schools – *Lese-* or *Schreibschulen*) generally enjoyed less attractive quarters, less regular tax disbursements, less qualified teachers, and were ultimately designed for rudimentary literacy and vocational training for local children.[96]

Secondly, alongside these city schools, new territorial or princely schools (*Landes-*, *Fürstenschulen*) were established – both to train budding bureaucrats to serve in the princely retinue and to prepare gifted students for ongoing work in the universities. These territorial schools were "an innovation" of the Reformation and a critical means of extending the services and consolidating the power of the local prince or duke.[97] The territorial schools were designed to complement, rather than compete with, the existing city schools; indeed many princes and dukes made periodic disbursements to the city schools to ensure that they would continue to cooperate in the region's educational system.

In the typical case, the territorial schools were established by the initiative (and where necessary with the funding) of the territorial prince and council, regulated by territorial legislation, and supervised by itinerant superintendents commissioned by the territorial council. Frequently these territorial schools provided the only forms of elementary and secondary education in the countryside. In the cities, they often served as "interim boarding schools" (*Pädagogia*) to which poor, but gifted Latin

---

[95] For a list of the new lower schools founded under Evangelical inspiration see Georg Mertz, *Das Schulwesen der deutschen Reformation im 16. Jahrhundert* (Heidelberg, 1902), 192–204.

[96] See Ernst C. Helmreich, *Religious Education in German Schools: An Historical Approach* (Cambridge, MA, 1959), 14–16.

[97] Friedrich Paulsen, *German Education Past and Present*, trans. T. Lorenz (New York, 1912), 65.

school and vernacular school students were sent to prepare them for university life. Alongside these Latin and vernacular schools, a large number of private tutorial schools continued to flourish in the cities – despite the best efforts of the city councils to stamp them out.[98]

Urban public schools: The example of Brunswick

The 1528 school law drafted by Johannes Bugenhagen for the city of Brunswick provides a typical and influential example of the new urban legislation.[99] The law demonstrates neatly both the reformers' penchant for amalgamating their fresh principles with traditional institutional forms and the local magistrates' proclivity for seeking to regulate their new schools in minute detail.

The preamble to the school law offers a crisp distillation of the reformers' pedagogical principles, peppered throughout with biblical citations and homiletic appeals. "It is an equitable and Christian right," the preamble begins, "that children are baptized into God's grace," "that they are taught to distinguish right and wrong," and that they "receive the fruits of the Spirit and the knowledge of Christ." It is the reciprocal duty of parents and magistrates to provide such education. Some teaching must occur in the home and in the church. But the most important education must take place in the school. Parents must send their children to school, even though it may be more lucrative to keep them at home and even though it may appear dangerous to expose them to new ideas and uncertain career plans. The preamble ends with a resounding rendition of the reformers' belief in the religious and civic utility of education:

Before all else, therefore, it is considered necessary . . . to establish good schools and to employ honorable, well-grounded, scholarly masters and assistants to the honor of God the Almighty for the welfare of youth and the satisfaction of the entire city. In these schools, poor, ignorant youth may be properly trained, learn the Ten Commandments, the Creed, the Lord's Prayer, and the Christian sacraments with as much explanation as is suitable for children. They may also learn to sing the psalms in Latin, and to read passages every day from the Latin Scriptures. In addition, they may study the humanities from which one learns

---

[98] See, e.g., Strauss, *Luther's House of Learning*, 316 (showing how the Nuremberg city council fought unsuccessfully with the private tutorial schools throughout the sixteenth century, and ultimately in 1613 consolidated forty-eight such schools into a private guild); Helmreich, *Religious Education*, 21 (stating that, in Munich in 1560, some sixteen illegal private tutorial schools competed for students with the three established Latin schools).

[99] The statute is printed in Vormbaum, *Schulordnungen*, 1:8–18 and Richter, 1:106–19.

to understand such matters. And not merely that, but also that in time there may come good schoolmasters, good preachers, good jurists, good physicians, God-fearing, decent, honorable, well-grounded, obedient, sociable, scholarly, peaceable, sober but happy citizens, who henceforth may train their children in the best way, and so on the children's children. This God requires of us.[100]

The ordinance makes extensive provision for Latin boys' schools, devoting seven of its ten articles to their governance. Two Latin schools are to be permanently established for the city, each housed in a former cathedral school and each staffed, as a minimum, with a rector, chorister, and assistant. The law sets out in copious detail the responsibility, authority, moral standards, skills, salary, and room and board provisions of each school official, and the division of responsibility among them. It lays down the procedures to be followed by the city council to adjudicate any disputes among school officials, students, and members of the community (particularly parents of schoolchildren). It prescribes a curriculum, which is, in the statute's words, "more or less as Philip Melanchthon has described it."

The Brunswick law repeats Melanchthon's plans for a tripartite division of classes and regimen of textbooks with little deviation, though it encourages officials to supplement Melanchthon's exclusive diet of Latin with some offerings in Greek, Hebrew, and German. The law orders that school assistants collect tuition fees from parents in accordance with each family's means. Aristocratic parents must pay double fees for each student sent. Most parents must pay single fees. Some parents may commute their tuition payment by offering room and board to another student. Others may seek, with the city council's help, "some pious, rich folks who will make scholarly donations to bright, poor boys." "Those who are so poor that they can pay nothing, and yet would willingly bless their children [with education] may go to the general treasurer in the precinct [who] will keep a record of such children and bring them to the schoolmaster [for free education]." When students reach the ages of twelve and sixteen, the schoolmaster must judge whether they should either continue to pursue higher education or take up "an honorable or satisfactory vocation" with the skills they have learned. Only a very small number of students should be encouraged to continue university studies after their sixteenth year and so "be dedicated to the godly service of other people in spiritual affairs as well as the temporal affairs of government."

---

[100] Vormbaum, *Schulordnungen*, 1: 8–9.

The Brunswick law also provides, more cryptically, for vernacular boys' and girls' schools. Only officially licensed vernacular schools are permitted in the city; unofficial private tutors and private schools (*Winkelschulen*) are strictly prohibited. The law authorizes an unspecified number of boys' schools designed primarily "to teach something good from the Word of God about the Decalogue, the Creed, Lord's Prayer, the two sacraments . . . and Christian songs." Two German schoolmasters are appointed by the city council, given a basic salary, and authorized to collect fees from their students. Nothing is said about curriculum, facilities, schoolmaster responsibilities, and the like for these schools.

The vernacular girls' schools receive considerably lengthier statutory treatment, since they were a wholly new creation in the city. Four girls' schools are established for the city. Schoolmistresses "grounded in the Gospel and of good repute" are to be appointed as "Christian servants of the entire city," devoted to teaching the young girls. The city council must pay them a basic salary, which they may supplement with fees collected from students who have the means to pay. The law waxes at some length on the limited mission and curriculum of the girls' schools. Girls are to attend them "one or at most two hours per day" for "a year or at most two years." The young girls "need to learn only to read, and to hear some exposition of the Decalogue, the Creed, and the Lord's Prayer, and [the sacraments]. They also ought to learn to recite some passages from the New Testament concerning the Creed, the love and patience of the cross, and some sacred history . . . and Christian songs." With such training, young girls will be capable of becoming "useful, skillful, happy, friendly, God-fearing, not superstitious or stubborn, housewives who can control their servants and train their children."

The Brunswick law assigns to the Church and its clergy discrete roles to play in the educational process. Churches are to open their doors each morning and evening without fail so that the children can follow a regimen of reading Scripture, singing Christian psalms and hymns, and offering vespers and matins under the direction of the chorister or pastor. This method of daily devotional exercises, the statute declares, will "render the children accustomed to going to the Holy Scriptures as if to a play."[101] Clergy who serve as school superintendents are to give mid-week lessons on the Holy Scripture in the school or in the public square – such

---

[101] This final section "Vam singende unde lesende de Scholekynderen in der Kerken," appears in Frederick Koldewy, "Braunschweigische Schulordnungen," *Monumenta Germaniae Pädagogica*, 62 vols. (Berlin, 1886–1938), 1:27ff., but does not appear in the Vormbaum printing of the same statute.

lessons to be in Latin to distinguish them from sermons, which are delivered in German during worship services. Churches are required to provide various forms of material aid to students, to hire students and graduates of the local schools as acolytes and choir members, and to furnish accommodations to newly-wed school assistants who have need. The "most distinguished pastor" of the community, together with five members of the city council and the city treasurer, is required to make semi-annual inspection visits to each of the city schools to ensure they are adhering to their charges "in every particular."

The Brunswick law also makes some provision for broader public participation in the educational process. Public libraries are to be established, at city expense, near each of the schools in the city. The libraries are to house the writings of the great Church Fathers, Ambrose, Augustine, Jerome, and other doctors who have written on Scripture, and to be open to all members of the community.[102] The law authorizes the construction of a public lecture hall (*lectorium*), and the regular delivery of public lectures on sundry topics. Two jurists are to be hired by the city to deliver lectures thrice weekly on the *Institutes* and the Code of Justinian's *Corpus iuris civilis*, and for "whatever other purpose the city council and the deacon deems proper." One or more medical doctors are to give thrice-weekly lectures on matters of hygiene, diet, and care of the poor and the sick, and also to participate in care for the sick and hospitalized in the community. School rectors, superintendents, and their brightest students are to give daily biblical expositions that are designed "not so much for the instruction of their students as for the [spiritual] enhancement of their listeners."[103] Through these and other means, the entire community would be imbued with religious and civic learning.

Bugenhagen's 1528 statute for Brunswick was quickly held up in Evangelical circles as a model. Both Luther and Melanchthon praised it heartily for its skillful appropriation and reification of Evangelical pedagogical learning, and saw to its wide dissemination throughout Germany

---

[102] See Richter, 1:106, 113, for article "Van der librye." See also "Schulordnung aus der hambergischen Kirchenordnung" (1529), art. 5, reprinted in Vormbaum, *Schulordnungen* 1:18, 25, which Bugenhagen had included in his penultimate draft of the Brunswick law, but slightly revised in the promulgated law.

[103] An article "Vom Lectorio" was included in the penultimate draft of the Brunswick school law, but dropped from the promulgated law. The same article appears, verbatim, in Bugenhagen's Hamburg School law, in Sehling, 5:488, 499, passed in 1529 and eventually became part of the practice in Brunswick. For purposes of illustrating the range of typical provisions in these early city laws, I include discussion of this provision under the Brunswick law.

and Scandinavia.[104] The next two generations of city councilmen and their advisors made ready use of its structure and language in crafting their own legislation. It was a common feature of the city school laws passed before 1559 to begin with a recitation of Evangelical pedagogical principles, often laced with the favorite theological themes of local religious leaders. The city school ordinances typically then made detailed provision for the structure, teaching, curriculum, and maintenance of the Latin schools, the establishment of vernacular boys' and girls' schools, and often featured staggered tuition rates and/or various forms of aid for poor students, public libraries, and public lectures on law, medicine, theology, and the arts.

Local magistrates offered their own variations on the Brunswick school law, driven in part by pragmatics, in part by their own principles. Though such variations range broadly over time and across jurisdictions, a few general trends are evident in the available urban statutes and case studies.

First, many of the larger cities began to insist on increasing professionalization of their Latin schools. Minimal educational requirements for teachers and superintendents became more stringent, moral and lifestyle standards more rigorous. The city school laws after the 1540s insist regularly that only university-trained theologians be employed as rectors and superintendents, and that well-trained jurists and judges participate in the inspection of the schools. Officially sanctioned textbooks became increasingly the norm. City councils began to insist on more routinized teaching and evaluation techniques and more refined differentiations among classes of students. Johannes Sturm's ten-class lower school in Strasbourg was a brilliant exception to the usual division of classes into four or five groups.

Secondly, the disparities between the Latin schools, on the one hand, and the vernacular boys' and girls' schools, on the other, became increasingly acute. In many cities and towns, funding for the facilities, materials, and teachers of the vernacular schools dropped off appreciably. Statutory attention also waned. (The 1543 revision of the Brunswick school law, for example, quite unlike its 1528 prototype, makes no provision for the funding or maintenance of the vernacular schools, even though the six vernacular schools in place in the city were floundering badly.) As a consequence, the vernacular schools in several cities simply closed; several

104 See letters in Eike Wolgast, ed., *D. Bugenhagens Briefwechsel* (Hildesheim, 1966), and broader discussion in Luise Schorn-Schütte, " 'Papocaesarismus' der Theologen? Vom Amt des evangelischen Pfarrers in der frühneuzeitlichen Stadtgesellschaft bei Bugenhagen," *AFR* 79 (1988): 230.

others became little more than grand apprentice programs, run voluntarily by well-meaning, but untrained tailors, shoemakers, carpenters, and church custodians.[105]

Thirdly, over time, the city councils made heavier use of local parish churches as their administrative agencies of education. In the larger cities, pastors were expected to lecture and offer counseling in the local schools. Consistories were expected to help in soliciting school funds, securing student housing, and supervising schoolteachers and superintendents. Church buildings were to be available for use by the schoolmasters, in the (rather common) case of overflow at the schools. Choristers, paid by the Church, were expected to participate in the musical instruction of the schools.

In the smaller towns, where formal schooling was harder to establish, the magistrates leaned even more heavily on the local church. The church sanctuary on Sunday became the schoolhouse during the week. The parsonage became the rooming house for poor, gifted students. Local pastors and sextons were to hold periodic instruction in Scripture, the catechism, singing, and sundry humanistic texts, so that the young were not entirely neglected.

Territorial public schools: the example of Württemberg

While Johannes Bugenhagen's 1528 school law for the city of Brunswick provided a model of the new urban legislation, Johannes Brenz's 1559 school law for the duchy of Württemberg provided a model of the new territorial legislation.[106] Like Bugenhagen, Brenz incorporated into this law a preambulary apologia for state education, followed by detailed provision for various lower schools, and the responsibilities of Church, state, and community to them. Unlike Bugenhagen, however, Brenz proceeded far more formally and self-assuredly, armed with the expertise harvested from the first two generations of educational reform in Lutheran

---

[105] See, e.g., Helmreich, *Religious Education*, 15–16; id., "Joint School and Church Positions in Germany," *Lutheran School Journal* 79 (1943): 157.

[106] Reprinted with some omissions in Vormbaum, *Schulordnungen*, 1:68–165 and in complete form in August L. Reyscher, ed., *Vollständige, historisch, und kritisch bearbeitete Sammlung der Württembergischen Gesetze* (Württemberg, 1828–51) with relevant school materials 8:106ff.; 11 / 1:2ff.; 11 / 2:24ff. The Württemberg school ordinance forms part of the larger Württemberg church ordinance, which Brenz and several others drafted. The statute incorporates large sections of the legislation promulgated by the duchy in the previous decade: Brenz's Württemberg Confession (1551), the liturgical church order (1553), the marriage court ordinance (1553), the welfare ordinance (1552), and, most importantly, Brenz's cloister ordinance (1556).

Germany. Gone from the Württemberg school law are the intermittent biblical quotations and homiletic appeals that marked the Brunswick law and its progeny. Gone, too, are the plaintive entreaties to magistrates and citizens to cooperate in this tender new enterprise. In nearly a hundred pages of densely written text, the Württemberg school ordinance firmly commands and finely routinizes the school system of the duchy.

The preamble to the ordinance focuses directly on the utility of education for the three estates of the earthly kingdom. "[U]pright, wise, learned, skillful, and God-fearing men belong to the holy preaching office, to the secular magistracy and administrative offices, and to domestic life," the preamble begins. "[S]chools are the proper means ordained and commanded by God, wherein such people may be educated." "[O]ur forefathers [devoted] a considerable portion of their temporal goods to monasteries and foundations to the support of schools and studies." In our day, we devote our resources to public schools, and command that they "be put into effect throughout the principality without fail and with all industry and serious attention."

The ordinance tolerates no deprivation of education for any child and no diversity in the methods and media of instruction. School attendance is compulsory. The statute insists that "special care be taken that in each and every community . . . from the foremost cities to the hamlets in our principality," schools are available and accessible to the children. The form of instruction should be identical everywhere, for "diversity in teaching methods and textbook authors is . . . more of a hindrance than a help" in pedagogy. The statute thus provides a "uniform and universal" educational program with "distinct divisions [of the schools] into classes," and detailed instructions for "textbook authors, hours, recitations, and the like by which our officials must regulate everything." School officials shall "by no means change anything to suit themselves," the statute warns. "Every school shall accord with every other."

No exact uniformity in education was forthcoming. The Württemberg school law provides for four forms of lower education that intermixed traditional and newly established institutions: (1) Latin schools, (2) cloister schools, (3) vernacular schools, and (4) territorial boarding schools.

Latin boys' schools (*Partikularschulen*) provided the foundation for the new school system. Existing Latin schools in the cities were to be maintained, alongside new Latin schools established in every village and town. Ideally, each Latin school was to be divided into five classes through which students could advance at their own pace. In reality, the smaller villages often could offer only the first two or three classes (and were thus often called *Trivialschulen*). The most able "graduates" from these schools could then pursue training in the school of a larger neighboring city, or in the five-class interim boarding school. The ordinance sets out a detailed, uniform curriculum and calendar for each of the five classes. The curriculum blends religious and humanistic instruction in familiar Evangelical patterns. Many of the texts that Melanchthon had prescribed in his 1528 *Instructions* are assigned, together with Melanchthon's own textbooks on grammar, rhetoric, and dialectics, his exegesis of Proverbs and his Latin catechism, and a host of other books. Each class was to begin and end its day with prayer and song, with devotions and a brief meditation to be offered at lunchtime. Each hour of the day was designated for the teaching of a discrete subject, with exact specifications for how the subject was to be taught. Teachers were strictly prohibited to depart from this regimen.

The ordinance dwells at some length on the morality and discipline of the Latin schoolboys. While the young are "still gentle and amenable," the statute reads, they must be inculcated with the "godly morality that Scripture imparts." The statute distills this godly morality into a seven-part rule respecting the students' attendance, dress, work habits, and the like. Families and churches must aid the school in disciplining the young. Schoolmasters must keep parents and pastors apprised of their disciplinary patterns, particularly with more delinquent youths. Parents must visit the schools regularly to see the behavior of their children and confirm the schoolmasters' discipline when it is meted out. Pastors must offer special counsel to delinquent and incorrigible youths, and use their sermons and lectures to inculcate and illustrate Christian morality for parents and students alike.

Latin schoolmasters and their assistants must be "learned, God-fearing, industrious, and indefatigable." No one was better able to measure their credentials than the local church council led by the head pastor. Candidates for teaching positions were to be carefully screened concerning their education, family background, moral scruples, and above all their religious convictions. They had to be conversant with both the basic Lutheran dogma of the Augsburg Confession, and the particular local formulations of that doctrine set down in the official confession and catechism of the duchy. Promising candidates were escorted by local consistory officials to Tübingen, where they offered a lecture and disputation before the theology faculty at the university. Those who passed this test returned to the local community, and as a final step to their induction, read aloud before representatives of the city council and consistory court the full text of the Württemberg school ordinance. After they were inducted into their offices, they were subject to monthly inspections and quarterly examinations by the local pastor and three "learned men" of the community.

While the Latin schools in Württemberg provided general education for a substantial fee, the "cloister schools" (*Klosterschulen*) usually provided theological education for free. The cloister schools, among Brenz's most provocative innovations,[107] were boarding schools housed in former cloisters throughout the duchy that had been appropriated by the magistrates. They were designed for the "sole purpose of . . . training young men to become teachers and preachers in the Church." Their doors were to be open only to able adolescent boys, of good Christian stock, presented to the superintendent by a local pastor or noble. Some of these boys could be plucked from the Latin schools, but generally they were to be boys of precocious ability but of too humble a means to attend the Latin schools. The cloister schools were to charge these students little, if any, tuition fees on condition that their parents or guardians sign an elaborate adhesion contract consenting to the ministerial training they would receive.

For all the anti-monasticism of Brenz and the other early reformers, the Württemberg law prescribed a veritable monastic experience in these cloister schools. The boys were to be housed together, away from their families, and under the watchful eye of a superintendent and/or schoolmaster. Their time was to be spent on a regimen of daily chores, devotional exercises, and reading, writing, and speaking. The school law sets forth in painstaking detail a carefully graduated curriculum. Alongside the conventional training in the liberal arts, the students were to receive special, in-depth training in Scripture, Church history, formal theology, homiletics, liturgy, hymnology, and the like. The law sets out elaborate lists of moral imperatives to be mastered and by which the boys were to be measured. It also assigns long passages of Scripture, the catechism, prayers, and liturgical rites to be memorized and recited faithfully. After four or five years of such training, all students were equipped, at minimum, to hold minor ecclesiastical appointments throughout the duchy – as sextons, assistants, catechism instructors, and the like. Others could be assigned a pastoral tutor, and slowly groomed for a pastoral office or higher ecclesiastical administration. The best students were

---

[107] Estes, *Johannes Brenz*, 16. Brenz first set out his idea for such cloister schools in a 1529 letter to Margrave George of Brandenburg-Ansbach. See Brenz, *Anecdota Brentiana: Ungedruckte Briefe und Bedenken von Johannes Brenz*, ed. Theodor Pressel (Tübingen, 1868), 33.

to compete for stipends to pursue advanced theological training in Tübingen, whose graduates were equipped for full-fledged pastorates, schoolmaster positions, and, for the very best, professorial positions in the theology faculties.

The Württemberg law makes brief provision for the German vernacular schools, with little departure from conventional norms. Separate boys' and girls' schools were to be established so that all the young "may be well instructed and trained in the fear of God, right doctrine, and good conduct." Basic literacy training was critical – to teach the students proper mastery of the alphabet, good grammar, legible penmanship, and proper pronunciation of the local dialect. Such training was critical so that the students could master not only Scripture, but especially the catechism and confession prescribed by the Württemberg church ordinance.

Two "interim boarding schools" (*Pädagogia*), newly established in Stuttgart and Tübingen, served multiple pedagogical needs. They provided advanced training for students whose local Latin schools did not offer all five classes of instruction. They offered pre-university training and screening for Latin school, and some cloister school, graduates whose university credentials were somewhat suspect. They also eventually came to serve as an elite training ground for young students (particularly of distinguished families) who aspired to high bureaucratic positions in the duke's retinue.[108]

Brenz's 1559 Württemberg school law established a model of an integrated school system in sixteenth-century Germany, and emerged as a pristine institutional appropriation of the reformers' educational ideals.[109] The traditional varieties of independent Church schools, city schools, and private schools were integrated into a common public school system subject to the central rule of a Christian magistrate. The great varieties of curricula and teaching methods previously offered were reduced to common forms and foci that balanced religious and humanistic instruction. The traditional disparities in educational opportunities were relieved by the opening of schools to all children, boys and girls, rich and poor, rural and urban alike. The traditional deprecation of learning in the lay estates gave way to new opportunities for training in literacy and literature for all citizens. In place was an educational system that was

---

[108] Raeff, *The Well-Ordered Police State*, 139.
[109] A similar comprehensive system, modeled in large part on the Württemberg school ordinance, was established by the church ordinance of Saxony (1580), in Vormbaum, *Schulordnungen*, 1:230; Sehling, 1/1:359.

predicated on Evangelical educational ideals, and positioned to perpetuate Evangelical learning and leadership for generations to come.

The law on the books, of course, is not the law in action. The many close studies of the actual working of the new educational system, in Württemberg and in several other cities and territories in sixteenth-century Germany, suggests that the new territorial and city laws provided an ideal form that could not be fully realized.[110] Tax records reveal a perpetual bickering over endowment disbursements, schoolteachers' salaries, school maintenance costs, and the like. School and Church visitation records suggest ongoing problems with delinquent and ignorant teachers, self-serving inspectors and pastors, student delinquency, parental interference in the schools, and the like. Court records are filled with disputes between and among schoolteachers, parents, and civil magistrates over everything from payments in arrears to prostitution rings. Census records give evidence of continued illiteracy among substantial portions of the population.

This evidence, drawn from local studies, properly softens some of the overly bright assessments of the Evangelical reformers' educational reforms offered by champions of Luther and of the Reformation.[111] It does not, however, suggest that the Evangelical reformers' new system of education was a failure, as some recent writers have argued.[112] The evidence of alleged failure is drawn principally from records that are barometers of discontent and dissent, naturally disposed to reflect strongly negative impressions. It reflects the conventional problems of every educational system in action – including our own. Such evidence must be balanced against the incontrovertible fact that the Lutheran Reformation permanently transformed German education into a system that was considerably more public, more egalitarian, more pluralistic, and more

[110] See, e.g., Ludwig von Friedeburg, *Bildungsreform in Deutschland: Geschichte und gesellschaftlicher Widerspruch* (Frankfurt am Main, 1989); "Symposium on Education in the Renaissance and Reformation," *Renaissance Quarterly* 43 (1990): 1; Goebel, ed., *Luther in der Schule;* Scott H. Hendrix, "Luther's Impact on the Sixteenth Century," *Sixteenth Century Journal* 16 (1985): 3; R. A. Houston, *Literacy in Early Modern Europe: Culture and Education, 1500–1800* (New York/London, 1988); James Kittelson, "Successes and Failures of the German Reformation: The Report from Strasbourg," *AFR* 73 (1982): 153; Klaus Leder, *Kirche und Jugend in Nürnberg und seinem Landgebiet: 1400–1800* (Neustadt, 1973); Geoffrey Parker, "Success and Failure During the First Century of the Reformation," *Past and Present* 136 (1992): 43; Wright, "Evaluating the Results."

[111] See, e.g., F. V. N. Painter, *Luther on Education* (St. Louis, MO, 1928), 168 (describing Luther's 1524 sermon on education as "the most important educational treatise ever written" and Luther "as the greatest not only of religious, but of educational reformers").

[112] See critical reviews of Strauss's *Luther's House of Learning* by Steven Ozment, *Journal of Modern History* 51 (1979): 837; Lewis W. Spitz, *American Historical Review* 85 (1980): 143; Mark U. Edwards, Jr., *History of Education Quarterly* 21 (1981): 471.

humanistic than any that came before, and that the populace was rendered more literate, learned, and advanced than it was before.[113] The
basic law and structure of education born of the Lutheran Reformation
remained at the cornerstone of education for more than three centuries
thereafter, not only in Germany but in many other parts of Protestant
Europe as well.[114]

SUMMARY AND CONCLUSIONS

Prior to the sixteenth century, the Catholic Church had established a
refined system of religious education for Western Christendom. Cathedrals, monasteries, chantries, ecclesiastical guilds, and large parishes offered the principal forms of lower education, governed by general and
local canon law rules of the Church. Young students were trained in
the trivium and quadrivium, and taught the creeds, catechisms, and
confessional books. Gifted graduates were sent on to Church-licensed
universities for advanced training in the core faculties of law, theology,
and medicine. The foundation of this Church-based educational system
lay in Christ's Great Commission to his apostles and their successors "to
teach all nations" the meaning and measure of the Christian faith. The
vast majority of students were trained for clerical and other forms of
service in the Church.

The Lutheran Reformation transformed this pan-European system of
Church-based education into a local and national system of state-based
education in Germany. Luther, Melanchthon, Bugenhagen, Brenz, and
other leading Protestant reformers castigated the Church both for its professional monopolization of education and for its distortions of religious
and humanistic learning. They introduced, in its place, a "secular" system
of public education that featured both (1) "laicization" (*Verbürgerlichung*),
the leveling of traditional social distinctions between clergy and laity in
defining the goods and goals of education; and (2) "temporalization"
(*Verweltlichung*), the predominant use of civil officials and civic concerns

---

[113] Cf. Karl Holl, "Die Kulturbedeutung der Reformation," in id., *Gesammelte Aufsätze*, 1:518;
H. G. Haile, "Luther and Literacy," *Publications of the Modern Language Association* 91 (1976), 817;
id., *Luther: An Experiment in Biography* (Princeton, NJ, 1980), 81–92.

[114] For recent literature, see, e.g., Golz and Mayrhofer, eds., *Luther and Melanchthon*; Karin Maag, ed.,
Melanchthon in Europe: His Work and Influence Beyond Wittenberg (Grand Rapids, MI, 1999); Heinz
Scheible, "Die Reform von Schule und Universität in der Reformationszeit," *Luther-Jahrbuch*
66 (1999): 266; id., ed., *Melanchthon in seinen Schülern*; and the collections of texts in Karl Ernst
Nipkow and Friedrich Schweitzer, eds., *Religionspädagogik: Texte zur evangelischen Erziehungs- und
Bildungsverantwortung seit der Reformation*, 2 vols. (Munich/Gütersloh, 1991–94).

to organize and operate the schools.[115] In the reformers' view, the state magistrate, as "father of the community," was primarily responsible for the education of the community. Education was to be mandatory for boys and girls alike, fiscally and physically accessible to all, and marked by both formal classroom instruction and civic education through community libraries, lectures, and other media. The curriculum was to combine biblical and Evangelical values with humanistic and vocational training. Students were to be stratified into different classes, according to age and ability, and gradually selected for any number of secular and religious vocations.

The theological reformers of the sixteenth century built on the work of the legal reformers of the fourteenth and fifteenth centuries. The system of state-run public education that they established built squarely on the Latin and vernacular schools already established in larger cities. The system of state-run charities and guilds to support poor students built on the prior practice of princes, guilds, and monasteries to maintain educational endowments. The curricula of the lower schools kept religion at their core, and retained the seven liberal arts as well as a number of texts prescribed by the Catholic canon law.

The reformers, however, cast these traditional pedagogical principles and practices into their own distinctive ensemble, grounded in the two-kingdoms theory. Over time, the Christian magistrate replaced the Church cleric as the chief protector and cultivator of the public school and university. The state's civil law replaced the Church's canon law as the chief law governing education. The Bible replaced the scholastic text as the chief handbook of the curriculum. German replaced Latin as the universal tongue of the educated classes in Germany. The general callings of all Christians replaced the special calling of the clergy as the *raison d'être* of education. Education remained fundamentally religious in character. But it was now subject to broader political control and directed to broader civic ends.

Despite their differences, however, both the Protestant and Catholic traditions of education assumed the presence of a religious establishment – one established set of religious beliefs and values to be transmitted in the classroom, one preferred cadre of ecclesiastical structures and officials to help administer the schools. After decades of bitter fighting, both traditions also came to see that the co-existence of two or more

---

[115] The phrases are from Liermann, *Handbuch des Stiftungsrechts*, 124–5; see also Cohn, "Church Property in the German Protestant Principalities."

religious communities within the community required some form of accommodation of the educational needs of religious non-conformists. The Religious Peace of Augsburg (1555) confirmed the power of the prince to establish his own preferred form of Lutheran or Catholic faith in his polity, under the principle of *cuius regio, eius religio*. But it also guaranteed to non-conformist Lutherans or Catholics the right to offer private religious education in the home, and the right of students to emigrate freely to a more confessionally congenial territory for their education.[116] After several more decades of religious warfare, the Peace of Westphalia (1648) extended this same principle of accommodation to Calvinist communities, and over time to the growing plurality of faiths in Germany.[117]

---

[116] Reprinted in Ehler and Morrall, eds., *Church and State Through the Centuries*, 164–73.
[117] Reprinted in ibid., 189–93.

Concluding reflections

A century ago, most Protestants viewed Martin Luther as the faithful David who felled the papal Goliath with the single stones of sacred Scripture. Most Catholics viewed Luther as the seven-headed demon who destroyed Western Christendom with his heretical ranting. For most Protestants, Luther was the great prophet of modern liberty who freed Western law and culture from the oppressive rule of the Catholic Church. For most Catholics, Luther was the grim priest of secularism, who cut off Western law and culture from their essential religious roots.[1]

Today, such confessional caricatures of Luther and the Reformation are happily fading. Most Protestants have now begun to recognize that the Lutheran Reformation was part and product of a whole series of late medieval reform movements, and that the new Evangelical churches depended upon Catholic theology and canon law for many of their cardinal ideas and institutions. Most Catholics have now begun to recognize Luther as a loud but inspired prophet for an alternative Christian worldview, a shrill but shrewd architect of a new biblical theology of human nature, social pluralism, and religious liberty, much of which the modern Catholic Church now embraces.[2]

The sixteenth-century Lutheran Reformation did bring fundamental changes to German spiritual life. The Lutheran Reformation radically resystematized dogma. It truncated the sacraments. It revamped spiritual symbolism. It vernacularized the Bible and the worship service. It transformed corporate worship and congregational music. It gave new emphasis to the pulpit and the sermon. It expanded catechesis and

---

[1] On various images of Luther, see, e.g., Peter N. Brooks, ed., *Seven-Headed Luther* (Oxford, 1983); Edwards, *Printing, Propaganda, and Martin Luther*; Jacques Maritain, *Three Reformers: Luther – Descartes – Rousseau* (New York, 1947); Robert Scribner, *For the Sake of Simple Folk: Popular Propaganda for the German Reformation* (Cambridge, 1981); James Stayer, *Martin Luther, German Saviour: German Evangelical Theological Factions and the Interpretation of Luther, 1917–1933* (Montreal, 2000).

[2] See sources and discussion in my "A Dickensian Era of Religious Rights: An Update on *Religious Human Rights in Global Perspective*," *William and Mary Law Review* 42 (2001), 726ff. and my "The Goods and Goals of Marriage."

religious instruction. It truncated clerical privileges and Church properties. It dissolved ecclesiastical foundations and endowments. It outlawed
the cult of religious artifacts. It rejected the veneration of non-biblical
saints and the cult of the dead. It outlawed the payment of indulgences
and mortuaries. It discouraged religious pilgrimages. It reduced the number of holy days. It lightened spiritual rules of diet and dress. It reformed
ecclesiastical discipline and Church administration, and much more.

To be sure, some of these spiritual changes built on two centuries
of reformist agitation by late medieval humanists, conciliarists, pietists,
nominalists, nationalists, and others. And, to be sure, some of the spiritual changes introduced by the Lutheran Reformation had parallels
in Catholic reform movements, especially during and after the Council of Trent (1545–63). But it was especially the Lutheran Reformation
that brought these earlier reformist efforts to institutional fruition and
expression in Germany. The spiritual changes that the reformers introduced were cast into a unique Evangelical ensemble and transmitted to
later generations in scores of thick confessions, catechisms, creeds, and
church ordinances.

The Lutheran Reformation also brought fundamental changes to
German legal life, sometimes in direct expression of the new Lutheran
theology. Lutheran reformers pressed to radical conclusions the theological concept of the magistrate as the father of the community, called
by God to enforce both tables of the Decalogue on his political children.
This idea helped to trigger a massive shift in power and property from the
Church to the state, and ultimately introduced enduring systems of state
established churches, schools, and social welfare institutions. Lutheran
reformers replaced the traditional idea of marriage as a sacrament with a
new idea of the marital household as a social estate to which all persons
are called, clerical and lay alike. On that basis, the reformers developed a new civil law of marriage, featuring requirements of parental
consent, state registration, church consecration, and peer presence for
valid marital formation as well as absolute divorce on grounds of adultery, desertion, and other faults, with subsequent rights to remarriage.
Lutheran reformers replaced the traditional understanding of education as a teaching office of the Church with a new understanding of the
public school as a "civic seminary" for all persons to prepare for their
distinctive vocations. On that basis, magistrates replaced clerics as the
chief rulers of education, civil law replaced canon law as the principal
law of education, and the general callings of all Christians replaced the
special calling of the clergy as the principal goal of education. Lutheran

reformers developed a theory of the essential union of law and equity in the conscience of the Christian judge. On that basis, they developed innovative new theories of practical legal reasoning and pious judicial activism, and advocated the merger of Church courts and state courts, of legal procedures and equitable remedies. Lutheran reformers introduced a new theology of the civil, theological, and educational uses of the law. On that basis, they developed arresting new theories of divine law, natural law, and civil law, and an integrated theory of the retributive, deterrent, and rehabilitative functions of law and authority.

To be sure, some of these legal changes, like some of the spiritual changes introduced by the Lutheran Reformation, had antecedents in late medieval life and analogues in contemporaneous Catholic movements. Particularly important for the Lutheran reformation were the "legal reformations" issued by fifteenth-century German cities and territories that sought both to truncate some of the power, property, and privilege of the Catholic Church, and to transplant some of its learned canon law procedures, structures, and institutions into civil law. And, to be sure, a good deal of the medieval canon law that the Lutheran reformers had set out to spurn and burn found its way back into the private, public, and criminal laws of Reformation Germany. But, again, it was the Lutheran Reformation that cast this medieval legal inheritance into a unique new legal ensemble in Germany that was preserved in hundreds of legal monographs, consilia, cases, and ordinances crafted by Lutheran jurists and theologians.

THE LEGAL LEGACY OF THE LUTHERAN REFORMATION

Nearly half a millennium after it first broke out in the little town of Wittenberg, the Lutheran Reformation still has a shaping influence on Western law.

A good deal of our modern Western law of marriage, education, and social welfare, for example, still bears the unmistakable marks of Lutheran Reformation theology. Today, in most Western legal systems, marriage is still viewed as both a civil and a spiritual institution, whose formation and dissolution require special legal procedures. Parents must still consent to the marriages of their minor children. Peers must still attest to the veracity of the marital oath. Pastors or political officials must still confirm the marital union, if not consecrate it. Divorce and annulment still require a special public proceeding before a tribunal, with proof of support for dependent spouses and children.

Today, in most Western legal systems, basic education remains a fundamental right of the citizen to receive and a fundamental duty of the state to provide. Literacy and learning are still considered a prerequisite for individual flourishing and communal participation. Society still places a heavy burden on those who shirk education voluntarily. The state is still considered to be the essential monitor of civil education, which task it discharges directly through its own public or common schools or indirectly through its accreditation and supervision of private schools.

Today, in most Western legal systems, care for the poor and needy remains an essential office of the state and an essential calling of the citizen. The rise of the modern Western welfare state over the past century is in no small measure a new institutional expression of the Lutheran ideal of the magistrate as the father of the community called to care for all his political children. The concurrent rise of the modern philanthropic citizen is in no small measure a modern institutional expression of Luther's ideal of the priesthood of all believers, each called to give loving service to neighbors. Sixteenth-century Lutherans and twenty-first-century Westerners seem to share the assumption that the state has a role to play not only in fighting wars, punishing crime, and keeping peace, but also in providing education and welfare, fostering charity and morality, facilitating worship and piety. They also seem to share the assumption that law has not only a basic use of coercing citizens to accept a morality of duty but also a higher use of inducing citizens to pursue a morality of aspiration.

A good deal of our modern Western struggle with law, however, is also part of the legal legacy of the Lutheran Reformation. For example the Lutheran reformers removed the Church as the spiritual ruler of Germany in expression of their founding ideals of religious liberty. But they ultimately anointed the state as the new spiritual ruler of Germany in expression of their new doctrines of Christian republicanism. Ever since, Germany and other Protestant nations have been locked in a bitter legal struggle to eradicate state establishments of religion and to guarantee religious freedom for all – a struggle that has still not ended in modern-day Germany.[3] Similarly, Lutheran reformers removed clerics as mediators between God and the laity, in expression of St. Peter's teaching of the priesthood of all believers. But they ultimately interposed husbands between God and their wives, in expression of St. Paul's teaching of male headship within the home. The Lutheran reformers

---

[3] See Martin Heckel, "The Impact of Religious Rules on Public Life in Germany," in Johan van der Vyver and John Witte, Jr., eds., *Religious Human Rights in Global Perspective: Legal Perspectives* (The Hague/Boston/London, 1996), 191ff.

outlawed monasteries and cloisters. But these reforms also ended the vocations of many single women, placing a new premium on the vocation of marriage. Ever since, Protestant women have been locked in a bitter legal struggle to gain fundamental equality both within the marital household and without – a struggle that has still not ended in more conservative Protestant communities today.

Luther's legal legacy therefore should be neither unduly romanticized nor unduly condemned. Those who champion Luther as the father of liberty, equality, and fraternity might do well to remember his ample penchant for elitism, statism, and chauvinism. Those who see the reformers only as belligerent allies of repression should recognize that they were also benevolent agents of welfare. Prone as he was to dialectic reasoning, and aware as he was of the inherent virtues and vices of human achievements, Luther would likely have reached a comparable assessment.

Such circumspection becomes doubly imperative in drawing connections between sixteenth-century Lutheranism and twentieth-century Nazism. It is, of course, tempting to follow many modern critics who draw direct and easy lines from Luther to Hitler, from Luther's horrible 1543 sermon *On The Jews and Their Lies* to Hitler's horrible slaughter of the Jews in the ghettoes and the death camps.[4] Such unfathomable tragedies as the Holocaust demand villains to become a bit understandable, and so giant a German personality as Luther is a natural and easy target to single out.

But we need remind ourselves of elementary facts and elementary law before drawing this indictment. The elementary facts are that Luther's late-life railings against the Jews were quite in contrast to his earlier solicitude for the Jews, and quite in keeping with a millennium and more of vicious anti-Judaism and anti-semitism in the Christian tradition.[5] Luther certainly added his ample share of vitriol to this Christian tradition of anti-semitism, and for that he deserves ample condemnation – doubly so given that he knew his words would inspire his followers. But Luther's words were no more harsh than those of many other Protestant, Catholic, and Orthodox Christians before and after him who condemned the Jews and called for all manner of savage abuses against them. And Luther did not act on his words in a way that many Christians before him had done, and after him would do, in their many brutal campaigns of persecution, ghettoization, pogromization, ostracism, and plain slaughter of the Jews.

---

[4] *LW* 47:121–306.
[5] See, e.g., Oberman, *The Roots of Anti-Semitism*; Edwards, *Luther's Last Battles*, 115ff.; Eric W. Gritsch, "Luther and the Jews: Toward a Judgment of History," in Harold H. Ditmanson, ed., *Stepping-Stones to Further Jewish–Lutheran Relations: Key Lutheran Statements* (Minneapolis, 1990), 104.

To indict Luther for the horrors of the Holocaust is not only to strain elementary facts but also to strain elementary law. The statutory period on homicide in most Western jurisdictions is no more than three years, usually only a year and a day. However diabolical a defendant's actions, he or she can be indicted for homicide only if the victim dies of those actions within the statutory period. This rule sometimes produces outrageous decisions at the margins – when victims die a day or two after the statutory period has expired, or when defendants glory in their escape from liability by the mere accident of chronology. But the point of a statutory period is for a community to have closure. Nearly four hundred years elapsed between Luther's horrible sermon and the Nazis' horrible actions.

Moreover, an indictment for homicide depends upon proof of a clear causal chain between the defendant's culpable action and the victim's ultimate death. The defendant's action must be the cause-in-fact of the victim's death – an action without which the deaths would not have occurred. The defendant's conduct must also be the proximate cause of the victim's death – close enough in time, space, and foreseeability, without intervening conduct by third parties. It is unquestionable that Luther's late-life railings against the Jews were a link in the chain of causation that ultimately brought on the Holocaust. But it was but one link in a causal chain of many thousands of links, and very far removed in time, space, and foreseeability from the actual horrors of the Holocaust.

Perhaps the statutory period on genocide, unlike that of homicide, should be infinite, not limited. Perhaps long chains of causation should be used to hang in memory, not to exonerate in casuistry, all those Christian hatemongers against the Jews, however distant in time and cause from the actual events of the Holocaust. Perhaps the counsel of emotion is better than the court of law to deal with so evil a tragedy. Perhaps so. But for all his rhetorical braggadocio, I think Luther would have been as horrified as any of us to see what the Holocaust had wrought. In the hundred-plus thick volumes of his writings that we have before us, there is precious little to indicate that he would have condoned diabolical savagery of this proportion.

THE THEOLOGICAL LEGACY OF THE LUTHERAN REFORMATION

Nearly half a millennium after it first broke out, the Lutheran Reformation also still has a shaping influence on Western theology. Lutheran churches to this day still hold firmly to many of the cardinal theological teachings of the Lutheran Reformation: *sola fidei*, *sola gratia*, and *sola Scriptura*, the priesthood of all believers, the distinctions between Law and Gospel, between faith and works. The great Evangelical catechisms, confessions, and creeds forged in the Reformation ring with as much power for a Lutheran today as they did for a Lutheran in 1530. The majestic hymns that Luther crafted still bring tingles to many modern Protestant worship services. The timeless language of Luther's German Bible and German Mass captures the imagination of a modern German Protestant as much as the magisterial language of the King James Bible and the *Book of Common Prayer* captures the imagination of a modern English Protestant.

Moreover, the Lutheran Reformation continues to shape a good deal of modern Protestant theology and ethics. Particularly Luther's founding ideas of human nature, human equality, and human liberty have shaped many Protestants' theological instincts and reflexes about some of the deepest questions of modern individual and corporate life.

First, Luther's founding doctrine of *simul iustus et peccator*, that humans are at once sinners and saints, renders many Protestants instinctively skeptical about too optimistic a view of human nature, and too easy a conflation of human dignity and human sanctity. Such views take too little account of the radicality of human sin and the necessity of divine grace. They give too little credibility to the inherent human need for discipline and order, accountability and judgment. They give too little credence to the perennial interplay of the civil, theological, and pedagogical uses of law, to the perpetual demand to balance deterrence, retribution, and reformation in discharging authority within the home, church, state, and other associations. They give too little insight into the necessity for safeguarding every office of authority from abuse and misuse. A theory of human dignity that fails to take into account the combined depravity and sanctity of the person, many Protestants believe, is theologically deficient and politically dangerous.

This cardinal insight into the two-fold nature of humanity was hardly unique to Martin Luther, and is readily amenable to many other formulations. Luther's formula of *simul iustus et peccator* was a crisp Christian distillation of a universal insight about human nature that can be traced to the earliest Greek and Hebrew sources of the West. The gripping works of Homer, Hesiod, and Pindar are nothing if not chronicles of the perennial dialectic of good and evil, virtue and vice, hero and villain in the ancient Greek world. The very first chapters of the Hebrew Bible paint pictures of these same two human natures, now with Yahweh's imprint on them. The more familiar picture is that of Adam and Eve who were created equally in the image of God, and vested with a natural right and duty to perpetuate life, to cultivate property, to dress and keep the creation (Genesis 1:26–30; 2:7, 15–23). The less familiar picture is that of their first child Cain, who murdered his brother Abel and was called into judgment by God and condemned for his sin. Yet "God put a mark on Cain," Genesis reads, both to protect him in his life, and to show that he remained a child of God despite the enormity of his sin (Genesis 4:1–16).[6] One message of this ancient Hebrew text is that we are not only the beloved children of Adam and Eve, who bear the image of God, with all the divine perquisites and privileges of Paradise. We are also the sinful siblings of Cain, who bear the mark of God, with its ominous assurance both that we shall be called into divine judgment for what we have done, and that there is forgiveness even for the gravest of sins we have committed.

Luther believed that it is only through faith and hope in Christ that we can ultimately be assured of divine forgiveness and eternal salvation. He further believed that it was only through a life of biblical meditation, prayer, worship, charity, and sacramental living that a person could hold his or her depravity in check and aspire to greater sanctity. I believe that, too, as do many Christians today. But this is not to say that, in this life, Christians have the only insights into the two-fold nature of humanity, and the only effective means of balancing the realities of human depravity and the aspirations for human sanctity. Any religious tradition that takes seriously the Jekyll and Hyde in all of us has its own understanding of ultimate reconciliation of these two natures, and its own methods of balancing them in this life. And who are we Christians to say how God will ultimately judge these?

Luther also believed that the ominous assurance of the judgment of God is ultimately a source of comfort not of fear. The first sinners in the Bible – Adam, Eve, and Cain – were given divine due process: they were confronted with the evidence, asked to defend themselves, given a chance to repent, spared the ultimate sanction of death, and then assured of a second trial on the Day of Judgment, with appointed divine counsel – Christ himself, the self-appointed "advocate before the Father" (1 John 2:1). The only time that God deliberately withheld divine due process, Luther reminds us, was in the capital trial of His Son – and that was the only time it was and has been necessary. The political implications of this are very simple for Protestants: if God gives due process in judging us, we should give due process in judging others. If God's tribunals feature

---

[6] This is but one of numerous interpretation of the story of Cain and Abel. For alternatives, see Ruth Mellinkoff, *The Mark of Cain* (Berkeley/Los Angeles, 1981); Claus Westermann, *Genesis 1–11: A Commentary*, repr. (Minneapolis: Augsburg Publishing House, 1990).

at least basic rules of procedure, evidence, representation, and advocacy, human tribunals should feature at least the same. The demand for due process is a deep human instinct, and it has driven Protestants over the centuries, along with many others before, with, and after them, to be strident advocates for procedural rights.

Second, Luther's doctrine of the lordship and priesthood of all believers renders many Protestants instinctively jealous about liberty and equality – but on their own quite distinct theological terms. In the modern Western tradition, liberty and equality are generally defended on grounds of popular sovereignty and unalienable rights. The American Declaration of Independence (1776) proclaimed it a "self-evident truth" "that all men are created equal [and] . . . are endowed with certain unalienable rights." The Universal Declaration of Human Rights (1948) proclaimed "[t]hat all men are born free and equal in rights and dignity." Protestants can resonate more with the norms of liberty and equality in these documents than with the theories of popular sovereignty and unalienable rights that generally undergird them.

The heart of the Protestant theory of liberty is that we are all lords on this earth. We are utterly free in the sanctuary of our conscience, entirely unencumbered in our relationship with God. We enjoy a sovereign immunity from any human structures and strictures, even those of the Church and the clergy when they seek to impinge on this divine freedom. Such talk of "sovereign immunity" sounds something like modern liberal notions of "popular sovereignty." And such talk of "lordship" sounds something like the democratic right to "self-rule." Protestants have thus long found ready allies in liberals and others who advocate liberty of conscience and democratic freedoms on these grounds. But, when theologically pressed, many Protestants will defend liberty of conscience not because of their own popular sovereignty, but because of the absolute sovereignty of God, whose relationship with His children cannot be trespassed.

The heart of the Protestant theory of equality is that we are all priests before God. "You are a chosen race, a royal priesthood, a holy nation, God's own people" (I Peter 2:9; cf. Revelation 5:10, 20:6). Among you, "[t]here is neither Jew nor Greek, there is neither bond nor free, there is neither male nor female; for ye are all one in Christ Jesus" (Galatians 3:28; cf. Colossians 3:10–11; Ephesians 2:14–15). These and many other biblical passages, which Luther highlighted and glossed repeatedly, have long inspired a reflexive egalitarian impulse in Protestants. All are equal before God. All are priests who must serve their neighbors. All have vocations that count. All have gifts to be included. This common calling of all to be priests transcends differences of culture, economy, gender, and more.

Such teachings have always led a few Protestant groups, from Luther's day onwards, to experiment with intensely communitarian states of nature where life is gracious, lovely, and long. Most Protestant groups, however, view life in such states of nature as brutish, nasty, and short, for sin invariably perverts them. Structures and strictures of law and authority are necessary and useful, most Protestants believe. But such structures need to be as open, egalitarian, and democratic as possible. Hierarchy is a danger to be indulged only so far as necessary. To be sure, Lutherans and other Protestants over the centuries have often defied these founding ideals, and have earnestly partaken of all manner of elitism, chauvinism, racism, anti-semitism, tyranny, patriarchy, slavery, apartheid, and more. And they have sometimes engaged in outrageous hypocrisy and casuistry to defend such pathos. But an instinct for egalitarianism – for embracing all persons equally, for treating all vocations respectfully, for arranging all associations horizontally, for leveling the life of the earthly kingdom so none is obstructed in access to God – is a Lutheran gene in the theological genetic code of Protestantism.

Third, and finally, Luther's notion that a person is at once free and bound by the law has powerful implications for our modern understanding of human rights. For Luther, the Christian is free in order to follow the commandments of the faith – or, in more familiar and general modern parlance, a person has rights in order to discharge duties. Freedoms and commandments, rights and duties, belong together in Luther's formulation. To speak of one without the other is ultimately destructive. Rights without duties to guide them quickly become claims of self-indulgence. Duties without rights to discharge them quickly become sources of deep guilt.

Protestants have thus long translated the moral duties set out in the Decalogue into reciprocal rights. The First Table of the Decalogue prescribes duties of love that each person owes to God: to honor God and God's name, to observe the Sabbath day of rest and worship, to avoid false gods and false swearing. The Second Table prescribes duties of love that each person owes to neighbors: to honor one's parents and other authorities, not to kill, not to commit adultery, not to steal, not to bear false witness, not to covet. Church, state, and family alike are responsible for the communication and enforcement of these cardinal moral duties, Protestants have long argued. But it is also the responsibility of each person to ensure that he and his neighbors discharge these moral duties. This is one important impetus for Protestants to translate duties into rights. A person's duties toward God can be cast as the rights of religion: the right to honor God and God's name, the right to rest and worship on one's Sabbath, the right to be free from false gods and false oaths. Each person's duties towards a neighbor, in turn, can be cast as a neighbor's right to have that duty discharged. One person's duties not to kill, to commit adultery, to steal, or to bear false witness thus gives rise to another person's rights to life, property, fidelity, and reputation. For a person to insist upon vindication of these latter rights is not necessarily to act out of self-love. It is also to act out of neighborly love. To claim one's own right is in part a charitable act to induce one's neighbor to discharge his or her divinely ordained duty.[7]

The great American jurist Grant Gilmore once wrote: "The better the society the less law there will be. In Heaven, there will be no law, and the lion will lie down with the lamb. In Hell, there will be nothing but law, and due process will be meticulously observed."[8] This is a rather common Protestant sentiment, which Luther did much to propound in some of his early writings. But a Protestant, faithful to Luther's later and more enduring insights, might properly reach the exact opposite projection. In Heaven, there will be pure law, and thus the lamb will lie down with the lion. In Hell, there will be no law, and thus all will devour each other eternally. Heaven will exalt due process, and each will always receive what's due. Hell will exalt pure caprice, and no one will ever know what's coming.

---

[7] For modern examples among Protestant writers, see Lutheran World Federation, *Theological Perspectives on Human Rights* (Geneva, 1977); Wolfgang Huber and Heinz Eduard Tödt, *Menschenrechte: Perspektiven einer menschlichen Welt* (Stuttgart, 1977); Wolfgang Vögele, *Menschenwürde zwischen Recht und Theologie: Begründungen von Menschenrechte in der Perspektive öffentlicher Theologie* (Gütersloh, 2000); Walter Harrelson, *The Ten Commandments and Human Rights* (Philadelphia, 1979).

[8] Grant Gilmore, *The Ages of American Law* (Chicago, 1977), 110–111.

Bibliography

Albrecht, F., *Verbrechen und Strafen als Ehescheidungsgrund nach evangelischem Kirchenrecht* (PhD Diss., Munich, 1903)

Alexander, Frank S., "Validity and Function of Law: The Reformation Doctrine of *usus legis*," *Mercer Law Review* 31 (1980): 509

Althaus, Paul, *The Ethics of Martin Luther*, trans. Robert C. Schultz (Philadelphia, 1972)

The Theology of Martin Luther, trans. Robert C. Schultz (Philadelphia, 1966)

Andreas, Willy, *Deutschland vor der Reformation*, 5th edn. (Berlin, 1932)

Apel, Johann, *Defensio Johannis Apelli ad Episcopum Herbipolensem pro svo conivgio* (Wittenberg, 1523)

Apeldoorn, L. J. van, *Nicolaas Everaerts (1462–1532) en het recht van zijn tijd* (Amsterdam, 1935)

Aquinas, Thomas, *Opera omnia Sancti Thomae Aquinatis Doctoris Angelici* (Rome, 1882–)

Summa contra Gentiles, trans. V. J. Bourke (Notre Dame, IN, 1975)

The Summa Theologiae, trans. by English Dominican Fathers, 5 vols. (London, 1912–36)

Atkinson, James, *The Trial of Luther* (New York, 1971)

Baron, Hans, "Religion and Politics in the German Imperial Cities during the Reformation," *English Historical Review* 52 (1937): 405

Barraclough, Geoffrey, *The Origins of Modern Germany* (New York, 1957)

Bauer, Clemens, "Der Naturrechtsvorstellungen des jungeren Melanchthon," in *Festschrift für Gerhard Ritter zu seinem 60. Geburtstag* (Tübingen, 1950), 244

"Melanchthons Rechtslehre," *AFR* 42 (1951): 64

Baylor, Michael G., *Action and Person: Conscience in Late Scholasticism and the Young Luther* (Leiden, 1977)

Becker, Gisela, *Deutsche Juristen und ihre Schriften auf den römischen Indices des 16. Jahrhunderts* (Berlin, 1970)

Bell, Susan G., "Johan Eberlin von Günzburg's *Wolfaria*: The First Protestant Utopia," *Church History* 36 (1967): 122

Benecke, Gerhard, *Society and Politics in Germany, 1500–1700* (London, 1974)

Benert, Richard Roy, "Inferior Magistrates in Sixteenth-Century Political and Legal Thought" (PhD Diss., University of Minnesota, 1967)

Benson, Robert L. and Giles Constable, eds., *Renaissance and Renewal in the Twelfth Century* (Cambridge, MA, 1982)

Berman, Harold J., *Faith and Order: The Reconciliation of Law and Religion* (Atlanta, 1993)

Law and Revolution: The Formation of the Western Legal Tradition (Cambridge, MA, 1983)

"The Interaction of Spiritual Law and Secular Law: An Historical Overview with Special Reference to Sixteenth-Century Lutheran Germany," in Hoeflich, ed., *Lex et Romanitas*, 149

Berman, Harold J. and Charles J. Reid, Jr., "Roman Law in Europe and the *Jus Commune*: A Historical Overview with Emphasis on the New Legal Science of the Sixteenth Century," *Syracuse Journal of International Law and Commerce* 20 (Spring, 1994): 1

Berman, Harold J. and John Witte, Jr., "The Transformation of Western Legal Philosophy in Lutheran Germany," *Southern California Law Review* 62 (1989): 1573

Bettenson, Henry and Chris Maunder, eds., *Documents of the Christian Church*, 3rd edn. (Oxford, 1999)

Beyer, Hermann W., *Luther und das Recht: Gottes Gebot, Naturrecht, Volksgesetz in Luthers Deutung* (Munich, 1935)

Biel, Gabriel, *Sermones dominicales* (Hagenau, 1510)

Binder, Joseph, "Zur Hermeneutik der Rechtslehre Martin Luthers," *Archiv für Rechts- und Sozialphilosophie* 51 (1965): 337

Blaurer, Ambrosius and Thomas Blaurer, *Briefwechsel der Brüder Ambrosius und Thomas Blaurer 1509–1548*, 3 vols. (Freiburg im Breisgau, 1908–12)

Böhmer, Heinrich, "Luther und der 10. Dezember 1520," *Luther-Jahrbuch* 2/3 (1920/1): 7

Bornkamm, Heinrich, *Das Jahrhundert der Reformation: Gestalten und Kräfte* (Göttingen, 1966)

"Iustitia dei in der Scholastik und bei Luther," *AFR* 4 (1942): 1

Luther and the Old Testament, trans. Eric W. Gritsch and Ruth C. Gritsch (Philadelphia, 1969)

Luther im Spiegel der deutschen Geistesgeschichte (Heidelberg, 1955)

Brady, Thomas A., *et al.*, eds., *Handbook of European History, 1400–1600* (Leiden/New York, 1994)

Brecht, Martin, "Anfänge reformatorischen Kirchenordnungen bei Johannes Brenz," *ZSS KA* 96 (1969): 322

"Die gemeinsame Politik der Reichsstädte und die Reformation," *ZSS KA* 63 (1977): 180

Martin Luther, 3 vols., trans. James L. Schaaf (Philadelphia/Minneapolis, 1985–93)

Breen, Quirinius, " 'Loci communes' and 'Loci' in Melanchthon," *Church History* 16 (1947): 197

Brenz, Johannes, *Anecdota Brentiana: Ungedruckte Briefe und Bedenken von Johannes Brenz*, ed. Theodor Pressel, (Tübingen, 1868)

Wie in Eesachen vnnd den fellen so sich derhalben zutragen nach Götlichem billichem rechten christenlich zu handeln (Nuremberg, 1529)

Brooke, Christopher N. L., *The Medieval Idea of Marriage* (Oxford/New York, 1991)

Brooks, Peter N., ed., *Seven-Headed Luther* (Oxford, 1983)

Bruce, Gustav M., *Luther as an Educator* (Westport, CT, 1979)

Brundage, James A., *Law, Sex, and Christian Society in Medieval Europe* (Chicago, 1987)

Brunner, Otto, *et al.*, eds., *Geschichtliche Grundbegriffe. Historisches Lexicon zur politisch-sozialen Sprache in Deutschland*, 5 vols. (Stuttgart, 1984)

Bucer, Martin, *Common Places of Martin Bucer*, trans. and ed. D. F. Wright (Aberdeen, 1972)

    De Regno Christi (1550), in Wilhelm Pauck, ed., *Melanchthon and Bucer* (Philadelphia, 1969), 174

    Martin Bucers Deutsche Schriften, 7 vols., ed. Robert Stupperich (Gütersloh, 1960)

Buchholz, Stephen, "Justus Henning Böhmer (1674–1749) und das Kirchenrecht," *Ius Commune* 18 (1991): 37

Buckland, W. W., *Equity in Roman Law* (London, 1911)

Bugenhagen, Johannes, *Vom ehebruch und weglauffen* (Wittenberg, 1539, 1541)

    Von dem ehelichen Stände der Bischoffe vnd Daiken (Wittenberg, 1525)

    Was man vom Closter leben halten sol (Wittenberg, 1529, 1545)

Bullinger, Heinrich, *Der christlich Ehestand* (Zurich, 1540)

Burmeister, Karl H., *Das Studium der Rechte im Zeitalter des Humanismus im deutschen Rechtsbereich* (Wiesbaden, 1974)

Burnett, Amy, "Church Discipline and Moral Reformation in the Thought of Martin Bucer," *Sixteenth Century Journal* 22 (1991): 439

    The Yoke of Christ: Martin Bucer and Christian Discipline (Kirksville, MO, 1994)

Capito, Wolfgang, *Das die Pfaffhait schuldig sey Burgelichen Ayd zuthün. On verletzung jrer Eeren* (1525)

Cargill Thompson, W. D. J., *The Political Thought of Martin Luther* (Brighton, Sussex, 1984)

Carlebach, Rudolf, ed., *Badische Rechtsgeschichte* (Heidelberg, 1906)

Caron, Pier Giovanni, "Aequitas et interpretatio dans la doctrine canonique aux xiiie et xive siècles," *Monumenta Iuris Canonici Series C* 4 (1971): 131

Caspary, Gerard E., *Politics and Exegesis: Origen and the Two Swords* (Berkeley, CA, 1979)

Cassirer, Ernst, *The Individual and the Cosmos in Renaissance Philosophy*, trans. Mario Domandi (Philadelphia, 1963)

    The Myth of the Modern State, trans. Charles W. Hendel (New Haven, CT, 1946)

    The Problem of Knowledge: Philosophy, Science, and History Since Hegel, trans. William H. Woglom and Charles W. Hendel (New Haven, CT, 1950)

Cau, C. *et al.*, *Groot Placaetboeck*, 11 vols. (Louvain, 1658–1797)

Chemnitz, Martin, *Loci theologici* (1581), trans. J. A. O. Preus (St. Louis, MO, 1989)

Chrisman, Miriam, *Conflicting Visions of Reform: German Lay Propaganda Pamphlets, 1519–1530* (Atlantic Highlands, NJ, 1996)
Lay Culture, Learned Culture: Books and Social Change in Strasbourg, 1480–1599 (New Haven, CT, 1982)
Coakley, Sarah, *Christ without Absolutes: A Study of the Christology of Ernst Troeltsch* (Oxford, 1988)
Cohn, Henry J., "Church Property in the German Protestant Principalities," in Kouri and Scott, eds., *Politics and Society in Reformation Europe*, 158
The Government of the Rhine Palatinate in the Fifteenth Century (Oxford, 1965)
Cohrs, Ferdinand, *Die evangelischen Katechismusversuche vor Luthers Enchiridion*, 4 vols. (Berlin, 1900–2)
Coing, Helmut, *Die Frankfurter Reformation von 1578 und das Gemeine Recht ihrer Zeit* (Weimar, 1935)
Die Rezeption des römischen Rechts in Frankfurt am Main (Frankfurt am Main, 1962)
"Zur romanistischen Auslegung von Rezeptionsgesetzen," *ZSS KA* 69 (1936): 264
Coing, Helmut, ed., *Handbuch der Quellen und Literatur der neueren europäischen Privatrechtsgeschichte*, 4 vols. (Munich, 1973–77)
Cole, P. R., *A History of Educational Thought* (London, 1931)
Congar, Yves, *Tradition and the Life of the Church*, trans. A. N. Woodrow (London, 1964)
Congar, Yves and Bernard D. Dupuy, eds., *L'Episcopat et l'église universelle* (Paris, 1962)
Couvreur, Gilles, *Les pauvres ont-ils des droits?* (Rome, 1961)
Cranz, F. Edward, *An Essay on the Development of Luther's Thought on Justice, Law, and Society* (Cambridge, MA/London, 1959)
Dahm, Georg, "On the Reception of Roman and Italian Law in Germany," in Strauss, ed., *Pre-Reformation Germany*, 281
D'Arcy, Eric, *Conscience and its Right to Freedom* (New York, 1961)
Dawson, John P., *The Oracles of the Law* (Ann Arbor, MI, 1968)
Deferrari, R. J., ed., *St. Augustine: Treatises on Marriage and Other Subjects* (New York, 1955)
Delius, Hans-Ulrich, *Augustin als Quelle Luthers: Eine Materialsammlung* (Berlin, 1984)
Diehl, Wilhelm, "Martin Bucers Bedeutung für das kirchliche Leben in Hessen," *Schriften des Vereins für Reformationsgeschichte* 22 (1904): 39
Dieterich, Hartwig, *Das protestantische Eherecht in Deutschland bis zur Mitte des 17. Jahrhunderts* (Munich, 1970)
Dietrich, Hans, *Evangelisches Ehescheidungsrecht nach den Bestimmungen der deutschen Kirchenordnungen des 16. Jahrhunderts* (Berlin, 1892)
Dietze, Hans-Helmut, *Oldendorp als Rechtsphilosoph und Protestant* (Königsberg, 1933)
Dilthey, Wilhelm, *Gesammelte Schriften*, 23 vols. (Leipzig, 1921)
Dooyeweerd, Herman, *Encyclopaedie der Rechtswetenschap*, 2 vols. (Amsterdam, 1946)

DuBoulay, F. R. H., *Germany in the Later Middle Ages* (London, 1983)

Duchrow, Ulrich, *Christenheit und Weltverantwortung: Traditionsgeschichte und systematische Struktur der Zweireichelehre* (Stuttgart, 1983)

Duggan, Lawrence G., *Bishop and Chapter: The Governance of the Bishopric of Speyer to 1552* (New Brunswick, NJ, 1978)

"The Church as an Institution of the Reich," in Vann and Rowan, eds., *The Old Reich: Essays on German Political Institutions*, 149

Ebel, Wilhelm, *Geschichte der Gesetzgebung in Deutschland* (Göttingen, 1958)

Studie über einem Goslarer Ratsurteilsbuch des 16. Jahrhunderts nebst einem Urkundenanhang (Göttingen, 1961)

Ebeling, Gerhard, *Word and Faith*, trans. J. Leitsch (Philadelphia, 1963)

Eby, Frederick, *The Development of Modern Education in Theory, Organization, and Practice*, 2nd. edn. (New York, 1952)

Eby, Frederick, and Charles F. Arrowood, *The History and Philosophy of Education, Ancient and Medieval* (New York, 1940)

Edwards, Mark U., Jr. *Luther's Last Battles: Politics and Polemics, 1531–1546* (Ithaca/London, 1983)

Printing, Propaganda, and Martin Luther (Berkeley/Los Angeles, 1994)

"The Reception of Luther's Understanding of Freedom in the Early Modern Period," *Luther-Jahrbuch* 62 (1995): 104

Eells, Hasting, *The Attitude of Martin Bucer Toward the Bigamy of Philip of Hesse* (New Haven, CT, 1924)

Ehler, Sidney Z. and John B. Morall, *Church and State Through the Centuries* (Westminster, MD, 1954)

Ehrle, Franz, *Beiträge zur Geschichte und Reform der Armenpflege* (Freiburg im Breisgau, 1881)

Eisermann, Johannes *see* Ferrarius, Johann Monatus

Elert, Werner, *Law and Gospel*, trans. Edward H. Schroeder (Philadelphia, 1967)

Emme, Barbara and Dietrich Emme, eds., *Martin Luther: Traktat über das kirchliche Asylrecht* (Regensburg, 1985)

Enderle, Wilfred, "Die katholischen Reichsstädte im Zeitalter der Reformation und der Konfessionsbildung," *ZSS KA* 106 (1989): 228

Ernst, August and Johann Adam, *Katechetische Geschichte des Elsasses bis zur Revolution* (Strasbourg, 1897)

Estes, James M., *Christian Magistrate and State Church: The Reforming Career of Johannes Brenz* (Toronto, 1982)

Estes, James, M., ed., *Whether Secular Government Has the Right to Wield the Sword in Matters of Faith* (Toronto, 1994)

Etudes d'Histoire du droit canonique dédiées à Gabriel le Bras, 2 vols. (Paris, 1965)

Everardus, Nicolaus, *Loci argumentorum legales* (Amsterdam, 1603)

Falk, F., "Luthers Schrift an die Ratsherren der deutschen Städte und ihre geschichtliche Wirkung auf die deutschen Schulen," *Luther-Jahrbuch* 19 (1937): 55

Fell, A. London, *Origins of Legislative Sovereignty and the Legislative State*, 4 vols. published to date (Königstein/Cambridge, MA, 1983–)

Ferrarius, Johann Monatus (Johannes Eisermann), *A Woorke of J. Ferrarius Mona-*
tus touchynge a Good Orderynge of a Common Weale (London, 1559)
    Ad titulum Pandectarum de regulis iuris commentarius (Louvain, 1537, 1546)
    Adnotationes in IIII. Institutionum Iustiniani (Marburg, 1532)
    Collectanea in usus feudorum, in *Tractatus universi iuris* (Frankfurt am Main, 1554),
    vol. 10/2
    Commentarius, omnibus qui in iure foro(que) iudicario versantur (Marburg, 1542;
    Frankfurt am Main, 1600)
    De republica bene instituenda paraenesis (Basel, 1556)
    Processus iudiciarii, ad mores nostros accommodati (Hamburg, 1608)
    Progymnasmata forensia sive processus iudiciarii recepti libri V (Marburg, ca. 1542,
    1556)
    Tractatus de iudiciorum prae-exercitamentis, et iis, quae ad ius decentis officii atque etiam
    causas disceptantium modestius studium pertinent (Frankfurt am Main, 1554, 1600)
    Von dem gemeinen Nutze (Marburg, 1533)
    Was . . . Philips Landtgraue zue Hessen . . . als ain Cristlicherfürst mit den Closterper-
    sonen, pfarrherren, un abgötischen bildnissen, in seiner gnaden fürstenthumbe, auss
    Gottlicher geschrifft fürgenomemen hat (Ausburg, 1528)
Festschrift für Erich Ruppel zum 65. Geburtstag (Hanover, 1968)
Festschrift für Gerhard Ritter zu seinem 60. Geburtstag (Tübingen, 1950)
Fichtner, Paula Sutter, *Protestantism and Primogeniture in Early Modern Europe*
    (New Haven, CT, 1989)
Field, Lester L., *Liberty, Dominion, and the Two Swords: On the Origins of Western*
    Political Theology (Notre Dame, IN, 1998)
Fild, H., *Justitia bei Melanchthon* (Theol. Diss., Erlangen, 1953)
Finnis, John, *Aquinas: Moral, Political, and Legal Theory* (Oxford, 1998)
Fischer, Thomas, *Städtische Armut und Armensfürsorge im 15. und 16. Jahrhundert*
    (Göttingen, 1979)
Florentinus, Paulus, *Breviarium decretorum et decretalium* (Louvain, 1484)
Franzen, August, *Zölibat und Priesterehe in der Auseinandersetzung der Reformationszeit*
    und der katholischen Reform des 16. Jahrhundert (Münster, 1969)
Friedberg, Emil, *Das Recht der Eheschliessung in seiner geschichtlichen Entwicklung*, repr.
    (Aalen, 1968)
    Lehrbuch des katholischen und evangelischen Kirchenrechts (Leipzig, 1909)
Friedberg, Emil, ed., *Corpus iuris canonici*, 2 vols. (Leipzig, 1879–81)
Friedmann, Robert, *The Theology of Anabaptism* (Scottdale, PA, 1973)
Friesen, Joseph, *Geschichte des kanonischen Eherechts bis zum Verfall der Glossenliteratur*,
    2nd. edn., repr. (Aalen, 1963)
Frostin, Per, *Luther's Two Kingdoms Doctrine: A Critical Study* (Lund, 1994)
Fuller, Lon L., *The Morality of Law*, rev. edn. (New Haven, CT, 1964)
Gawthrop, Richard and Gerald Strauss, "Protestantism and Literacy in Early
    Modern Germany," *Past and Present* 104 (1984): 31
Gedeon, Andreas, *Zur Rezeption des römischen Privatrechts in Nürnberg* (Nuremberg,
    1957)
Gehrke, Heinrich, *Die Rechtsprechung- und Konsilienliteratur Deutschlands bis zum Ende*
    des alten Reichs (Frankfurt am Main, Univ. Fachber. Rechtwissen. Diss., 1972)

Genzmer, Erich, "Kleriker als Berufsjuristen im späten Mittelalter," in *Etudes d'histoire du droit canonique dédiées à Gabriel le Bras*, 2:1207

Gesschen, B., *Zur ältesten Geschichte und ehegerichtslichen Praxis des Leipziger Konsistoriums* (Leipzig, 1894)

Gerson, Jean, *Opusculum tripartitum de praeceptis decalogi, de confessione, et de arte moriendi* (Paris, 1487)

Gilmore, Grant, *The Ages of American Law* (Chicago, 1977)

Gilmore, Myron P., *Humanists and Jurists: Six Studies in the Renaissance* (Cambridge, MA, 1963)

Göbler, Justin, *Der Rechten Spiegel* (Frankfurt am Main, 1550)

Goebel, Klaus, *Luther in der Schule: Beiträge zur Erziehungs- und Schulgeschichte: Pädagogik und Theologie* (Bochum, 1985)

Golz, Reinhard and Wolfgang Mayrhofer, eds., *Luther and Melanchthon in the Educational Thought of Central and Eastern Europe*, trans. Arista Da Silva and Alan Maimon (Rutgers, NJ, 1999)

Gough, J. W., *The Social Contract* (Oxford, 1963)

Grabner, J., *Ueber Desertion und Quasi-desertion als Scheidungsgrund nach dem evangelischen Kirchenrecht* (PhD Diss., Leipzig, 1882)

Gratian, *The Treatise on Laws with the Ordinary Gloss*, trans. Augustine Thompson and James Gordley (Washington, DC, 1993)

Greschat, Martin, *Martin Bucer: Ein Reformator und seine Zeit* (Munich, 1990)

Grimm, Harold J., *Lazurus Spengler: A Lay Leader of the Reformation* (Columbus, OH, 1978)

   "Luther's Contribution to the Sixteenth-Century Organization of Poor Relief," *AFR* 61 (1970): 222

   "Luther's Catechisms as Textbooks," in Grimm and Hoelty-Nickel, eds., *Luther and Culture*, 119.

   "The Reformation and the Urban Social Classes in Germany," in Olin *et al.*, eds. *Luther, Erasmus, and the Reformation*, 75

Grimm Harold J., and Theodore Hoelty-Nickel, eds., *Luther and Culture* (Columbus, OH, 1960)

Grisez, Germain, *The Way of the Lord Jesus: Living a Christian Life*, 2 vols. (Quincy, IL, 1993)

Gritsch, Eric W. "Luther and the Jews: Toward a Judgment of History," in Harold H. Ditmanson, ed., *Stepping-Stones to Further Jewish–Lutheran Relations: Key Lutheran Statements* (Minneapolis, 1990), 104.

   Martin – God's Court Jester: Luther in Retrospect (Philadelphia, 1983)

   "Martin Luther and Violence: A Reappraisal of the Neuralgic Theme," *Sixteenth Century Journal* 3 (1992): 37

Gross, Hans, "The Holy Roman Empire in Modern Times: Constitutional Reality and Legal Theory," in Vann and Rowan, eds., *The Old Reich: Essays on German Political Institutions*, 1

Grubb, Judith Evans, *Law and Family in Late Antiquity: The Emperor Constantine's Marriage Legislation* (Oxford, 1995)

Grumbach, Argula von, *Ein Christennliche Schrift einer erbaren Frawe vom Adel* (Bamberg, 1523).

Grund und Ursach auss gotlichen Rechten, warumb Prior und Convent in Sant Annen Closter zu Augspurg jren standt verendert haben (Augsburg, 1526)

Wye ein Christliche Fraw des Adels . . . in Gotlicher schrifft, wolegrundtenn Sendbrieffe, die hohenschul zu Ingolstadt, und das sie eynen Evangelischen Jungeling, zu widersprechung des wort Gottes (Erfurt, 1523)

Grünberger, Hans, "Die Institutionalisierung des Sittendiskurses durch Humanismus und Reformation im 15. und 16. Jahrhundert" (unpublished ms.)

"Institutionalisierung des protestantischen Sittendiskurses," *Zeitschrift für historische Forschung* 24 (1997): 215

Grundmann, Siegfried, ed., *Für Kirche und Recht: Festschrift für Joh. Heckel* (Cologne, 1959)

Günzburg, Johann Eberlin, *Johann Eberlin von Günzburg, Ausgewählte Schriften*, ed. Ludwig Enders (Halle, 1896)

Haalk, W., "Die Rostocker Juristenfakultät als Spruchskollegium," *Wissenschaftliche Zeitschrift der Universität Rostock* 3 (1958): 401

Haile, H. G., *Luther: An Experiment in Biography* (Princeton, NJ, 1980)

"Luther and Literacy," *Publications of the Modern Language Association* 91 (1976): 816

Hain, Ludwig, *Repertorium bibliographicum in quo libri omnes ab arte typographica inventa usque ad annum MD typis expressi ordine alphabetico vel simpliciter enumerantur vel adcuratius recensentur*, 4 vols. (Milan, 1948)

Halbach, Silke, *Argula von Grumbach als Verfasserin reformatorischer Flugschriften* (Frankfurt am Main, 1992)

Hänel, Albert, "Melanchthon der Jurist," *Zeitschrift für Rechtsgeschichte* 8 (1869): 249

Harrelson, Walter, *The Ten Commandments and Human Rights* (Philadelphia, 1979)

Harrington, Joel F., *Reordering Marriage and Society in Reformation Germany* (Cambridge, 1995)

Härter, Karl, "Entwicklung und Funktion der Polizeigesetzgebung des Heiligen Römischen Reiches Deutscher Nation im 16. Jahrhundert," *Ius Commune* 20 (1993): 61

Hartfelder, Karl, *Philipp Melanchthon als Praeceptor Germaniae* (Berlin, 1899)

Hartmann, Julius and Karl Jäger, *Johann Brenz nach gedruckten und ungedruckten Quellen* (Hamburg, 1840)

Hartung, Fritz, "Imperial Reform, 1485–1495: Its Course and its Character," in Strauss, ed., *Pre-Reformation Germany*, 73

Harvey, Judith W., "The Influence of the Reformation on Nürnberg Marriage Laws, 1520–1535" (PhD Diss., Ohio State University, 1972)

Haverkamp, Alfred, ed., *Haus und Familie in der spätmittelalterlichen Stadt* (Tübingen, 1984)

Hay, Denys, *Europe in the Fourteenth and Fifteenth Centuries* (New York, 1966)

Heckel, Johannes, "Das *Decretum Gratiani* und das deutsche evangelische Kirchenrecht," *Studia Gratiana* 3 (1955): 483

Gesammelte Aufsätze, ed. Siegfried Grundmann (Cologne, 1964)

Im Irrgarten der Zwei-Reiche-Lehre (Munich, 1957)

Lex charitatis: Eine juristische Untersuchung über das Recht in der Theologie Martin Luthers (Munich, 1953)

Heckel, Martin, *Gesammelte Schriften: Staat, Kirche, Recht, Geschichte*, 4 vols. (Tübingen, 1989–97)

"The Impact of Religious Rules on Public Life in Germany," in van der Vyver and Witte, eds., *Religious Human Rights in Global Perspective*, 191

Hegendorf, Christoph, *Die zehen Gepot der glaub, und das Vater unser, für die kinder ausgelegt* (Wittenberg, 1527)

Heimpel, Hermann, "Characteristics of the Late Middle Ages in Germany," in Strauss, ed., *Pre-Reformation Germany*, 43

Helmholz, R. H., *Canon Law and English Common Law* (London, 1983)
The Ius Commune in England: Four Studies (Oxford, 2001)
Marriage Litigation in Medieval England (Cambridge, 1974)
The Spirit of the Classical Canon Law (Athens, GA/London, 1996)

Helmholz, R. H., ed., *Canon Law in Protestant Lands* (Berlin, 1992)

Helmreich, Ernst C., "Joint School and Church Positions in Germany," *Lutheran School Journal* 79 (1943): 157
Religious Education in German Schools: An Historical Approach (Cambridge, MA, 1959)

Hemming, Nicolaus, *De lege naturae apodicta methodus* (Wittenberg, 1563)
De methodis libri duo (Wittenberg, 1559)
D. Nicolai Hemming . . . Opuscula theologica (Geneva, 1586)
Enchiridion theologicum (Leipzig, 1579)
Libellus de conjugio, repudio, et divortio (Leipzig, 1578)

Hendrix, Scott H., *Luther and the Papacy: Stages in a Reformation Conflict* (Philadelphia, 1981)
"Luther's Impact on the Sixteenth Century," *Sixteenth Century Journal* 16 (1985): 3.
"Luther on Marriage," *Lutheran Quarterly* 14/3 (2000): 335
"Masculinity and Patriarchy in Reformation Germany," *Journal of the History of Ideas* 56 (1995): 177

Henkel, Nikolaus, *Deutsche Übersetzungen Lateinischer Schultexte: Ihre Verbreitung und Funktion im Mittelalter und in der frühen Neuzeit* (Munich, 1988)

Hering, Carl Joseph, ed., *Staat, Recht, Kultur: Festgabe für Ernst von Hippel zu seinem 70. Geburtstag* (Bonn, 1965)

Hesse, Hans, *Evangelisches Ehescheidungsrecht in Deutschland* (Bonn, 1960)

Hillerbrand, Hans J., *Landgrave Philip of Hesse* (New York, 1967)

Hintz, Ernst Ralf, *Learning and Persuasion in the German Middle Ages* (New York/London, 1997)

Hoeflich, Michael, ed., *Lex et Romanitas: Essays for Alan Watson* (Berkeley, CA, 2000)

Holborn, Hajo, *A History of Germany: The Reformation* (New York, 1967)
"Luther and the Princes," in Olin, *et al.*, eds., *Luther, Erasmus, and the Reformation*, 67

Holl, Karl, *Gesammelte Aufsätze zur Kirchengeschichte*, 7th edn., 3 vols. (Tübingen, 1948)

Horn, Norbert, *Aequitas in den Lehren des Baldus* (Cologne, 1968)

Hostiensis, *In Primum . . . Sextum Decretalium Librum Commentaria* (Venice, 1581)

Houston, R. A., *Literacy in Early Modern Europe: Culture and Education, 1500–1800* (New York/London, 1988)

Huber, Wolfgang and Heinz Eduard Tödt, *Menschenrechte: Perspektiven einer menschlichen Welt* (Stuttgart, 1977)

Hugh of St. Victor, *On the Sacraments of the Christian Faith*, trans. R. Deferrari (Cambridge, MA, 1951)

Hugo, John J., *St. Augustine on Nature, Sex, and Marriage* (Chicago, 1969)

Huschke, Rolf B., *Melanchthons Lehre vom Ordo politicus* (Gütersloh, 1968)

Janssen, Johannes, *History of the German People at the Close of the Middle Ages*, 15th Germ. edn., 2nd rev. Engl. edn. trans. M. A. Mitchell and A. M. Christie, 14 vols. (London 1905)

Joachimsen, Paul, "*Loci communes*: Eine Untersuchung zur Geistesgeschichte des Humanismus und der Reformation," *Luther-Jahrbuch* 8 (1926): 27

Joest, Wilfred, *Gesetz und Freiheit: Das Problem des tertius usus legis bei Luther und die neutestamentliche Parainese* (Göttingen, 1968)

Jonas, Justus, *Der Briefwechsel des Justus Jonas*, 2 vols., ed. Gustav Kawerau (Halle, 1884–5)

Junghaus, Helmar, "Die evangelische Ehe," in Treu, ed., *Katherina von Bora*, 1

Junghaus, Helmar, ed., *Leben und Werk Martin Luthers von 1526 bis 1546*, 2 vols. (Berlin, 1983)

Jütte, Robert, "Andreas Hyperius (1511–1564) und die Reform des frühneuzeitlichen Armenswesens," *AFR* 75 (1984): 113

Obrigkeitliche Armensfürsorge in der deutschen Reichsstädten der frühen Neuzeit (Cologne/Vienna, 1984)

Kantorowicz, Ernst H., *The King's Two Bodies: A Study in Medieval Political Theology* (Princeton, 1957)

Karant-Nunn, Susan C., "The Reality of Early Lutheran Education: The Electoral District of Saxony – A Case Study," *Luther-Jahrbuch* 57 (1990): 128

The Reformation of Ritual: An Interpretation of Early Modern Germany (London and New York, 1997)

"The Transmission of Luther's Teachings on Women and Matrimony: The Case of Zwickau," *AFR* 77 (1986): 31

Kaufmann, Thomas, "Martin Chemnitz (1522–1586): Zur Wirkungsgeschichte der theologischen Loci," in Scheible, ed., *Melanchthon in seinen Schülern*, 183

Kawerau, Gustav, ed., *Zwei älteste Katechismen der lutherischen Reformation von P. Shultz und Chr. Hegendorf* (Halle, 1890)

Kelley, Donald R., *Foundations of Modern Historical Scholarship: Language, Law, and History in the French Renaissance* (New York, 1970)

Kern, Arthur, ed., *Deutsche Hofordnungen des 16. und 17. Jahrhunderts*, 2 vols. (Berlin, 1905–7)

Kirn, Paul, "Der mittelalterliche Staat und das geistliche Gericht," *ZSS KA* 46 (1926): 162

Kirstein, Roland, *Die Entwicklung der Sponsalienlehre und der Lehre vom Eheschluss in der deutschen protestantischen Eherechtslehre bis zu J.H. Böhmer* (Bonn, 1966)

Kisch, Guido, *Consilia: Eine Bibliographie der juristischen Konsiliensammlungen* (Basel, 1970)

    Erasmus und die Jurisprudenz seiner Zeit: Studien zum humanistischen Rechtsdenken (Basel, 1960)

    Melanchthons Rechts- und Soziallehre (Berlin, 1967)

    "Melanchthon und die Juristen seiner Zeit," in *Mélanges Philippe Meylan: recueil de travaux*, 2 vols. (Lausanne, 1963), 2:135

Kittelson, James M., "Successes and Failures of the German Reformation: The Report from Strasbourg," *AFR* 73 (1982): 153

Kittelson, James M., and Pamela J. Transue, eds., *Rebirth, Reform, and Resilience: Universities in Transition, 1300–1700* (Columbus, OH, 1984)

Klaasen, Walter, *Anabaptism in Outline: Selected Primary Sources* (Scottsdale, PA, 1981)

Kling, Melchior, *Das gantze sachsich Landrecht, mit Text und Gloss* (Leipzig, 1572)

    In praecipuos, & eos qui ad usum forensem prae caeteris faciunt. Secundi libri, Antiquarum Decretalium Titulos Commentaria (Frankfurt am Main, 1550)

    Matrimonialium causarum tractatus, methodico ordine scriptus (Frankfurt am Main, 1543, 1553)

Klingebeil, Stefan, *Von Priesterehe . . . mit Vorrede Mart. Luther* (Wittenberg, 1528)

Knemeyer, Franz Ludwig, "Polizei," in Brunner *et al.*, eds., *Geschichtliche Grundbegriffe*, 4:875

Knobler, Abby Phyllis, "Luther and the Legal Concept of the Poor in the Sixteenth Century German Church Ordinances" (Ph.D. Diss., UCLA, 1991)

Knoche, Hansjürgen, *Ulrich Zasius und das Freiburger Stadtrecht von 1520* (Karlsruhe, 1957)

Köbner, Richard, "Die Eheauffassung des ausgehenden deutschen Mittelalters," *Archiv für Kulturgeschichte* 9 (1911): 136

Kock, Karl, *Studium Pietatis: Martin Bucer als Ethiker* (Neukirchen-Vluyn, 1962)

Koehne, Carl, *Der Ursprung der Stadtverfassung in Worms, Speier und Mainz* (Berlin, 1890)

    Die Wormser Reformation vom Jahre 1499 (Berlin, 1897)

Köhler, K., *Luther und die Juristen: Zur Frage nach dem gegenseitigen Verhältnis des Rechtes und der Sittlichkeit* (Gotha, 1873)

Köhler, Walter, "Die Anfänge des protestantischen Eherechtes," *ZSS KA* 74 (1941): 271

    "Luther als Eherichter," *Beiträge zur sächsischen Kirchengeschichte* 47 (1947): 18

    Zürcher Ehegericht und Genfer Konsistorium, 2 vols. (Leipzig, 1932–1942)

Kohler, Josef and Willy Scheel, eds., *Die peinliche Gerichtsordnung Kaiser Karls V. Constitutio Criminalis Carolina*, repr. (Aalen, 1968)

Kohls, Ernst-Wilhelm, *Die Schule bei Martin Bucer in ihrem Verhältnis zu Kirche und Obrigkeit* (Heidelberg, 1963)

"Evangelische Bewegung und Kirchenordnungen in oberdeutschen Reichsstädten," *ZSS KA* 53 (1967): 110

Evangelische Katechismen der Reformationszeit vor und neben Martin Luthers kleinem Katechismus (Gütersloh, 1971)

"Martin Bucers Anteil und Anliegen bei der Abfassung der Ulmer Kirchenordnung im Jahre 1531," *Zeitschrift für evangelisches Kirchenrecht* 15 (1970): 333

Koller, Heinrich, ed., *Reformation Kaiser Siegmunds* [1438] (Stuttgart, 1964)

Kouri, E. I. and Tom Scott, eds., *Politics and Society in Reformation Europe: Essays in Honor of Sir Geoffrey Elton on his Sixty-Fifth Birthday* (New York, 1987)

Kratsch, Dietrich, *Justiz-Religion-Politik: Das Reichskammergericht und die Klosterprozesse im ausgehenden sechzehnten Jahrhundert* (Tübingen, 1990)

Krause, Otto W., *Naturrechtslehre des sechzehnten Jahrhunderts. Ihre Bedeutung für die Entwicklung eines natürlichen Privatrechts* (Frankfurt am Main, 1982)

Kroon, Marijn de, *Studien zu Martin Bucers Obrigkeitsverständnis* (Gütersloh, 1984)

Kühn, Helga-Maria, *Die Einziehung des geistlichen Gütes im albertinischen Sachsen, 1539–1553* (Cologne/Graz, 1966)

Kunkel, Wolfgang, "The Reception of Roman Law in Germany," in Strauss, ed., *Pre-Reformation Germany*, 263

Kunkel, Wolfgang, Hans Thieme, and Franz Beyerle, eds., *Quellen der neueren Privatrechtsgeschichte Deutschlands*, 2 vols. (Weimar, 1936)

Kuntz, Paul G. and Marion L. Kuntz, eds., *Jacob's Ladder and the Tree of Life: Concepts of Hierarchy and the Great Chain of Being* (New York, 1987)

Kusukawa, Sachiko, *The Transformation of Natural Philosophy: The Case of Philip Melanchthon* (Cambridge, 1995)

Kuttner, Stephan, *Kanonistische Schuldlehre von Gratian bis auf die Dekretalen Gregors IX, systematisch auf Grund der handschriftlichen Quellen dargestellt* (Vatican City, 1935)

Ladner, Gerhard, *The Idea of Reform: Its Impact on Christian Thought and Action in the Age of the Fathers* (Cambridge, MA, 1959)

Lähteenmäki, Olavi, *Sexus und Ehe bei Luther* (Turku, 1955)

Landau, Peter, "Sakramentalität und Jurisdiktion," in Rau *et al.*, eds., *Das Recht der Kirche*, 2:58

Lane, Frank Peter, "Poverty and Poor Relief in the German Church Orders of Johann Bugenhagen, 1485–1558" (Ph.D. Diss., Ohio State University, 1974)

Langbein, John H., *Prosecuting Crime in the Renaissance: England, Germany, France* (Cambridge, MA, 1974)

Torture and the Law of Proof: Europe and England in the ancien régime (Chicago, 1977)

Lange, Hermann, "*Ius aequum* und *ius strictum* bei den Glossatoren," in Schrage, ed., *Das römische Recht im Mittelalter*, 89

Lau, Franz, "*Äusserliche Ordnung*" und "*Weltlich Ding*" in Luthers Theologie (Göttingen, 1933)

Lau, Franz, and Ernst Bizer, *A History of the Reformation in Germany to 1555*, trans. Brian A. Hardy (London, 1969)

Lazareth, William, *Luther on the Christian Home* (Philadelphia, 1960)

Learned, William S., *The Oberlehrer: A Study of the Social and Professional Evolution of the German Schoolmaster*, repr. (Cambridge, MA, 1986)

Leclercq, Jean, *Monks on Marriage: A Twelfth-Century View* (New York, 1982)

Leder, Klaus, *Kirche und Jugend in Nürnberg und seinem Landgebiet: 1400–1800* (Neustadt, 1973)

Lewis, Ewart, *Medieval Political Ideas*, 2 vols. (New York, 1954)

Liermann, Hans, "Das kanonische Recht als Gegenstand des gelehrten Unterrichts in den protestantischen Universitäten Deutschlands in den ersten Jahrhunderten nach der Reformation," *Studia Gratiana* 3 (1955): 539

Der Jurist und die Kirche: Ausgewählte kirchenrechtliche Aufsätze und Rechtsgutachten (Munich, 1973)

"Der unjuristische Luther," *Luther-Jahrbuch* 24 (1957): 69

Deutsches evangelisches Kirchenrecht (Munich, 1933)

"Evangelisches Kirchenrecht und staatliches Eherecht in Deutschland: Rechtsgeschichtliches-Gegenwartsprobleme," in Wurtenberger, ed., *Existenz und Ordnung*, 43

Grundlagen des kirchlichen Verfassungsrechts nach lutherischer Auffassung (Berlin, 1954)

Handbuch des Stiftungsrechts (Tübingen, 1963)

"Laizismus und Klerikalismus in der Geschichte des evangelischen Kirchenrechts," *ZSS KA* 39 (1952): 1

Liese, Wilhelm, *Geschichte der Caritas* (Freiburg im Breisgau, 1922)

Linck, Wenceslaus, *Ob die Geystlichen auch schuldig sein Zinsse, geschoss, etc. zügeben und andere gemeyne bärde mit zutragen. Eyn Sermon Auffs Euangelion Mat. 22. Ob sich getzymme dem Keyser Zinns geben* (Altenburg, 1524)

Lindberg, Carter, *Beyond Charity: Reformation Initiatives for the Poor* (Minneapolis, 1993)

"Do Lutherans Shout Justification But Whisper Sanctification?" *Lutheran Quarterly* 13 (1999): 1

The European Reformations (Oxford, 1996)

"The Future of a Tradition: Luther and the Family," in Wenthe *et al.*, eds., *All Theology is Christology*, 133

Lindberg, Carter, ed., *The Reformation Theologians* (Oxford, 2001)

Lohse, Bernhard, *Luthers Theologie* (Göttingen, 1995)

Mönchtum und Reformation: Luthers Auseinandersetzung mit dem Mönchsideal des Mittelalters (Göttingen, 1963)

Lombardus, Petrus, *Libri IV sententiarum* (1150), 2nd rev. edn. (Florence, 1916)

Lovejoy, Arthur, *The Chain of Being: A Study of the History of an Idea* (Cambridge, MA, 1933)

Lück, Heiner, "Wittenberg als Zentrum kursächsischer Rechtspflege: Hofgericht – Juristenfakultät – Schöffenstuhl – Konsistorium," in Oehmig, ed., *700 Jahre Wittenberg*, 213

Luke, Carmen, *Pedagogy, Printing, and Protestantism: The Discourse on Childhood* (Albany, NY, 1989)

Luther, Martin, *D. Martin Luthers Werke: Briefwechsel*, 17 vols. (Weimar, 1930–83)
 D. Martin Luthers Werke: Kritische Gesamtausgabe, 78 vols. (Weimar, 1883–1987)
 D. Martin Luthers Werke: Tischreden (Weimar, 1912–)
 Lectures on Romans [1516], trans. and ed. W. H. Pauck (Philadelphia, 1961)
 Letters of Spiritual Counsel, ed. Theodore G. Tappert (Philadelphia, 1955)
 Luther's Correspondence and Other Contemporary Letters, trans. and ed. Preserved
  Smith and Charles M. Jacobs (Philadelphia, 1918)
 The Table Talk or Familiar Discourses of Martin Luther, trans. W. Hazlitt (London,
  1848)
Lutheran World Federation, *Theological Perspectives on Human Rights* (Geneva, 1977)
Maag, Karin, ed., *Melanchthon in Europe: His Work and Influence Beyond Wittenberg*
  (Grand Rapids, MI, 1999)
McGovern, William M., *From Luther to Hitler: The History of Fascist-Nazi Political
  Philosophy* (Boston, 1941)
McGrath, Alister, *The Intellectual Origins of the European Reformation* (Oxford, 1987)
McHugh, John A. and Charles J. Callan, trans. and eds., *Catechism of the Council
  of Trent* (Rockford, IL, 1982)
McNeill, John T., "Natural Law in the Thought of Luther," *Church History* 10
  (1941): 211
MacFarlane, Alan, *Marriage and Love in England, 1300–1840* (Oxford, 1986)
Mack, Eugen, *Die kirchliche Steuerfreiheit in Deutschland seit der Dekretalengesetzgebung*,
  repr. (Aalen, 1965)
Macke, Peter, *Das Rechts- und Staatsdenken des Johannes Oldendorp* (Inaug. Diss.,
  Cologne, 1966)
Mackin, Theodore, *What is Marriage?* (New York, 1982)
Mager, Inge, "'Es is nicht gut dass der Mensch allein sei' (Gen 2, 18): Zum
  Familienleben Philipp Melanchthons," *AFR* 81 (1990): 120
Margarita decreti seu tabula martiniana (Erlangen, 1481)
Maritain, Jacques, *Three Reformers: Luther – Descartes – Rousseau* (New York, 1947)
Marsilius of Padua, *The Defensor Pacis Translated with an Introduction*, trans. and ed.
  Alan Gewirth (New York, 1956)
Martos, Joseph, *Doors to the Sacred: A Historical Introduction to Sacraments in the Catholic
  Church* (Garden City, NY, 1981)
Matheson, Peter, ed., *Argula von Grumbach: A Woman's Voice in the Reformation*
  (Edinburgh, 1998)
Maurer, Wilhelm, *Der junge Melanchthon zwischen Humanismus und Reformation*,
  2 vols. (Munich, 1969)
 Die Kirche und ihr Recht: Gesammelte Aufsätze zum evangelischen Kirchenrecht
  (Tübingen, 1976)
 Luthers Lehre von den drei Hiearchien und ihr mittelalterlicher Hintergrund (Munich,
  1970)
 "Reste des kanonischen Rechtes im Frühprotestantismus," *ZSS KA* 95 (1965):
  190
 "Von Ursprung und Wesen kirchlichen Rechts," *Zeitschrift des evangelischen
  Kirchenrechts* 5 (1956): 1
Mauser, Konrad, *Explicatio erudita et utilis X. tituli inst. de nuptiis* (Jena, 1569)

May, Georg, *Die geistliche Gerichtsbarkeit des Erzbishofs von Mainz im Thüringen des späten Mittelalters* (Tübingen, 1950)

Die Stellung des deutschen Protestantismus zu Ehescheidung, Wiederverheiratung und kirchlicher Trauung Geschiedener (Paderborn, 1965)

Meinhold, Peter, *Philipp Melanchthon: Der Lehrer der Kirche* (Berlin, 1960)

Melanchthon, Philip, *De arbore consanguinitatis et affinitatis, sive de gradibus* (Wittenberg, 1540)

Dialectices Philippi Melanchthonis (Louvain, 1534)

Handtbuchlein wie man die Kinder zu der geschrifft vnd lere halten soll (Wittenberg, 1521/1524/1530)

Loci communes theologici (1521), in Pauck, ed., *Melanchthon and Bucer*, 18

Melanchthon on Christian Doctrine: Loci Communes 1555, trans. and ed. Clyde L. Manschrek (New York/Oxford, 1965)

Melanchthons Briefwechsel, 10 vols., ed. Heinz Scheible (Stuttgart, 1977–87)

Melanchthons Werke, 28 vols., in G. Bretschneider, ed., *Corpus Reformatorum* (Brunswick, 1864)

Melanchthons Werke in Auswahl, ed. Robert Stupperich, 6 vols. (Gütersloh, 1951)

Orations on Philosophy and Education, ed. Sachiko Kusukawa (Cambridge, 1999)

Mellinkoff, Ruth, *The Mark of Cain* (Berkeley/Los Angeles, 1981)

Mertz, Georg, *Das Schulwesen der deutschen Reformation im 16. Jahrhundert* (Heidelberg, 1902)

Merzbacher, Friederich, "Johann Oldendorp und das kanonische Recht," in Grundmann, ed., *Für Kirche und Recht*, 223

Michaelis, Karl, "Ueber Luthers eherechtliche Anschauungen und deren Verhältnis zum mittelalterlichen und neuzeitlichen Eherecht," in *Festschrift für Erich Ruppel zum 65. Geburtstag* (Hanover, 1968), 43

Mikat, Paul, "Bemerkungen zum Verhältnis von Kirchengut und Staatsgewalt am Vorabend der Reformation," *ZSS KA* 93 (1981): 300

Mirbt, Carl, ed., *Quellen zur Geschichte des Papsttums und des römischen Katholizismus*, 2nd edn. (Tübingen/Leipzig, 1901)

Moeller, Bernd, *Imperial Cities and the Reformation: Three Essays*, trans. and ed. H. C. Erik Midelfort and Mark U. Edwards, Jr. (Philadelphia, 1972)

"Wenzel Lincks Hochzeit: Über Sexualität, Keuscheit und Ehe in der frühen Reformation," *Zeitschrift für Theologie und Kirche* 97 (2000): 317

Moeller, Bernd, ed., *Studien zum städtischen Bildungswesen des späten Mittelalters und der frühen Neuzeit* (Göttingen, 1983)

Molitor, Erich, *Die Reichreformbestrebungen des 15. Jahrhunderts bis zum Tode Kaiser Friedrichs III* (Breslau, 1921)

Mollatt, Michel, ed., *Etudes sur l'histoire de la pauvreté* (Sorbonne, 1974)

Monner, Basilius, *Tractatus duo. I. De matrimonio. II. De clandestinis conjugiis*, 2nd. edn. (Jena, 1604)

Monumenta Germaniae Pädagogica, 62 vols. (Berlin, 1886–1938)

Moore, Cornelia Niekus, *The Maiden's Mirror: Reading Materials for Girls in the Sixteeth and Seventeenth Centuries* (Wiesbaden, 1987)

Moraw, Peter, *et al.*, "Reich," in Brunner, *et al.*, eds., *Geschichtliche Grundbegriffe*, 5:423

Morrison, Karl Frederick, *The Mimetic Tradition of Reform in the West* (Princeton, 1982)

The Two Kingdoms: Ecclesiology in Carolingian Political Thought (Princeton, 1964)

Müller, Gerhard, "Martin Luther and the Political World of his Time," in Kouri and Scott, eds., *Politics and Society in Reformation Europe*, 35

"Philipp Melanchthon zwischen Pädagogik und Theologie," in Reinhard, ed., *Humanismus im Bildungwesen des 15. und 16. Jahrhundert*, 95

Müller, W., ed., *Freiburg im Mittelalter* (Baden, 1970)

Muther, Theodor, *Aus dem Universitäts- und Gelehrtenleben im Zeitalter der Reformation* (Erlargen, 1866; repr. Graz, 1966)

Doctor Johann Apell. Ein Beitrag zur Geschichte der deutschen Jurisprudenz (Königsberg, 1861)

Zur Geschichte der Rechtswissenschaft und der Universitäten in Deutschland (Jena, 1876; repr. Amsterdam, 1976)

New Cambridge Modern History, 16 vols. (Cambridge, 1957–79)

Niebuhr, Reinhold, *The Nature and Destiny of Man*, 2 vols. (New York, 1964)

Nipkow, Karl Ernst and Friedrich Schweitzer, eds., *Religionspädagogik: Texte zur evangelischen Erziehungs- und Bildungsverantwortung seit der Reformation*, 2 vols. (Munich/Gütersloh, 1991–1994)

Noonan, John T., *Canons and Canonists in Context* (Goldbach, 1997)

"Marital Affection in the Canonists," *Studia Gratiana* 12 (1967): 489

The Scholastic Analysis of Usury (Cambridge, MA, 1957)

Oberman, Heiko A., *The Dawn of the Reformation: Essays in Late Medieval and Early Reformation Thought* (Edinburgh, 1986)

Forerunners of the Reformation: The Shape of Medieval Thought (New York, 1966)

The Harvest of Medieval Theology: Gabriel Biel and Late Medieval Nominalism (Cambridge, MA, 1963)

The Impact of the Reformation (Grand Rapids, MI, 1994)

Luther: Man Between God and Devil, trans. Eileen Walliser-Schwarzbart (New Haven, CT, 1983)

The Roots of Anti-Semitism in the Age of Renaissance and Reformation, trans. J. I. Porter (Philadelphia, 1984)

"University and Society on the Threshold of Modern Times: The German Connection," in Kittelson and Transue, eds., *Rebirth, Reform, and Resilience*, 19

O'Donovan, Oliver, *The Desire of the Nations: Rediscovering the Roots of Political Theology* (Cambridge, 1996)

Oehmig, Stefan, ed., *700 Jahre Wittenberg* (Weimar, 1995)

Oldendorp, Johann, *Actionum iuris civilis loci communes, ad usum forensem secundum aequissimas Legislatorum sententias bona fide accommodati* (Cologne, 1539)

Collatio juris civilis et canonici, maximam afferens boni et aequi cognitionem (Cologne, 1541)

Consiliorum et responsorum doctorum et professorum facultatis juridicae in academia Marpurgensi (Marburg, 1606)

De copia verborum et rerum in iure civili (Cologne, 1542)

De iure et aequitate forensis disputatio (Cologne, 1541)

Ein Ratmannen-Spiegel von Joh. Oldendorp (Rostock, 1971)

Iuris naturalis gentium et civilis isagoge (Antwerp, 1539)

Lexicon iuris (Franfurt am Main, 1546/1553)

Loci communes iuris civilis ex mendis tandem et barbarie in gratiam studiosorum utiliter restituti (Louvain, 1545; rev. ed., Louvain, 1551)

Loci iuris communes (Frankfurt am Main, 1546)

Opera omnia (Basel, 1559; facs. repr. Graz, 1968)

Rationes sive argumenta, quibus in iure utimur (Rostock, 1516)

Responsio ad impiam delationem parochorum Coloniensium de communicatione sacramenti corporis et sanguinis Christi sub utraque specie, cum exemplo litterarum, quas Phil. Melanthon dedit ad Joh. Old. (Marburg, 1543)

Topicorum legalium . . . exactissima traditio (Marburg, 1545; Louvain, 1555)

Van radtslangende, wo men gude Politie und ordenunge ynn Steden und Landen enholden möghe (Rostock, 1530)

Wahrhafftige entschuldige Doct. Johann Oldendorp, Syndici tho Rostock, wedder de mortgirigen uprorschen schantdichter und falschen klegen (Rostock, 1533)

Wat byllich und recht ist (Rostock, 1529)

Olin, John C. *et al.*, eds., *Luther, Erasmus, and the Reformation* (New York, 1969)

O'Malley, John W., *Trent and all That: Renaming Catholicism in the Early Modern Era* (Cambridge, MA, 2000)

Omphalius, Jakob, *De civili politica libri tres* (Cologne, 1563)

Ozment, Steven, *The Age of Reform, 1250–1550: An Intellectual and Social History of Late Medieval and Reformation Europe* (New Haven, CT, 1980)

Ancestors: The Loving Family in Old Europe (Cambridge, MA, 2001)

The Bürgermeister's Daughter: Scandal in a Sixteenth-Century German Town (New York, 1996)

Flesh and Spirit: Private Life in Early Modern Europe (New York, 1999)

Protestants: The Birth of a Revolution (New York, 1992)

The Reformation in the Cities: The Appeal of Protestantism to Sixteenth-Century Germany and Switzerland (New Haven, CT, 1975)

When Fathers Ruled: Family Life in Reformation Europe (Cambridge, MA, 1983)

Painter, F. V. N., *Luther on Education* (St. Louis, MO, 1928)

Parker, Geoffrey, "Success and Failure During the First Century of the Reformation," *Past and Present* 136 (1992): 43

Pauck, Wilhelm, ed., *Melanchthon and Bucer* (Philadelphia, 1969)

Paulsen, Friedrich, *German Education Past and Present*, trans. T. Lorenz (New York, 1912)

Geschichte des gelehrten Unterrichts auf den deutschen Schulen und Universitäten vom Ausgang des Mittelalters bis zur Gegenwart, 3rd edn. (Leipzig, 1919)

Pawlas, Andreas, *Die lutherische Berufs- und Wirtschaftsethik: Eine Einführung* (Neukirchen-Vluyn, 2000)

Pelikan, Jaroslav, "Foreword," in John Witte, Jr. and Frank S. Alexander, eds., *The Weightier Matters of the Law: Essays on Law and Religion* (Atlanta, 1988), ix

    Obedient Rebels: Catholic Substance and Protestant Principle in Luther's Reformation (New York, 1964)

    Reformation of Church and Dogma (1300–1700) (Chicago, 1984)

    Spirit versus Structure: Luther and the Institutions of the Church (New York, 1968)

    " '*Verius servamus canones*': Church Law and Divine Law in the Apology of the Augsburg Confession," *Studia Gratiana* 11 (1967): 367

Peters, Albrecht, *Kommentar zu Luthers Katechismen*, 5 vols. to date (Göttingen, 1990–)

Pettke, O., "Zur Rolle Johann Oldendorps bei der offiziellen Durchführung der Reformation in Rostock," *ZSS KA* 101 (1984): 339

Petzold, Klaus, *Die Grundlagen der Erziehungslehre im Spätmittelalter und bei Luther* (Heidelberg, 1969)

Ploese, Detlof and Günter Vogler, eds., *Buch der Reformation. Ein Auswahl zeitge-noessischer Zeugnisse (1476–1555)* (Berlin, 1989)

Po-Chia Hsia, R., *Social Discipline in the Reformation: Central Europe 1550–1750* (London and New York, 1989)

Politische Reichshandel. Das ist allerhand gemeine Acten Regimentssachen und weltlichen Discursen (Frankfurt am Main, 1614)

Prest, Wilfried, ed., *Lawyers in Early Modern Europe and America* (London, 1981)

Pullan, Brian, *Rich and Poor in Renaissance Florence: The Social Institutions of a Catholic State to 1620* (Oxford, 1971)

    "Support and Redeem: Charity and Poor Relief in Italian Cities from the Fourteenth to the Seventeenth Centuries," *Continuity and Change* 3 (1988): 177

Raeff, Marc, *The Well-Ordered Police State: Social and Institutional Changes Through Law in the Germanies and Russia, 1600–1800* (New Haven, CT, 1983)

Rashdall, Hastings, *The Universities of Europe in the Middle Ages*, rev. edn., 3 vols., ed. F. M. Powicke and A. B. Emden (London/Oxford, 1936)

Ratzinger, Georg, *Geschichte der kirchlichen Armenpflege*, 2nd edn. (Freiburg im Breisgau, 1884)

Rau, Gerhard, *et al.*, eds., *Das Recht der Kirche*, 3 vols. (Gütersloh, 1994–97)

Rautenberg, Werner, ed., *Johann Bugenhagen: Beiträge zu seinem 400. Todestag* (Berlin, 1958)

Regan, Augustine, "The Perennial Value of Augustine's Theology of the Goods of Marriage," *Studia Moralia* 21 (1983): 351

Reicke, Bo, *Die Zehn Worte in Geschichte und Gegenwart* (Tübingen, 1973)

Reid, Charles J., "The Canonistic Contribution to the Western Rights Tradition," *Boston College Law Review* 33 (1991): 37

Reinhard, Wolfgang, ed., *Humanismus im Bildungswesen des 15. und 16. Jahrhunderts* (Weinheim, 1984)

Renz, Horst and Friedrich-Wilhelm Graf, eds., *Protestantismus und Neuzeit* (Gütersloh, 1984)

Repertorium aureum mirabili artificio contextum continens titulos quinque librorum decretalium (Cologne, 1495)

Reu, Johann M., *Quellen zur Geschichte des kirchlichen Unterrichts in der evangelischen Kirche Deutschlands zwischen 1530 und 1600* (Gütersloh, 1904–35)

Reyscher, August L., ed., *Vollständige, historisch, und kritisch bearbeitete Sammlung der Württembergischen Gesetze* (Württemberg, 1828–51)

Rice, Edward Lloyd, "The Influence of the Reformation in Nuremberg's Provisions for Social Welfare, 1521–1528" (PhD Diss., Ohio State University, 1974)

Richter, Aemilius, *Beiträge zur Geschichte des Ehescheidungsrechts in der evangelischen Kirche* (Aalen, 1958)

Richtes, Aenilius, ed., *Die evangelischen Kirchenordnungen des sechzehnten Jahrhunderts*, repr., 2 vols. (Nieuwkoop, 1967)

Riggenbach, Bernard, *Johann Eberlin von Günzburg und sein Reformprogramm* (Tübingen, 1874)

Rost, Julius Robert, *Die pädagogische Bedeutung Bugenhagens* (Inaug. Diss., Leipzig, 1890)

Rowan, Steven W., "Jurists and the Printing Press in Germany: The First Century," in Tyson and Wagonheim, eds., *Print and Culture in the Renaissance*, 74

Ulrich Zasius: A Jurist in the German Renaissance, 1461–1535 (Frankfurt am Main, 1987)

Safley, Thomas Max, "Canon Law and Swiss Reform: Legal Theory and Practice in the Marital Courts of Zurich, Bern, Basel, and St. Gall," in Helmholz, ed., *Canon Law in Protestant Lands*, 187

Let No Man Put Asunder: The Control of Marriage in the German Southwest, A Comparative Study, 1550–1600 (Kirksville, MO, 1984)

Sarcerius, Basilius [Erasmus], *Corpus juris matrimonialis. Vom Ursprung, Anfang und Herkomen des Heyligen Ehestandts* (Frankfurt am Main, 1569)

Scanlan, James D., "Husband and Wife: Pre-Reformation Canon Law on Marriages of the Officials' Courts," in *An Introduction to Scottish Legal History* (Edinburgh, 1958)

Schäfer, Rudolf, "Die Geltung des kanonischen Rechts in der evangelischen Kirche Deutschlands von Luther bis zur Gegenwart," *ZSS KA* 5 (1915): 165
"Die Versetzbarkeit der Geistlichen im Urteil der evangelischen-theologischen Autoriäten des 16. Jahrhunderts," *ZSS KA* 9 (1919): 99

Schaff, Philip and Henry Wace, eds., *A Second Library of Nicene and Post-Nicene Fathers of the Christian Church*, 2nd. ser., repr. 14 vols. (Grand Rapids, MI, 1952–56)

Schaich-Klose, Wiebke, *D. Hieronymus Schürpf: Leben und Werk des Wittenberger Reformationsjuristen, 1481–1554* (Tübingen, 1967)

Schatt, Heinrich, *Das priester ee nit wider des Gottlich, gaystlich, unnd weltich recht sey* (Augsburg, 1523)

Schatzgeyer, Kaspar, *De vera libertate evangelica* (Tübingen, 1527)

Scheel, Willy, *Johann Freiherr zu Schwarzenberg* (Berlin, 1905)

Scheible, Heinz, *Das Widerstandsrecht als Problem der deutsche Protestanten 1523–1546* (Gütersloh, 1969)

"Die Reform von Schule und Universität in der Reformationszeit," *Luther-Jahrbuch* 66 (1999): 266

Melanchthon: Eine Biographie (Munich, 1997)

"Philip Melanchthon," in Lindberg, ed., *The Reformation Theologians*

Scheible, Heinz, ed., *Melanchthon in seinen Schülern* (Wiesbaden, 1997)

Schiele, F. M., "Luther und das Luthertum in ihrer Bedeutung für die Geschichte der Schule und der Erziehung," *Preussisches Jahrbuch* 31 (1908): 383

Schmelzeisen, Gustav Klemens, *Polizeiordnung und Privatrecht* (Münster/Cologne, 1955)

Schmidt, Gustav L., *Justus Menius, Der Reformator Thüringens nach archivalischen und andern Quellen*, 2 vols. (Gotha, 1867)

Schmidt, Heinrich Richard, *Konfessionalisierung im 16. Jahrhundert* (Munich, 1992)

Reichsstädte, Reich, und Reformation: Korporative Religionspolitik 1521–1529/30 (Stuttgart, 1986)

Schmitt, Jean-Claude, *Les citations bibliques et canoniques dans les traités médiévaux sur la pauvreté (XIVe–XVe siècles)* (Paris, 1994)

Schneidewin, Johannes, *In institutionum imperialium titulum X. De nuptiis . . . .* (Frankfurt am Main, 1562, 1571)

Schorn-Schütte, Luise, "'Papocaesarismus' der Theologen? Vom Amt des evangelischen Pfarrers in der frühneuzeitlichen Stadtgesellschaft bei Bugenhagen," *AFR* 79 (1988): 230.

Schoss, Carl Wolfgang Huismann, *Die rechtliche Stellung, Struktur und Funktion der frühen evangelischen Konsistorien nach den evangelischen Kirchenordnungen des 16. Jahrhunderts* (Inaug. Diss., Heidelberg, 1980)

Schrage, E. J. H., ed., *Das römische Recht im Mittelalter* (Darmstadt, 1987)

Schroeder, H. J., ed., *Disciplinary Decrees of the General Councils: Text, Translation, and Commentary* (St. Louis, 1937)

Schulz, Kurd, "Bugenhagen als Schöpfer der Kirchenordnung," in Rautenberg, ed., *Johann Bugenhagen*, 51

Schürpf, Hieronymus, *Consilia seu responsa* (Basel, 1559)

Schwab, Hans-Rüdiger, *Philipp Melanchthon, Der Lehrer Deutschlands: Ein biographisches Lesebuch* (Munich, 1997)

Schwahn, Walter, ed., *De falsa credita et ementita Constantini Donatione declamatio* (Stuttgart, 1994)

Schwanhäusser, Gertrud, *Das Gesetzgebungsrecht der evangelischen Kirche unter dem Einfluss des landesherrlichen Kirchenregiments im 16. Jahrhundert* (Munich, 1967)

Schwarz, Reinhard, "*Ecclesia, oeconomia, politia*: Sozialgeschichte und fundamentalethische Aspekte der protestantischen Drei-Stände Lehre," in Renz und Graf, eds., *Protestantismus und Neuzeit*, 3:78

Schwarzenberg, Johann Freiherr von, *Beschwerung der alten teüfelischen Schlangen mit dem göttlichen Wort* (Zwickau, 1527)

Der Zudrincker und Prasser Gesatze, Ordenung und Instruction (Oppenheim, 1512)

Diss Büchlyn Kuttenschlang genant die Teuffels lerer macht bekant (Nürnberg, 1526)

Ein schöner Sendbrieff des wolgepornen und Edeln herrn Johannsen herrn zu Schwartzenberg an Bischoff zu Bamberg aussgangen (Nürnberg, 1524)

Schwerhoff, Gerd, "Blasphemie vor den Schranken der städtischen Justiz: Basel, Köln, und Nürnberg im Vergleich (14. bis. 17. Jahrhundert)," *Ius Commune* 25 (1998): 39

Schwinges, Rainer C., *Deutsche Universitätsbesucher im 14. bis 15. Jahrhundert. Studien zur Sozialgeschichte des alten Reiches* (Stuttgart, 1986)

Scribner, Robert W. [Bob], *For the Sake of Simple Folk: Popular Propaganda for the German Reformation* (Cambridge, 1981)

"Germany," in Scribner *et al.*, eds., *The Reformation in National Context*, 4

"Police and the Territorial State in Sixteenth Century Württemberg," in Kouri and Scott, eds., *Politics and Society in Reformation Europe*, 103

Scribner, R. W., *et al.*, eds., *The Reformation in National Context* (Cambridge, 1994)

Seebass, Gottfried, *Das reformatorische Werk des Andreas Osiander* (Nürnberg, 1967)

Seeberg, Reinhard, "Luthers Anschauung von dem Geschlechtsleben der Ehe und ihre geschichtliche Stellung," *Luther-Jahrbuch* 7 (1925): 77

Sehling, Emil, *Kirchenrecht* (Leipzig, 1908)

Sehling, Emil, ed., *Die evangelischen Kirchenordnungen des 16. Jahrhunderts* (Leipzig, 1902–1913), vols. 1–5; continued under the same title (Tübingen, 1955–), vols. 6–16

Selderjhuis, H., *Marriage and Divorce in the Thought of Martin Bucer*, trans. John Vriend and Lyle D. Biersma (Kirksville, MO, 1999)

Shäfer, Rudolf, "Die Versetzbarkeit der Geistlichen im Urteil der evangelisch-theologischen Autoritäten des 16. Jahrhunderts," *ZSS KA* 9 (1919): 99

Sibeth, Uwe, *Eherecht und Staatsbildung: Ehegesetzgebung und Eherechtsprechung in der Landgrafschaft Hessen(-Kassel) in der frühen Neuzeit* (Darmstadt, 1994)

Sichelschmidt, Karla, *Recht aus christlicher Liebe oder obrigkeitlicher Gesetzesbefehl? Juristische Untersuchungen zu den evangelischen Kirchenordnungen im 16. Jahrhundert* (Tübingen, 1995)

Sigmund, Paul E., "The Influence of Marsilius of Padua on xvth-Century Conciliarism," *Journal of the History of Ideas* 23 (1962): 392

Skinner, Quentin, *The Foundation of Modern Political Thought*, 2 vols. (Cambridge, 1978)

Smith, Helmut Walser, *German Nationalism and Religious Conflict: Culture, Ideology, Politics, 1870–1914* (Princeton, NJ, 1995)

Sockness, Brent W., *Against False Apologetics: Wilhelm Herrmann and Ernst Troeltsch in Conflict* (Tübingen, 1998)

Sohm, Rudolph, *Das Recht der Eheschliessung aus dem deutschen und kanonischen Recht geschichtlich entwickelt*, repr. (Aalen, 1966)

Kirchenrecht (Leipzig, 1892)

Sohm, Walter, "Die Soziallehren Melanchthons," *Historische Zeitschrift* 115 (1916): 68

Sohm, Walter, *et al.*, eds. *Urkundliche Quellen zur hessischen Reformationsgeschichte*, 4 vols. (Marburg, 1957)

Söllner, Alfred, "Die causa in Konditionen- und Vertragsrecht des Mittelalters bei den Glossatoren, Kommentaren, und Kanonisten," *ZSS* (*Rananische Abteilung*) 77 (1960): 182

Spengler, Lazurus, *Ain kurtzer Begriff vnd Underrichtung aines gantzen wahrhaften Christlichen wesens* (Wittenberg, 1522)

Ein kurtzer auszug auss den Babstlichen recht der Dekret und Decretalen/Inn denn artickeln die ungeverlich Gottes wort un dem Evangelio gemetz seind/oder zum wenigstens nit wider streben (Nürnberg, 1530)

Ein kurczer auszug auss den Bebstlichen rechten der Decret und Decretalen . . . mit einer schönen Vorrhede Mart. Luth. (Wittenberg, 1530)

Sperl, Adolf, *Melanchthon zwischen Humanismus und Reformation* (Munich, 1959)

Spiegel, Jacob, *Lexicon iuris civilis* (Basel, 1554)

Spitz, Lewis W., "The Importance of the Reformation for the Universities: Culture and Confessions in the Critical Years," in Kittelson and Transue, eds., *Rebirth, Reform, and Resilience*, 42

"Reformation," in Philip P. Wiener, ed., *Dictionary of the History of Ideas*, 5 vols. (New York, 1973), 4:60

The Religious Renaissance of the German Humanists (Cambridge, MA, 1963)

Spitz, Lewis W., ed., *The Reformation – Material or Spiritual?* (Boston, 1962)

Sprengler-Ruppenthal, Anneliese, "Bugenhagen und das kanonische Recht," *ZSS KA* 75 (1989): 375

"Das kanonische Recht in Kirchenordnungen im 16. Jahrhundert," in R. H. Helmholz, ed., *Canon Law in Protestant Lands* (Berlin, 1992), 49

"Zur Rezeption des römischen Rechts in Eherecht der Reformation," *ZSS KA* 112 (1978): 363

Staehelin, Adrian, *Die Einführung der Ehescheidung in Basel zur Zeit der Reformation* (Basel, 1957)

Stayer, James, *Martin Luther, German Saviour: German Evangelical Theological Factions and the Interpretation of Luther, 1917–1933* (Montreal, 2000)

Stein, Albert, "Luther über Eherecht und Juristen," in Junghaus, ed., *Leben und Werk Martin Luthers*, 1:171

Steinbecker, Carl R., *Poor Relief in the Sixteenth Century* (Washington, DC, 1937)

Stelzenberger, Johannes, *Syneidesis, Conscientia, Gewissen* (Paderborn, 1963)

Stephenson, Carl and Frederick G. Marcham, eds., *Sources of English Constitutional History*, rev. edn. (New York/San Francisco, 1972)

Stintzing, Roderich von, *Das Sprichwort 'Juristen böse Christen' in seiner geschichtlichen Bedeutung* (Bonn, 1875)

Geschichte der deutschen Rechtswissenschaft, Erste Abtheilung (Munich/Leipzig, 1880)

Geschichte der populären Literatur des römisch-kanonischen Rechts in Deutschland am Ende des fünfzehnten und im Anfang des sechszehnten Jahrhunderts (Leipzig, 1867)

Ulrich Zasius: Ein Beitrag zur Geschichte der Rechtswissenschaft im Zeitalter der Reformation (Basel, 1857)

Stobbe, Otto von, *Geschichte der deutschen Rechtsquellen*, repr., 2 vols. (Aalen, 1965)

Stölzel, Adolf, *Die Entwicklung des gelehrten Richtertums in den deutschen Territorien*, 2 vols. (Berlin, 1901, 1910)

Störmann, Anton, *Die städtischen Gravamina gegen den Klerus am Ausgange des Mittelalters und in der Reformationszeit* (Münster, 1916)

Strauss, Gerald, *Law, Resistance and the State: The Opposition to Roman Law in Reformation Germany* (Princeton, NJ, 1986)

Luther's House of Learning: Indoctrination of the Young in the German Reformation (Baltimore, MD, 1978)

Strauss, Gerald, ed., *Manifestations of Discontent in Germany on the Eve of the Reformation* (Bloomington, IN, 1971)

Pre-Reformation Germany (New York, 1972)

Strohm, Christoph, "Die Voraussetzungen reformatorischer Naturrechtslehre in der humanistischen Jurisprudenz," *ZSS KA* 86 (2000): 398

Stupperich, Robert, *Philip Melanchthon: Gelehrter und Politiker* (Zürich, 1996)

Sturm, Johannes, *De institutione scholastica opuscula selecta*, in Vormbaum, ed., *Die Evangelischen Schulordnungen des sechzehnten Jahrhunderts*, 1:653

Suppan, Klaus, *Die Ehelehre Martin Luthers. Theologische und rechtshistorische Aspekte des reformatorischen Eheverständnisses* (Salzburg, 1971)

Swanson, Guy E., *Religion and Regime: A Sociological Account of the Reformation* (New York, 1967)

Sweeney, James R. and Stanley A. Chodorow, eds., *Popes, Teachers, and Canon Law in the Middle Ages* (Ithaca, NY, 1989)

"Symposium on Education in the Renaissance and Reformation," *Renaissance Quarterly* 43 (1990): 1

Telle, Emile V.-, *Erasme de Rotterdam et le septième sacrement* (Geneva, 1954)

Tentler, Thomas N., *Sin and Confession on the Eve of the Reformation* (Princeton, NJ, 1977)

Thieme, Hans, "Die 'Nuewen Stattrechten und Statuten der löblichen Staat Fryburg' von 1520," in Müller, ed., *Freiburg im Mittelalter*, 96

Thomson, John A. F., *Popes and Princes, 1417–1517* (London, 1980)

Tierney, Brian, *The Crisis of Church and State, 1050–1300* (Englewood Cliffs, NJ, 1964)

Foundations of the Conciliar Theory: The Contribution of the Medieval Canonists from Gratian to the Great Schism, new enlarged edn. (Leiden/New York, 1998)

The Idea of Natural Rights: Studies on Natural Rights, Natural Law, and Church Law, 1150–1625 (Atlanta, 1997)

Medieval Poor Law: A Sketch of Canonical Theory and its Application in England (Berkeley/Los Angeles, 1959)

The Origins of Papal Infallibility, 1150–1350 (Leiden, 1972)

Religion, Law, and the Growth of Constitutional Thought: 1150–1650 (Cambridge, 1982)

Tietz, Gerold, *Verlobung, Trauung, und Hochzeit in den evangelischen Kirchenordnungen des 16. Jahrhunderts* (PhD Diss., Tübingen, 1969)

Todd, John M., ed., *Problems of Authority* (Baltimore, MD, 1962)

Tonkin, John, *The Church and the Secular Order in Reformation Thought* (New York, 1971)

Towns, Elmer L., "Martin Luther on Sanctification," *Bibliotheca Sacra* 125 (1969): 114

Tracy, James D., ed., *Luther and the Modern State in Germany* (Kirksville, MO, 1986)

Treggiari, Susan, *Roman Marriage: Iusti Coniuges from the Time of Cicero to the Time of Ulpian* (Oxford, 1991)

Treu, Martin, ed., *Katherina von Bora, die Lutherin* (Wittenberg, 1999)

Triglott Concordia: The Symbolic Books of the Ev. Lutheran Church German–Latin–English (St. Louis, MO, 1921)

Troeltsch, Ernst, *Die Soziallehren der christlichen Kirchen und Gruppen* (Berlin, 1912)

Ernst Troeltsch: Writings on Theology and Religion, ed. Robert Morgan and Michael Pye (Louisville, KY, 1977)

Gesammelte Schriften, 4 vols., ed. Hans Baron (Tübingen, 1922–5)

Protestantism and Progress: A Historical Study of the Relation of Protestantism to the Modern World, trans. W. Montgomery (New York, 1912)

Religion in History, trans. and ed. James Luther Adams and Walter F. Bense (Minneapolis, 1991)

The Social Teachings of the Christian Churches, trans. Olive Wyon, 2nd impr. (London, 1949; original edn. 1911)

Vernunft und Offenbarung bei Johann Gerhard und Melanchthon (Berlin, 1891)

Troje, Hans Erich, *Graeca Leguntur: Die Aneignung des byzantinischen Rechts und die Entstehung eines humanistischen Corpus iuris civilis in der Jurisprudenz des 16. Jahrhunderts* (Cologne/Vienna, 1971)

"Konrad Lagus (ca. 1500–1546): Zur Rezeption der Loci-Methode in der Jurisprudenz," in Scheible, ed., *Melanchthon in seinen Schülern*, 255

Trüdinger, K., *Luthers Briefe und Gutachten an weltliche Obrigkeit zur Durchführung der Reformation* (Münster, 1975)

Trusen, Winfried, *Anfänge des gelehrten Rechts in Deutschland. Ein Beitrag zur Geschichte der Frührezeption* (Wiesbaden, 1962)

Tyson, Gerald P. and Sylvia S. Wagonheim, eds., *Print and Culture in the Renaissance: Essays on the Advent of Printing in Germany* (Newark, NJ, 1986)

Uhlhorn, G. W., *Die christliche Liebestätigkeit in der alten Kirche* (Stuttgart, 1882–1890)

van der Vyver, Johan and John Witte, Jr., eds., *Religious Human Rights in Global Perspective: Legal Perspectives* (The Hague/Boston/London, 1996)

Vann, James and Steven W. Rowan, eds., *The Old Reich: Essays on German Political Institutions, 1495–1806* (Brussels, 1974)

Viehweg, Theodore, *Topik und Jurisprudenz*, 2nd edn. (Munich, 1963)

Vitoria, Francisco de, *Political Writings*, ed. Anthony Pagden and Jeremy Lawrance (Cambridge and New York, 1991)

Vögele, Wolfgang, *Menschenwürde zwischen Recht und Theologie: Begründungen von Menschenrechten in der Perspektive öffentlicher Theologie* (Gütersloh, 2000)

Voigt, Alfred, "Die juristische Hermeneutik und ihr Abbild in Melanchthons Universitätsreden," in Carl Joseph Hering, ed., *Staat, Recht, Kultur: Festgabe für Ernst von Hippel zu seinem 70. Geburtstag* (Bonn, 1965), 265

von Beust, Joachim, *Tractatus de iure connubiorum et dotium ad praxin forensem accommodatus* (Frankfurt am Main, 1591)

von Bonin, Burkhard, *Die praktische Bedeutung des ius reformandi: Eine rechtsgeschichtliche Studie* (Stuttgart, 1902)

von Friedeburg, Ludwig, *Bildungsreform in Deutschland: Geschichte und gesellschaftlichter Widerspruch* (Frankfurt am Main, 1989)

von Gierke, Otto, *Political Theories of the Middle Age*, trans. F. W. Maitland, repr. (Cambridge, 1958)

    The Development of Political Theory, trans. Bernard Freyd (New York, 1966)

von Hutten, Ulrich, *Ulrich von Huttens Schriften*, ed. Eduard Boecking, repr., 5 vols. (Aalen, 1963–6)

von Kaltenborn, Carl, *Die Vorläufer des Hugo Grotius auf dem Gebiete des ius naturae et gentium sowie der Politik im Reformationszeitalter* (Leipzig, 1848)

von Schulte, Johannes Friedrich, *Lehrbuch des katholischen und evangelischen Kirchenrechts* (Kieken, 1886)

Vormbaum, Reinhold, ed., *Die evangelischen Schulordnungen des sechzehnten Jahrhunderts*, 3 vols. (Gütersloh, 1860)

Weigand, Rudolf, *Die bedingte Eheschliessung im kanonischen Recht* (Munich, 1963)

    "Ehe- und Familienrecht in der mittelalterlichen Stadt," in Haverkamp, ed., *Haus und Familie in der spätmittelalterlichen Stadt*, 173

Weigand, Rudolf, ed., *Die Naturrechtslehre der Legisten und Dekretisten von Irnerius bis Accursius und von Gratian bis Johannes Teutonicus* (Munich, 1967)

Wendel, François, *Le mariage à Strasbourg à l'époque de la réforme 1520–1692* (Strasbourg, 1928)

Wengert, Timothy J., *Law and Gospel: Philip Melanchthon's Debate with John Agricola of Eisleben over Poenitentia* (Carlisle, 1997)

    Philip Melanchthon's Exegetical Dispute with Erasmus of Rotterdam (New York/Oxford, 1998)

Werminghoff, Albert, "Die deutschen Reichskriegssteuergesetze von 1422 bis 1427 und die deutsche Kirche," *ZSS KA* 5 (1915): 1

Wenthe, Dean O. *et al.*, eds., *All Theology is Christology: Essays in Honor of David P. Scaer* (Fort Wayne, IN, 2000)

Werner, Heinrich, ed., *Die Reformation des Kaiser Sigismund: Die erste Reformschrift eines Laien vor Luther* (Berlin, 1908)

Westermann, Claus, *Genesis 1–11: A Commentary*, repr. (Minneapolis: Augsburg Publishing House, 1990)

Whitford, David, "The Right of Resistance in the Theology of Martin Luther, With Specific Reference to the Magdeburg Confession of 1550" (Ph.D. Diss., Boston University, 1999)

Wiater, W., "'The Church and the School Should Have the Same Doctrine': State, Church and School According to Philip Melanchthon," in Golz and Mayrhofer, eds., *Luther and Melanchthon in the Educational Thought of Central and Eastern Europe*, 59

Wieacker, Franz, *Privatrechtsgeschichte der Neuzeit*, 2nd. rev. edn. (Göttingen, 1967)

Wilpert, Paul, ed., *Lex et Sacramentum im Mittelalter* (Berlin, 1969)

Winckelmann, Otto, "Die Armenordnungen von Nürnberg (1522), Kitzingen (1523), Regensburg (1523), und Ypern (1525)," *AFR* 11 (1914): 1

Das Fürsorgewesen der Stadt Strassburg vor und nach der Reformation bis zum Ausgang des sechzehnten Jahrhunderts, repr. (New York, 1971)

Wingren, Gustaf, *The Christian Calling: Luther on Vocation*, trans. Carl C. Rasmussen (Edinburgh, 1957)

Winkler, Benedict, *Principiorum iuris libri quinque* (Leipzig, 1615)

Witte, John, Jr., "A Dickensian Era of Religious Rights: An Update on *Religious Human Rights in Global Perspective*," *William and Mary Law Review* 42 (2001): 707

From Sacrament to Contract: Marriage, Religion, and Law in the Western Tradition (Louisville, KY, 1997)

"The Goods and Goals of Marriage," *Notre Dame Law Review* 76 (2001): 1019

"Moderate Religious Liberty in the Theology of John Calvin," *Calvin Theological Journal* 31 (1996): 359

Witte, John, Jr. and Frank S. Alexander, eds., *The Weightier Matters of the Law: Essays on Law and Religion* (Atlanta, 1988)

Witte, John, Jr. and Thomas C. Arthur, "Three Uses of the Law: A Protestant Source of Criminal Punishment?" *Journal of Law and Religion* 10 (1994): 433

Wohlhaupter, Eugen, *Aequitas canonica. Eine Studie aus dem kanonischen Recht* (Paderborn, 1931)

Wolf, Erik, *Grosse Rechtsdenker der deutschen Geistesgeschichte*, 4th edn. (Tübingen, 1963)

Wolf, Erik, ed., *Quellenbuch zur Geschichte der deutschen Rechtswissenschaft* (Frankfurt am Main, 1949)

Wolf, Günther, ed., *Luther und die Obrigkeit* (Darmstadt, 1972)

Wolgast, Eike, *Die Religionsfrage als Problem des Widerstandsrechts im 16. Jahrhundert* (Heidelberg, 1980)

"Reform, Reformation," in Brunner *et al.*, eds., *Geschichtliche Grundbegriffe*, 5:313

Wolgast, Eike, ed., *D. Bugenhagens Briefwechsel* (Hildesheim, 1966)

Wolter, Udo, "Amt und Officium in mittelalterlichen Quellen vom 13. bis 15. Jahrhundert: Eine begriffs-geschichtliche Untersuchung," *ZSS KA* 78 (1988): 246

"Die Fortgeltung des kanonischen Rechts und die Haltung der protestantischen Juristen zum kanonischen Recht in Deutschland bis in die Mitte des 18. Jahrhunderts," in Helmholz, ed., *Canon Law in Protestant Lands*, 13

Ius canonicum in iure civili (Cologne/Vienna, 1975)

Wrede, A., *Reichsakten unter Kaiser Karl V* (Gotha, 1896)

Wright, D. F., ed., *Martin Bucer: Reforming Church and Community* (Cambridge, 1994)

Wright, William J., *Capitalism, the State, and the Lutheran Reformation: Sixteenth-Century Hesse* (Athens, OH, 1988)

"Evaluating the Results of Sixteenth Century Educational Policy: Some Hessian Data," *Sixteenth Century Journal* 18 (1987): 411

"Reformation Contributions to the Development of Public Welfare Policy in Hesse," *Journal of Modern History* 49 (1977): DI145

"The Impact of the Reformation on Hessian Education," *Church History* 44 (1975): 182

Wurtenberger, Thomas, ed., *Existenz und Ordnung: Festschrift für Erik Wolf* (Frankfurt am Main, 1962)

Yamin, George J., Jr., *In the Absence of Fantasia: Troeltsch's Relation to Hegel* (Gainesville, FL, 1993)

Yasukata, Toshimasa, *Ernst Troeltsch: Systematic Theologian of Radical Historicality* (Atlanta, 1986)

Zasius, Ulrich, *Von wahrer und falscher Jurisprudenz* [1529], ed. Erik Wolf (Frankfurt am Main, 1948)

Ziehen, E., *Frankfurt, Reichsreform und Reichsgedanke 1486–1504*, repr. (Vaduz, 1965)

Zimmermann, Walter, *Die Reformation als rechtlich-politisches Problem in den Jahren 1524–1530/31* (Göttingen, 1978)

Index

Agricola, Johann, 53
Agricola, Rudolph, 263
Aktenversendung process, 37, 133, 181
Althusius, Johannes, 162
Ambrose, 282
Andreae, Johannes, 36, 75 n.96, 80
Apel, Johann, 62–3, 81, 180, 200 n.3, 264
Aquinas, Thomas, 28, 53, 121, 204, 208–10, 219
Aretinus, Angelus, 75 n.96
Aristotle, 141, 146, 156 n.168, 165, 219, 263, 264, 265
Augsburg, 54,
  Peace of (1555), 4, 43, 71, 85, 132, 137 n.97, 174, 292
  reformation ordinance (1537), 190
Augsburg Confession (1530), 122, 185, 286
Apology of (1531), 72, 122, 185, 217–18
  see also Melanchthon, Philip
Augustine, 90, 203–5, 217, 219, 226, 282

Baden
  legal reformation (1511), 44
  territorial ordinance (1495), 47
Bamberg
  reformation of criminal law (1507), 44
baptism, sacrament of, 38, 58, 169, 183
Bavaria, 49
  legal reformation (1518), 44
Berman, Harold J., xvii
Berthold, Johannes von Bruder, 36
bigamy, *see* polygamy
Blaurer, Ambrosius, 250 n.172
Blaurer, Thomas, 69
Bohemia, 43
Boniface VIII, Pope, 109
Brandenburg, 43
  laws of, 189
Bremen, reformation ordinance (1534), 190
Brenz, Johannes, 15, 180, 250 n.179, 251
  on church order, 71

on education, 275, 284–9
reformation ordinances of, 189
Brunswick (Braunschweig),
  reformation ordinances (1528/31/43), 176, 189, 190, 273 n.79
  school law, 279–84
  see also Bugenhagen, Johannes
Bucer, Martin, 15, 180
  on celibacy, 62
  on Christian commonwealth, 153–4
  on divorce and remarriage, 228–9, 246, 251
  on education, 263–4, 265 n.34, 275
  on marital love, 221
  on polygamy, 225–6
  on uses of law, 104 n.74
  reformation ordinances of, 189–90
Bugenhagen, Johannes, 15, 69, 84, 176, 180, 185
  on education, 268, 272–5, 278–84
  on marriage and divorce, 249–51
  reformation ordinances of, 185, 190
Bullinger, Heinrich, 220–1

Calvin, John and Calvinism, xii, 27, 89, 140, 292
Capito, Wolfgang, 60
Castro, Paulus de, 75 n.96
catechisms, 274–5
  see also education; Luther, Martin
Cato, 273
celibacy and monasticism, 1, 2, 48, 59, 61–3, 199–201, 205–6, 222–4
  see also marriage
charity
  see Eisermann, Johannes; Luther, Martin; Melanchthon, Philip; social welfare
Charlemagne, Emperor, 177
Charles IV, Emperor, 42
Charles V, Emperor, 167, 187–8
Chemnitz, Martin, 139